The Forgotten Marlins

A Tribute to the 1956–1960 Original Miami Marlins

Sam Zygner

THE SCARECROW PRESS, INC.
Lanham • Toronto • Plymouth, UK
2013

Published by Scarecrow Press, Inc.
A wholly owned subsidiary of The Rowman & Littlefield Publishing Group, Inc.
4501 Forbes Boulevard, Suite 200, Lanham, Maryland 20706
www.rowman.com

10 Thornbury Road, Plymouth PL6 7PP, United Kingdom

British Library Cataloguing in Publication Information Available

Library of Congress Cataloging-in-Publication Data

Zygner, Sam.
The forgotten Marlins : a tribute to the 1956–1960 original Miami Marlins / Sam Zygner.
pages cm
Includes bibliographical references and index.
ISBN 978-0-8108-9138-8 (pbk. : alk. paper) -- ISBN 978-0-8108-9139-5 (electronic)
1. Miami Marlins (Baseball team : 1956–1960)—History. 2. Minor league baseball—Florida—Miami—History. I. Title.
GV875.M47Z94 2013
796.357'6409759381—dc23
2013004549

This book is dedicated to my wife, Barbra, for without her faith in my abilities, positive encouragement, and never-ending patience this book would not have been possible. I love you with all my heart.

In Memory of Anne Marie Zygner

Contents

Introduction

On a balmy Opening Day afternoon on Monday, April 5, 1993, forty-five-year-old Charlie Hough stood perched on the mound ready to throw the first-ever pitch for major league baseball's latest, shiny, new-out-of-the-box entry to the National League: the Florida Marlins. The hometown team, decked out in their novel white uniforms trimmed in black and teal, sported the aptly named game fish on their caps that was seemingly springing from its woolly backdrop. The Marlin emblem seemed like an appropriate logo for the team housed inside Joe Robbie Stadium, just scant miles from the ocean the fighting fish calls home. Among the 42,334 fans in attendance that memorable day, there were probably few who had any realization that behind the catchy name of their hometown team there was a history dating back to 1956, when the original Miami Marlins made their indelible mark on the city.

It seemed apropos that one of baseball's senior citizens, Hough, also became one of the Marlins' first star players. Yet it was only thirty-seven years before the newest edition of Marlins took the field that an even more elderly baseball legend, forty-nine-year-old Satchel Paige, would make his own grand entrance, sparking excitement for baseball in Miami that had never been seen before. Under the guidance of legendary baseball maverick Bill Veeck; an optimistic new owner, Sid Salomon Jr.; a cast of youngsters mixed with grizzled veterans hanging on for one more chance at their big league dream; and an iconic superstar popularly known as "Satch," a city starved for sports got its first taste of what big-time baseball would be.

This book is the concise history of the five-year run of one of the most colorful minor league franchises to ever have graced the diamond and that resided in a state-of-the-art playing field known simply as Miami Stadium. It's a story of the highs and lows of a team that reached its zenith on a sweltering evening in August 1956, playing in, of all places, a football venue, in one of the most famous minor league games in history. What began as a love affair would, in time, end in a bitter separation. Dogged by financial losses and dwindling fan interest, the team would be forced to relocate, leaving a lower level of minor league baseball to follow. Although the Miami Marlins only burned bright for five years as a member of the International League, before their demise, the club did play a key role in paving the way for major league baseball's arrival in

South Florida by opening the local fans' eyes to the possibilities of supporting baseball at its highest level.

Over the course of two years, I had the honor and opportunity to interview several of the surviving ballplayers, the original batboy, and the son of a legendary broadcaster who shared their personal accounts and experiences relating to the Miami Marlins. Although each of the aforementioned men made their own unique contribution to the team, by far the one man who made the greatest impression, and left the most lasting mark on all, was one of the greatest pitchers, whom many consider the greatest hurler in the history of baseball—the iconic Satchel Paige. Without exception, everyone that I interviewed who played alongside Paige remembered fondly, with quite a few chuckles and guffaws, sharing the field and participating in off-the-field exploits with the man they simply referred to as "Satch."

Along with Paige, a cast of other characters populated various Marlins rosters, including an infamous group of pitchers, or, as they became more popularly known, "The Dalton Gang," and a happy-go-lucky hurler whose name became synonymous with falling short of his enormous potential due to his excessive drinking and partying: Mickey McDermott, who left more than a few victims in his wake.

Journey with me back to the mid-1950s to a paradisiacal city where warm Atlantic Ocean waves lap on shore to greet sunbaked tourists, Dwight Eisenhower resides in the White House, and concerns over communist threats from an emerging leader in Cuba, Fidel Castro, are an unwelcome distraction from everyday life. Have fun and "Let's Play Ball!"

Preface and Acknowledgments

I began this journey on January 24, 2010. Having decided to write a book at the age of fifty-one, I launched on this labor of love after a few months of struggling to find a subject that spoke to me personally. Leading up to writing this book, I mulled over several ideas in my mind, none of which particularly inspired me. I found that it was kind of like trying on, and buying, a new pair of shoes. You select a style that fits just right, but they look like they came off the clearance rack at Goodwill. Conversely, you find a second pair that looks like something out of *GQ* magazine, but they fit so poorly you might as well wear the box they came in.

Eventually I had an epiphany, and the story that I wanted to tell was right in front of my nose the whole time. I live in Miami, Florida, and we have a professional baseball team down south here called the Marlins, an adopted name from a long-ago predecessor. I said to myself, although not out loud so as not to provoke any strange looks, "Why not write about those original Marlins?" Who were the first Miami Marlins, and what was their story?

To begin, I had a vague notion that baseball legend Satchel Paige had plied his trade in Miami as a member of the original Marlins. Second, I knew that baseball maverick and recently deposed St. Louis Browns owner Bill Veeck had taken a brief sabbatical in 1956 and dabbled in promoting Miami baseball before his triumphant return to the big leagues in Chicago as owner of the White Sox. Other than that, most of my knowledge concerning the Marlins was pretty sketchy. So I began to look into every nook and cranny that I could find where information concerning the team was hiding. I began by researching on microfilm old newspaper accounts. Then I turned to the trusty Internet and followed by checking out books at the library or purchasing them online. With my appetite more than sufficiently whetted, I began to thirst for firsthand accounts from the actual participants, and so I began compiling names of the ballplayers who were still around and were willing to share their tales. This was the most exciting step I took in the process, tracking down ballplayers from all over the country. I spoke with most of them by phone, and they shared with me their exploits on the diamond; more than a few were surprised that my focus was on their time in Miami. Since many had played in the big leagues they were quite used to being asked how was it playing with the Phillies, or the Orioles, or whatever team they had become associated with during their stay in the big leagues. As I collected more and more interviews, it did nothing but inspire me even more to record the history of a team that time had forgotten.

Over the course of doing several interviews I am proud to say that I was able to build some interesting personal relationships, not only with several of the ballplayers but also with others who participated in one form or another with the Marlins. I would like to thank all of those men scattered throughout the four corners of the United States who once proudly wore the uniform of the Miami Marlins, or were their opponents in a few cases, for sharing their time and relating their exploits and personal experiences through conversations mostly on the telephone, including Jim Archer, Bob Bowman, Richard Bunker, Leo Burke, Mel Clark, Angelo Dagres, Billy DeMars, Dick Getter, Johnny Gray, Dallas Green, Fred Hopke, Earl Hunsinger, Wilbur Johnson, Steve Korcheck, Bob Kuzava, Stu Locklin, Clinton "Butch" McCord, Bob Micelotta, Albie Pearson, Tom Qualters, Ron Samford, Ray Semproch, Jack Spring, Ben Tompkins, Bob Usher, Vito Valentinetti, Fred Van Dusen, Robert Willis, and George Zuverink.

My heartfelt gratitude goes out to two ballplayers especially: Richard Bunker and Wilbur Johnson. Richard and his lovely wife Barbara were kind enough to allow my wife and me into their home and Richard shared photos and memories from his time in Miami. Richard and I have kept in touch by phone and through many conversations he has imparted countless stories and experiences that he had as a member of the team. Also, Wilbur Johnson, an unsung baseball-lifer who devoted over fifty years to the game as a minor league infielder, minor league manager, and longtime scout, regaled me with more than a few conversations over the phone and offered his own unique perspective on the Marlins based on his personal experiences, especially when it came to Satchel Paige.

There were also those who provided input, but weren't ballplayers. I would like to acknowledge and thank May Abrams (wife of Cal Abrams), Tim Anagnost (batboy), Bill Durney Jr. (son of Bill Durney), and Michael Sass (an avid fan of the Marlins as a kid) for contributing their thoughts and experiences from that time long ago. One person who gave me the most unique view of the Marlins was Tim Anagnost, who served as the original batboy for the Marlins in 1956 and came back for an encore performance in 1957 when the then-batboy was ill. Tim was one of the first people I had a conversation with and he entertained me with several tales relating to Satchel Paige, along with many of the other ballplayers whom he had a personal relationship with while serving the team. To this day Tim still has his uniform. It is still as fresh and crisp as his memories from way back then.

I cannot forget Dawn Hugh, archives manager, and her assistant Ashley Trujillo from the HistoryMiami Archive and Research Center, who were invaluable in assisting me in locating several photographs that appear in the book. They both worked very hard on this project and I owe a debt to them for their diligent efforts.

I would also like to express my gratitude to Christen Karniski, Patricia Stevenson, and all the fine people at Scarecrow Press for guiding me through the publishing experience. Their hard work and dedication to seeing this project come to completion is greatly appreciated.

I am thankful to the Society for American Baseball Research and baseball-reference.com for their continued support of baseball research and dedication to the ongoing commitment to continue bringing baseball's rich history to light. I am proud to say I am member of SABR and have a platform to share my love of baseball with all of you. And not to be forgotten are all of the folks who painstakingly compile statistics at baseball-reference.com to make available more baseball statistics than ever I can digest. Thank you.

And last, but not least, I thank my wife, Barbra, to whom this book is dedicated. Through her support and understanding I was able to spend the time I needed to work on this book and tell this story. Barbra also played a key role in helping me locate ballplayers whose professional careers consisted of only time in the minor leagues and were especially hard to find. Her technical advice and guidance were invaluable, and without her I doubt I could have reached a successful conclusion. Barbra, you are the light of my life.

Part I

1956

ONE

Let's Play Ball, Sport Shirt Bill, and Satch's Grand Entrance

The corner of Northwest 23rd Street and 10th Avenue is abuzz. The enormous twenty-foot blaring reddish-orange neon lights spelling out M.I.A.M.I. S.T.A.D.I.U.M. above the entrance greet the throng of fans as they approach the ticket-takers, waiting anxiously to tear their tickets. It is spring in Miami and everything feels new. The aroma of roasting peanuts and sizzling wieners wafting through the air blends with the familiar sounds of barking vendors hawking their programs. Everybody is eager to see their newest home team, and the anticipation brought on by the reputation of renowned showman, promoter, and flamboyant executive vice-president with the colorful nickname "Sport Shirt Bill" Veeck leaves everyone so excited that the actual game seems almost secondary. The feeling in the air is Opening Day baseball and it's as familiar as your own broken-in fielder's mitt.

The city of Miami and/or Miami Beach had served as the home for a host of teams in the past, including the likes of the renowned barnstorming Ethiopian Clowns and minor league teams with such colorful names as the Flamingos, Hustlers, Seminoles, Tourists, Sun Sox, Tigers, and Wahoos. However, none of these clubs were above the lowest rungs of the ladder of the minor leagues. In fact, the highest level that any Miami team had achieved prior to 1956 was Class B as members of the famed Florida International League (IL).[1] Although the major leagues have been part of the rites of spring since 1920, going back to the arrival of the Boston Braves, for the first time in the history of the city by the sea, the fair citizens of Miami would be supplied with a full season of baseball that truly began to epitomize what this energetic "boomtown" city deserved. The fans now had a team that was the newest member of the Triple-A International League, only one step below the big leagues.[2]

3

In the center of all this excitement was the blonde, top-tufted, and always outgoing Veeck himself. "Sport Shirt Bill," as the press liked to call him, loathed ties, and used the hollowed out portion of his wooden leg to flick his cigarette ashes in while reclining, all so familiarly, in his favorite office chair. Characterized as a combination circus ringmaster and Madison Avenue ad man, Veeck was unique to his time. While fellow baseball executives felt they were above knowing the fans that they profited from, Veeck instead sought them out. Always gregarious, Veeck's glowing personality ingratiated him to everyone who crossed his path—that is, except for the dyed-in-the-wool baseball establishment types, who were threatened by his decades-ahead-of-his-time approach to promoting baseball. But to the throngs of baseball aficionados across the country, he was an antiestablishment hero.

The more that Veeck endeared himself to the fans, the more he was despised by the people who ran major league baseball, hiding behind their holier-than-thou facades. Put simply, he lived for promoting the game that he loved and was very good at it. There was little that the common man found standoffish in Veeck, and so in touch with the fans was this iconic legend that it was not uncommon to see him at any game working the crowd and conversing with anyone willing to let him bend his ear.

An inquisitive youth, the young Veeck grew up around baseball and it was as much a part of his life as fine cuisine is to a world-class chef. Veeck's father, William Veeck Sr., served as the longtime president of the Chicago Cubs, and young Veeck was weaned by his father on all the inner workings of the national pastime. The lessons he was taught as a youngster, going back to when he began selling popcorn and hawking tickets at the gates of Wrigley Field, carried on through to adulthood. His first recognizable position was serving as the Cubs treasurer, a position that he held until 1941, which further laid the groundwork for one of the most dynamic marketing minds ever to grace baseball's landscape.

In the spring of 1956, Tom Qualters, a then impressionable, up-and-coming, highly prized prospect for the Phillies, was new to Miami and preparing for his first season with the Marlins. He remembers with fondness the first time he met the baseball legend and the unique circumstances in which he signed a contract to play in Miami. Veeck, as usual, was just as much at ease with his players as he was with the fans he adored and left an impression on Qualters that is still vivid today.

> *Tom Qualters*: I went in there and signed a damn contract. I'd heard about Bill Veeck my whole life and I didn't know he had a wooden leg. So I knocked on the door and he says, "Come in." So I walked in the door and here is this leg laying on the table right in front of him. You know we shake hands and everything. He's smoking a cigar and we're just chit-chatting, talking. And he's flicking his ashes in this wooden leg. It had an indentation right where your calf would be, kind of

hollowed out a little bit, and here's where he's flicking all of his ashes. He's sitting there talking and I'm thinking, "What the hell is this?" That was Bill Veeck. He was a great person and great guy.[3]

Veeck wasted no time upon arriving in Miami to ensure the success of the team. He found speaking engagements wherever possible and opened up his promotional bag of tricks early on by exposing the community to Marlins baseball. Player and management involvement was a must with Veeck along with plentiful amounts of glad-handing. Veeck never traveled alone and recruited his cronies, partners in crime, to help him guarantee the success of baseball in Miami. One person who was essential in Veeck's promotional strategies was broadcaster and PR man "Big Bill" Durney, whose history dated back to Veeck's arrival in St. Louis as owner of the Browns, including being a key assistant in the famous Eddie Gaedel promotion that had the midget pinch-hitting in a game that gained nationwide attention. The velvet-voiced former KMOX and St. Louis Browns play-by-play man served as the team's relations and promotional director during the inaugural season and would eventually land the job of being the play-by-play man for the Marlins before the 1957 season would break.

Besides good working partners, Veeck also had a clear understanding of the importance that the relationship between kids and their parents had in driving the team's success. Put simply, the youth were instrumental in encouraging dad and mom to attend games with them, and the result was more paying customers at the box office. One of Veeck's earliest conceptions was a contest to be sponsored by one of the city's largest newspapers, the *Miami Herald*, that allowed youngsters to vie for the title of team batboy. It was a chance for any adolescent in the Miami area to submit a twenty-five-words-or-less essay describing why he wanted to serve in this position for the Marlins. All entrants were awarded two ducats for a future home game as part of the submittal process, thus guaranteeing numerous responses. The contest drew hundreds of entries, with the top ten finalists being awarded season tickets. From the lucky ten, the final two contestants picked would vie for the top prize of representing the home team as their batboy. Winning the contest in the end was a thirteen-year-old youngster named Timmy Anagnost from Miami proper. Before making the final decision, Bill Veeck asked young Tim to come into a conference room where the Marlins brass was waiting to interview him. Young Tim was politely told to sit down and relax, but in his nervous state of mind Anagnost replied, "That's easy for you to say," which promptly brought down the house with appreciative laughter.[4] They had found their guy.

To further drum up excitement, the team sponsored another contest, also through the *Miami Herald*, to involve the fans in a "Name the Team" contest. Each entrant was to submit his or her personal choice. The reward for submittal of an entry was a ticket to a future ball game, with one winning lucky customer obtaining season tickets. The most popular name was chosen and accepted by team ownership. Although the *Miami Herald* drew hundreds of responses, ultimately the moniker chosen was to be "Marlins," a fighting game fish that made its home in the waters off of South Florida. It was the perfect name and edged out the previous Miami Stadium's tenant signature label, Sun Sox.

Although Veeck was garnering most of the headlines, the two men most instrumental in bringing baseball to Miami were St. Louis investment banker Sid Salomon Jr. and his partner Elliot Stein. Anxious to launch their flagship team in style, they were the parties responsible for seeking out and acquiring the services of the blackballed former major league owner and all-around maverick Veeck, who would serve as the team's executive vice-president and promoter. Although major league owners, at least for the time being, had found a way to keep Veeck from shaking up the status quo in the big leagues since forcing him out as owner of the St. Louis Browns, now, left to his own devices, there was no one and nothing stopping him from opening up his crackerjack box full of tricks in the minor leagues.

One of Veeck's strategies was his belief that all promotions should be kept secret. This left the customer anticipating what would happen next, and as a fan you never knew what to expect on any given day or night when you passed through the gates. Sometimes a few morsels of information would be leaked to the press, but Veeck understood, better than anyone, that a strategically placed tease drew fannies into the seats. When asked by *Miami News* reporter Norris Anderson prior to opening night what promotions were in store, Veeck predictably replied, "If there is a surprise in tonight's business at *Miami Stadium* I'm looking forward to what it will be."[5]

In total, 8,816 fans pushed their way through the turnstiles into Miami Stadium on Wednesday, April 18, 1956. Although Salomon, Stein, and Veeck were expecting upward of ten thousand paying customers and General Manager Eddie Stumpf had been even more optimistic in projecting fifteen thousand, sadly the actual numbers would fall short. Stumpf announced to the press, "Of course that depends on how many general admission seats we sell. There are a lot left but we will be open for business all day."[6] Nevertheless, the hierarchy couldn't be too disappointed, as the park was near its capacity. Unfortunately, it was later found out that some fans had stayed away, figuring that all the seats had been sold out.

It was a near-perfect night for hardball. With temperatures hovering around the mid-sixties, and only a gentle breeze blowing in from the southeast, the numerous gentleman in their tidy suits and ties, some topped off with Bogart hats, and women in their latest spring dresses and shawls slowly drifted into their assigned seats under the one-of-a-kind cantilevered roof of Miami Stadium. These were the days before gaudily printed T-shirts, faded jeans, and shorts adorned the crowds. A baseball game was enjoyed for the game itself, not the rock concert production it would ultimately become.

The milling ladies and gents scrutinized the visiting Buffalo Bison's squad and hometown Marlins going through their pregame warm-up rituals. Others stared with curiosity at the odd tension wire strung eighty feet above the ground in right centerfield that stretched 150 feet from Erecter Set–style light tower to light tower. They must have wondered, what did this character Veeck have up his sleeve after all?

Without delay the night's entertainment got under way. Perched above the stadium on a ramp built on one of the outfield towers was former Ringling Brothers Circus entertainer Josephine Bromine, ready to perform her death-defying tightrope walk across the wire that had drawn so much inquisitiveness. Although there were a few squeamish individuals in the crowd who couldn't watch, the majority who did were thrilled as Josephine gingerly made her way from one end to the other without the hint of calamity befalling her.

There was still more to come. What would a Veeck promotion night be without fireworks? Before catching their collective breaths, the fans were quickly treated to an on-the-field red and green pyrotechnic greeting, "Hi Fans," accompanied by rockets of various hues shot in the air. Unsuspected by all in attendance, besides the baseball game they came to see, the best was yet to come, and the fireworks were just beginning.

The PA announcer then read off the starting lineups. To add drama to the evening's festivities the stadium was darkened and each starting player in the Marlins lineup was introduced by spotlight at his respective position. Without hesitation the home plate umpire belted out, "Play Ball," and the spanking new Miami Marlins, decked out in their crisp white home uniforms trimmed in blue and orange, blue sanitary socks, and blue caps with the prominent large "M," took to the field.

Opening Day Starting Lineups:

Buffalo Bisons	*Miami Marlins*
CF George Bullard	CF David Mann
SS Billy DeMars	2B Ben Tompkins
RF Joe Brovia	RF Mel Clark
1B Luke Easter	3B Sid Gordon
LF Johnny Blatnik	1B Ed Bouchee
3B Bill Serena	LF Ed Mierkowicz
2B Lou Ortiz	SS Bob Micelotta

C Phil Tompkinson	C Gus Niarhos
P Bill Froats	P Thornton Kipper
Manager: Phil Cavarretta	Manager: Don Osborn

The top of the first inning went quietly when the visiting Bisons failed to tally a run. In the bottom half of the inning the Marlins first-ever batter David Mann stepped up to the plate, no doubt with a few opening-night butterflies, but the crowd was more interested by the going-ons along the first base line. To the delight of everyone, the crazy antics of the "Clown Prince of Baseball," Max Patkin, were creating a hilarious distraction. Following an unsuccessful career as a minor league pitcher, the pencil-thin, rubber-necked Patkin, in order to stay close to the game he loved, began to develop his nationally famous comedy act. His sideline pranks were perfected in major and minor league ballparks all across the country and gained him nationwide fame. Taking his usual position in the area around the first-base coaching box, Patkin took to his unusual contortions and mocking of opponents and umpires, much to the delight of all attendees.

Just when it seemed that Veeck's bag of tricks had been exhausted, a two-man bubble-shaped helicopter began to circle the stadium. To the amazement of everyone, both locals and ballplayers, the whirlybird slowly lowered itself onto the infield just behind the pitcher's mound. The ensuing windstorm created quite a furor as the ladies in their box seats, many of them wearing their best Sunday dresses, were soon assaulted by the infield dirt and dust. The Marlins infielders were forced to shield their eyes from the blowing loam and Kipper hastily retreated from the pitcher's mound for safer ground. Although most of the folks at field level thought of sending Veeck a dry-cleaning bill, they were soon to be delighted by the most pleasant of surprises.

The fans and the players were shocked—but thrilled—to see a pencil-thin older black gentleman stepping out from the side of the helicopter in a Marlins uniform and a blue silk warm-up jacket. Only Veeck, Marlins management, and a few knowledgeable fans recognized the baseball legend who had just exited the whirlybird. It was a complete surprise to his teammates and the crowd that had no idea of what transpiring. A few in the audience could be heard to say, "Oh my God, it's Satchel Paige!"[7]

Mel Clark, the starting right fielder, Wilbur Johnson, a utility infielder, and Jack Spring, a left-handed pitcher watching from the sidelines, recalled the night that Paige made his grand entrance.

> *Mel Clark*: I'll tell you, in the first game he arrived in a helicopter. Yes, I was in right field when the helicopter came and started coming down. It just kept coming down and our pitcher [Thornton Kipper] was looking around for cover you know. He got out of the way or it would have landed on the mound. Satchel walked over to the dugout and told the

manager [Don Osborn], he said, "My name is Satchel Paige and I'm here ready to pitch."[8]

Wilbur Johnson: A helicopter comes right over the stadium, flies around the stadium and lands right around home plate, at the pitcher's mound. And out comes Satchel Paige in his uniform. And none of the players knew he was coming, we never met the guy before; he never went to spring training. . . . The fans were all dressed up. These women, it was a beautiful night, they had these white dresses on and they were dressed to kill . . . that helicopter landed on the dirt part of the mound and it shot dust all over the stands.[9]

Jack Spring: We had heard some rumors about something that was going on, but even the players didn't know officially. It was just that something special was going to happen and then, you know, here comes this helicopter landing out there.

At the time I was a relief pitcher. I was out in the bullpen out along the left field line as I recall, and here he came out there and he said, "Holy man." It was one of those bubble fronts you know where they open. His eyes were as big as saucers.[10]

Known as "Money Bags," Tom Qualters, a Phillies $40,000 "bonus baby," was a nervous youngster on the sidelines that eventful day. He remembered, just like it was yesterday, his feelings after Paige had exited the helicopter and walked slowly to the bullpen where his rocking chair awaited him.

Tom Qualters: You know in those days the club was run by Bill Veeck. . . . In my case the Philadelphia organization had a working agreement and sent a lot of ballplayers there [Miami], and if they made the team OK, and if they didn't they would go someplace else.

So it was a long shot, in my mind, for me to make that ball club. I had only played a half a year of Class B ball . . . so I go down there and I'm really working my tail off. There were many ex-major league players on the club and they start cutting guys, and cutting guys, and I'm hanging on.

Finally it comes, Opening Day. I'm still there and I'm absolutely amazed I made the ball club. All of the sudden here comes a helicopter in and it lands beside the mound and who comes out but Satchel Paige. And I thought, "You old son-of-a-gun, you just took my job," you know [laughing]. And it had turned out that they had cut another guy; it wasn't me.

So, in the aftermath of that Satch and I became very, very close.[11]

Joe Ryan, the anxious Marlins business manager, was worried that the stunt wasn't going to come off. He had lost contact with the pilot and knew he was running low on fuel. "I was so scared . . . that pilot and me was like husband and wife until we landed," Paige vividly recalled.[12]

Paige told the tale of how that night's promotion came off in his book, *Maybe I'll Pitch Forever*:

> That opening night game, Mr. Veeck decided to fly me into the ballpark in a helicopter. They got me to the airfield where the helicopter was and it looked to me like nothin' but a big lawn mower.
>
> I hopped out of that plane and those Miami fans went crazy. And they wanted to see me pitch too. But I didn't get in that first game. I just took me a rocking chair ride. Mr. Veeck'd given me a big rocking chair to sit in out in the bullpen and I made good use of it. [13]

While Paige was settling into his new surroundings—and getting accustomed to his new rocking chair in the bullpen that Veeck had arranged for him—the Bisons struck first blood in the third inning. A double by Phil Tompkinson, followed by a pair of walks, and another double by International League (IL) legend Luke Easter plated two runs off of starting pitcher Thornton Kipper. It was cause for concern to the now restless hometown rooters.

The Marlins eased some of fans' fears by striking back quickly in the bottom of the third frame. After retiring David Mann, Bisons' starter Bill Froats walked Ben Tompkins and Mel Clark, setting up the first RBI by a Marlin when Sid Gordon sent a screeching liner to center field that bounced off centerfielder George Bullard's glove, scoring Tompkins. Ed Bouchee followed with a resounding triple, bringing home both base runners and giving the Marlins a 3–2 lead.

Seeing enough of Froats, manager Phil Cavarretta signaled to the bullpen and called on six-foot-two right-hander Harry Nicholas to snuff the rally. Much to the chagrin of Cavarretta, pinch-hitter Larry Novak, batting for Ed Mierkowicz, drove the first offering by Nicholas off of the right field light post, increasing the home team's lead to 5–2. Although Cavarretta argued to try to overturn the blast, claiming it was off the wall, the umpires were not persuaded and the call stood. Novak was the proud recipient the first-ever Marlins home run.

The Bisons added another run in the top of the fourth, but the rest of the night would belong to Miami. After they scored one run in the fifth inning, the atmosphere got a little heated during the sixth inning. After Mann got caught in a rundown between first and second base an argument ensued with the umpire. Bisons left fielder Johnny Blatnik took exception to Mann and his rants. Blatnik had had enough with the delay and told Mann to stop showboating and get off of the field. According to accounts in the *Miami Herald*, Mann swung first at Blatnik, and before you could say "seventh-inning stretch," the brouhaha was on. Although the fisticuffs led to a consensus no decision, both Blatnik and Mann were summarily tossed from the game and play was resumed. [14]

The Marlins weren't done yet. In the eighth inning the offense exploded for four runs, all with two outs. Reliever Fred Hahn, who was the fourth pitcher of the night for the Bisons, allowed singles to both Clark and Gordon. Walks to Bouchee and Novak followed, scoring Clark, and then one of three passed balls on the night plated Gordon. To put the icing on the cake, pepper pot shortstop Bob "Mickey" Micelotta tripled, driving in two more runs and finishing the offensive outburst for the hometown Fish.

The *Miami News* recognized Gordon, who reached base all five of his at-bats, including three walks, and Micelotta, with two singles, a triple, and his fine defensive play, as the stars of the game. Bob Greenwood would record the first win for the team in relief.[15] The final tally showed 10–3 in favor of the hometown boys. The fans left happy and all was well in the Magic City—at least for the time being.

NOTES

1. *Miami, Florida Minor League City Encyclopedia*, 2010, baseball-reference.com.
2. Kevin M. McCarthy, *Baseball in Florida* (Sarasota, FL: Pineapple Press, 1996).
3. Tom Qualters, phone interview with the author, March 5, 2010.
4. Tim Anagnost, interview with the author, May 9, 2010.
5. Norris Anderson, "Sports Today," *Miami News*, April 18, 1956.
6. Norris Anderson, "Baseball Returns Tonight," *Miami News*, April 18, 1956.
7. Keith Sherouse, "Marlins to Get More Help; Veeck's 'Circus' Thrills Fans," *Miami News*, April 19, 1956.
8. Mel Clark, phone interview with the author, March 15, 2010.
9. Wilbur Johnson, phone interview with the author, March 11, 2010.
10. Jack Spring, phone interview with the author, March 16, 2010.
11. Qualters interview.
12. Larry Tye, *Satchel: The Life and Times of an American Legend* (New York: Random House, 2007), 234.
13. David Lipman and Satchel Paige, *Maybe I'll Pitch Forever* (Garden City, NY: Doubleday, 1962).
14. Eddie Storin, "Brawl Game Comment: Did Veeck Plan Fight?" *Miami News*, April 19, 1956.
15. Luther Evans, "Fisticuffs Enliven Contest," *Miami Herald*, April 19, 1956.

TWO

In the Beginning, and the Dalton Gang

The IL had survived the challenging years of World War II, while at the same time several other minor leagues had died on the vine. Following the war, the IL enjoyed the postwar economic boom and continued to remain solid. However, as the boom faded and the country settled into normalcy, there was an increasing concern following the 1953 season as fan interests continued to wane and attendance began to lag. Even the strongest of IL cities were struggling at the gate.

Frank Shaughnessy, who had served as the IL president since 1936, was increasingly showing interest in new locales where he could relocate struggling affiliates. On the top of the list of floundering teams was the Philadelphia Phillies affiliate in Syracuse, the longtime Chiefs who had drawn a paltry 84,931 fans in 1955, the lowest figure in the league.[1]

Ever since Havana, Cuba, had been adopted into the league, there had been an increased focus by league fathers toward the warmer climes to the south, and Miami was definitely on their radar. What soon transpired would fix both problems, that being the replacing of a floundering team and awarding ownership with a new and dynamic club poised to swell the attendance coffers and create promotional excitement that no IL team would again experience.[2]

Bill Veeck recalled in his landmark biography *Veeck—As in Wreck* that Sid Salomon Jr. and Elliot Stein came into ownership of the Miami franchise in the most unusual of circumstances. At the time both Salomon Jr. and Stein were in Columbus, Ohio, to close a deal on a restaurant Salomon Jr. owned and intended to sell to Louie Jacobs. By coincidence the rival American Association was having its minor league meetings at the same location and had just voted down moving the Toledo club to Miami. In the course of the conversation between the two men, the always opinionated Salomon commented on what a mistake it was for the AA to

13

pass up such a golden opportunity. Salomon Jr., who owned a home in Miami and was a self-proclaimed baseball fan, commented, "If I could buy a club I wouldn't hesitate to move it to Miami." Martin Haske, the owner of the IL's Syracuse club, sitting at an adjoining table, overheard Salomon's comments and tapped him on the shoulder and said, "OK, you've just bought yourself a club."[3]

As soon as Salomon Jr. realized the gravity of the situation he had gotten himself and Stein into, he immediately turned to his old friend Veeck for guidance and help. "I am about to give some very good advice," Veeck said. "Go back to the restaurant, tap the shoulder of the guy at the table on the other side of you and ask him if he wants to buy a ball club. If that doesn't work, go out into the street and try to spot some lamb walking by. If you don't have a buyer by nightfall, see if you can't give it to somebody. Believe me, it will be cheaper."[4]

However, Salomon Jr. was not to be persuaded otherwise and had already sold himself on the viability of a successful team in Miami. Even though he had yet to secure a ballpark or working agreement with the city, he was so enthusiastic about the possibilities that he talked his friend Veeck into coming south and running the club (mind you, without pay). Veeck would later assist in the negotiations with the city to secure a location and terms that were acceptable. Veeck later admitted, "It was kind of fun operating on a small minor-league scale again." It must have reminded him of his early days when he cut his teeth as a first-time owner of a Triple-A club in Milwaukee.[5] One thing that would come to define the Marlins more than anything else, at least in the first season, was fun.

On December 21, 1955, IL league president Shaughnessy put his final stamp of approval on the transfer of the Philadelphia Phillies Syracuse Chiefs affiliate to Miami by sending the new owners a wire, thus consummating the deal for the price of $100,000; Salomon, a successful St. Louis investment banker, agreed to all the terms.[6]

Syracuse had been experiencing attendance problems for many years. The problem was twofold: the Chiefs' lack of success in the win column, and the negative perception by the public of the team as a whole due to the poor conduct of its players. The last time that Syracuse had finished first in the IL was in 1897, and the team usually found itself in the middle or end of the pack in the standings. Even more damaging was a highly publicized incident that occurred in June of 1955. After a particularly frustrating game, words were exchanged between a couple of ballplayers and a local sportswriter in a neighborhood bar. The situation grew increasingly heated until a physical altercation broke out between sportswriter Norm Hannon of the *Syracuse Post-Standard* and Chiefs pitchers Dick Farrell and Seth Morehead. The results weren't pretty and Hannon suffered a broken nose and had a severe cut above his eye that required five stitches to close. Farrell and Morehead came out unscathed—at least physically—but from a PR standpoint the team's image in the community took a beating.[7]

Farrell and Morehead were part of a trio that became more popularly known by their teammates as the "Dalton Gang," named after an infamous group of rowdy bank robbers that once terrorized the Midwestern United States. The third member of the group, although not involved in the altercation, was pitcher Jim Owens. The "Dalton Gang" would gain later fame—or infamy, depending on your point of view—for their antics and practical jokes in Miami.

Jack Spring, who was part of the pitching staff with Farrell, Morehead, and Owens on the 1955 Chiefs, recalled the trouble that the players and even the wives faced after the ugly altercation.

> *Jack Spring*: Well, I guess you'd call it that, yeah. They got into a little hot water up in Syracuse and almost got us run out of town. Farrell got in a fight in a bar and beat some guy up pretty good. It turns out the guy was some kind of sportswriter for the local newspaper.
>
> We in fact, I was married and my wife was there, and the other married guys' wives were afraid to go out in public because they might get recognized . . . the baseball players didn't have a very good reputation in Syracuse after that incident. They were called the "Dalton Gang."[8]

However, most of the "Dalton Gang's" exploits were of a lighter nature and in general served as a tension reliever in the clubhouse. They were just the sort of ballplayers that self-professed oddballs like Jim Bouton and Bill "Spaceman" Lee would have approved.

> *Wilbur Johnson*: But they called them the "Dalton Gang." I don't care if it was on the field, or off the field, they were doing something. They were an amazing group of guys. They never stopped.[9]
>
> *Bob Micelotta*: Seth Morehead, and uh, Dick Farrell and Jimmy Owens. Yeah, they were good pitchers and thing is they liked to drink beer. And they were the wild bunch. They enjoyed beer and relaxing. That was a bunch of guys, the "Dalton Gang"; it didn't strike me right away but they were a wild bunch.[10]
>
> *Jack Spring*: "Skeeter" Newsome was our manager up in Syracuse and he was kind of a naïve old guy, but a nice guy. He called this meeting when we got to Havana and said, "Look guys the manager of the team that just left told me that you guys got to be careful because Havana is planting these gals around to keep you guys out all night to be tired and not able to play. You gotta look out for these plants." Well, the "Dalton Gang" almost broke the door off getting out of the room going to look for the plants. [laughing heartily] That was the "Dalton Gang."[11]

First baseman Bouchee recalled in Dan Peary's *We Played the Game* that the "Dalton Gang's" exploits never stopped even during the Marlins' first spring training in Plant City, Florida. While staying at a local hotel, Bouchee found himself in the bathroom catching up on the daily news when Farrell began to take potshots with his .45 through the door. "You've never seen somebody hit the floor so fast in your life," said a startled Bouchee. He also explained, "I don't know if they were actually disruptive but they were always in the office of the general manager." [12]

Despite the tarnished reputation of the club, throughout the late months of 1955 and January of 1956 some team supporters in Syracuse tried, in what would turn out to be a vain effort, to block the Chiefs' move to Miami. The Chiefs and/or Stars (as the team had been known prior to 1928) had been part of the IL since 1885 with the exception of two gaps from 1902 through 1917 and 1928–1932. [13] Some marriages are hard to break up even under the worst circumstances, and so a few loyal local supporters did try their best to save the beaten horse, but it was not meant to be.

The *Miami News* proudly announced in their January 29 edition that General Eddie Stumpf, along with Marlins management, had completed a deal with Mayor Otis Andrews, City Manager T. J. McCall, and Commissioner Henry S. Moody to lease Miami Stadium. Pitchers and catchers were expected to report to spring training in Plant City, Florida, on March 10 with the remaining squad to arrive no later than March 12. The schedule reflected a twenty-four-game warm-up before the regular season with the first game to be played on March 18 against the Charleston Senators of the AA. All negotiations with the city fathers of Plant City went off without a hitch. According to Stumpf, "The Plant City officials have agreed to meet all of our wishes and the citizens are going all out to see that our stay will be happy and successful." As a show of goodwill, the Marlins management agreed to turn over all receipts to spring training games to support the local Little League program. [14]

As predicted by the local sportswriters, the leading candidate for the skipper's job, Don Osborn, was taking over the managerial reins from Skeeter Newsome. Osborn's managerial style was compared to the legendary Al Lopez by General Manager Stumpf: "Osborn is a solid baseball man, a great fundamentalist and real student of pitching." Added Stumpf, "He is even tempered and works well with his men." [15]

Osborn brought with him ten years of minor league managerial experience, a record of producing winners wherever he went, and a reputation as an excellent evaluator and developer of pitchers. Osborn, who had starred as a hurler in the Pacific Coast League during the early and mid-1940s, had been paying his dues in the lower rungs of the minors with stops along the way in such outposts as Vancouver (Capilanos), Macon (Peaches), Nashville (Volunteers), Spokane (Indians), Mattoon (Phillies), and Schenectady (Blue Jays). Osborn assessed his responsibilities by saying, "I feel that managing Miami is the most responsibility I've had with any of the clubs I've managed in the last ten years. Miami is used to big league sports and the baseball future in Miami depends a lot upon the success of the 1956 management and player personnel." [16]

Although Osborn was confident that he would do well with his new club, there were definitely areas that needed improvement if he were to develop a playoff quality team. Osborn was quick to point out that his handling of pitchers was a high priority and in the offensive department he was an advocate of playing for the big inning. He confidently announced, "I feel many of the younger players on the Miami roster are ready for Triple A ball and some are not, but my clubs have always shown good competitive spirit and every player will have a chance to make the Miami club if he has the desire and ability." [17]

NOTES

1. Jimmy Burns, "Miami Gate Spins as Marlins Spurt," *Sporting News*, June 20, 1956, 27.

2. Bill O'Neal, *International League: A Baseball History 1884–1991* (Austin, TX: Eakin Press, 1992), 154–61.

3. Ed Linn and Bill Veeck, *Veeck—As in Wreck* (New York: University of Chicago Press, 1961), 311–12.

4. Ibid.

5. Ibid.

6. United Press Release, "Shaughnessy Okays Sale of Syracuse," December 21, 1955. As seen in the *Palm Beach Post*, December 22, 1955.

7. Dink Carroll, "Playing the Field: The Trouble in Syracuse," *Montreal Gazette*, July 8, 1955.

8. Jack Spring, phone interview with the author, March 16, 2010.

9. Wilbur Johnson, phone interview with the author, March 11, 2010.

10. Bob Micelotta, phone interview with the author, October 23, 2012.

11. Spring interview, March 16, 2010.

12. Danny Peary, *We Played the Game* (New York: Black Dog & Leventhal Publishers, 1994), 363.

13. *Syracuse, New York Minor League City Encyclopedia*, 2010, baseball-reference.com.

14. *Miami News*, "Plant City Chosen as Camp Site," January 29, 1956.

15. Ibid.

16. Baseball-reference.com.

17. Norris Anderson, "Osborn Chosen Marlins Manager," *Miami News*, January 29, 1956.

THREE

Cardwell, Satch, and Hope for the Best

The success of opening night was history. The fans in attendance were thrilled by the circus atmosphere—not to mention a hometown victory— but management was a bit disappointed by the turnout. An expected crowd of at least ten thousand was forecasted but that estimate fell short. However, there was no sense in crying over spilled milk. After the dust had settled, more pressing concerns quickly came to light as the team slumped and their early performance sent up warning flares more glaring than the opening-night fireworks.

By dropping the next five of six games at home to the Buffalo Bisons and Rochester Red Wings, the hometown boys found themselves resting at seventh place in the standings. Manager Don Osborn had figured on a quick start out of the gate. Instead, he found the team heading south in the standings. The offense was so pathetic that it could only scratch out sixteen runs over those same six games. The Marlins had holes and what they needed most was a bopper in the middle of the lineup to drive in runs, and a quality lead-off hitter who could set the table. Although the former Giant, Brave, and Pirate Sid Gordon was hitting for average, at thirty-eight years old his range in the field had clearly evaporated and his power was waning. Ed Bouchee at first base, Ben Tompkins at second, and Bob Micelotta at short were solid, but Gordon found himself frequently substituted late in the game by scrappy tobacco-chewing utility man Wilbur "Moose" Johnson or thirty-five-year-old veteran Don Richmond. Compounding the team's hitting problems was a knee injury to the Marlins' hottest hitter, Bouchee, who found himself among the league leaders in batting average. The injury would keep Bouchee on the sidelines for almost a week.[1]

Prior to the season, Phillies pitching coach Whitlow Wyatt assessed the Marlins staff by saying, "I never saw so many good young pitchers in baseball camp." He added, "It's the best crop I've ever worked with."[2] The staff, considered the team's strength—although young, with the exception of Paige at forty-nine—had been inconsistent and ineffective, seemingly trying to still find their "sea legs." Don Cardwell (twenty), Seth Morehead (twenty), Jim Owens (twenty-two), and Jack Spring (twenty-three) were all considered to be on track to join the Phillies within the next year. Another one of the main starters counted on to stabilize the staff, Dick "Turk" Farrell, would be lost until at least June with a broken ankle. The previous season with the Chiefs he posted a 12–12 record with a 3.94 ERA.[3] Farrell was also high on the list of Phillies prospects expected to make the big leagues.

On top of everything else, the Marlins rooters began to wonder if Satchel Paige was just a sideshow gimmick, merely sitting in his rocking chair enjoying the game from his comfortable perch in the bullpen, or if he was really going to show his stuff. The general consensus was, even if he did pitch, the well-traveled veteran might not have anything left in his proverbial tank. What the fans, and his teammates, soon found out was that it was no joke and "Old Satch" was the "Real McCoy." In fact, he would prove to be even more of a force than anyone could have imagined in their wildest dreams. But Paige, and the many who had competed against or played with the ageless veteran, all knew that Miami was about to get all that it had bargained for, plus interest.

One of Bill Veeck's first moves after arriving in Miami was to sign Paige to a contract for $15,000 plus a percentage of the gate. Veeck knew that Satch was still effective as a pitcher and would not only boost attendance but also help the team in the win column. Nevertheless, not everyone was sold on Paige, including Osborn, who was opposed to signing the lanky, free-spirited pitcher. Veeck resorted to the same strategy that he used with Lou Boudreau, his then player-manager of the Cleveland Indians in 1948, to convince him that Paige would help the team. A natural horse-trader, Veeck made a deal with Osborn to line up his best nine hitters to face the ageless wonder. If any hitter could register a solid hit off of Paige, he would pay the hitter $10 and send Satch on his way. Satch proceeded to mow down all nine batters, and in the process changed the mind of Osborn, who was, to say the least, very impressed.[4]

Osborn, a strict disciplinarian with his players, knew he had a unique situation with Paige. The question posed was how would he deal with a baseball nomad while maintaining some semblance of authority on his team? Just shy of his fiftieth birthday, it was a lock that Paige was going to live by his own rules. Osborn understood this and that he would have to make concessions, but trusted that his players would understand that the same rules that applied to them didn't pertain to Paige.

Jack Spring: He [Osborn] was pretty understanding about it. Of course, you know, Satch being nearly fifty years old, if not already fifty. And so he [Osborn] kind of went along because he looked at his stats which were outstanding and he knew he would help the team. He had a great season and he kind of pitched when he wanted to pitch . . . he treated him a little different than the young guys.[5]

On April 22, Paige made his Marlins debut in the second game of a Sunday twin bill. The two games combined would last a total of seven and a half hours. As per the league mandate, the first game of a double-header consisted of the mandatory nine innings, with the second game at night to be played in an abbreviated seven-inning format. It was no doubt a relief to Paige to finally see some action.

In the opener the Marlins squandered several opportunities before finally bowing to the Red Wings in the eighteenth inning 10–6. The Marlins threw away an excellent opportunity in the seventeenth inning when, after a Micelotta double, Gus Niarhos singled to right field with the apparent game winner. Manager Osborn frantically waved Micelotta home, hoping to end the marathon, but to the chagrin of the Miami fans and players alike, Micelotta was gunned down at home plate by a perfect peg from right fielder Tom Burgess. Osborn later lamented, "I'll take all the blame for that one."[6]

In the second game the Marlins got their revenge. Paige's performance was brief but critical. With two outs in the bottom of the seventh Paige laboriously slogged his way from bullpen to the mound. It was classic Paige, never in a hurry. As he was famously quoted many times, "I never rush myself. See, they can't start the game without me." Paige now squared off against highly regarded St. Louis Cardinals prospect Mel Nelson. Paige uncorked a pitch that backstop Niarhos let get away for a passed ball, moving two Red Wing base runners to second and third. The crowd was in the mood of "here we go again," but as Paige had done so often in the past, he upset Nelson's timing with a perfectly placed fastball that coaxed the twenty-year-old centerfielder to ground it back to the mound. Paige calmly threw to Jim Westlake at first and pitcher Cardwell's second win of the season was secure. Unfortunately, many of the 3,486 spectators had departed and weren't there to witness his debut performance. However, they would get the chance to see "Old Satch" much more as the season wore on.[7]

Marlins management received some much-needed good news on the same day of the doubleheader from the parent club, the Philadelphia Phillies. Hometown rooter's hopes were buoyed when it was announced that their newest acquisition, Bob Bowman, was being shipped back to Miami to join the club. Bowman had proven to be a more than capable middle-of-the-order hitter, blasting out twenty dingers and eighty-three ribbies the previous season with Syracuse, and he was just what the doctor ordered to revive a so far moribund offense.

After sinking to 2–6, the Marlins ran off a six-game win streak, only to be rudely interrupted by a 6–5 loss to Montreal in the final game of a fifteen-game homestand. Osborn, who had been using Paige only sparingly in relief, awarded him his first start of the season on April 29, in the second game of a doubleheader. It was to be vintage Paige.

A total of 5,536 paying customers found their way into Miami Stadium in short-sleeve weather to see the forty-nine-year-old legend. Veeck, always the promoter, was pronouncing Paige to be a more advanced fifty-six years old. Veeck never skipped a beat. It only took one hour and thirty-eight minutes and eighty-three pitches to dispatch the Royals, who were held to four puny hits. Paige, who exhibited his usual pinpoint control, struck out four Royals and only walked two, without giving up a single run or extra base hit. Right fielder Bowman did his part by driving in two runs—one with his second homer of the evening—earning Paige his first win of the season by the score of 3–0. After the game Paige confidently bragged, "I wasn't tired at all. Pitching a full game is easier than pitching relief because you get a chance to use all your pitches." [8]

Paige's control and command of the strike zone was the impetus for what legends are made. To several of Paige's new teammates, his command was simply a source of amazement and something that they had never experienced, and never would again.

Paige was known to use various articles at his disposal as a home plate, and he even would throw balls through a hole in the outfield fence from great distances to prove his prowess with the horsehide. Always the showman, Paige also exhibited his skills on the sidelines to his many admirers who watched starry-eyed in disbelief from the stands.

> *Bob Bowman*: The kids [referring to the young pitchers on the staff], when they were out running in the outfield before the game, he'd go out with the pitchers and run and stuff. They always had something going. If there was a knot hole in the fence for a home run thing, I think it was in Columbus, Ohio, Satch would throw the ball through that hole from a pitching distance. They always had something going on.
>
> He'd warm up over cigarette packs sometimes and hit the corners. Oh yeah. He would try almost anything. [9]

> *Mel Clark*: I enjoyed him so much. These young ballplayers, catchers, when he'd warm up he'd want to warm up throwing over a cigarette for home plate down in the bullpen. That was his home plate: a cigarette. . . . It was funny. [10]

> *Earl Hunsinger*: Absolutely, you know, you hear the stories about him putting a gum wrapper on home plate and throwing across it is absolutely true. I saw him do it. [11]

Wilbur Johnson: Satchel Paige did throw hard but what he used for home plate was a paper cup. He threw that thing over that paper cup nineteen out of twenty times.[12]

Ben Tompkins: He'd come to spring training on his first day and he'd put a Dixie cup on the ground. That was home plate and would warm up throwing over the Dixie cup. But it was amazing.[13]

Jack Spring: I remember a couple of times he would go get a paper cup, and he would smash it down so that it was flat, and then he'd get his warm-up catcher. Quite often it was "Gussie" Niarhos, and he'd bring him down right in front of the stands where the people were and then he'd say, "OK, you're right here." He's set the cup down right on the ground in front of him [Niarhos] and that was his home plate. And then he'd pace off his, however many paces, for his distance and he'd warm up right there in front of the stands with the cup for home plate.[14]

Two old war horses, Paige and Niarhos, soon developed a special rapport that only a pitcher and catcher can understand. Micelotta remembers the simplistic understanding the two veterans had.

Bob Micelotta: He had a strange relationship [with] Gus Niarhos, who was the catcher. At one time he was the bullpen catcher for the Yankees. And old Gus never gave him a signal to Satch for a curveball; he just sat up. He squatted down put his glove down and Satch just threw to it.[15]

Brimming with confidence, the Marlins began their first road swing of the year heading north to Buffalo, Rochester, Toronto, Montreal, and Columbus. Most of the ballplayers were used to traveling by charter plane, although the rookies had mostly traveled by bus at their prior minor league stop. In the IL all teams traveled by chartering flights, most because of the distance between cities. However, as many of the ballplayers remember, the planes were not always first class.

Bob Bowman: We flew just about everywhere we went. . . . The flying was, I think with airlines; it was Regina Airlines; kind of Mickey Mouse DC-4s.

One night we had to stop in Pittsburgh and let some people off, or something. And we took off from Pittsburgh. The airport sets on top of a mountain or hill and when we took off one of the engines cut out and we were actually below the airport when the engine cut out and it was kind of scary.

Regina Airlines, I think that's what it was, Regina Airlines. [laughing heartily] It was kind of a little Mickey Mouse.[16]

Paige was known to have his reservations about flying, but one ballplayer in particular, Gus "Gussie" Niarhos, had to acquire a little courage every time before he boarded the plane. Spring remembers the veterans, especially Niarhos and his fear of flying:

Jack Spring: Mel [Clark] was a little older. He had been in the big leagues a little bit. He, and Cal Abrams, and the catcher Gus Niarhos. One thing I remember about Gus, one of the funny things that happened, in those days we flew a charter service out of Purdue, Indiana called Purdue Airlines. They flew these pre–World War II airplanes— DC-3s. And so we would go out to the airport for the first trip, and of course we don't go through the terminal, we go out to some hangar somewhere. And the pilot, they got a bathroom scale sitting on the tarmac there and they're sitting the bags on a [pause] "Hey '35' put that one up front," and then "put that in the rear." Old Gussie Niarhos, he was just down from the big leagues, and the big show, and here we are at an old airplane weighing our bags and he just like fainted on the tarmac; there, of course. [laughing] "Oh my god we're going to fly on that." [laughing even harder]

It was quite an experience flying in those things. I don't think they went eight hundred miles and we would have to land and fuel them up. Yeah that was something. It was a little better when we didn't take them over to Havana. We went over there kind of first class for those games. [17]

Wilbur Johnson: Oh, Gus Niarhos. Oh yeah, Gus. He played with us for a little while but he was afraid to fly. He wouldn't fly, but they said, "You got to fly." And, you know, we have to get to all of these cities in the International League. And what did he do? He got drunk and would pass out. And then, so then, they said, "We can't tolerate this," so he joined me later and played with Schenectady. It was Schenectady or Williamsport and he ended up being the catcher there because it was a bus league. [18]

Winning and losing streaks would soon become a trademark of the Marlins, and they began their first road trip by losing nine of their first ten games. The Fish were colder than the winter lake effect in Buffalo. What was even more disconcerting was that seven of the nine losses were by one run. Some of the blame was placed on Bowman, who, after an impressive start, was mired in a miserable oh-for-twenty-seven slump. [19]

Jimmy Burns, sports editor for the *Miami Herald*, succinctly stated in regards to the team's play, "Pretty promises about strengthening this Miami club must be redeemed in a hurry—or else." Ben Tincup, a pitching coach, and Eddie Miller, infield coach, were dispatched from the parent Phillies to help get the club back on track. [20] On May 17, the Phillies sent some reinforcement in strong-armed outfielder Glen Gorbous after acquiring longtime Philadelphia fan favorite Elmo Valo, who had just been released by the crosstown Athletics. [21] The rocket-armed Gorbous gained a level of notoriety the following year when he threw a baseball 445 feet, 10 inches, breaking the previous world record held by Don Grate. Gorbous was a member of Omaha Cardinals of the AA when he broke the record on August 1, 1957, which he holds to this day. [22]

Sid Salomon Jr. fulfilled his earlier promise of bringing Miami a winner. One of his first major moves was signing eight-year major league veteran outfielder Cal Abrams. Abrams, who grew up in the Brooklyn Dodgers organization and later played for Cincinnati, Pittsburgh, Baltimore, and the Chicago White Sox, was an old hand who brought a proven bat (ML stats: .269, .386 OBP)[23] and provided stability to the clubhouse. Abrams would make his first appearance on May 11 in Montreal. He quickly paid dividends by reaching base twice along while delivering his first hit. Although not fleet of foot, or the purveyor of great power, Abrams was an outstanding fly-chaser and an on-base machine that was just what the Marlins needed at the top of the order to set the table. Abrams would finish the season with 119 walks in 129 games and a .422 OBP.[24] "You can't be a pennant contender in this league with a rookie in centerfield," said Buffalo manager Phil Cavarretta. "He's an old pro who knows what he's doing. A guy like that gives a club a lot of confidence out there."[25] Confidence is just what Abrams would help to instill in the Marlins, and his influence quickly became apparent during their soon-to-be turnaround.

Veeck and Salomon Jr. were just beginning to wheel and deal by putting the needed pieces in place. The fans in the Magic City may have reason to be concerned, but better days were ahead. Miami was yet a force to be reckoned with in the IL.

NOTES

1. *Sporting News*, May 9, 1956, 26.
2. Norris Anderson, "Phillies and Marlins 'Happy' With Young Pitching Talent," *Miami News*, February 24, 1956.
3. Baseball-reference.com.
4. Mark Ribowsky, *Don't Look Back: Satchel Paige in the Shadows of Baseball* (New York: Simon & Schuster, 1994), 309–10.
5. Jack Spring, phone interview with the author, March 16, 2010.
6. Howard Kleinberg, "Marlins Play 7½ Hours without Finding Hitter," *Miami News*, April 23, 1956.
7. Ibid.
8. "Ancient Satch Keeps Rollin' Blanks Royals in Miami Bow," *Sporting News*, May 9, 1956, 26.
9. Bob Bowman, phone interview with the author, February 22, 2010.
10. Mel Clark, phone interview with the author, March 15, 2010.
11. Earl Hunsinger, phone interview with the author, March 15, 2010.
12. Wilbur Johnson, phone interview with the author, March 11, 2010.
13. Benjamin Tompkins, phone interview with the author, March 2, 2010.
14. Jack Spring, phone interview with the author, March 16, 2010.
15. Bob Micelotta, phone interview with the author, October 23, 2011.
16. Bowman interview, February 22, 2010.
17. Spring interview.
18. Johnson interview.
19. *Sporting News*, May 16, 1956, 30.
20. *Sporting News*, May 23, 1956, 28.

21. "Player Transactions," *Sporting News*, May 30, 1956, 38.

22. *Sporting News*, August 14, 1957, 35.

23. Gary Gillette and Pete Palmer, *The ESPN Baseball Encyclopedia*, 5th ed. (New York: Sterling, 2008).

24. Baseball-reference.com.

25. Norris Anderson, "The Miami Story," *Miami News*, August 4, 2010.

FOUR

Marlins Swim into Contention

The Marlins returned home to the friendly confines of Miami Stadium on May 18 for a nine-game homestand to play host to Richmond, followed by Columbus. The opener against the Virginians—or Vees, as they were more popularly known—found the Marlins hovering only a half game above the IL basement at 11–17. Only the Havana Sugar Kings, at 10–17, had a worse mark.

Prior to the series, the Marlins announced their intention to maintain Hall-of-Famer Jimmie Foxx as a full-time coach.[1] The barrel-chested Foxx was no longer the svelte six-foot, two-hundred-pound Adonis of his playing days when he established himself as one of baseball's premier sluggers; still, he was an imposing figure. Now gray around the temples and a little wider in girth, Foxx had been struggling with a drinking problem dating back to when he was a ballplayer. His post-baseball career had been a rocky one as he jumped from job to job, mostly living on his name and past fame. With the help of Veeck and Osborn, he was getting yet another chance. Early in the season Foxx had been only assisting Don Osborn during home games, but now would travel with the team on the road as well.[2] Foxx's role was critical, since he took it upon himself to impart his wealth of batting knowledge as one of the game's all-time greatest hitters and share it with his players. One of his first projects was showing Ed Bouchee and Bob Bowman how to narrow their batting stances to give them more control with the bat. As the season wore on, Foxx would receive praise for his mentoring.[3]

Foxx's arrival must have been cause for celebration, judging by the team's performance. The Marlins were led by Don Cardwell's nine strike-outs, guiding his team to a 3–1 victory over the Vees. Satchel Paige picked up the save and Cal Abrams was the offensive difference maker, driving in two runs. Nevertheless, Miami's woes continued during the remainder

27

of the series as they dropped the next three games, while in the process being outscored 19–5. In the second game of the Sunday doubleheader, Paige lost his first decision of the year to Richmond's Carlton Post. Paige's teammates failed to plate a single run, and managed only a paltry three hits, dropping the tilt 2–0. A sparse crowd of only 3,221 showed up. Team ownership blamed the game being televised as the reason for the low turnout.[4] It was to be the low point of the season.

The Marlins lived up to their reputation as a streaky team for the rest of the month. First, they took four out of five games from Columbus, including shutting out the Jets in three of the meetings. The Marlins nearly garnered a fourth shutout on May 24, behind Gene Snyder, who pitched shutout ball into the eighth inning before being relieved by Paige, who yielded a solo run in the ninth inning that led to a 6–1 final.

In the previous night's double dip, Seth Morehead crafted a four-hit, 5–0 shutout in the twilight game, and Cardwell came back in the night-cap, hurling a five-hit, 7–0 shutout. In the process Cardwell recorded his fourth win against no losses and tallied his forty-seventh strikeout in forty-nine innings worked. During this same series the pitching staff had a dominating stretch, only allowing one earned run over thirty-eight innings.

Upon Miami's return from the road, they took two of three from Richmond, and then six out of eight from Havana in an away and home series with the last four games played in the inhospitable environs of Havana's Gran Stadium. One of the keys to the Marlins' recent reversal of fortunes was Bowman's resurgence with the bat. Foxx's coaching was paying dividends. Following an earlier 0–27 slump, Bowman went on a tear going 13–27, including slamming his first grand slam of the year that helped sink the Vees on May 27, 7–6.[5]

The Marlins headed off to Havana to close out May and kick off June. Since joining the league in 1954, the beautiful tropical paradise of sun, sand, and beautiful brown-skinned Latin women (look out for the "Dalton Gang") had quickly established itself as the favorite road trip stop in the IL. From 1946–1953, Havana had participated in the six-team Class B Florida International League, winning four pennants and two playoff titles, but was hungry for a higher grade of competition.[6]

Following the 1953 season, Bobby Maduro, the successful Cuban entrepreneur, approached Frank Shaughnessy and the IL fathers with an offer that they couldn't refuse. A major concern to the IL was travel costs that each team would incur and rampant gambling interests that were commonplace in and around the game. Maduro overcame both objections by offering $60,000 in travel expenses to compensate teams for their expenses and had four hundred gamblers arrested on their opening day in the league, sweeping the problem away. In addition, the use of Gran Stadium and its thirty-five-thousand seating capacity offered ample room for attendance, accompanied by an avid and boisterous fan base that was especially attractive to a league dealing with lagging atten-dance.[7]

> *Jack Spring*: I loved it. . . . You know the people were happy . . . they had bands and drummers up in the stands. They were really having a big time. I really enjoyed playing there. . . . They drew really good crowds . . . it was a luxurious place as far as we were concerned.[8]

The Marlins had begun to scratch and crawl their way up the stand-ings beginning in late May by taking four out of five from Columbus in Miami, then sweeping three games from Richmond on the road before returning home again and taking three out of four from Havana.

As was the custom that season, Miami would play a home/road series with Havana. Upon returning to Miami the Marlins lost their last game of May rather convincingly to the Sugar Kings, 11–1, behind the crafty hurl-ing of right-hander and ex-Chicago Cub Vicente Amor.

June started out promisingly enough as the Marlins bounced back in the second game of the series as Cardwell and Paige combined to coast to an easy 7–2 victory. Bowman, Cardwell, Gorbous, and Micelotta all ho-mered in the game in front of three thousand screaming supporters.

Gene Snyder and Angelo LiPetri held the Sugar Kings to four hits for the second night in a row, as the Marlins cruised 3–0. Snyder was pulled after five and a third innings because of control problems resulting in five walks, a hit batsman, and a wild pitch. LiPetri was up to the task and closed the game out while striking out three and stingily allowing no free passes. The heroes of the game were Wilbur Johnson, Bob Micelotta, Ben Tompkins, and Ed Bouchee, who in total accounted for three double plays and an errorless defense.

The *pièce de résistance* was the final game at Miami Stadium with Paige squaring off against lefty Charlie Rabe. Rabe had about as much luck against Paige as he did against major league hitters, failing to win a single contest during his brief stay in the big show. "Old Satch" only hung around for five innings, letting Seth Morehead do the cleanup work in a tidy 5–2 win. Abrams and Micelotta each drove in a couple of runs to spur the offense.[9] The Marlins were beginning to gel.

By June 9 the Marlins had reached the .500 mark. The month of June would prove to be kind as the team registered nineteen wins in thirty contests. The Marlins had closed the gap on first-place Montreal, leaving them only six games behind the frontrunners and in first division. The once moribund offense scored in double figures five times, including a doubleheader sweep in Buffalo on June 15, winning by scores of 10–2 and 11–3.[10]

Further good news for the pitching corps was Dick Farrell's return from a broken ankle suffered during spring training. Farrell made his first appearance on June 10, pitching a scoreless inning in relief in the opening game of a doubleheader, a 3–2 win over Buffalo.[11] Farrell would soon join the starting rotation.

Just like chili made from scratch, where the conglomeration of ingredients form a tasty dish, the Marlins were finding a winning combination in the sum of their parts. While the "Dalton Gang" was keeping the mood loose in the clubhouse with their pranks, the veterans like Abrams, Gordon, Micelotta, Niarhos, and Tompkins were making sure the team didn't stray too far off course. On top of everything else, Paige was fitting in with his charges like the last piece of a jigsaw puzzle.

Paige, always the consummate teammate, found himself the recipient of many of the pranks the "Dalton Gang" pulled, but wasn't remiss in dishing them out in return. Paige understood, better than anyone, that the tension of a long season had to be released in small doses or else everything would explode. The players, and even the batboy, remembered the never-ending hijinks.

> *Tim Anagnost*: The things that Satchel Paige, that they did to him. For some reason they must have liked him a lot because you don't do this to people you don't like. . . . They once, they had these stand-up lockers and they were opened, and they nailed his uniform to the wall of the locker. They nailed down his shoes to the floor. They nailed his cap down. . . . I never saw him get mad at anybody. There never was any animosity toward each other.[12]

> *Wilbur Johnson*: [laughing while remembering Paige] Oh yeah, he was a character. He loved to play. He loved to play with that Jim Owens and Seth Morehead. They would throw buckets of water at each other. Then sometimes they would miss and they would get another bunch of guys in the locker next to them.[13]

> *Tom Qualters*: They were a bunch of crazy guys. Holy Mackerel! I'll tell you what. You never knew what was going to happen next. I mean, it was in the clubhouse, in the motel, it was everywhere we went. . . . Oh my god, it never stopped. These young guys were the guys pulling it off. They were pulling it off on the older veterans and stuff. They didn't care about anything.
>
> I mean, they were absolutely nuts. They were good guys, but oh man, you had to cover your back all the time because you didn't know what was happening. They picked on Satch a lot, but Satch loved it because they gave him all their attention. They nailed his shoes to the floor and all kinds of crap. He'd come in and get dressed, and he'd be sitting around, and the first thing he'd do was shake out his uniform to make sure there were no bugs or big beetles in his sanitary socks. And then they'd nail his hat to the locker . . . It was just nonstop and they did this with everybody.[14]

Although Paige was a victim of many pranks, he was also quick to get his revenge and his teammates loved him for it. Satch was the fun-loving free spirit and was the antithesis to his manager Osborn. Osborn took his baseball very seriously, but although he and Paige were polar opposites in their philosophy, they had a great deal of respect for each other.

Hunsinger, a member of the Marlins in 1956 and 1957, remembered his manager pulling the team aside. Osborn told everyone when Paige signed with the team that he didn't have to follow the same rules that he always set down. "Fellas," Osborn explained, "I'm breaking one of my rules. Normally we treat everybody the same but because of Satchel's age don't be surprised if he doesn't show up until the fifth or sixth inning, or something." Hunsinger amusingly recounted, "Sure enough that would be when Satchel would show up."[15]

Osborn was a strict manager, but the special relationship and admiration he had for Paige was not more evident than an incident that occurred on June 11. This vintage Paige episode occurred after Paige had failed to catch the team's charter flight to Rochester. General Manager Eddie Stumpf claimed that Paige told him that he overslept,[16] but according to Paige in his autobiography, *Maybe I'll Pitch Forever*, he got mixed up on his times.

> That took about every penny I had. When I got to Rochester, I got up to Don Osborn's room fast. "That's too bad," he said. He was burning good.
>
> "It sure does take a piece of change to get up here."
>
> "Why, I got here with a dollar and a half and that wasn't even cab fare to the hotel. I ain't even got eatin' money, Don, and I suspect I'll have to speak to somebody about that."
>
> "What'd you do with that dollar and a half?" Don asked me. He still was mad.
>
> "I got me a little coffee and rolls when I got in."
>
> Don just looked at me for a minute. Then he started grinning. He wasn't hot anymore, that was for sure. I felt a lot better.
>
> "You gonna get me some eatin' money?" I asked.
>
> "We'll get you some."[17]

Osborn understood all too well that Paige couldn't be controlled, and hoping to contain him was almost too much to ask; it was like trying to catch the wind in the palm of your hand. But Paige was the least of his concerns; with the team on a roll and a long season still ahead, the Marlins were a team hotter than the noonday sun on Miami Beach. Paige was 5–3 with a 1.83 ERA, good enough for third in the league. The only pitcher with a lower ERA was Tom Qualters at 1.76 with a 4–3 mark.[18] Not to be forgotten was Cardwell, sporting a glossy 9–1 record, who had established himself as the ace of the staff. Cardwell would later go on to a successful major league career (102–138, 3.92), including hurling a no-hitter on May 15, 1960 for the Chicago Cubs, and in the process blanking the St. Louis Cardinals 4–0.[19] Cardwell was also a key member of the World Champion 1969 Miracle Mets staff.

With Cardwell and Paige pitching lights out, and the offense coming to life, you could feel the excitement in the air in the Magic City and it wasn't the humidity. The Marlins had turned the corner.

NOTES

1. *Sporting News*, May 30, 1956, 29.
2. Ibid., 32.
3. *Sporting News*, June 27, 1956, 34.
4. *Sporting News*, May 30, 1956, 30.
5. *Sporting News*, June 6, 1956, 27–28.
6. Bill O'Neal, *International League: A Baseball History 1884–1991* (Austin, TX: Eakin Press, 1992), 276–77.
7. Rory Costello, "Bobby Maduro," 2009, www.bioproj.sabr.org.
8. Jack Spring, phone interview with the author, March 16, 2010.
9. *Sporting News*, June 13, 1956, 38.
10. *Sporting News*, June 27, 1956, 32.
11. *Sporting News*, June 20, 1956, 28.
12. Tim Anagnost, personal interview with the author, May 9, 2010.
13. Wilbur Johnson, phone interview with the author, March 11, 2010.
14. Tom Qualters, phone interview with the author, March 5, 2010.
15. Earl Hunsinger, phone interview with the author, March 15, 2010.
16. Jimmy Burns, "Satch's Nap Proves Costly; Has to Buy Own Air Ducat," *Sporting News*, June 20, 1956, 28.
17. David Lipman and Satchel Paige, *Maybe I'll Pitch Forever* (Garden City, NY: Doubleday, 1962).
18. *Sporting News*, July 4, 1956, 29.
19. Gary Gillette and Pete Palmer, *The ESPN Baseball Encyclopedia*, 5th ed. (New York: Sterling Publishing, 2008).

FIVE

The View Looks Pretty Good from Up Here

Don Osborn had to feel good. Satchel Paige hadn't missed any of the team flights since the Columbus incident, and the Marlins were closing in on the IL top spot. July found Osborn's charges in Toronto against the veteran-laden Maple Leafs. Although Montreal was residing at the top of the standings, Toronto was considered by many to be the favorite to take the IL. The roster was loaded with veterans with major league experience, like former Yankee third sacker Loren Babe, Phillies "Whiz Kid" and second baseman Mike Goliat (1956 IL MVP), 1950 NL Rookie of the Year Sam Jethroe, Hector Rodriguez, Ed Stevens, and Archie Wilson. Unlike the rest of the league, the majority of the players filling Toronto's roster were over thirty years of age, and of the thirty-two players who appeared in games during the season, eighteen were north of their thirtieth birthday. One of the reasons the Leafs carried so many senior ballplayers was that they were independent of any major league affiliation, and thus had more freedom to sign veterans versus depending on youngsters trying to climb their way up the ladder to the big show. And the second reason was that team owner Jack Kent Cooke had deep pockets and was willing to spend cash to field a competitive team. Toronto was typically a league leader in attendance and they were frequent visitors when it came playoff time.

Miami had already split the first leg of the northern road swing with Montreal, taking two of four games. The longtime Dodgers farm team that once boasted Jackie Robinson as its "favorite son" had been playing the Marlins almost straight up all season, winning seven of the fifteen meetings. A cause of concern for the Marlins was an injury to Bob Bowman, a result of a hairline chip on his ribs from a sliding injury that later would be determined to be a torn rib cartilage. Bowman had put together

33

his most impressive month of the season, compiling thirty-one ribbies on twenty-nine hits. His bat was one the Marlins could scarcely afford to lose. Bowman would finish the month only one behind Luke Easter's seventeen for the IL lead in the home run race.[1]

The Marlins got off on the right foot against the Leafs, beating them in the opener in Maple Leaf Stadium 2–1 behind the stellar pitching of Bob Greenwood, who raised his record to 4–4. Greenwood, who hadn't started a game since May 7, held his opponents to a mere four hits.[2] It would be Greenwood's final win before being shipped off to San Diego and the Pacific Coast League later in the season.

The first two days of July proved to be fatiguing for the road-weary Marlins as they faced back-to-back doubleheaders. In the first game of the July 1 twin bill the Marlins fell in a heartbreaker 10–9 in ten frames. Brooklyn-born Angelo LiPetri took the loss in relief. Ben Tompkins, a former star quarterback at the University of Texas, blasted two home runs and collected four RBIs that went for naught in a losing effort.

On a brighter note, Don Cardwell pitched seven shutout innings in the second game to earn a 3–0 shutout win. It was Cardwell's tenth win against a solitary loss, leaving him only one win behind the league leader, Lynn Lovenguth.[3] Lovenguth, who had amassed an impressive eleven wins to this point, would finish the season winning the IL's version of the Cy Young Award as pitcher of the year, with twenty-four wins. Ironically, Lovenguth had spent the previous year with Syracuse, but had been let go by the Phillies prior to the 1956 season in favor of younger prospects coming up through the system.

The July 2 twilight game, on Canadian Dominion Day, found the Marlins taking their worst defeat of the season, 18–4. In front of a crowd of 9,068 faithful Leafs rooters, Lovenguth would get one of his most satisfying victories of the season, collecting his twelfth win and his eighth in a row. He found more than ample support from his teammates to the tune of twenty-three hits. Starter Gene Snyder was chased after only two and a third innings but didn't take the loss. Instead, Thornton Kipper took the defeat in relief and Tom Qualters had the indignity, while Osborn gave the relief staff some rest, of giving up the final nine runs, seven of which were earned, before the game mercifully ended.

Seth Morehead started, and lost, the night game 2–1 that was played in only one hour and forty-eight minutes. It was Morehead's seventh loss against only two wins for the season. Morehead continued to play the role of the Marlins' hard-luck pitcher. A two-run dinger by second-sacker Goliat proved to be the difference maker.[4]

Miami moved on to Richmond, losing three of four games before closing out the road trip sweeping Columbus in four, then taking two of three in Havana from the Sugar Kings. For the rest of the month of July Miami either took or tied every series they played, and by the end of July they found themselves in a first-place tie with Toronto.

When the going gets tough, the tough get going. So it was with Paige, as once again he proved to be invaluable in the clutch. On July 29 against Montreal in the first game of an afternoon doubleheader, the Marlins moved into first place for the first time all season. Recently acquired Tony Ponce, who started the game and worked the first seven innings, left with the score knotted at 4–4. Paige, who was quickly becoming known as the Marlins' best Sunday pitcher, toiled the last six innings before the Marlins finally broke the tie and drove across a run on an Ed Bouchee single, breaking the deadlock in the thirteenth inning. Paige lifted his record to a glossy 8–3.

Unfortunately, the Marlins followed the heart-stopping first game by dropping the second game 5–4. Jack Spring remembers that Sid Salomon Jr. had drawn up this special day-night doubleheader in hopes of improving attendance and earning a little extra cash at the gate. This, of course, went over with the players like a lead balloon. However, Spring also remembered how generous and apologetic Salomon Jr. was with everyone, and how he showed his charitable nature.[5]

> *Jack Spring*: They decided to try a split doubleheader on a Sunday. Play one in the afternoon and the other at six or seven in the evening. I'm pretty sure it was Sid, wrote a little note to every player about the inconvenience of this on a Sunday . . . he included money. I don't remember what it was; $20. You could probably take your family to dinner for $20 in those days. [laughing] But anyway it was a little thank you for the inconvenience of doing that [*Sporting News* reported it was $25].[6]

Salomon Jr., who deeply loved a variety of sports, was considered one of the most generous owners in the minor leagues. Salomon had a long history of munificence going back to his financial interest with Bill Veeck, including his sojourn with the St. Louis Browns, and was known to be almost parental with his players and employees.

Salomon Jr. understood the value of hard work and showed appreciation for the efforts of those in his employ. Holding down as many as five jobs as a youth, he began selling insurance at the tender age of nineteen and soon became a repeated member of the exclusive *Million Dollar Round Table*. After making his fortune, he couldn't escape his love of athletics and later became the owner of a new hockey franchise in 1967, the St. Louis Blues. His efforts laid the groundwork for one of the most successful franchises in the history of the NHL.[7] Many of the positive traits he had as an owner reflected on the players, who appreciated the first-class operation that he operated, almost comparable to their big-league experiences.

> *Bob Bowman*: I have a lot of good memories about Miami. The year, in general, was a little bit different than what I was used to. There was

more attention paid by the ownership and management than we were used to. But everybody I knew on the ball club really enjoyed the year.[8]

Jack Spring: Sid Salomon was really a nice guy. One thing I remember he did, they had a party at his home. This was quite a luxurious place. I never saw it, but all of the wives were invited to a poolside party at his home and they gave a little charm; a Marlin cutout. It probably was the size of a fifty-cent piece in those days. It had a Marlin stamped out of it and it had a very small diamond for an eye. It was really a charm on a necklace, and he gave each of the wives one of those.[9]

The next night against Buffalo, Paige once again answered the call and saved the day, this time for Dick Farrell. With the potential tying run on first with two outs, Paige entered the game for Farrell, who was suffering the effects of fatigue from another South Florida steaming summer night. It only took the minimum amount of pitches before the wily veteran fanned Norm Sherry on three straight pitches. Final tally read Marlins 6, Bisons 5, and Farrell had his seventh win against only three losses for the season.[10]

The Marlins' continued turnaround could be attributed to several moves in July that bolstered the team and their hopes of grabbing an inaugural season pennant. Salomon proudly announced, "We promised before the season that if were within striking distance around the Fourth of July, we would go all out to bring a pennant to Miami. And that's just what we we're trying to do." The first two of four moves orchestrated by the team occurred on July 7. To find relief for the overworked veteran backstop Gus Niarhos, the Marlins acquired two catchers: Ray Holton from Louisville, and Toby Atwell from Omaha of the AA. Although Atwell was summarily sold to Milwaukee of the AA, Holton would quickly establish himself as the alternating catcher for the rest of the season with Niarhos. In addition, the Marlins got reacquainted with pitcher Jim Owens, returned from the parent Phillies, who found himself reunited with the "Dalton Gang." It was hoped that Owens would add depth to the starting rotation.

The biggest player swap of the month, also on July 7, involved four players. Pitcher Thornton Kipper and utility infield Wilbur Johnson (on option) along with cash were sent to Louisville. The Marlins then acquired thirty-four-year-old veteran pitcher Tony Ponce (9–7, 4.46) from Louisville and on option from the Washington Senators infielder Pompey "Yo-Yo" Davalillo.[11]

However, the dealing wasn't done yet. The most far-reaching deal made by the Marlins was consummated on July 26 when the Sugar Kings agreed to sell Woody Smith to Miami for $15,000 cash. To casual fans of baseball, memories of the first Marlins mostly revolve around the exploits of Satchel Paige. However, to Miamians who remember those lexicon days, the player who would come to best exemplify the face of the

Marlins was the man from University City, Missouri: Forrest Elwood Smith. The ruggedly Hollywood handsome Smith would have fit the mold perfectly as a leading man in 1950s and 1960s Western movie flicks, riding on his white stag and saving settlers from some unknown fate. One of his many legacies would be being one of only two players to represent the Marlins every season during their five-year stay in the IL. Always a gentleman, he was well liked by both male fans and female supporters. "Woody," as he was widely known, earned a reputation for always keeping his thick, dusty brown locks combed to perfection and satisfying his admirers' expectations. The beloved Smith would later return to Miami to manage Class A ball for four seasons from 1969–1972, winning four straight Florida State League championships, and even made a few plate appearances during his stay as skipper. His work ethic, hustle, and personal connection with the fans of Miami formed a symbiotic relationship of mutual admiration enjoyed by both parties.

> *Earl Hunsinger*: Woody was not only the favorite of the players, but of the fans too. Woody was very outgoing, hustled all of the time, and never slacked up. He was a third baseman and I'll never forget, you know, after each groundout you used to throw the ball around the infield. The third baseman always throws it back to the pitcher, and Woody, when he threw the ball back to you, always had something good to say. He was quite a gentleman.[12]

Smith wasted no time making a lasting impression in his first appearance. The hometown faithful were delighted as he knocked out four hits in four at-bats, helping the Marlins defeat the visiting Leafs 4–3. Even more impressive was the fact that Smith did it against league-wins leader Lovenguth in the midst of his finest season as a professional.[13]

Smith's sale to the Marlins sent tremors throughout the league. Even Toronto's ever-confident manager, Bruno Wetzel, was predicting Miami to be his team's biggest competition going into the final weeks of the season. Smith, who had been unhappy in Havana, was rejuvenated, and, according to Montreal manager Greg Mulleavy, "Smitty is liable to hit ten or fifteen home runs in Miami Stadium because everything there is in favor of right-handed pull hitters." Mulleavy went as far as to say the acquisition of Smith should clinch the pennant for the Marlins.[14]

As the beginning of August rolled around, it found the Marlins tied with Toronto for first place with a record of 62–46 and the Rochester Red Wings lurking only two games behind the front-runners at 59–47. Montreal had begun to fade and was now resting five and a half games back at 58–53. Optimism was bountiful in the Magic City but there were still more than forty games left to play and Montreal, Rochester, and Toronto still had something to say about it. Pennant fever was in the air and the sprint to the finish was turning out to be closer than the presidential race between Harry Truman and Adlai Stevenson. And just around the corner was the game that would forever symbolize the Miami Marlins in the hearts of baseball fans everywhere.

NOTES

1. *Sporting News*, July 11, 1956, 35–36.
2. Ibid., 38.
3. Ibid., 35.
4. Ibid., 35, 38.
5. *Sporting News*, August 8, 1956, 27–28.
6. Jack Spring, phone interview with the author, March 16, 2010.
7. Bob Broeg, *One Hundred Greatest Moments in St. Louis Sports* (St. Louis: Missouri History Museum, 2000), 133.
8. Bob Bowman, phone interview with the author, February 22, 2010.
9. Spring interview.
10. *Sporting News*, August 8, 1956, 27–28.
11. *Sporting News*, July 18, 1956, 34.
12. Earl Hunsinger, phone interview with the author, March 15, 2010.
13. *Sporting News*, August 8, 1956, 28.
14. Jimmy Burns, "Marlins Deaf to First-Year Pennant Warning by Betzel," *Sporting News*, August 8, 1956, 28.

SIX

Life Is a Bowl of Oranges

Tuesday, August 7, 1956, will arguably go down as one of the most famous minor league games in baseball history. Not because it was a classic do-or-die match-up for the pennant, or a colossal effort by its participants that lent itself to legend, but because the event was such a spectacle that the people in Miami who saw the game remembered it in the same vein that New Yorkers would remember "Thomson's Shot Heard Round the World," or how Bostonians recall Carlton Fisk's 1978 World Series blast that snuggled itself just inside the foul pole.

The game, or should I say event, was Barnum & Bailey, a night at the Oscars, and American Bandstand all rolled into one juicy, sweet nougat Field of Dreams. At center stage of the circus big top was Bill Veeck and his star attraction, Satchel Paige. It was Veeck at his pure best, using the same tried-and-true formula that previously worked for him when he was the owner of the Cleveland Indians to fill seats when on the night of August 20, 1948, 78,382 packed into Municipal Stadium, or as it was known at times, Cleveland's "The Mistake by the Lake," setting a then all-time attendance record for a night game.

Veeck had his sights set squarely on surpassing the minor league record of 56,391 established in Jersey City on April 17, 1941. To break the record he realized that he would have to pull out all the stops and billed the event as "The Baseball Party to End All Baseball Parties." As with any production, you need a star and a stage to carry out the action. Veeck had his star, the great Paige, and he rented the biggest stage he could find in Miami: the world-famous Orange Bowl.

Miami had just finished a road series with their season-long nemesis, the Rochester Red Wings. Rochester's sweep of the Marlins meant that the Wings had now won thirteen of the sixteen meetings between the two IL contenders. Osborn's crew was reeling as they returned home to face the Columbus Jets. Usually "money in the bank" pitchers, Don Cardwell and the reliable Dick Farrell had failed to come up aces in the recent away series and the Miamians were looking to Paige to reverse their fortunes. More disturbingly, the Marlins' bats had once again fallen silent and took the majority of the blame for the most recent five-game losing streak. In three of the four games against the Wings, the Marlins had plated only one run, and the only game that they produced more than a single tally was a five-run outburst in a 12–5 loss.

The cockles of the collective hearts of the Marlins must have been warmed upon seeing the largest crowd, up to this time, that the city of Miami had ever seen for a game of hardball. Announced as a charity game with proceeds to benefit the Columbus Club, Veeck had arranged, through promoter Coy Poe, a star-studded cast of entertainers that included the likes of Cab Calloway, the Russ Morgan Band, Helen O'Connell, Patricia Manville, Martha Raye, Ginny Simms, Margaret Whiting, Gloria De Haven, Merv Griffin, and four Dixieland bands sprinkled in for good measure. With festivities to begin two and a half hours before the start of the game, the required fifty-five cents to enter was more than worth the price of admission.

Joining the cavalcade of stage, screen, and music stars were some baseball royalty as well. The crown prince of baseball, Max Patkin, returned again to delight the crowd with his zany antics, and IL president Frank Shaughnessy, Minor League president George Trautman, and Hall-of-Famer Dazzy Vance were all accorded royal boxes with a view of the joust that was about to take place on the field.[1]

Paige had pitched in more big games in his career than most players had played games. To the wily veteran, it was just another day in the office. However, Paige did have an initial reservation prior to the game. With memories of Opening Night still in his mind, he addressed those concerns with his friend Veeck. "There ain't gonna be any parachutin' or anything like that for me?" inquired Paige. Veeck assured him there were no concerns beyond pitching the biggest game in the short life of the Marlins.[2] That was all that Paige needed to hear.

Orange Bowl Game Starting Lineups:

Columbus Jets	*Miami Marlins*
CF Bill Kern	CF Cal Abrams
3B Johnny Lipon	2B Ben Tompkins
2B Curt Roberts	1B Ed Bouchee
LF Russ Sullivan	RF Bob Bowman
RF Ben Downs	3B Woody Smith
1B Butch McCord	LF Glen Gorbous

C Billy Shantz   C Gus Niarhos

SS Russ Rose   SS Bob Micelotta

P Bob Kuzava   P Satchel Paige

Manager: Nick Cullop   Manager: Don Osborn

Both teams warmed up on the field and were acutely aware of the odd dimensions of their new playing field. In order to accommodate such a large crowd, the Orange Bowl venue was necessary, but in turn, putting a baseball field on a football field made for some unique configurations and ground rules. The right field fence was situated only 216 feet from home plate and the left field fence was only 250 feet away. A twelve-foot screen was placed from the right field line running toward centerfield that ran 165 feet around the perimeter of the outfield. Any ball that was hit over the screen was awarded a ground rule double unless it hit above the north ramp. In left field, balls hit between the bleachers in the west end zone were also to be ruled ground rule doubles unless they cleared the first ramp.[3] When Dazzy Vance was asked if he would be at all interested in toeing the rubber in the Orange Bowl, he politely replied, "No, not unless somebody digs a hole where the pitcher's mound is, so I can duck."[4] Even the Baker Bowl was cavernous compared to these proportions.

Bob Bowman was the starting right fielder; having no choice but to play in the shallow right field of the Orange Bowl, he looked more like a second baseman playing deep on a shift than a fly-chaser patrolling right. Bowman literally had his back up against the wall.

> *Bob Bowman*: We played in the Orange Bowl. We had 56,000 [actually 51,713] people at a Triple-A baseball game, which was very unusual. Of course, we had a big charity night and Margaret Whiting, and I'm trying to think of the others that performed. Satchel pitched that night and it was really interesting. The configuration of the ball field that they put into the Orange Bowl was interesting. In fact, I was playing right field and threw a guy out on a base hit. I threw him out at first. You know the fence was so shallow that I was playing almost a deep second base. [chuckling][5]

It was a typical summer Florida night. Scattered showers throughout the day had weighed the evening down with excess moisture left hanging in the air. The eighty-degree temperature was a mirage, as the humidity was thick and it probably seemed more like ninety-five degrees, exacerbated by the fact that people were sitting elbow to elbow.

Paige set down the visiting Jets quietly in the first inning. Ben Tompkins got the action started in the bottom of the same inning for the Marlins, with nobody on base, by driving a Bob Kuzava offering 365 feet into the left field stands. Tompkins, the bespectacled former University of

Texas star baseball and football player who looked more like a college professor than the athletic second baseman he was, to this day remembers this as one of the highlights of his baseball career. Ironically, it would be the only home run of the evening and would stand as the only one ever hit in the Orange Bowl.

In the third inning, the Marlins added to their lead. Woody Smith singled but was forced out at second base on a fielders' choice by Glen Gorbous. Gus Niarhos followed by doubling to left field, but Gorbous, who would have normally scored, was held at third, since Russ Sullivan was forced to play so shallow. Bob Micelotta was intentionally walked so that Kuzava could face the weak-hitting Paige.[6]

Although Paige was long past his best days as a hitter, he still took great pride in doing well at the plate. To this day Tim Anagnost remembers how Paige was anything but lackadaisical when it came to swinging the wood and was particular about his own bat.

> *Tim Anagnost*: He took his hitting very seriously, but he never got any hits. . . . He took it so seriously that he would put "SP" on the handle end of his bat. . . . All the position players had their names inscribed on their bats just like the big leaguers . . . pitchers did not have that. But Satchel Paige had found a bat apparently that he liked, and I can't recall whose bat it was but he had put "SP," in magic marker, on the handle of the bat so that anytime that he got into a game, starting or as a reliever, I had to make sure and get that bat."[7]

What followed couldn't have been better scripted even by Hollywood writing standards. Kuzava, the crafty veteran who had previously pitched in two World Series with the Yankees, had a strike already on Paige, and was looking to ease another one past the grizzled veteran. The crowd collectively leaned back in their seats and more than a few clamored toward the concession stands. It looked as if the Jets were going to escape the inning unscathed, when all of a sudden a crack of the bat shattered the air like a gunshot during hunting season. Paige sent a screaming line drive into centerfield, skipping past the centerfielder, Kern, who was probably just as shocked as everyone else. It was off to the races.

> *Tim Anagnost*: I think it probably went in the gap in left field. And the ball just kept rolling and rolling because left field [actually center field] had to be four hundred feet [actually estimated at 330 feet] or more instead of the normal dimensions. So the ball just kept rolling. It got past the outfield and he had to go chase it down.
>
> The bases were loaded and all three runs score, and I'm thinking to myself, I'm watching and looking to my left, and seeing the ball rolling. I said, "I can't believe it, Satchel Paige has just hit an inside the park home run." . . . And I look back and Satchel Paige is walking into second base. Anyone else would have been rounding third . . . you could almost trot around but he was literally walking into second base.

Kuzava was stunned, but found humor in the moment. One of his teammates later exclaimed, "Yeah, he got sore because he walked [Bob] Micelotta to get to him." It would turn out to be the game breaker the Marlins needed. Kuzava remembers the pitch as a fastball although Paige later claimed it was a curveball. Either way, the results were the same.

> *Bob Kuzava:* I'm laughing because Satchel Paige hit a double off of me. Leroy hit a double and he stood at second base and he was laughing at me and I laughed back at him. He was a great guy.
>
> [Asking Kuzava what pitch he threw] Oh, it was probably a fastball. I was trying to get ahead of him and throw a strike. He hit it and got a double.[8]

Columbus scored their first run in the seventh inning on a Butch McCord RBI single. Paige had already begun to wilt and by the top of the eighth inning he was spent. With no outs in the eighth, pinch-hitter Dick Getter and lead-off man Kern hit back-to-back singles. Paige then coaxed Johnny Lipon into a double play grounder to Tompkins, leaving Getter looming dangerously at third. The rubber-armed but weary Paige allowed the next batter, Roberts, to single, scoring Getter and cutting the lead to 4–2. Don Osborn had seen enough and it was obvious that the heat and excitement of the evening was taking its toll. "You're looking tired. Don't worry. You've shown them plenty. Go on in and take a rest," said Osborn. The manager signaled toward the bullpen and Paige was headed for the showers. Jack Spring trotted in, took his few warm-up tosses, and then proceeded to retire the last four Jet batters he faced in order to end the game. The Marlins did add a couple of insurance runs in the bottom of the eighth, padding their lead to 6–2. Tompkins started the scoring by doubling, and advanced to third on Ed Bouchee's single to right field. Bowman then singled up the middle, bringing in Tompkins. Bouchee later scored from third on a Smith sacrifice fly to finish the scoring. History had been made and Paige had prevailed again.[9]

The final score showed the Marlins on top 6–2. To everyone's surprise, the expected orgy of home runs and scoring never materialized. Paige so dominated the Jets that they could only muster seven hits total, including a scant three extra base hits that were all doubles. On the same night Toronto edged Montreal in twelve innings 5–4, maintaining their two-game lead over the second-place Fish.[10]

Most important, Bill Veeck and Sid Salomon Jr. had proved to the naysayers who had doubted they would be successful that baseball was a viable product in Miami. They indirectly planted the seed that thirty-seven years later would come to fruition in the form of major league baseball's entry of the Florida Marlins. But the predecessors, just like their successors, found that success would be hard earned. Despite the excitement of a pennant race, after the Orange Bowl game the crowds dwindled like an orchid in the South Beach sun. Salomon Jr., Veeck, and all the Marlins' front office staff envisioned surpassing Toronto's 1955 attendance mark of 350,742.[11] What they would find was that the endless distractions of white sandy beaches and sleepy, intimate night clubs, along with the constant threat of afternoon summer rains, would doom their optimistic vision. It became increasingly evident to Salomon Jr. and his protégés that the early advice that Veeck had so sagely shared ("Go back to the restaurant, tap the shoulder of the guy at the table on the other side of you and ask him if he wants to buy a ball club. If that doesn't work, go out into the street and try to spot some lamb walking by. If you don't have a buyer by nightfall, see if you can't give it to somebody. Believe me, it will be cheaper") had considerable merit.[12] Down the road, however belated it was, Salomon Jr. would heed "Sport Shirt Bill's" advice and shed himself of the team after only one year.

The Marlins showed the effects of partying the night before, and their play was compared by the *Miami News* as lifeless as the flag hanging in centerfield. Despite the fine defensive play of Glen Gorbous, and a strong effort by Dick Farrell, the Marlins fell to the Jets in a heartbreaker, 2–1, missing out on a chance to make up a half-game on Toronto, who suffered a rainout.

Of more concern to the team was the suspension of Jim Owens. Apparently the "Dalton Gang" had partied a little too hard the night after the Orange Bowl party and Owens found himself suspended for breaking training rules. According to *The Sporting News*, Owens and Don Osborn were involved in a physical altercation that left Owens cut on his forehead.[13]

Owens and his drinking problem had come to the surface. He had a reputation as a hard drinker with a propensity to find a good time wherever he landed but now his dirty laundry was in all of the newspapers. Qualters remembered, while a member of the Phillies the next season, that Owens's problem would come to a head again, leading to a decision that affected his career in baseball.

> *Tom Qualters*: Roy Hamey is the general manager, Mayo Smith the manager, and the coaching staff; I guess everyone was in there. And Roy Hamey says to Owens, "We've about had it with you. You're going to have to make up your mind what you're going to be. You can either be an alcoholic or a ballplayer; you can't be both. Now we want an answer and we want it right now. What's it going to be?" And he [Owens] looked around at everybody and said, "Can I have a couple of days to think it over?" [laughing]
>
> I mean, here's a guy, if there ever was a major league pitcher, this guy is it. . . . Yeah, that's the story. I wasn't in the room but that's the story.[14]

Since being returned from Philadelphia, the Marlins had cemented a four-man rotation of Cardwell, Farrell, Morehead, and Owens to fuel their recent success. Now without Owens, the team would have to turn to either the recently acquired veteran righty Tony Ponce, the sore-armed Tom Qualters, or the control-challenged Gene Snyder.[15]

The suspension of Owens was an ominous sign and cause for concern. It was going to be a tooth-and-nail battle to the end and the Marlins could ill afford to lose an important cog in their wheel. Besides the antics, what was disconcerting to Marlins management was the night after the big party the Marlins only attracted 2,074 fans to Miami Stadium.[16] Although the all-time minor league attendance record fell short, many considered it broken. The 1941 Jersey City game found curious customers purchasing ducats to the tune of over fifty-six thousand, but almost half of those customers failed to attend the actual game based upon the stadium capacity; the actual fans estimated at the park were in the neighborhood of thirty thousand. Based upon the turnstile count Miami felt that they were the proud holders of the single-game attendance record. Although Salomon and Veeck had visions of fans dancing in their heads, the reality was that success was fleeting and more often than not most of those seats would be left empty.

NOTES

1. Larry Tye, *Satchel: The Life and Times of an American Legend* (New York: Random House, 2007), 235; Jimmy Burns, "Marlins Set 57,713 Gate High at Orange Bowl Game," *Sporting News*, August 15, 1956, 15; Norris Anderson, "Crowds Not New to Satchel Paige," *Miami News*, August 7, 1956.

2. David Lipman and Satchel Paige, *Maybe I'll Pitch Forever* (Garden City, NY: Doubleday, 1962), 271–72.

3. Norris Anderson, "Extravaganza (and Baseball) May Draw Record Attendance," *Miami News*, August 7, 1956.

4. Morris McLemore, "No Homer Shower," *Miami News*, August 8, 1956.

5. Bob Bowman, phone interview with the author, February 22, 2010.

6. Norris Anderson, "Marlins Claim Record; 51,713 See 6–2 Victory," *Miami News*, August 8, 1956.

7. Tim Anagnost, personal interview with the author, May 9, 1956.

8. Bob Kuzava, phone interview with the author, May 15, 2010.

9. Norris Anderson, "How They Scored," *Miami News*, August 7, 1956; Lipman and Paige, *Maybe I'll Pitch Forever*, 274.

10. Anderson, "How They Scored"; Lipman and Paige, *Maybe I'll Pitch Forever*, 274.

11. Anderson, "Marlins Claim Record; 51,713 See 6–2 Victory."

12. Ed Linn and Bill Veeck, *Veeck—As in Wreck* (New York: University of Chicago Press, 1961), 311–12.

13. *Sporting News*, August 22, 1956, 36.

14. Tom Qualters, phone interview with the author, March 5, 2010.

15. Norris Anderson, "Owens' Status with Marlins Doubtful; Replacement Due," *Miami News*, August 9, 1956.

16. Ibid.

SEVEN

The Race for the Pennant and the Playoffs

Coach Jimmie Foxx summed it up best prior to the Richmond series: "And it's getting that time of the season when you've got to be winning those close ones."[1] Coming off two straight one-run losses to Columbus, the Marlins found themselves in third place and three games behind the league-leading Maple Leafs. On a happier note, Jim Owens had made amends with the team, his teammates, and the fans by issuing a statement.

> I am certainly sorry that the whole thing happened. It was a terribly sad thing for me to do and any punishment given to me is deserved.
>
> I want to assure the Marlin management, my teammates, and the fans of Miami that it will never happen again. I realize what a spectacle I made of myself, and I am ashamed of my actions.
>
> I am sorry that I set such a bad example for the kids. I guess I feel worse about that than anything else. My only hope now is that I can get back in uniform and help the Marlins win the pennant.[2]

Although $250 lighter in the pocket, Owens was reinstated and allowed to play in the Richmond series. Owens, also known as the "Bear," would be quickly forgiven by the fans and team members. After all, how could anyone be mad with the man with the lovability of a big teddy bear and a fastball that would put the fear of God into even the most courageous hitter?

After taking the first game from Richmond 2–0 behind the four-hit pitching of Don Cardwell and Larry Novak's two-run, 330-foot shot that just cleared the left field wall,[3] Owens was handed the ball the next night for the second game against longtime Yankee farmhand Jim Coates. Coates was especially unpopular in Miami. "The Marlins really didn't like Coates. I guess he had thrown at a few of their guys or something," remembered Tim Anagnost. And they were anxious to take out their pound of flesh from the six-foot-four, lanky right-hander.

Owens stepped up by scattering eight hits over eight innings, but once again the Marlins' bats were quiet as a church mouse. Hoping to create a spark, Don Osborn had inserted Yo-Yo Davalillo at second base in place of Ben Tompkins. Osborn was expecting that Davalillo, who had recently returned from an injury, would provide a capable bat behind Abrams at the top of the order. Unfortunately for Davalillo, he failed to get a hit and the Marlins fell 2–1 to Coates, who picked up only his fourth win against eleven losses. Davalillo wasn't all to blame, as the middle of the order accounted for only a solitary Ed Bouchee single.[4]

August proved to be the most frustrating month that the Marlins had faced since April. The prophetic words of Foxx about winning close games proved to be true. Over the course of the month the team would win only four one-run games while dropping ten. Despite the moves to shore up the offense, the strategy had failed to pull the team out of its offensive doldrums. In key series with Rochester the Marlins won only one of four meetings at home. The lone victory came in the first game of a twi-night doubleheader. Osborn once again turned to the ancient mariner to turn the tide and Paige once again responded, allowing only a lone single to Tommy Burgess. Although only striking out three Red Wings, Paige did not allow a walk, and the defense was nearly flawless, with the exception of an error by Woody Smith.[5]

A critical four-game series now lay ahead with Toronto. The hopes of Miami were best exemplified by skipper Don Osborn, who lamented, "This is the series we have to win to stay in the race." He added, "The only thing to do is beat Toronto face to face. That's what we're here for." Now tied with Rochester three and a half games behind the Maple Leafs for first place, the team felt that nothing less than taking the series was necessary if the Marlins were to make a run for the pennant. Manager Bruno Betzel bluntly stated, "We're shooting for the works."[6] And so the gauntlet was laid down.

Upon arriving in Toronto the Marlins were greeted rather rudely by fifty-degree weather following a tortuous ten-hour flight. Paige, who despised pitching in the cold, was notorious for warming up in the clubhouse on chilly days, and sometimes would only show up at the park when he felt he was needed. Paige, looking for a warm spot after arrival at the airport, quipped, "This is mighty cool for a pitchin' man."[7]

The Marlins received a frosty welcome the next night in Maple Leaf Stadium. The first game matched Jim Owens against the Leafs' Eddie Blake. With newly acquired Cuban slugger Carlos Paula in tow—acquired August 18 from Louisville after Glen Gorbous was placed on the disabled list for a severely sprained thumb—the Marlins were hoping that his powerful bat (.342, 16 HR, 55 RBI) would add some needed punch down the stretch. In addition, Sid Gordon, the Opening Day third baseman who had been recently serving as coach, was reactivated to lend support.

The effects of the long trip quickly manifested themselves as the Marlins could only scratch out a sixth-inning Bouchee single against the crafty Blake, who went the full seven innings while earning his second straight shutout and garnering his fifteenth victory of the season. Catcher Carl Sawatski and third baseman Loren Babe each drove in a pair of runs to lead the Leafs to a 6–0 victory. Disappointingly, Paula failed to deliver in his first three at-bats and the usually reliable Owens was pulled after five and two-thirds innings after allowing nine enemy hits.

In the nightcap, the listless Marlins continued their struggles. Miami's ace Cardwell was sent out to the mound to stem the tide against six-foot-three righty Don Johnson. Cardwell helped his own cause getting things going by driving in two runs with a home run in the top of the fourth inning and staking the Marlins to a 2–0 lead. Despite only hitting .183 during the season, Cardwell had a propensity to drive in runs when they counted and would ultimately finish the season with seventeen ribbies—not bad for a pitcher.[8]

Cardwell struggled late in the game and finally yielded to Gene Snyder in the bottom the eighth with two outs and the score tied 4–4. Although Snyder escaped the eighth inning unscathed, he was only able to retire one batter in the ninth inning before right fielder Lew Morton singled in the winning run, sending the Marlins down in flames.[9] The mood in the locker room was lower than the Washington Senators in the September standings, to say the least.

With the two losses the Marlins dropped into a fourth-place tie with Montreal, leaving Rochester in sole possession of second place. Skipper Osborn boldly predicted that the Marlins would take the next two games, one of them a makeup curfew affair, and was confident that Seth Morehead was his man.

Although Morehead would ultimately finish the season leading the IL in strikeouts, bad luck had followed him all season, including five losses by the score of 2–1. Osborn was calling on him not only to close out the makeup curfew game in which the Marlins held a 3–0 lead but also to pitch the regularly scheduled game to close out the series.[10] It was a tall order for the lefty from Texas, but one that he was up to the task to complete.

Morehead was able to close out the July 7 curfew game but was tested in the late game. Abrams started things off in the third inning, coaxing a walk from Leafs' right-handed starter Pete Wojey. Bouchee followed by driving a shot into the gap in right center field, plating Abrams before finally chugging into third with a triple. Bouchee later scored on a Woody Smith drive, which resulted in a double play but allowed the Marlins to take a 2–0 lead.

In the seventh inning Wojey again ran into trouble. Ray Holton led off the inning with a single and moved to third on Morehead's sacrifice and a Leafs' error. Abrams flunked his assignment to drive in Holton, but the next batter, Bouchee's, sacrifice fly was driven long enough to the outfield to bring Holton home and provide an insurance run that was desperately needed.

Throughout the game Morehead struggled but remained composed, scattering nine hits and walking three. Nevertheless, "lady luck" was on his side this time and the only run the Leafs could muster was in the third inning when Hector Rodriguez was able to score on Mike Goliat's ringing double from second. Morehead had stranded ten Leafs base runners and in the process earned a hard fought 3–1 victory. Sadly, the win would be Morehead's final one of the season.[11]

Osborn and his club were optimistic as they left Toronto for Montreal for a three-game stand. The Marlins took two of three games, including a rare offensive outburst in the final game, crowning the Royals 11–7. Miami split the next series in Richmond by winning two games and found themselves tied with Rochester three and a half games behind the still-front-running Maple Leafs at the conclusion of August.

September failed to bring the Marlins any relief as they split another road series with the Columbus Jets, winning two of the four games. The road-weary Miamians were looking forward to a respite and return to the friendly confines of Miami Stadium. Their next opponent, the Havana Sugar Kings, whom they had already dominated by winning eleven of fourteen meetings so far, was a more than welcome match-up and one the team hoped would continue to improve their position in the standings. The Marlins were poised to close the gap on Toronto.

Returning to Miami to begin a five-game series with their archrival Sugar Kings, the Marlins knew that every game from there until the end of the season was a must-win situation. In addition, Osborn's crew still had a season-ending three-game series in Havana and Toronto, and Rochester still had something to say before the pennant and playoff positions were determined.

The Marlins' offense seemed up to the task, having just scored twenty-five runs in the recent four-game series against Columbus. However, there were some concerns, including the fact that slugger Bob Bowman had only hit two round-trippers since tying for the league lead back on July 3. It was obvious that the earlier rib injury was affecting Bowman's performance. He would ultimately finish the season with nineteen home runs.

A large Labor Day crowd of 6,441 boisterous—some might say rowdy—fans greeted the visiting Marlins with anything but friendly intentions. Osborn sent out Paige in the short game of the double-dip to face thirty-six-year-old Sugar Kings' Jehosie Heard. Heard, who in 1954 had been the first black pitcher to appear in a Baltimore Orioles uniform,[12] was in the twilight phase of his career and had struggled mightily with his new club since being acquired from the Double-A Tulsa Oilers.[13] The match-up appeared to strongly favor the visiting Marlins, but the shrewd five-foot-seven veteran and ex-Negro Leaguer must have relished the chance to pitch against a legend and he wanted to prove that he still had some magic up his tattered sleeves.

Uncharacteristically, Paige started out as slow as one of his strolls from the bullpen. The Sugar Kings tallied two runs in the first inning on RBI singles by Hal Bevan and Juan Delis. That would turn out to be more than they would need. Heard was in rare form, and seemingly reinvigorated, looked more like a twenty-two-year-old rookie than the thirty-six-year-old veteran that he was. The Marlins scratched out only two hits, consisting of Bouchee and Gorbous singles. Heard was sharp; despite walking three, he stranded all five Marlins runners while striking out two. Although Paige had not allowed a walk in his five innings of work, the ten singles he gave up, coupled with two Woody Smith errors, proved to be his undoing as the Sugar Kings earned a well-deserved 2–0 victory.[14]

In the late game, Osborn trotted out his prize filly Cardwell to stem the tide against the Sugar Kings' little five-foot-six left-hander, Emilio Cueche. Cardwell was up to the task but, surprisingly, Cueche, who had mostly been used in relief all season, matched him inning for inning. The team's hitting woes continued and after the regulation nine innings nothing but goose eggs showed up on the scoreboard.[15]

The Marlins continued to threaten in extra innings by putting runners in scoring position, but failed in their efforts to drive them in, stranding runners in all six of the extra frames. Finally, in the fourteenth inning, Sugar Kings skipper Nap Reyes had seen enough, and it was obvious that Cueche was fatigued. Reyes signaled to the bullpen and called on the forty-five-year-old ex-Washington Senator and Cuban Winter League legend Connie Marrero to save the day, which he did, silencing the Marlins once again.

Cardwell had pitched probably his best game of the season. He had walked only three enemy batters, and while he had only struck out six Sugar Kings, he had allowed only seven hits (none for extra bases) before turning over the reins in the fifteenth inning to Tom Qualters.[16] This was the perfect situation for Paige to enter, but he was obviously fatigued from the first game and Qualters was fresh. Osborn trotted out to the mound and summoned Qualters. The Havana humidity was taking its toll in more ways than one and both teams were showing signs of exhaustion. The floodgates were about to be opened when the Sugar Kings loaded the bases and chased Cardwell to the showers. The key hit that put the nail in the Marlins' coffin was a two-RBI single by first-sacker Nino Escalera, before Qualters was able to retire the side. Marrero was brilliant in the bottom of the inning and earned the victory, essentially closing the door on the Marlins' pennant hopes. Sadly, the Marlins, who missed countless opportunities during the course of the game, stranded sixteen runners.[17]

The four-game homestand against Havana turned out to be a disaster and sealed the fate of the Marlins' scant pennant hopes. All in all it was the culmination of a seven-game losing streak. Many years later Pittsburgh Pirates Andy Van Slyke complained while enduring one of the worst slumps of his career, "Right now I couldn't drive home Miss Daisy."[18] Osborn's charges could relate as they were shut out in three of the four games, which included a string of thirty-three innings, without scoring a single tally against a Sugar Kings team that they had dominated all season long.

The last home game of the season was unhappily a disappointing 1–0 loss as Jim Owens went into the tenth inning before giving up a game-winning RBI single to Danny Morejon. It was only one of two hits that Morejon would garner as a Sugar King that season.

On a happier note, the season finale produced a small but appreciative crowd of 1,518 loyal fans. It would turn out to be the smallest turnout at Miami Stadium all season. It was a night of recognition for a successful season and in a vote held by writers and broadcasters covering the team, Cal Abrams was voted Most Valuable Player and Satchel Paige Most Valuable Pitcher. Both received trophies and a raucous round of applause. In a tight race for most popular player, Bowman narrowly edged out pepper pot shortstop Bob Micelotta and was rewarded with a wristwatch.[19]

To this day, Abrams' wife May still proudly displays in her home the trophy that her husband won during his eventful season in Miami. And Bowman still possesses the wristwatch, although not in the same condition that it was when he originally accepted it.

> *Bob Bowman*: I did receive the most popular player that year. I got a wristwatch.
>
> [Do you still have it?]
>
> I've got pieces of it and made it into a kind of collage, or whatever you want to call it.[20]

Leaving the next day for Havana, all that was left to wonder was where the Marlins would finish in the pennant race. The Marlins played better, taking two out of three from Havana, but it was too late and in the end they may have done themselves a disservice not finishing lower in the standings. By season's end, Toronto pulled away from the pack and finished the season at 86–66, two games ahead of Rochester, five and a half games in front of Miami, and six games north of Montreal. By finishing third place, the Marlins lost home field advantage and drew their nemesis Rochester in the first round of the playoffs.

Final Standings:

	W	L	GB
Toronto	86	66	—
Rochester	83	67	2
Miami	80	71	5½
Montreal	80	72	6
Richmond	74	79	12½
Havana	72	82	16
Columbus	69	84	18½
Buffalo	64	87	22½

Fate had played a cruel trick on Miami. Many pundits felt that the Marlins would be better off matching up against the pennant-winning Maple Leafs, with whom the Marlins had played almost straight up during the season, winning ten of twenty-one games. On the other hand, in a fairly well-balanced IL, the only other mostly one-sided series during the season was Montreal's, who took seventeen of twenty-two games from Havana. The Marlins closed out their ledger 5–16 against Rochester. Had the Marlins taken the season series from the Red Wings, they would have won the pennant.

Why the Marlins had struggled so mightily against the Red Wings was anyone's guess. Osborn gave his prognosticators a clue that the chief reason for the Marlins' struggles against Rochester was their speed. The day before going into the series the serious manager stated, "Rochester's terrific speed has beaten us all season." He added succinctly on sharing his strategy, "It's simple—just keep 'em off the bases. They've got at least seven men in their lineup that can steal bases on you. They don't have to sacrifice or use the hit and run like we do."[21] Oddly enough, the Red Wings only totaled thirty-three stolen bases during the season, five more than the Marlins' total, although they did have the reputation around the IL for not being afraid to take an extra base under manager Dixie Walker's command.

The first game of the playoffs against Rochester pitted Owens (5–7, 2.86) against Gary Blaylock (8–5, 3.02). The Marlins' struggles continued from the start. In the bottom of the first inning, after Ron Plaza reached first, Tompkins snagged a sizzling liner only to have the next batter, Tom Burgess, move Plaza into scoring position. Joe Cunningham followed with a single, scoring Plaza. Gene Green followed with another single, and before you could say lickity-split, the Red Wings were on top 2–0. The 4,180 Rochester rooters were as cheery as ducks in placid water. The crew from Florida's level of frustration was rising.

The Marlins didn't pose any threats to Blaylock until the sixth inning, when Abrams led off with a triple. Gorbous followed by hitting a fly ball to right field that looked like a surefire sacrifice fly. However, Gorbous, who could appreciate a strong arm more than anyone, saw Abrams confidently heading for home only to be gunned down at the plate on a perfect throw from Green to backstop Dick Rand. Once again, the Marlins' bats went as limp as wet noodles. Osborn must have wondered if the Miami humidity was weighing down his club's bats. Cunningham added another run batted in with a double in the seventh, bringing Eddie Kasko home, and later in the game, when Larry Novak, batting for Woody Smith, popped up weakly, the final tally showed the Marlins losing 3–0.[22] A Philadelphia Phillies farm manager sent to gauge the Marlins' playoff performance lamented, "And you can't win in these playoffs on pitching alone."[23] In other action, Toronto beat Montreal 4–2 to take a 1–0 lead in their series kicking off in Toronto.

Skipper Osborn had been hailing his pitching as so strong that they would need only two or three runs to beat their opponent. Apparently the Red Wings took exception to these comments and proceeded to school Miami starter Dick Farrell (12–6, 2.50) on the finer points of slugging.

Bouchee, the most consistent hitter all season for the Marlins, got his club off on the right foot, slugging a 345-foot two-out home run in the top of the first inning, spotting his crew to a 1–0 lead. The Red Wings wasted no time scoring four runs in the bottom of the first inning and chased starter Farrell with only one out in the second inning, lighting him up for seven runs before Qualters was called in to stop the bleeding.[24]

By the third inning the Marlins had dug themselves into a 9–1 hole. Before the smoke had cleared the Red Wings had lit up the scoreboard for twelve runs and twenty hits. Starter Cot Deal (15–7, 4.39) had done his job by going the route and the offense was more than up to the task as every Red Wing batter collected at least one hit. Kasko alone had terrorized the four Marlin pitchers for five hits in six at-bats. Montreal knotted their series with Toronto as little chunky right-hander Bill Harris outdueled IL Pitcher of the Year Lynn Lovenguth 3–1. That series was now tied at one game apiece.[25]

Confidence in the clubhouse must have been low as the third game in Rochester approached. The team was placing their hopes on season-long hard-luck starter Seth Morehead (8–13, 2.87) to reverse their fortunes. Trotting out the mound for the Red Wings would be French-born Duke Markell (10–10, 3.07).[26]

It looked like business as usual in the first inning when the Marlins once again went scoreless and the Red Wings quickly tallied a couple of scores. To Walker, known as the "People's Cherce" while playing in Brooklyn, he must have thought he was playing the Philadelphia Phillies of old based upon how one-sided the series had been so far. All remained quiet until the bottom of the eighth inning, when Abrams finally got something going for Miami, doubling to right centerfield and advancing to third on a Tompkins infield out. Bouchee drove a seeing-eye single past Plaza and the Marlins had cut the Red Wings' lead to 2–1, keeping their hopes alive.

In the bottom of the eighth, Paige finally made his first appearance of the series. So far Osborn had not had the right moment to use the clutch services of his reliable veteran, but now was the time with the season hanging in the balance. For Paige, pitching in clutch was like taking a walk in the park. Paige responded by mowing down the Rochester hitters in order, including one strikeout, leaving the door open for his teammates. It was now up to Rochester reliever Mel Wright (5–6, 3.05).

In the top of the ninth inning, after Smith was retired, Gorbous doubled to right field. Micelotta, struggling to find a base hit the entire series, finally singled to left, tying the score. Larry Novak was sent up to pinch-hit for Niarhos, who quickly grounded out, moving Micelotta to third, only ninety feet away with the go-ahead run. Walker chose to stay with the usually reliable righty Wright to face right-handed batter Yo-Yo Davalillo, who was called on to pinch-hit for Paige.[27]

Osborn would have rather sent up a left-handed batter against Wright but was forced to go with the right-handed hitting Davalillo since he had already exhausted all of his left-handers on the bench. Davalillo, only a .253 hitter on the season and pretty much a stranger to drawing a walk or collecting an extra base hit, left much to be desired in this critical situation. The Wings' skipper must have felt pretty confident that he would escape the inning with a tie until, to the surprise of everyone, Yo-Yo smacked a single to center, putting the Marlins up 3–2. All that was left now was for Angelo LiPetri (4–4, 2.95) to come in and close the door, which he did, striking out the sides and earning the Miamians their first victory. Going back to his last appearance against Havana, LiPetri had now struck out six enemy batters in a row.[28] Now the question was, could the Marlins carry their momentum back to Miami Stadium and swing the pendulum their way?

Lest we forget, back in Montreal the Maple Leafs tamed the Royals 12–1. First baseman Chuck Stevens led the way with four hits while driving in four runs, putting Toronto back up in the series two games to one.

Upon returning to Miami both teams enjoyed their one day of rest before returning to action. Toronto had once again beat Montreal 12–6, extending their lead in the series to three games to one. A confident Osborn knew he could ill afford to fall behind the Red Wings and announced prior to game four, "Don Cardwell will start tonight, but I'll use every pitcher I have if necessary to win this series." The Red Wings would counter with Blaylock, who had so masterfully shut down the Marlins in the first game.[29]

In what appeared to be a good omen, Cardwell had escaped the first frame unscathed, the first time the Marlins had accomplished this feat in the series thus far. Both teams were quiet through the first two innings, until the Red Wings erupted for a couple of runs in the third, all on a Cunningham bases-loaded single. Miami countered, scoring an unearned run when Red Wings' shortstop Kasko mishandled a ball, leading to a gift run that brought Abrams across the plate.

Trailing 2–1, Cardwell began to feel the pressure and came unglued in the fifth inning, allowing two additional runs before being pulled for Farrell. Although Farrell had been the staff's mainstay down the stretch, he had little success, allowing three more Red Wings to cross the plate, virtually sealing the fate of Miami. By the time the damage was assessed Rochester had increased their lead to 7–1 on five unanswered runs, leaving their opponents' hopes as limp as yesterday's wash.[30]

The inability of the Marlins to hit with runners in scoring position continued to cast a dark shadow on Osborn's crew. The 5,929 fans who were praying for a change of fortunes came to see their hometown boys in hopes they would break through. Nevertheless, Blaylock once again was masterful and ended up in the win column, striking out ten Marlins and walking only a pair. With a commanding 3–1 lead in the series, the "fat lady" was indeed ready to sing.

Walker called again on his thirty-three-year-old veteran Deal to, pardon the expression, "seal the deal" in game five. The Oklahoma native had suffered his share of struggles during the regular season, including bouts of control problems resulting in eighty-one walks in 205 innings of work. (He also led Red Wings' pitchers in home runs allowed with twenty-two.) Deal seemed to find his second wind facing the listless Miami lineup. Osborn countered with the burly Owens to stem the tide.[31]

Deal quickly found himself in trouble in the first inning, loading the bases with no outs. If there ever was a chance for Miami to start to turn the tables, this was the moment. With slugger Bowman coming to bat, the hometown cheering was reaching a massive crescendo; for sure, this was the moment when the offensive slump would end. However, Bowman's struggles with the bat continued as he grounded weakly into a double play, plating the first run of the game. The once powerful slugger, who was once tied with Luke Easter for the league lead in home runs in July, continued to struggle at the plate. Novak followed by grounding out to end the inning. The result was a solitary run and a missed chance to put the Red Wings away early.[32]

Rochester tied the score in the fifth inning on three singles by Allie Clark, Deal, and Plaza. To add insult to injury, Deal scored the winning run in the seventh inning on Kasko's single, resulting in a 2–1 Red Wings win. Only 2,182 rabid rooters bothered to show up to see the season come to a merciful halt.[33]

And so the books closed on the 1956 season. If it was any consolation, the Red Wings went on to edge the pennant-winning Maple Leafs four games to three for the IL championship, but were swept in the Junior World Series by the Indianapolis Indians in four games.[34] With all the bluster about attendance, despite drawing poorly at the end of the season, Salomon, Veeck, and management in general had to be pleased as the turnstiles turned to the rate of 287,385 clicks of the gate for the year.[35]

For all their valiant efforts the Marlins' players received a $2,500 share for their playoff appearance and third-place finish. Even the batboy Tim Anagnost was voted a partial share of the playoff booty.[36] So pleased with their pleasant surroundings in the Magic City, Bouchee, Novak, and Micelotta announced at the close of the season that they would be staying in Miami to reside during the winter months.[37]

One young man who wouldn't be returning to Miami Stadium was the big slugger from Washington State. Bouchee had made quite an impression on the Phillies' brass, and in 1957 he would displace Marv Blaylock as the starting first sacker. Although fellow rookie Jack Sanford (19–8, 3.08) garnered Rookie of the Year honors, some would argue that Bouchee had a better season, as he led all National League rookies in games played (154), at-bats (574), hits (168), doubles (35), triples (8), tied teammate Harry Anderson in home runs (17), runs (78), RBIs (76), walks (84), batting average (.293), slugging percentage (.470), and on-base percentage (.396). Less impressive was ace Don Cardwell, who struggled through a 4–8 campaign and 4.92 ERA.[38]

Sadly, the "Dalton Gang" would ride off into the sunset, bound for greener pastures with the parent club in Philadelphia, never to return. Farrell—or, as he would more popularly become known as a ballplayer, "Turk"—became the parent Phillies' top reliever in 1957 (10–2, 10 SV's 2.38). Seth Morehead also made the Phillies roster and spent the season with the big club with less than spectacular results (1–6, 92.1 innings, 5.85), while Jim "Bear" Owens found himself in a uniform of a different color (olive drab) after being called to active military duty. The city of Miami would not see the likes of them again.[39]

Not asked to return for another season would be Hall-of-Famer Jimmie Foxx and player-coach Sid Gordon. Foxx had been popular with the players but his continued drinking was disconcerting to Marlins management, who already had enough distractions.

Bob Micelotta remembered Foxx and how he usually stayed to himself. Always good with kids, he did help many Marlins with their batting, offering tips from his own years of experience.

> *Bob Micelotta*: Jimmie Foxx. But I guess you know that Jimmie Foxx was our first base coach in the first year. A very quiet man. A very nice guy. Just a real quiet fella, you know.[40]

Although kept quiet to the public, Osborn had not gotten along well with Gordon since he was named as a coach. Management, who had signed him for $13,000 at the beginning of the season, was just trying to recoup their investment, but came to the realization by the close of the season that sometimes personalities just don't jibe. With the expiration of Gordon's contract, ownership accommodated Osborn, who would fill the position with one of his own choices. After all, how could you say "no" to the IL Manager of the Year?[41]

More profound changes were yet to come. Marlins fans could take solace in knowing that Paige was coming back for another season with a new cast of characters and more than a few familiar faces. Although the playoffs and late-season slump were disappointing, in baseball hope always springs eternal, and the mood was optimistic for a new season to begin.

NOTES

1. Norris Anderson, "Marlins 'Hitters' Getting Get Morning Batting Drill," *Miami News*, August 10, 1956.

2. Ibid.

3. *Sporting News*, August 22, 1956, 35.

4. Ibid., 36.

5. Jimmy Burns, "Satchel—48 or 56—Pitches Like Kid in One-Hit Victory," *Sporting News*, August 22, 1956, 36 and p. 36 boxscore.

6. Norris Anderson, "Cardwell and Morehead to Face Leafs Tonight," *Miami News*, August 21, 1956.

7. Ibid.

8. *Sporting News*, August 29, 1956, 28, 32.

9. Ibid.

10. Norris Anderson, "Marlins Back in Race after Winning 2 Games," *Miami News*, August 23, 1956.

11. Ibid.

12. Clarence Watkins, *Baseball in Birmingham: Images of Baseball* (Charleston, SC: Arcadia Publishing, 2010), 53.

13. Baseball-reference.com.

14. *Sporting News*, September 12, 1956, 30.

15. Ibid.

16. Ibid.

17. Ibid.

18. Bruce Shlain, *Baseball Inside Out* (New York: Penguin, 1992), 34.

19. *Sporting News*, September 19, 1956, 39–40.

20. Bob Bowman, phone interview with the author, February 22, 2010.

21. Norris Anderson, "Osborn Picks Dick Farrell to Oppose Wings Tonight," *Miami News*, September 12, 1956.

22. Norris Anderson, "Rochester's Speed Worrying Marlins," *Miami News*, September 11, 1956.

23. Anderson, "Osborn Picks Dick Farrell to Oppose Wings Tonight."

24. Norris Anderson, "Marlins Back in Playoff Battle," *Miami News*, September 14, 1956.

25. Norris Anderson, "Morehead Gets Chance to Stop Marlins Slump," *Miami News*, September 13, 1956.

26. Anderson, "Marlins Back in Playoff Battle."

27. Ibid.

28. Ibid.

29. Norris Anderson, "Osborn Ready to Work His Entire Pitching Staff," *Miami News*, September 15, 1956.

30. *Sporting News*, September 26, 1956, 36.

31. Ibid.

32. Ibid.

33. Ibid.

34. Bill O'Neal, *International League: A Baseball History 1884–1991* (Austin, TX: Eakin Press, 1992), 410.

35. *Sporting News*, September 19, 1956, 33.

36. Norris Anderson, "Sports Today," *Miami News*, September 9, 1956.

37. Norris Anderson, "3 Marlins Plan to Live in Miami," *Miami News*, October 3, 1956.

38. David Nemec and Dave Zemen, *The Baseball Rookies Encyclopedia* (Washington, DC: Brassey's, 2004).

39. Gary Gillette and Pete Palmer, *The ESPN Baseball Encyclopedia*, 5th ed. (New York: Sterling, 2008).

40. Bob Micelotta, phone interview with the author, October 23, 2011.

41. Jimmy Burns, "Osborn, Int Pilot of Year, Reported Asking 15 G's Pay," *Sporting News*, October 10, 1956, 34.

Part II

1957

EIGHT

Just What's in Storer

It had been almost a year since Bill Veeck had tried to dissuade Sid Salomon Jr. from jumping headlong into the fray of owning a minor league team. Salomon Jr.'s position as president of the Miami Marlins was increasingly time-consuming. Also, a recent bout of severe sinus attacks in November resulted in him being admitted to Mount Sinai Hospital to treat the ailment, further motivating him to shed his responsibilities and concentrate on other business interests.[1] Salomon Jr. and his associates were already putting the word out, ever so subtly, to any potential investor sniffing around for a team to buy, that his team was available.

The reality of the situation was that Salomon Jr. had absorbed losses in the amount of $100,000. Much of the optimism that was so prevalent from the beginning, when he purchased the team, had been sanded down to the bare wood realities. Furthermore, Bill Veeck had announced that he was retiring to his ranch in New Mexico, although temporarily; he was becoming active in trying to purchase the Ringling Brothers circus. Although it never came to fruition, it would have been an interesting match, to say the least.

Also pressing were the issues tied up with the leasing and/or purchasing of Miami Stadium from Jose Aleman Jr. and drawing fans into the seats. There was the question of whether or not the city of Miami would be a buyer and if it purchased the ballpark, how would the stipulations of a new lease affect the club. In addition, the challenge of drawing people into the seats during the inclement summer months of heavy rains, and the omnipresence of various distractions that the city of Miami uniquely offered, were all factors in the viability of constructing a consistent base of paying customers needed to ensure profitability. All of the variables were weighing heavily on Salomon's mind. Many years later the various owners of the Florida Marlins would find out just how fickle the baseball fan base was in South Florida by wrestling with these same aforementioned issues.

Stepping into the picture was radio and television magnate George B. Storer. A self-made millionaire who started in the business world with his brother-in-law J. Harold Ryan, he found success by purchasing gas stations, strategically placing them in profitable locations, and earning handsome profits by selling his product at prices below his competitors. The bottom line was a handsome return on his investment. He later entered the communication industry by purchasing a radio station in order to promote those very same gas stations, and eventually found out that the communications medium was far more profitable than filling gas tanks and refocused his efforts there, eventually amassing even a greater fortune buying several radio and television outlets.

Storer and Salomon's paths had crossed before when Storer had tried unsuccessfully to outbid Salomon and purchase the Syracuse Chiefs in 1955 from then-owner Martin Haske. Storer had in his mind to own a baseball team ever since his youth, and now when the opportunity presented itself again he couldn't resist. At an Orange Bowl committee luncheon held during the end of November 1956, Oscar Dooly, a Miami broker who represented Aleman Jr. and Salomon, presented the idea to Storer and the negotiating was on. Within a matter of five days, on December 5, all interested parties sat down including Salomon, Elliot Stein, and Bill Veeck, and together they hammered out an agreement transferring ownership to Storer for an estimated $250,000. On December 7, the group flew to Jacksonville and received a promise from Philadelphia Phillies general manager Roy Hamey that the Phillies would continue their working agreement with the Marlins and the deal was sealed. Salomon Jr. happily stated, "We got a satisfactory profit on our investment." He added, "There was no bickering over any of the terms."[2] Both parties walked away with what they wanted.

Although the ownership of Miami Stadium was still up in the air, Storer was secure in the fact that either way he would have a place to play. The question was whether it would be under the watchful eye of Aleman Jr. or the city of Miami. The back-and-forth negotiations continued with Aleman Jr. standing firm on his offer to sell his $2 million field of dreams for $850,000 to whoever was interested. There was even talk of Storer assisting in the purchasing and/or financing of the stadium.

Storer was confident in the current Marlins front-office personnel and the only change in command came when Eddie Stumpf stepped down as general manager to be later replaced by Joe Ryan, who had served as the team's business manager during the inaugural season.[3] Along with Don Osborn, Eddie Miller—a former major league star shortstop—was named as coach to lead the Marlins into the 1957 with high hopes. "I want some guys who can hit the ball and run," said Osborn, who was predicting a pennant or bust.[4] Already popular veterans Cal Abrams and Satchel Paige announced that they would be returning to enjoy another season.

Early predictions by the *Sporting News* had the Toronto Maple Leafs as favorites and the Marlins as contending for a playoff spot. The consensus by Jimmy Burns in predicting the upcoming IL pennant race was as follows:

> Satchel Paige's promise to return takes care of the relief pitching. Manager Osborn again figuring on strong pitching staff from Phillies. Cal Abrams, who was chosen most valuable player last season, and Jim Greengrass bought from Phillies offer strong outfield. Catching and keystone combination are question marks.[5]

As March rolled around, the Marlins began to trickle into their new spring training environs in Stuart, Florida. It was a wetter than normal spring, but not too damp for the oldest man on the roster to report early. The most surprising development of this spring training was the early arrival of the colorful Paige. "Satch" made it known that he was toting with him the much-heralded snake oil that he used to soothe his ageless arm and was more than ready for another season. Osborn trumpeted his glee on seeing the veteran in camp. Paige glibly stated to the press, "I've already contacted my Indian friend who makes my special snake oil . . . and I hear Stuart is a fine place for spring training . . . good fishing, I mean."[6]

In an attempt to beef up their catching deficiencies, the Marlins signed forty-year-old long-beard Clyde McCullough to share backstop duties with their other veteran receiver, Johnny Bucha. McCullough, coming off of a sixteen-year major league career with the Chicago Cubs and Pittsburgh Pirates, mostly as a backup, was an adept handler of pitchers and expected to bring stability to the young corps of chuckers breaking camp. Bucha, projected to alternate with McCullough, was an old school, stout, and hard-nosed receiver who had a penchant for blocking the plate and standing down base runners who dare challenged him. In his book *Out of the Park*, Ed Mickelson recalls a play and how Bucha was one of the toughest men he ever met in baseball:

> John was not a large man, only 5'9", 180 pounds, but he was really put together. He loved to receive the ball from an outfielder and block the plate, tagging out the incoming runner. Bucha reveled in this kind of contact and he guarded home plate with ferocity beyond description. I remember vividly a play that occurred in Rochester in a game against Montreal. . . . The runner neglected to slide and tried to barrel into John, who was crouching. Bucha flexed his knees, bent slightly at the waist and lowered his right shoulder and caught the unfortunate runner square in the gut. The runner's speed was used against him as Bucha catapulted him into the air.[7]

Bucha would also serve double duty as the team barber. Earl Hunsinger remembered, with great delight, how Bucha took great pride in trimming everyone's locks before and after the game: "Johnny was getting up in age but Johnny was the clubhouse barber. He cut everybody's hair on the team."[8] Osborn was hoping Bucha would be as effective in cutting down enemy base stealers as he was at trimming his teammates' manes.

Other holdovers from 1956 were Ben Tompkins, Bob Micelotta, Woody Smith, Abrams, and Larry Novak, who were all tabbed as starters. The veterans mixed with several new faces, including Cuban Francisco "Pancho" Herrera (14 HR, .286) from Schenectady (A), built like a brick wall at six feet, three inches, 220 pounds, and twenty-one-year-old lightning-fast centerfielder Don Landrum (1 HR, .282); both would prove to be impact players in 1957. Wilbur "Moose" Johnson, or "Shorty," as he was called by Paige, returned from his hiatus in Louisville with the expectation of filling the role of a reserve infielder.

Johnson, who toiled eight years and managed six years in the minor leagues before becoming a successful major league scout with the Phillies and Toronto Blue Jays, played in three of the five seasons the Marlins were in Miami. Johnson has a treasure trove of stories and experiences gathered along his trek riding the baseball highway. One of the more colorful aspects of his career was his ability to gather nicknames. For one, Paige always referred to Johnson as "Shorty." Sadly, nicknames have become a thing of the past with most players today.

> *Wilbur Johnson*: Well, I was a little guy. I wasn't very big. After the game we used to drink some beer and I was one of the young guys that hung around. McCullough would always stay in there [the clubhouse] with a couple of players and he'd talk baseball. I would sit by him and he'd say, "Who's that little moose going by here all the time." They put it [Moose] on my sweatshirt and that's where I ended up with my nickname, "Moose" Johnson, in baseball. My wife didn't like it, she called me "Wib," but I ended up being "Moose" in the baseball world.[9]

Once again, the pitching staff was considered the Marlins' strongest suit with a mixture of veterans blended in with prospects on the fast track from Schenectady (A). Returning for their second tours of duty were John Anderson, Bob Conley, Earl Hunsinger, Angelo LiPetri, Tom Qualters, Gene Snyder, and Paige. Qualters and Snyder were projected to mostly serve as starters, while the newcomers Richard Bunker, Hank Mason from Schenectady, and Ray Semproch from Wilson (B) were expected to round out the rest of the young, but talented, staff.

Although Paige was considered a distraction by management, he generally was regarded as a stabilizing and helpful influence on the young pitchers on the team. One hurler in particular remembers the sage advice he was given by Paige early during the 1956 season that played an important role in saving his career.

> *Tom Qualters*: We're in a game and it's very early in the season. I can't remember the circumstances but, this was my first shot. Here I am in Triple-A baseball and it felt like to me that I had made the majors. From the time I was a little kid I was never afraid of anything, or anybody, as long as I had a couple of rocks in my pocket; which I carried all the time, or a baseball in my hand. I had absolutely no fear of anything.
>
> And I come in the game, and I get there on the mound, and most of these guys I'm playing against are ex-major players. And I've listened to the radio and I recognized all of the names of different guys, from different teams. And all of the sudden I'm on the mound, and I'm taking my warm-up tosses and I get the shakes. I mean I become petrified. I know I haven't felt anything like that before in my life. And you can't bullshit another ballplayer, you know. Ballplayers can sense that. They can see it where nobody else can.
>
> Somehow or another, I got them out. I threw the ball up there and they hit it at somebody, or whatever, and I get out of the inning. I went home that night and I'm trying to figure out how I can quit and go home. Not because of the fans or anything like that, just that I couldn't stand the thought of players on the team thinking that I was a coward. I mean that was something that I had never gone through before. I was just totally lost.
>
> So, we're in the bullpen the next night. Of course, I'm sitting beside Satchel and a couple of innings go along. Finally he comes to me and hits me on the leg and says, "What's the matter, son?" I don't know what to do so I just told him the truth and I told him what happened. And he started laughing. He said, "I'm going to tell you something, son." He said, "Those sons-of-a-bitches can beat ya, but they can't eat ya."
>
> Geez, they called down there and it's me again. So I get back up there and I take up my warm-up tosses right on the mound and I'm standing there getting the shakes again. I thought that's it, the sons-of-a-bitches can beat me but you can't eat me, and I got them out.
>
> But Satch, without a question, saved my career.[10]

Expectations were especially high in the Marlins camp for the trio of hurlers named Anderson, Bunker, and Mason from the 1956 Eastern League pennant winners Schenectady Blue Jays (A). Anderson had made only four appearances during the 1956 season in Miami but had been impressive at Schenectady (A), going 8–5 with a 2.10 ERA and only walking thirty batters in 154 innings. Mason, who made four appearances for Syracuse (AAA) in 1955, had failed to impress the first time, but was recalled to Miami to reward his breakout season (15–11, 2.28). However, the real gem looked to be Bunker. The Notre Dame graduate had a sterling rookie pro season in Schenectady (A), winning seventeen games and losing eight in 202 innings, while keeping his ERA at a minuscule 2.09

and allowing only 7.3 hits per nine innings of work.[11] Under Osborn's tutelage, all three were expected to make their marks in the big leagues soon.

With the conclusion of the rites of spring, the Marlins headed a hop-skip-and-a-jump down the road to the friendly surroundings of Miami Stadium. They were prepared for their second season in the "Magic City" with a mixture of familiar faces and peach-fuzz-faced rookies. Cumulatively, the squad's eyes were set to conquer the rough-and-tumble IL. However, their opponents had other ideas, and the road ahead was going to be a bumpy one.

NOTES

1. Norris Anderson, "Osborn's Contract Still Not Signed," *Miami News*, November 22, 1956.
2. *Sporting News*, December 19, 1956, 28.
3. *Sporting News*, March 20, 1957, 28.
4. *Sporting News*, December 5, 1956, 34.
5. *Sporting News*, February 13, 1957, 28.
6. *Sporting News*, March 13, 1957, 36.
7. Ed Mickelson, *Out of the Park* (Jefferson, NC: McFarland, 2007).
8. Earl Hunsinger, phone interview with the author, March 15, 2010.
9. Wilbur Johnson, phone interview with the author, March 11, 2010.
10. Tom Qualters, phone interview with the author, March 5, 2010.
11. Baseball-reference.com.

NINE

Thoroughbred Staff Gets Out of the Gate Fast

As was the custom, the beginning of the 1957 IL season found the eight teams opening up their season in its farthest southern climes: Rochester at Richmond, Buffalo at Columbus, Montreal at Havana, and defending champions Toronto at Miami.

Second-year manager Don Osborn proudly announced his surprise Opening Day starter as Roman "Ray" Semproch from his impressive stable of young arms. A relative veteran in a group of up-and-coming pitchers in their early twenties, Semproch, who preferred to be called Ray, had been in the Marlins' spring training camp in Plant City the previous season only to be disappointed when the team reassigned him to pitch Class B ball for the Wilson Tobs of the Carolina League. The then twenty-five-year-old right-hander considered ending his baseball career and returning to his hometown in Ohio. Upon leaving camp he was heard lamenting, "I guess I'll give up baseball now." He added, "I better go back to Cleveland and get myself a job." Wise beyond his years, and fortunately for Osborn, Semproch changed his mind and now found himself only one rung on the ladder below the big show after performing well during the preseason.[1]

The Philadelphia Phillies brass were pleased with the performance of Semproch, who had been impressive the year before, showcasing an effective slider and sinker in Wilson that surely caught the eye of his evaluators. Despite his 13–13 record, he sported a nifty 2.91 ERA in 210 innings worked, while giving up only 162 hits.[2] Military service had interrupted his career from 1952 to 1954 but he was now well rested and ready to prove himself.

Although Semproch masked his disappointment at pitching at the lower levels of Phillies minor league system, he remembered his old manager, Charlie Gassaway, who taught him a little bit of baseball wisdom as his mentor, and the trying season and lack of run support that he received while chasing his major league dream.

> *Ray Semproch*: I just went into the military, you know, and I came home. Like I said, for Wilson I just couldn't get the runs. And I don't know, I went thirty-five innings without a walk and Charlie Gassaway came out. I had a runner on who got a single and Charlie wanted me to walk a guy, or I forgot, the runner was on second base. Anyway, there was a runner on second base and Charlie came out to the mound and he wanted me to walk the next hitter. And I blew my gasket, and I said, "Charlie, I got thirty-five innings with no walks and you're going to make me walk a guy." "Oh," he said, "this is the game. This is how the game is played." I had to walk him and the next guy hit into a double play. So it was worthwhile. But that was funny.[3]

Semproch was hoping that his new teammates would prove to be less offensively challenged and stepped to the rubber on a breezy April 17 evening to face an imposing Toronto Maple Leafs lineup.

Opening Day Starting Lineups:

Toronto Maple Leafs	Miami Marlins
CF Jack Daniels	CF Don Landrum
LF Sam Jethroe	2B Wilbur Johnson
1B Rocky Nelson	LF Cal Abrams
2B Mike Goliat	RF Jim Greengrass
3B Stan Jok	3B Woody Smith
RF Bill Antonello	1B Pancho Herrera
SS Hector Rodriguez	SS Bob Micelotta
C Ebba St. Claire	C Clyde McCullough
P Don Johnson	P Ray Semproch
Manager: Dixie Walker	Manager: Don Osborn

Under a blanket of stars, with just a touch of cool breeze tickling the lazy palm trees just beyond the outfield fence, the velvet voice of Bill Durney and his equally smooth sidekick, Miami's own future legendary announcer Sonny Hirsch, could be heard coming across the few crackling transistor radios sprinkled throughout the buzzing crowd. The opening night festivities were more reminiscent of a football game than hardball on the green, as the one-hundred-piece Miami High School Marching Band along with a cabal of majorettes entertained the opening night throng. Orange Bowl beauty queens waved at the crowd, fireworks brightened the night, and the Marlins' number-one fan, sight-impaired concessionaire Joe Yates, threw out the first ball to kick off the season in style. In a short time, no more poetic words were heard than when the home plate umpire hollered, "Let's Play Ball!"

Although several local dignitaries were in attendance, the most notable celebrity was Leafs owner Jack Kent Cooke, who made the flight down from Toronto to Miami with hopes of seeing his team begin the season on a winning note. Cooke was also interested in visiting with his friend George Storer. Both of them had once attempted to purchase the Detroit Tigers, only to be thwarted later in their valiant attempt by radio executive Fred Knorr.[4] Storer, along with General Manager Joe Ryan, had high hopes for a sellout. The expectations were for a crowd of nine thousand to push through the turnstiles, but unfortunately the prognosticators fell short in their prediction for the second season in a row. The final count registered at only 6,682.[5]

Both teams came out rather sluggish, with the exception of the starting pitchers, Semproch and Leafs veteran Don Johnson, who were in sharp early-season form. Toronto drew first blood in the third inning when Rodriguez reached first on a walk and advanced to second, stealing his first base of the season. St. Claire followed with a single, bringing in Rodriguez for the first run, and would himself later score on a Jethroe infield single that was bobbled by Wilbur "Moose" Johnson.

Miami answered in the fifth inning when Don Landrum singled to right field. After "Moose," who was playing in the place of injured Ben Tompkins, was retired, Abrams drew a base on balls, and Greengrass reached first on a Rodriguez error. With ducks on the pond, Johnson got a little too fine on his pitches and walked Smith, allowing Landrum to score. Johnson, the ex-Yankees, Browns, Senators, and White Sox hurler, then did his best Houdini impersonation and escaped from the jam, allowing just a single tally and leaving the Marlins trailing 2–1.

Semproch pitched masterfully through the first nine innings, allowing only two runs on four hits before yielding to Hank Mason. Miami knotted the score in the ninth inning when Landrum beat out an infield single, stole second, and later scored on a Greengrass sacrifice fly.

The marathon continued through sixteen innings. Both teams matched single runs in the fourteenth inning, but the game had to be called at the end of sixteen frames because the IL curfew took effect at 12:50 am. Francisco "Pancho" Herrera, or Frank, as the Miami press like to call him, wore both a hero's crown and a set of goat horns when in the fourteenth inning he saved the day by driving in Abrams on a single but was later thrown out at home trying to score the winning run. Herrera had run through Osborn's stop signal and was pegged easily at the plate by shortstop Rodriguez's pinpoint throw to backup catcher Mike Roarke. "I did everything but rope him to keep him on third, but he wanted to go, I guess," said Osborn. The outcome would be played out at a later date.[6]

The next evening Miami Stadium was inundated with rain, forcing a cancellation, but the Marlins finished out the series the following night on a high note when Tom Qualters hurled a complete game, holding the Leafs to a single score and earning a well-deserved 6–1 win. It was the second time in as many games that the Marlins starting pitcher had gone nine innings and was encouraging to Osborn, who didn't have a starter, as he recalled, go a full nine innings the previous season until Satchel Paige went the distance the fourteenth game of the season, blanking Montreal 3–0.[7]

Unlike the previous season, when the team came out of the gate slowly, this year's edition of the Marlins jumped out to a fast start. Most importantly, they were getting timely hitting from an assortment of players along with excellent pitching from four of their starting pitchers: Semproch, Qualters, John Anderson, and Dick Bunker. Even Satchel Paige got into the act, winning his first start of the season on April 28 when he topped Luke Easter and the Buffalo Bisons 7–1 in the second game of the doubleheader. Easter bragged that he and his cohorts would shell Paige, who he claimed was sixty-two years old. Although some sports scribes hinted that Easter was only kidding, Paige took the remarks seriously and bore down extra hard to silence Easter, who managed only one of the six hits his teammates accumulated in the loss.[8] Paige, as he usually did, got the last laugh.

The *coup de grâce* of the homestand was an impressive 5–4 win over the Bisons that started out looking like a surefire win for the visitors. Osborn called on Dallas Green to make his second start of the season despite the fact that he was hammered in his previous start in an 8–4 loss to Rochester. Green, who later made a name for himself as a successful major league manager and general manager, failed to survive the first inning. After only retiring one enemy batter, after two lead-off walks, Green yielded a three-run home run to Easter, spotting the visitors a 3–0 lead. Osborn had seen enough and called upon twenty-three-year-old righty Earl Hunsinger from Winfield, Alabama, to extinguish the fire.[9]

Hunsinger had been with the Marlins early on in 1956 before being sent down to Class-B ball in Wilson. The young righty earned his stripes after an impressive spring, combined with a fine season in the Carolina League where he went 14–9 with a 3.08 ERA, leading Osborn to ticket him for another season in Miami. Hunsinger would serve as a long reliever and part-time starting pitcher.

Depending on an excellent fastball, mixed in with a sharp curveball, Hunsinger quickly retired the Bisons and was mowing down batters like Lefty Grove in his prime. Before you could whistle "Shuffle Off to Buffalo," Hunsinger had fanned thirteen Bisons in only six and a third innings, breaking the Marlins' single-game strikeout record set the previous season when Seth Morehead whiffed eleven. All in all, eleven visitors went down swinging and two were called out standing like statues in a park.

By the eighth inning, despite allowing five walks and three hits, Hunsinger began to show some fatigue, but held the lead. Fortunately, the Marlins offense had erupted early in the contest and built a 5–3 lead, thanks to a five-run burst in the fourth inning.[10]

Osborn sauntered out to the mound and signaled for Semproch from the bullpen. "Sometimes a kid won't tell you when he's tired," said Osborn. "It was noticeable from the sideline that he was losing his stuff." Semproch went one and two-thirds of an inning, followed by Angelo LiPetri going the final two-thirds of an inning, closing out the game and earning the save.[11]

Hunsinger, a dominating high-school hurler, remembers his strikeout effort as his best performance in a Marlins uniform. It was especially thrilling since the man who scouted him in Alabama, Jack Sanford, was in attendance the night he set the record and witnessed his first victory as a member of the Marlins. Ironically, Hunsinger decided to forgo a scholarship to play college basketball and on Sanford's advice chose baseball instead.

> *Earl Hunsinger*: Yeah, I had a very good high-school career. In fact, my senior year I had six no-hit games. Well it wasn't the greatest competition. I lived in Winfield, Alabama, where the competition wasn't that great, but I'm proud of it.
>
> Well, I signed a baseball contract right out of high school in 1953. I signed a basketball scholarship to go the University of Alabama, but I decided I wanted to play baseball so I signed a minor league contract with Jack [Sanford] to play with the Phillies.[12]

By the end of April the Marlins were in first place percentage points ahead of Richmond in the standings and ready to hit the road. Most surprising to scribes and fans around the league was that the youngest pitching staff in the IL was not only winning but also doing it in impressive fashion. Storer, based on early season performances, must have been thinking that it was going to be interesting battling it out with his good friend Cooke for the pennant, but it's wise not to count your chickens before they've hatched.

NOTES

1. Norris Anderson, "Sports Today: Semproch Almost Gave Up Baseball," *Miami News*, April 17, 1957.

2. Baseball-reference.com.

3. Ray Semproch, phone interview with the author, April 11, 2010.

4. Norris Anderson, "Marlins, Leafs Try Again Tonight after 5-Hour Tie," *Miami News*, April 18, 1957.

5. Norris Anderson, "Marlins Face Leafs in Tonight's Opener," *Miami News*, April 17, 1957.

6. Anderson, "Marlins, Leafs Try Again Tonight after 5-Hour Tie."

7. Norris Anderson, "Winning Marlins Take on Royals," *Miami News*, April 20, 1957; Luther Evans, "Hunsinger Fans 13, Marlins Win, 5–4," *Miami Herald*, April 30, 1957.

8. Jimmy Burns, "Ol' Satch Makes Luke and Bisons Respect His Age," *Sporting News*, May 8, 1957.

9. Evans, "Hunsinger Fans 13, Marlins Win, 5–4"; Tommy Fitzgerald, "First-Place Marlins on Long Road Trip: Scout Who Found Rookie Proud of Him," *Miami News*, April 30, 1957

10. Evans, "Hunsinger Fans 13, Marlins Win, 5–4"; Fitzgerald, "First-Place Marlins on Long Road Trip."

11. Fitzgerald, "First-Place Marlins on Long Road Trip."

12. Earl Hunsinger, phone interview with author, March 15, 2010.

TEN

Settling into the Middle of the Pack and Herrera Goes Ballistic

The month of May began auspiciously enough as the Marlins began their northern road swing facing some unexpected frigid weather. Normally this spelled bad news, but Osborn had his troops prepared, everything short of bringing galoshes and bearskin coats. After splitting two games in Buffalo, the Miamians took three out of four from the Montreal Royals, and to the surprise of everyone swept all three games from their prior season's nemesis, the Red Wings, in Rochester. The pitching staff was firing on all eight cylinders and on the ready to take the mound even in the worst conditions. The lone exception was, of course, Satchel Paige, who notoriously avoided pitching in cold weather.

Gene Snyder was impressive, winning two games during the first three stops—one in relief and another starting. Osborn, who had been tinkering with the starting rotation, turned to Snyder in the first game of the Toronto series when Bob Conley faltered and was only able to last two innings while giving up three runs. Before a crowd of more than eighteen thousand, Snyder held the Maple Leafs in check, allowing only two runs over six innings of work as the Marlins rallied behind Clyde McCullough's three-run home run in the sixth inning. The final score showed the Marlins on top 8–6 as Ray Semproch closed out the win in relief of Paige, who preceded him.[1]

In Snyder's first start of the season on May 6, he gained his second win against no losses and topped Montreal by the score of 4–2. Snyder pitched a complete game and struck out six while only allowing three walks. Osborn showed that he wasn't afraid to tinker with the starting rotation and go with the hot hand, giving everyone on the staff the chance to succeed. Snyder was a special case because of the unpredictability of the control of his pitches. He was usually successful when in command of his pitches, but you never knew what to expect from him on any given night, and he usually struggled mightily when he had his fits of control-itis. Snyder would finish the season walking seventy batters in seventy-three innings of work and uncorking nine wild pitches.[2]

Other early key contributors were Bob Conley, the Marlins' win leader at three wins against no losses, with a 1.73 ERA in twenty-six innings worked, and Hank Mason, who continued to anchor the bullpen. Leading the Marlins' offensive attack were Pancho Herrera (.377, 3 HR, 17 RBIs) and Don Landrum (.347, 26 runs).

While in Montreal, the Marlins suffered their first major casualty of sorts away from the field when *Miami News* sports writer Luther Evans suffered a bloody head wound when a window in the press box fell on his "noggin," opening a wide gash. It was nothing a little bandage and antiseptic couldn't heal and Evans survived his bout with some amount of pain (no pun intended), but he didn't miss a beat covering the team by making his byline.

The Marlins also made their first major move of the season on May 8, acquiring the services of infielder Bobby Young from the Indianapolis Indians of the AA.[3] Young, who hit .339 the previous season, was expected to bring some offensive spark and veteran leadership to the once again offensively struggling team. Thus far, the middle infield of Bob Micelotta and Ben Tompkins, despite their stellar defense, had been unproductive in the run-producing department, and like Sid Salomon Jr. before, owner George Storer was committed to fielding a pennant-contending team.[4] At the same time the Marlins received some bad news when outfielder Chuck Essegian went on the disabled list with shoulder problems, joining the already walking wounded pitcher Angelo LiPetri (sore arm) and catcher Johnny Bucha (torn heel ligament).[5]

The road-weary Marlins returned to Miami Stadium to a rainout and day off before resuming play against Buffalo on May 12. Like a worn and tattered knit sweater, the Marlins began to show the telltale signs of unraveling. A doubleheader loss to Buffalo in front of 8,024 supporters was disconcerting enough as Gene Snyder suffered from his usual case of control-itis. In the first game of the doubleheader he lasted only three innings, giving up three runs, including a two-run home run blast to Luke Easter, and issued three free passes before hitting the showers.

Miami missed a golden opportunity in the bottom of the ninth. After loading the bases on a Landrum single to left, a Tompkins single to center, and Cal Abrams reaching on an error, Larry Novak hit a foul ball toward right field that was easily handled by Joe Caffie. Osborn took a chance and ordered Landrum to tag, only to be caught between home plate and a hard place by a laser throw from Caffie. The astute ex-major leaguer and veteran catcher Joe Astroth made a quick throw to Jim Baxes as Landrum retreated to third, while covering second base to catch Tompkins off base. Landrum broke for home again as Baxes quickly returned his throw home in time to nab Landrum trying to cross the plate. The rally was snuffed and the Bisons held on for a 4–3 win.

The second game results were even more distressing. What surprised the hometown folks most of all was that the usually reliable Paige was not able to earn the win in the split during the seven-inning second game of the double-dip affair. Paige started slowly by giving up three hits to the first three batters he faced—back-to-back doubles to Caffie and Baxes, followed by another single to Lou Ortiz that gave the Bisons a 2–0 lead. Of some consolation, Paige did retire his old rival Easter to thwart further damage. However, the harm was done and it would prove to be all the offense the visitors needed, as lefty starter Fred Hahn kept Miami in check, only giving up a single to Woody Smith and a double to Tompkins to earn the complete game win.[6]

Osborn was confident that his charges would turn the tide during their next series against the sixth-place Columbus Jets. Before leaving town Buffalo manager Phil Cavarretta assessed the Marlins pitching corps as the best staff in the league. However, they failed to live up to their reputation, dropping three of four games to the Jets while allowing a total of twenty-five runs. The Jets staff assessment by Cavarretta was more accurate, as starters Jack Brown and Ron Blackburn both blanked the home team during the series. Ironically, the shutouts were the only ones each respective hurler earned all year.[7]

Miami fared better at home against Richmond, taking two out of three. The biggest crowd for a Saturday game (6,238) of the season attended the May 18 match featuring marching bands, fireworks, and a brilliant pitching performance by Tom Qualters. The crafty right-hander scattered five hits while striking out five and walking three, earning a complete game win, his third victory against only one loss. Newly acquired Young, who appeared in his first game back on May 13, had his best game since joining the team, going 2–5 and driving in a run, all the while playing solid defense in place of Tompkins at second base. Young was one of seven Marlins to drive in at least one run in the 9–0 whitewashing of the Virginians.[8]

When Columbus returned for a second match-up in Miami Stadium against the Marlins to finish up the homestand, they swept the reeling Fish in four straight games. It was the most frustrating series of the season, as three of the losses were by one run, including a seventeen-inning loss to the Jets 3–2. Osborn and his crew must have been anxious to hit the road, considering they had won only three of thirteen games on their home turf. If there was a sign in the locker room that said, "Home Sweet Home," it was now residing in the closest trash bin.

By the end of May the Marlins found that they were just barely floating above the .500 mark and residing in fourth place at 21–20. To the surprise of most pundits around the IL, Richmond had established themselves as the front-runners with a glossy 28–15 record, a slim one-and-a-half-game lead over Toronto that was ever so precarious.[9]

Closing out May and going into June, a home/away series with rival Havana brought a considerable amount of apprehension as political unrest in Cuba became more and more omnipresent. Sugar Kings president Bobby Maduro, always the optimist, was doing his best to quell rumors of his team folding due to a nationwide mandate disallowing citizens to congregate. There was even talk of moving the team farther south and playing some home games in Panama, Puerto Rico, and Venezuela.[10]

Miami started out by taking two out of three at home before their first road trip to Havana. In order to motivate his pitching staff, skipper Osborn used a new form of carrot to get the horse to pull the cart while at the same time inspiring his troops. The offer was that any starting pitcher not allowing a walk in his start was to be issued a free steak dinner. Osborn had learned over his managerial career that the quickest way to a man's heart was through his stomach. Ironically, the first recipient was usually control-challenged Gene Snyder, who chucked his best game of the season on May 30, blanking the Sugar Kings 3–0 while scattering eight hits and upping his record to 3–2.[11]

While the Marlins' hurlers were bearing down to score their filet mignons, off the field, broadcaster Bill Durney and advertising man Ed Little were trying to cut down on not only their meat intake but also food in general. Heavyset "Big Bill" Durney had laid down the challenge by promising to dispatch thirty pounds, while 218-pound Mr. Little had a more cautious goal of losing fifteen pounds. Although neither party had announced what the winner would receive, they soon launched into a competition that even Osborn would have been proud of.[12] Regrettably, there is no record of who won the bet.

Bill Durney Jr., who served as one of the team's ballboys, and sometimes batting practice catcher for the Marlins, would later return to Miami following in his dad's footsteps in the capacity of GM for later Miami entries in the minor leagues. Durney Jr. also remembers his father's battle in controlling his weight and his battle with heart disease, having suffered five attacks before succumbing to the disease at the age of fifty-four.

> *Bill Durney Jr.:* Yeah, my dad was a big man. He was 6'2", and about 315 pounds, an ex-Marine, and he was a big, big man. I know he got his weight down to about 280. He cut down on his smoking and everything else, but I can remember him always saying that if he had to go any further than what he was doing, he might as well be dead.
>
> Yeah, it was probably about as far as it went too. As I remember, my dad pretty much stayed the same as far as I remember him.
>
> That brings back another memory. I wound up getting Ed Little's mother's car. It was one of my first cars.[13]

After losing the first game in Havana 7–2, Osborn made the decision to reinsert Semproch into the starting rotation for the next day's double-header. It was a move that proved fortuitous as the season unfolded. The staff was plagued with injuries all year and Osborn felt the time was right to see if his right-hander could recapture his early season form.

Semproch proved up to the June 1 challenge, holding the Cubans to only one run, striking out six and walking four in six and two-thirds innings. Semproch tired in the seventh inning before yielding to Satchel Paige, who promptly closed out the game. Young contributed with a double and a triple while driving in one of the three runs in a victorious 3–1 climax. Semproch earned his second win of the season.

Semproch remembered how providential his manager's decision proved to be not only for himself but for Osborn as well.

> *Ray Semproch*: Well, you know, I started off fairly well and all of the sudden I slumped off. In Triple-A, they get all of these pitchers from the majors back down and you were put on the side a little bit. . . . I think it was in July, or something like that they had a lot of injuries and he [Osborn] said, "Well, you're going back in the starting rotation." And he [Osborn] helped me. He watched me pitch and he says, "Just keep that sinker low and keep that slider on the outside and you'll be all right."
>
> I guess I was very successful because I ended up with a 12–4 record and I can't remember the ERA [2.76]. Is that what it was? I imagine it would be at Triple-A. [laughing] [14]

Despite all of Osborn's enticements to motivate the team, the Marlins continued to struggle. Although Semproch's start was promising, frustrations reached a high mark on June 2 between the first game and second game of the doubleheader at *El Gran Estadio del Cerro*, or, as it was more popularly known, Gran Stadium, when fisticuffs were seen flying not between the bitter rivals, but between teammates on the Marlins' side of the field. Osborn criticized his usually slick-field first baseman Herrera for making a poor effort on a ball hit through the infield, drawing the big Cuban's ire. The exchange visibly bothered the erstwhile slugger and stewing over what he perceived as a slight came to a head later. With Bob Conley on the mound in the bottom of the ninth trying to preserve the win, Herrera came over to Conley to remind him not to throw a change-up to the next batter, Sergio Garcia. The words between Conley and Herrera amounted to Conley less than politely reminding Herrera to go back to first base and leave the pitching to him. Conley promptly struck out Garcia to end the game and in short order between games Herrera reportedly went berserk in the clubhouse and threw a punch at Conley. [15] The repercussions would come later.

Herrera, who was batting over .300 and leading the club with ten home runs, decided he had had enough and expressed to Osborn that he would never play for him again. In essence, Herrera jumped the club and was absent for the second game of the doubleheader. Ironically, just minutes before the incident Miami had announced that backup first baseman and outfielder Clarence Maddern had been sold to Rochester. He would be pressed into action one more time before catching the next flight out of town.[16]

Without Herrera in the lineup, in the nightcap the Marlins were as droopy as a sail on a placid lake. They dropped the second game to Miguel "Mike" Cuellar, 2–0. The future Oriole and 1969 Cy Young Award winner held the boys from Miami to four hits, handing hard-luck Dick Bunker, with three wins, his fifth defeat of the season. Bunker would turn out to be the 1957 season's version of Seth Morehead. This was all despite his glossy 2.45 ERA.

Following the conclusion of the series the Marlins caught their flight back to Miami, minus their impetuous slugging first baseman. The Marlins' brass were showing obvious concerns about Herrera's return and welfare, including whether or not he would return to the club or jump to an outlaw league. It didn't take long before the Nicaraguan Summer League made a lucrative offer to the missing-in-action first sacker that immediately evoked a response from General Manager Joe Ryan, who stated, "If he shows he is sorry, and wants to come back, I think we can work something out." Osborn was harsher in his assessment when he pointedly remarked, "I naturally would like to have Frank back with us." He added, "He did a good job and is a capable first baseman, but it was inexcusable what he did in Havana—jumping the club between those games Sunday. Whatever happens, he will be fined."[17]

Miami was set to face off against Buffalo on June 4. Osborn had more important things to worry about than his AWOL first baseman, including keeping his team in the pennant race. With the dog days of summer just around the corner, and the mercury rising not only in the clubhouse but also in the air, there were many questioning if this team did indeed have the mettle to stand up to their competition in the IL.

NOTES

1. *Sporting News*, May 15, 1957, 29–30.
2. Ibid.
3. Jimmy Burns, "Marlins Buy Bobby Young," *Sporting News*, May 15, 1957.
4. *Sporting News*, June 5, 1957, 34.
5. *Sporting News*, May 15, 1957, 29–30.
6. Norris Anderson, "Marlins IL Lead Vanishes, Play Columbus Jets Tonight," *Miami News*, May 13, 1957; *Sporting News*, May 29, 1957, 31–32.
7. Anderson, "Marlins IL Lead Vanishes, Play Columbus Jets Tonight"; *Sporting News*, May 22, 1957, 34; *Sporting News*, May 29, 1957, 31–32.
8. Anderson, "Marlins IL Lead Vanishes, Play Columbus Jets Tonight"; *Sporting News*, May 22, 1957, 34; *Sporting News*, May 29, 1957, 31–32.
9. "International League Standings," *Miami News*, June 1, 1957.

10. Cy Kritzer, "Political Unrest Hits Cuban Gate," *Sporting News*, June 12, 1957.

11. *Sporting News*, June 12, 1957, 39–40.

12. Ibid., 40.

13. Bill Durney Jr., phone interview with the author, December 21, 2010.

14. Ray Semproch, phone interview with the author, April 11, 2010.

15. Jimmy Burns, "Herrera 'Jumps' Marlins Then Marks Return with Homer Blast," *Sporting News*, June 12, 1957, 39.

16. Burns, "Herrera 'Jumps' Marlins Then Marks Return with Homer Blast"; *Sporting News*, June 12, 1957, 40.

17. Norris Anderson, "Marlins Mason Will Face Bisons," *Miami News*, June 4, 1957.

ELEVEN

Let Bygones Be Bygones But Can Someone Hit the Ball?

"Let bygones be bygones." At least that was the fans' consensus as Pancho Herrera returned to Miami for the home opener against third-place Buffalo. Although a little lighter in the pocket due to an undisclosed fine, the prodigal son was back and remorseful for his misdeeds, ready to return to the lineup and contribute.

The 2,255 loyal Miami supporters in attendance were quick to forgive one of their favorite sons and greeted him with cheers when he came to bat in the second inning. Their show of support must have touched the big-hearted slugger and he rewarded the fans for their kindness with a solo shot homer in the second inning off Karl Drews's first offering in his first at-bat since skipping the team in Havana. To the delight of everyone, the blast staked the hometown favorites to an early 2–0 lead. Herrera, known for his kind nature, later expressed his thanks to the fans in his broken English by saying, "Fine people—the best." He also apologized to everyone involved by letting them know that everything was going to be okay.[1]

With everything returning to normalcy, the Marlins celebrated by adding to their lead in the third frame. Then the six-foot-four, tough-as-nails right-hander from Staten Island, Drews, uncharacteristically struggled early but would find his form as the game wore on. Drews, who started playing professional baseball back in 1939 in the Class-D Pennsylvania Association, had a reputation as a tough, crotchety, no-nonsense pitcher. As evidence of his toughness, Drews had a metal plate inserted in his head, the result of a collision in 1950 with Sam Mele that caused a serious skull fracture. Drews went through a deliberate routine that literally kept him from passing out. His regimen of bending over and tapping his knee before delivering each pitch was to purposely slow himself down. It was a constant battle between staying conscious and keeping enemy hitters in check.[2]

Seldom used as a starter, Hank Mason—perhaps exuding a little too much confidence with his 3–0 lead—imploded in the fourth inning, allowing six runs, including surrendering a Luke Easter monster shot that cleared the centerfield wall, traveled 370 feet, and plated a couple of the half-dozen runs the Bisons would tack on the board. Mason, the recipient of one of only two starts all year, was relieved by Bob Conley, but it was all to no avail as the Bisons held on to drop the Marlins 7–6. Three Marlins, in an odd show of power—Herrera, Micelotta, and Tompkins—all went deep but their efforts were in vain. Bobby Young was beginning to slump and Ben Tompkins, who pinch-hit for Young in the ninth inning, smashing a home run, was making a case for returning to his regular spot at second base.[3]

Despite the disappointing defeat there was some good news to be had. Two regulars returned to the club after prolonged stays on the injured reserve list. Fellow bashers Chuck Essegian and backstop/barber Johnny Bucha happily reported back to duty. Unfortunately for backstop Haywood Sullivan, who had been filling in for Bucha during his absence, he would soon find himself riding the pine before landing on the injured reserve list himself.[4]

After dropping two out of three to Buffalo, the Marlins' woes continued against the visiting Rochester Red Wings. The series opener featured one of the biggest crowds of the season. In all, 6,412 people flocked to Miami Stadium on one of those pleasant evenings that Miami is famous for. With temperatures hovering in the mid-seventies, and a cool ocean breeze lightly caressing the crowd, the annual Miami Goodwill Party was guaranteed to be one of the biggest draws of the year. Coy Poe, the entertainment organizer of the famous Orange Bowl game, served as the host and brought in the musical likes of Lord Flea and His Calypsonians, Babe Pier, and Pat Manville to amuse the festive crowd.[5]

Less than festive were the participants on the field as tempers began to boil on the diamond. Gene Snyder was cruising along going into the fifth inning, having allowed only a single base hit, when the wheels started to come ajar. Snyder promptly lost his up-to-this-point pinpoint control and walked, in order, Allie Clark, Tom Burgess, and Gary Geiger. With one out, the next batter, pitcher Gary Blaylock, seemed like a reprieve. Snyder, attempting to gain back his lost control, grooved a curveball down the pike and Blaylock sent the ball on a long trip over the left field wall. It was Blaylock's only home run of the season, but it was a killer. "You could call it my 'outside pitch,'" mused Snyder. "He put it outside the park, didn't he?"[6] Osborn was less than amused and removed his starting pitcher in favor of the diminutive Angelo LiPetri.

Miami countered in the bottom of the fifth inning when Tompkins singled in Bucha and Landrum, cutting the Red Wings' lead to 4–2. In the eighth inning Conley, who had replaced LiPetri to start the same inning, sent a message to the visitors throwing inside to catcher Gene Green. The ball grazed Green's wrist, but he was ruled out by the plate umpire. The ensuing argument caused a verbal brouhaha at home plate with umpire Pete D'Ambrosia in the center of the storm. Wings manager Cot Deal joined the fracas, but to no avail. D'Ambrosia's decision stood. Although the Marlins out-hit the Red Wings 9–3, they failed to prevail in the run column. Their inability to hit with runners in scoring position proved their undoing and the loss left the boys from Miami at 24–24 for the season, trailing first-place Richmond by seven and a half games. The win allowed Rochester to close the gap to one and a half games behind fourth-place Miami.[7]

What lay ahead was a dreaded northern road swing. Leaving town, Miami's next destination was Toronto. As was the case, the Marlins caught a chartered flight out of Miami airport to their next destination. Although most of the players were quite used to the travel, as usual, "Old Satch" had misgivings. Paige was never partial to flying and he instead used his favorite mode of transportation with four wheels. When he could, Paige would drive his own car—a Cadillac—or borrow his good friend Luke Easter's Cadillac to catch up with the team on their road trips.

> *Stu Locklin*: I played with Satchel Paige, of course, in Miami. You see he was a good friend of Luke Easter's going back to when I was with Cleveland. You know Luke and Satchel they both owned Cadillacs and every time they could they kind of shared their cars when they went home and away.[8]

Although the "Dalton Gang" had long since departed town you couldn't leave it past the current gaggle of players on the Marlins to still inject some jocularity and provide comic relief to cut the tension. On the second leg of the flight to Toronto, out of Idlewild Airport in New York, some of the players stashed a pressurized can of shaving cream in Paige's personal carry-on satchel. As you might have guessed, it didn't take long for the can's contents to escape. With the unnamed person, or partners, in crime watching, Paige reached into his bag to find some stomach-relief medicine, but instead found a bag full of shaving cream. With the white liquid oozing everywhere, and everyone in the plane's cabin in stitches, the quick-witted Paige lamented, "Who said you only get seventy shaves out of these cans?"[9]

Dick Bunker was an innocent bystander sleeping next to Paige when the incident occurred and remembers his reaction upon realizing what had happened.

> *Dick Bunker*: I'm sitting on the plane next him [Paige] going to Toronto and was sound asleep. You know it was early in the morning and I woke up and said, "What the hell?" All this white stuff is all over me.

His stuff blew on him from his satchel, his shaving cream, and it went
all over me too. That's a true story. Honest to God![10]

Everyone knew that Toronto was Paige's least favorite locale. In the
past he had openly expressed his distaste for the Canadian city, no doubt
from a negative encounter in his past or just plain contempt for the local
climate. It was also well known how much "Satch" hated the cold weather and in order to avoid the chill he would throw his warm-up pitches in
the locker room. Sometimes he was known to not even show up to pitch
if the mercury dropped to a low enough level on the thermometer. As
was the custom, every ball club set up a rocking chair in their bullpen for
Paige, which he usually occupied, but in Toronto he refused to sit and
joined his colleagues in the bullpen instead. Although it was a point of
contention with Toronto management, it was classic Paige and how he
dealt with those who he felt wronged him.

> *Wilbur Johnson*: Yeah, that rocking chair went to every ballpark. But he
> wouldn't sit in it in Toronto. They put it out there and he wouldn't sit
> in it. He had something against Toronto.[11]

Communications tycoon George Storer was becoming increasingly
concerned, not only with the team's lackluster performance on the field
and their poor showing at the gate but also with the fluctuating status of
ownership of Miami Stadium. Jose Aleman Jr., the strikingly handsome
and wealthy Cuban stadium owner, received the ballpark as a gift from
his doting father, which was built in 1947 at a cost of $2 million. His plan
was to bring a high-caliber level of baseball to Miami while at the same
time earning a handsome profit from leasing the stadium. At the time of
its construction, Miami Stadium was considered the jewel of the minor
leagues and a state-of-the-art venue that was the envy of clubs everywhere. One of the most impressive features of the ballpark was the cantilevered roof that sported beamless supports and provided an unob-
structed view of playing field. The unique roof design covered the majority of the spectator area, unlike the traditional flat or sloping roofs of
most ballparks, and wrapped around the infield portion of playing field
from first to third base. The arching roof protected fans from the rainy
weather, as well as providing much-needed shade that is so important
during the alternating sunny summer months in South Florida. Other
attractive creature comforts built in were the Dugout Club with an intimate, fully stocked wraparound bar, a players private lounge, and roomy
dressing rooms for both the home and visiting teams.[12]

Sometimes the best laid plans of mice and men are not always successful. Aleman Jr., who masterminded and who took great pains in oversee-
ing the stadium's construction, had high hopes that the ballpark would
bring personal rewards, recognition, and big-time baseball to the city he
loved. However, after eight years of sustained financial losses the dream
had turned into a nightmare and none of his goals had come to fruition.

Aleman Jr. was more than willing, after years of throwing money into what must have seemed like a bottomless pit, for anyone to take this albatross from around his neck. He openly made it known that he was willing to let his prize go to the highest bidder for $850,000.[13]

The most interested party was the City of Miami. Negotiations between the city and Aleman Jr. seemed endless, always going back and forth, with no agreement ever coming to fruition. The Miami city commission continually vacillated on whether the investment was viable, and Aleman Jr. was losing patience and even threatened to sell his stadium to anyone who could use the property for commercial use. Storer, who was leasing the park, even though he was once rumored to be interested in buying the stadium, was uncomfortable with that proposition and was forced to accept his position as a lessee on a year-by-year basis.[14]

Storer's frustration was becoming increasingly evident as the season wore on. Near the point of desperation, he went so far as to recommended an alternative plan to the city, proposing a second, smaller stadium be built at a cost of $700,000 with a proposed seating capacity of five thousand. In addition, his plan would allow for expanded seating some time down the road. According to Storer, his plan allowed for a more complementary lease agreement versus the $40,000 yearly fee that he was paying now.[15] The stadium issue would continue to be a cloud over the Miami team until their demise.

In response to declining attendance General Manager Joe Ryan announced that Sunday night games would be dropped in favor of afternoon tilts. Ryan felt that strategy would draw more kids and elderly ticket buyers to the games. Storer, like his predecessor Sid Salomon Jr., was already beginning to doubt the long-term viability of baseball in South Florida. So far the Marlins had drawn a paltry total of 107,243 paying customers in their first thirty-three home dates, considerably less than what Ryan and Storer had projected.[16]

As the month of June wore on, Storer and Osborn's frustrations must have hit a boiling point. It would prove to be the worst month of the season for the Marlins. Losing streaks of four and six games added to a disappointing 11–19 record for the month and a slide into seventh place further aggravated the situation.

In an all-too-familiar theme, the Marlins' anemic offense was the major focus of blame. A case in point, a four-game sweep at the hands of the Royals in Montreal from June 14 through June 16 found the Marlins hammered by the Royals to the tune of outscoring Miami 18–1. Even the ageless wonder Paige was sent to the locker room empty-handed following a disappointing loss, a seven-inning decision, 3–0, during the second game of a doubleheader.

As if there wasn't enough bad news, catcher Clyde McCullough was placed on the injured reserve list on June 4 (split finger),[17] backup catcher Haywood Sullivan on June 12 (right finger injury), and outfielder Larry

Novak on June 12 (wrenched stomach muscle), and southpaw Dick Bunker was called to return to his hometown of Norwood, Massachusetts, on June 15 for his draft examination, stretching the roster to its limit.[18]

In response to the several walking wounded the Marlins brought in a group of players to try to fill the gaps in an attempt to right their ship. Four ex-major leaguers were acquired on June 12 and 13: Jack Meyer was on temporary loan from the parent Phillies, Whitey Herzog was on option from the Washington Senators, and Howie Judson and Bubba Church were purchased from Seattle of the Pacific Coast League. Church was the most surprising acquisition, having been in retirement from baseball since 1955 and last appearing in the minor leagues pitching for Los Angeles of the Pacific Coast League. The former "Whiz Kid," feeling he still had something left in his tank, was hoping a strong showing in Miami would buy him a ticket back to the big leagues. Church, who had been working at building his insurance business, now found himself as insurance for the Marlins as the midpoint of the season quickly approached.[19] Just as frontline troops are glad to see reinforcements, so were the Marlins happy to see some fresh faces that carried with them a possibility of turning their losing ways around. Little did the Marlins and their supporters know that three of the four new faces were to play key roles in their second-half drive for a playoff spot.

NOTES

1. Tommy Fitzgerald, "Qualters Faces Buffalo Tonight: Herrera Returns Amid Cheers," *Miami News*, June 5, 1957.

2. Baseball-reference.com.

3. *Sporting News*, June 12, 1957, 40.

4. Ibid.

5. Jimmy Burns, "Poe, Veeck Plan '58 Park Shows: Seek Stage, Radio-TV Acts; Coy Draws 6,412 Crowd at Miami Stadium Party," *Sporting News*, June 19, 1957, 37; Norris Anderson, "Opposing Pitchers Clubbing Marlins," *Miami News*, June 8, 1957.

6. Ibid.

7. Ibid.

8. Stu Locklin, phone interview with the author, March 7, 2010.

9. "Paige's Sabotaged Satchel Gives Marlins Some Laughs," *Sporting News*, June 26, 1957, 32.

10. Richard Bunker, phone interview with the author, May 26, 2011.

11. Wilbur Johnson, phone interview with the author, March 11, 2010.

12. "Miami Stadium Situation Again Placed in Doubt," *Sporting News*, June 19, 1957, 37.

13. Ibid.

14. Ibid.

15. Ibid.

16. *Sporting News*, July 3, 1957, 38.

17. *Sporting News*, June 19, 1957, 34.

18. *Sporting News*, June 26, 1957, 32.

19. Ibid.

TWELVE

The Fish Rise from the Bottom

What began as a promising season was slowly spiraling downward. The lack of hitting—with the exception of Don Landrum and Pancho Herrera, who were both hovering just over the .300 mark, and the consistent performance of Cal Abrams—continued to be a sticking point and the reason the team was failing to stay in the pennant race with Buffalo, Toronto, and Richmond. George Storer stated prior to the season that he was committed to fielding a winning team and he was about to prove just how committed he was to that promise. Although some changes had already been made, more were coming down the pike.

An eighteen-game road trip that started out on June 25 in Buffalo and ended on July 11 in Havana showed the Marlins winning only eight of the contests. Richmond (49–39) had come back down to earth and now yielded the IL lead to Buffalo (51–34). Miami stood at 39–46, in sixth place, just percentage points behind their rival Havana, twelve games off the pace. On a more promising note, the final five wins on the most recent road trip were shared by newcomer Bubba Church, Saul Rogovin (recently purchased from the Philadelphia Phillies on July 8),[1] and Satchel Paige, who was rounding into his usual dominating midseason form after a slow start. Paige's resurgence was especially encouraging based on his uncharacteristic slow start.

The Marlins were excited about Rogovin's arrival. As recently as 1951, he led the American League with a sparkling 2.76 ERA, but six years later he was being used sparingly by the Phillies. The big six-foot right-hander from Brooklyn so far had appeared in four games and logged eight innings with an inflated 9.00 ERA. The Marlins' brass were hoping that with a change of scenery and a chance to work more innings that he might regain some of his old magic. Rogovin was probably a little bitter when finding out about his demotion but took it in stride: "I don't blame the Phillies. They have a bunch of promising kids who throw hard, but I never got a real chance."[2] To General Manager Ryan, the veteran was exactly the type of player he loved to have in his club.

Although Rogovin was in the twilight of his career, Paige, who had recently turned fifty-one years old, was continuing to amaze even his most strident critics, belying the prognosticators who thought he was slowing down and reaching the end of the road. Putting the icing on the cake, Paige received the ultimate birthday present on July 7 when he earned his fifth win of the season. Paige pitched the final four and a third innings in relief for starter Earl Hunsinger and reliever Dick Bunker, closing out the 4–3 win against Columbus. Jets batters were left befuddled by his hesitation pitches and pinpoint fast ones that left them shaking their heads like bobble-head dolls.[3]

The arrival of the new bodies was just in the nick of time, as the Marlins were informed, on Paige's birthday, that one of their mainstays, Jack Meyer, was to be recalled to the parent club, stretching the already taxed pitching staff again to its limits. Meyer's departure allowed Bob Conley to return from the inactive list. Two of Conley's teammates were still on the disabled list: relievers Angelo LiPetri, who would not return until July 24, and Hank Mason, who was scheduled for July 12.[4] Regardless of whatever difficulties he faced, Don Osborn continued to work his magic, juggling his pitching staff tactfully while waiting for his moribund offense to wake up and support the valiant staff that ranked third in the league in ERA.

Returning to their friendly confines of Miami Stadium on July 12, the Marlins opened up with a three-game series against the Columbus Jets, the same team Paige had just tamed the week before. Starting righty Howie Judson struggled in the opener and was pulled after only one-third of an inning, giving up five runs in the 6–3 loss. But encouragingly, Hank Mason pitched well in his first appearance since returning from an injury, going six and two-thirds innings and giving up a single run while striking out three and only walking two.[5] Making his debut against the Jets on the same day was future Hall-of-Famer Whitey Herzog, who doubled in his first game as a Marlin. No doubt Herzog was disappointed by his demotion, but nevertheless, being the competitor he was, anxious to prove himself and return to the big leagues. Although the loss was upsetting, the future St. Louis Cardinals and Kansas City Royals manager received an eye-popping introduction to another future member of the hallowed Hall, Satchel Paige. As Bunker recalls, Whitey was more than impressed.

> *Dick Bunker*: So Satch could throw the ball, you know, he had such great control that he could always throw it down where you couldn't get it. But anyway, we were in Columbus, Ohio, and we were playing Skidoodle. Satch and I were playing Skidoodle in right field. And that

morning in the paper we read where Whitey Herzog was going to join our team. . . . Okay, we were out in right field playing Skidoodle and Satchel came out, I mean Whitey came out. Whitey came out to the outfield and he introduced himself. And so, in right field there was this hole in the wall. And at one time I tried to put a ball through it, and you could just about squeeze a ball through it. And they had a big sign there and it said, "$10,000 if you ever hit a ball in a regulation game through this hole." The odds on that are probably fifty million to one.

So anyway, we were talking and Whitey said, "You know I heard about your great control, Satch. You see that hole out there? I'll bet you can't throw a ball through it."

And Satch says, "Well, what do you want to bet?" And then Satch says, "How about a case of Canadian Club?" That's what he drank, you know. He loved Canadian Club.

So, he stood about forty feet away and threw the first ball and it was pretty close. [dramatically pauses] The second ball, it went right through the hole, right through the hole. Whitey's jaw dropped about ten feet and said, "You've got to be kidding me." He threw the ball right through that hole.

That's another true story I'm telling you. That's amazing that you remember that Skidoodle game. I don't know if anybody even remembers what Skidoodle was. That's amazing, but that's a true story about Whitey.[6]

The following night's game was cancelled due to rain, but Miami came back to sweep the Jets in the July 14 doubleheader by the scores of 7–6 and 3–2. Tom Qualters won the first game in relief with Paige picking up the save. Paige, in his favorite predicament—a late-inning tough jam—gave up a lead-off single to Ken Toothman, allowing the Jets to close the gap to 7–6, then settled down and struck out Howie Goss and got Dick Hall to pop up to end the game. "I was throwin' them screwballs along with my usual rapid ones," said the ageless wonder, who added, "It was the same old usual me—there with all those people on the bases." Bucha, Landrum, and Herrera all drove in a pair of runs apiece as key contributors.[7]

In the nightcap, a rejuvenated Church held Columbus to five hits and walked a solitary batter, ending his streak of twenty consecutive innings without issuing a free pass. In addition, he earned his third win of the season. Clyde McCullough accounted for all three ribbies, providing his battery mate with all the offensive support he needed. The two victories lifted the Marlins back into fifth place, four and a half games behind Rochester.[8]

Richmond was next on the slate and Osborn made it known that it was imperative that the Marlins start beating the teams that they were behind in the standings if they had any chance of getting back into the IL race. Thus far the Marlins were a paltry 21–27 against the teams in front of them in the standings: Buffalo, Richmond, Rochester, and Toronto.

After six weeks on the IR, Osborn turned to the well-rested Bob Conley to continue their winning ways. In what would prove an ominous note, in the second inning, one-time Phillies prospect and cast-off Danny Schell belted a Conley offering 340 feet over the left field wall, giving his Vees a 1–0 lead, much to the chagrin of more than 2,500 paying fans. The Vees assault continued, and by the fifth inning the visitors had built a 6–2 lead; Osborn had seen enough. The Marlins failed to mount any kind of a rally and went on to lose the game by the same score. The lone bright spot was the Miami's bullpen of Ray Semproch, Mason, and Earl Hunsinger, all combining for four and a third innings of scoreless relief.[9]

The next evening the Marlins caught a much-needed break and by Osborn's own account a gift that the team sorely needed. The Virginians had staked themselves to a 4–2 lead going into the bottom of the ninth and the game looked all but in the bag. Behind the fine pitching of right-hander Marty Kutyna the Vees were brimming with confidence, and after Bobby Young and Bob Micelotta went down on strikes, the few remaining paying customers sprinkled in the stands began to find their way toward the exit gates.[10]

With light-hitting Bucha coming up, Kutyna ran the count to one and one, and was looking for him to swing at something out of the strike zone. The plan was a good one, considering that Bucha was hitting a paltry .225 at the time, but the hard-nosed catcher's bat had other ideas as it made contact with the high and wide delivery driving into right field for a single. Ben Tompkins was called on to pinch-hit for Qualters and he promptly followed up by driving a double in the gap, bringing Bucha home and cutting the lead to 4–3.[11]

The wily Richmond manager Eddie Lopat had seen enough and called upon his best southpaw reliever Carlton Post to face lefty-swinging Abrams. The eagle-eyed Abrams worked Post for a walk, bringing up Whitey Herzog. Herzog then hit what appeared to be a game-ending weak grounder down to the usually sure-handed first baseman John Jaciuk. The game looked like it was in the bag for the Vees, but instead Jaciuk did his best Bill Buckner impression and let the ball squirt through the infield, allowing Tompkins to score and tie the game.

Lopat called on Sonny Dixon to try to snuff the rally, but found the veteran Woody Smith up to the task. A scorching line drive down the third base line missed the glove of Jerry Lumpe to give the Marlins the win, and joy to the few attendees in the stands who stuck around to see the comeback. Osborn appreciatively acknowledged after the game, "It's a long time between gifts." He added, "We had given them a couple of runs on throwing errors in the third inning." A win was a win, no matter how they got it, and Osborn was only too happy to accept it. Qualters earned the win in relief, despite giving up a run in the top of the ninth. Moreover, doing a yeoman's job was starter Howie Judson, who hurled seven strong innings in the comeback win, giving up three runs—

although only one was earned—before having to yield to Qualters. It was Judson's best outing of the year.[12]

The next day, Richmond closed out the series by beating Miami, 2–1. Oppressive heat and the soggy field proved challenging for both clubs. The game was ultimately halted after eight innings and called off by the umpires on the account of rain and the added soaking from the night before. Over the course of the contest the field condition had become so bad that the umpiring feared that injury could occur due to the quagmire and slick conditions. This was much to the chagrin of the Marlins, a mere one run behind at the time. It was a bit of a payback as the Vees scored two runs in the top of the last inning, earning their own comeback win. Virginian starter Bill Bethel and relief ace Johnny James combined for the victory, scattering seven Marlins hits. Rogovin's gutsy complete game performance went to waste as he suffered his first loss since joining the club. So hot and muggy was the weather in the "Magic City" that in order to endure the stifling humidity Rogovin had to take salt tablets between innings to avoid dehydration.[13]

As promised by Storer, the team made additional moves to bolster the roster. Ironically, the most significant moves addressed the pitching staff, not the offense. In quick order it was announced that thirty-five-year-old Red Adams from the Los Angeles Angels, and thirty-two-year-old Windy McCall from San Francisco Seals—both from the Pacific Coast League (PCL)—had been purchased to bring experience to the Marlins' young staff.[14] Adams, a native Californian who pitched briefly for the Chicago Cubs in 1946, was a longtime PCL star who was now in the twilight of his career. As recently as 1955, he had been a starting pitching mainstay, going 12–12 with 2.05 ERA in 1955 with the Portland Beavers. Before closing out his career in 1958 with Sacramento, he would compile a work-man-like minor league record of 193 wins against 182 losses, almost all of which were accomplished while toiling in the PCL.[15] The Marlins were looking for Adams's experience to add depth to their bullpen.

McCall, carrying with him major league experience dating back to his days with the Red Sox, Pirates, and Giants, was also a native of California. "Windy," as his teammates liked to call him because of his propensity to never shut up, brought a 3–2 record and 4.93 ERA, splitting time between starting and relieving. He would ultimately make only twelve appearances down the stretch but provided valuable veteran leadership and a stabilizing presence in the locker room. He would also return to Miami the next season and prove to be a more than capable long relief specialist.[16]

In total, when taking Paige's age out of the equation, the Marlins went from the youngest pitching corps in the IL to among the oldest. Among the graybeards now were Adams (thirty-five), Rogovin (thirty-three), McCall (thirty-two), Church (thirty-two), and Judson (thirty-one).[17] Only the Toronto Maple Leafs, with seven pitchers over the age of thirty, had more senior citizens on their staff. Parting company upon the newly acquired veteran arrivals was Gene Snyder, demoted to Tulsa. The parent Phillies were in hopes that he would find his control.

The rest of the month of July proved to be kinder to the Marlins as they began their climb out of second division. On July 20, Ray Semproch celebrated his upcoming wedding and announced his engagement to the lovely Ms. Jerri Kral by halting Havana 5–1. Semproch, who allowed nine hits, also struck out six while giving out a single free pass to earn the 5–1 victory.[18]

Although rookies Pancho Herrera, Don Landrum, and Ray Semproch were continuing to make their marks, the veterans also had something to prove. On July 21 Judson earned his first win of the season, throttling Havana at home, 12–1, earning a complete game victory. In the process he retired the final thirteen Sugar Kings he faced. Unfortunately, Hunsinger failed in his bid to win the second game of the double dip, falling to Sugar Kings ace Mike Cuellar, 5–2, the recipient of his seventh win against a solitary defeat.[19] Hunsinger would soon join his teammate Gene Snyder in Tulsa.

Inspired by Judson's performance, Rogovin came out the next night against the Montreal Royals and turned the guests away, 7–3. Rogovin had goose eggs on the board until the sixth inning when with one out and Jimmy Williams on first base, right fielder Bob Wilson planted one of Rogovin's offerings just over the left field wall, cutting the Marlins' lead to 5–2. Osborn, not wasting any time, turned to Paige to close the door and preserve the win. Paige, as he so often did, was up to the task and allowed only one run and three hits while striking out four of the enemy during the ensuing three innings.[20] With some newfound confidence, the Marlins took three of four from the visiting Royals.

Toronto followed their Canadian neighbors for their July 26 opening game in Miami Stadium. They found a different team than they had last played in June. Manager Dixie Walker's team, which had been enduring some of their own hitting problems of late, were dispatched prior to the game for some extra batting practice. The results paid some dividends, but not in a timely enough fashion for the crusty old manager's taste. In one of the strangest performances of the year, starter Judson mixed an assortment of curves, sliders, and fastballs, scattering ten hits over the first seven innings before being relieved by Qualters in the eighth inning. Qualters was tagged for a couple of more base hits, but persevered to earn the save. In total the visiting Toronto Maple Leafs stranded thirteen runners and not one single hit went for extra bases.[21] Clyde McCullough's assessment of Judson after the game was simply, "Howie had trouble getting his curve over, but he sure showed he's a hard worker who can stand pressure." Osborn added, "Howie Judson hung in there pretty good didn't he?"[22] The final tally showed Marlins 3, Maple Leafs 0.

The five-game series, and last meeting between the two clubs in Miami against Toronto, proved to be the jump start the Marlins needed going down the stretch. By taking four out of the five contests the Marlins were poised to jump into first division. On July 30, Miami swept the front-running Buffalo Bisons in a double dip; teamed with fifth-place Havana's split of a doubleheader with Rochester in Havana, this victory allowed the Marlins to slip back into fourth place. Paige, who was called on to relieve Judson in the first game, arrived late for his appearance because he had fallen asleep. After being startled out of his hotel bed, he arrived at the ballpark just in time to strike out Joe Caffie and cement the win.[23]

Seemingly rejuvenated and ready to return to the road, the Marlins were anxious to take on their next comers, the always pesky Rochester Red Wings. The new Marlins were drawing the attention of the rest of the league and were making it known that this team was not out of the race yet. The question that begged for a response was this: "Is anyone in Miami taking notice?"

NOTES

1. *Sporting News*, July 17, 1957, 36.
2. Ralph Berger, "Saul Rogovin," 2009, www.bioproj.sabr.org.
3. "Paige Wins on Birthday," *Sporting News*, July 17, 1957, 36.
4. Ibid.
5. *Sporting News*, July 24, 1957, 32.
6. Richard Bunker, phone interview with the author, January 15, 2011.
7. Norris Anderson, "Marlins Now Fifth, Play Vees Tonight," *Miami News*, July 15, 1957.
8. *Sporting News*, July 24, 1957, 32; Anderson, "Marlins Now Fifth, Play Vees Tonight."
9. Tommy Fitzgerald, "'Tame' Wiesler Tames Marlins," *Miami News*, July 16, 1957.
10. Tommy Fitzgerald, "'Marlins Take Gift' Play Richmond Two," *Miami News*, July 17, 1957.
11. Ibid.
12. Fitzgerald, "'Marlins Take Gift' Play Richmond Two"; *Sporting News*, July 24, 1957, 32.
13. Norris Anderson, "Miami Drills Today, after More Base Hits," *Miami News*, July 19, 1957.
14. Anderson, "Miami Drills Today, after More Base Hits"; *Sporting News*, July 31, 1957, 38.
15. Baseball-reference.com.
16. Ibid.
17. *Sporting News*, July 31, 1957, 33.
18. Ibid.
19. Ibid., 38.
20. *Sporting News*, July 31, 1957, 33; Tommy Fitzgerald, "Royals Wilson Learns: Never Befriend an Ump," *Miami News*, July 23, 1957.
21. *Sporting News*, August 7, 1957, 39; Norris Anderson, "Leafs in Morning Workout," *Miami News*, July 27, 1957.
22. Anderson, "Leafs in Morning Workout."
23. Tommy Fitzgerald, "Marlins Luck Out, 3–1," *Miami News*, July 30, 1957.

THIRTEEN

Goodbye Cal, New Faces, and the Fight to Make the Playoffs

General Manager Joe Ryan worked feverishly to rework the Miami roster, having added several players and shed others, in the process spending some significant cash to bolster the team. Buffalo Bisons skipper Phil Cavarretta disgustedly chortled in response to his team's lack of efforts to acquire help, "Look at Miami buying those seven players, including pitchers Bubba Church and Saul Rogovin, and outfielders like Stu Locklin and Whitey Herzog and they're taking 'em away from us." What nobody saw coming came after the doubleheader in Buffalo on July 31. The announcement that star outfielder Cal Abrams had been sold to IL rival Toronto for $20,000 cash sent shock waves that were felt clear to South Beach. Although only seven games below Buffalo in the standings, and a mere two and a half games behind Toronto for the third-place position, many were left scratching their heads asking why the sale of such a vital piece of the team, at this stage of the pennant race, and why to one of their chief competitors?

Obviously the sale of Abrams was a response to fiscal concerns. The Marlins were hemorrhaging money and the recent player acquisitions had not responded as well as management had hoped toward building a winner and spurring attendance. Upon Abrams's departure the Marlins lost one of the few consistent bats that they possessed in their lineup, one of their most popular players, and one of the finest and most respected gentlemen ever to don a Marlins uniform. Ironically, Abrams would go and play an integral role in Toronto's push to win the IL and finished the season batting .278 with .386 OPB, his last season in professional baseball.[1]

As a small consolation the Phillies placed on loan to the Marlins twenty-seven-year-old first baseman and outfielder Marv Blaylock in hopes of providing some offensive contribution and to compensate for the loss of Abrams. Blaylock, displaced by ex-Marlin Ed Bouchee, had been the Phillies starting first baseman the previous season, but had spent most of the year riding the pine. The left-handed hitting Arkansas native was batting a paltry .154 with two homers and four ribbies in twenty-six at-bats at the time and Phillies management figured that gaining some at-bats might help him gain some lost form.[2] Osborn's intentions were to honor the Phillies' request and to insert him in the lineup to play right field in hopes he would regain his batting eye and provide some pop to the Marlins' otherwise lackluster offense.

As evidence of the team's financial problems, GM Joe Ryan announced that at the conclusion of the Toronto series, home attendance was down fifty-seven thousand paying customers from the previous season. This figure even took into account the Orange Bowl gala from the year before that accounted for 51,713, which was left out of the numbers.[3] The honeymoon that the once confident Storer had experienced at the beginning of the year was now proving to be short-lived, and the reality of the viability of profitable baseball in Miami was beginning to cause him some concern. Rumors had been swirling around the team, the most accepted being that Miami was changing affiliations for the 1958 season to the Boston Red Sox even though the Phillies were confident of reaching a complementary working agreement.[4]

Every win at this juncture of the season was increasingly crucial. On August 3, in front of a sparse crowd of just over 1,300 attendees, Miami crawled back to the .500 mark for the first time since June 8. It wasn't pretty, but for one of the few times all season the offense was firing on all eight cylinders. Locklin, Bobby Young, and Clyde McCullough all blasted home runs, highlighting a fifteen-hit attack that amounted to a 12–9 victory. At the top of the order, lead-off hitter Whitey Herzog provided the spark they were hoping for, gathering three hits, and Bobby Young followed with four more hits, providing the much-needed spark in an albeit ugly triumphant contest. Tom Qualters garnered his ninth win of the season in three and two-thirds innings of relief work in place of Judson, holding the Red Wings in check.[5]

The Marlins hold on .500 was all too brief, as they dropped the final two games at home to Rochester by scores of 3–2 and 2–1. Recipients of the defeats were newcomers Saul Rogovin and Windy McCall. Pancho Herrera (.308) and Don Landrum (.313) remained among the league leaders in hitting, while Ray Semproch had now established himself as the new staff ace, improving his record to 8–3, coupled with a shiny 2.86 ERA.[6] Semproch credited his most recent success to his old manager and former Cubs, Athletics, and Indians pitcher Charlie Gassaway, who suggested earlier in the year that he try to drop down and pitch with a more side-arm motion.[7] The results were positive, to say the least.

Returning home to play Buffalo and then Rochester, home sweet home proved to be troublesome as the Marlins salvaged a split with the Bisons but then dropped three out of four to Rochester. Sadly, even the reliable Semproch suffered a rare defeat during the second game of the August 11 doubleheader extra-inning affair, when he faltered during the eighth inning and allowed the Red Wings to push three runs across the plate in the top of the inning. Despite Paige's excellent relief work, Semproch's loss dropped his record to 8–4 in what would prove to be his final regular season loss. It was also announced before leaving town that Saul Rogovin would be placed on the disabled list to make room for the much-anticipated return of Dick Bunker.[8] Bunker had received a reprieve from his military six-month reserve program obligation until October and was anxious to rejoin his teammates.

Returning to the road, the reeling Marlins' bad luck continued in Montreal as the Royals took two out of three in Delorimier Stadium. The lone victory was a 10–3 thrashing of the Royals supplemented by Woody Smith's three hits and two RBIs, along with home runs by Johnny Bucha and Locklin. Conspicuously absent from the game was Satchel Paige.

Bad news seemed to be a constant companion of the Marlins as of late and had especially been unkind to its most recent victims: Bob Micelotta, who was in the midst of a zero for thirty-four slump, and Paige, whose luggage went AWOL somewhere between Miami and Montreal. Arriving with only his hi-fi set and typewriter intact, Paige failed to show up for the opening game of the series, played seventy-five miles away in Quebec City, drawing some harsh words from his usually forgiving manager Don Osborn.[9] Paige had tested the frustrated skipper's patience one too many times and as punishment he scheduled Paige, on short notice, the next night to start. The "Ancient One," usually up to the task, left his best stuff with his baggage, lasting only three innings and giving up three runs before feeling the hook.[10] The humiliating 7–0 loss dropped Paige to seven wins and six losses and left more than a few pundits scratching their heads.

Before returning home the Marlins salvaged a split in Toronto, taking two of the four games. After splitting the opening night twin bill the Marlins almost had the next night's game literally blow up in their faces. With the Leafs trailing by two runs, and with two runners edging off their bases in the eighth inning, Hector Rodriguez hit a sinking liner off of Paige, heading between Locklin and Landrum in left centerfield. As was the habit in Toronto, when the home town team scored, the fireworks attendant would set off fireworks to celebrate the scores. In this case the operator jumped the gun and set off the pyrotechnics prematurely, startling Landrum. Fortunately, the dazed Landrum regained his composure—although belatedly—in the nick of time to flag down the ball. Unfortunately, the delay from the scare had allowed two runs to score, and left Rodriguez at third base with a triple. Osborn immediately blew a fuse of his own and, after arguing with the umpires, promptly put the game under protest because of the interference.

Providentially, for the Marlins and league officials, Bucha doubled in the winning run in the tenth inning, giving the boys from Miami a much-deserved win and no further need to file the protest. [11]

With a chance to pick up valuable ground on the league contenders the next night, one of the most disheartening losses of the season came in the final game of the series. What started as a slugfest turned into a pitcher's duel between two relief aces: Bobby Tiefenauer and Paige. Paige, who entered the game in the ninth inning, remained strong for four and two-thirds innings before faltering in the fourteenth inning, allowing a 310-foot home run to Loren Babe that just cleared the right field fence. Osborn lamented after the thirteen-inning affair that the ball would have been an out in most parks and that Paige didn't deserve such a bad break. Regardless, the results were the same: a 9–8 loss. [12] Again, the Marlins' failure to win against the better teams in the league was increasingly becoming a stumbling block in their quest to gain a playoff spot. For the first time in his managerial career Osborn was looking at the possibility of finishing out of first division.

The Marlins were happy for a one-day respite from play thanks to the IL All-Star game break held on August 19. The only member of the Miami squad to appear in the game was Woody Smith. Smith represented his team well by garnering a single and double in five at-bats. He was responsible for the only run driven in as the IL stars fell to the Brooklyn Dodgers in a nail-biter, 2–1. [13]

Taking advantage of the time off to catch their collective breath, the Marlins kicked off their first road trip taking their first series since August 1 and toppling the Columbus Jets in two out of three games. However, their miseries soon returned when they followed up their success by losing all four games in Richmond and then two out of three more games in Columbus.

As August neared its conclusion, the trying month had left the Marlins reeling. Whatever aspirations were held for a pennant had long since been scrapped and now the team's goal was focused on earning a playoff berth. Returning home for a thirteen-game home stand, the Marlins were fortunate that they had only dropped as low as sixth place in the standings. Buffalo (79–59) and Toronto (78–61) found themselves in a heated race at the top of the IL with only one and a half games separating the Bisons from the Maple Leafs. The fast-starting Richmond Vees (73–64) were on the verge of falling out of the pennant race completely, now five and a half games off the pace, having lost twelve of their last fourteen games. The Marlins (64–72) had faded to fourteen games off the pace, but were remarkably still alive, out only a half-game behind Havana and one and half games behind Rochester for fourth place. As of late, Rochester had cooperated by losing eight straight games, keeping the hopes of the Miamians in their quest for the final playoff spot alive.

On August 27 the last-place Columbus Jets came to town to kick off a Marlins homestand in Miami Stadium before closing out the year with four games in Havana. The Marlins' chances hinged on putting some kind of winning streak together and wrest fourth place away from their closest competitors, the Sugar Kings and Red Wings. Osborn's forthright assessment to the sportswriters was concise and to the point: "The only way we're going to get in that first division is to beat 'em ourselves — We can't depend on someone else beating 'em for us." He added, "We've got to do it ourselves."[14] No one was expecting Havana or Rochester to lie down, but the Marlins were going to need a little help from Rochester and Havana.

Kicking off against Columbus with a twin bill, Osborn went with his two most reliable veterans: Church (4–4), to match up against the Vees lefty Don Kildoo (6–10) in the first game, and Judson (4–5), taking on righty Ron Blackburn (8–10) in the nightcap. Both games would prove to be classic pitchers' duels.[15]

With ominous thunderclouds threatening on the horizon on an otherwise pleasant Miami night, a meager crowd of 2,193 trickled into Miami Stadium. This wasn't what Storer envisioned, and an even more concerned General Manager Ryan paced nervously in the press box, contemplating what he could do to spur attendance. Even though his team was in second division, they were still very much alive in the hunt for the final playoff position; yet the fans were staying away in droves.[16]

Taking the hill for the first game of the double dip would be Church. Now thirty-two years old, Church was a key member of the 1950 Philadelphia Phillies club as a starting pitcher that won the National League pennant. During his 1950 rookie season, while facing Ted Kluszewski of the Cincinnati Reds, he was struck in the face by a vicious line drive and missed the rest of the season. Although he returned to the big leagues the next season, going 15–11 for the Phillies, his career began a slow decline that found him in the PCL by 1954. What looked like a long promising career was now nearing its conclusion. Having lost some of the zip on his once wicked fastball, he now relied more on control and guile to fool enemy hitters.

Church, appearing a little off his game, started the evening sluggishly, allowing a couple of base hits and an RBI single to Johnny Lipon in the first inning. The veteran right-sider settled down after the first two innings. Mixing his assortment of sharp curves and sinking fastballs, he started to find his rhythm and the Jets' hitters were befuddled. The Marlins knotted the score in the third inning when Dick Barone mishandled a hard hit grounder that allowed Church to score and bring the score to 1–1.[17]

Church continued to rely on his control and through eight innings he matched Kildoo inning for inning. Running out of gas, Jets skipper Ron Oceak opted to go with reliever George O'Donnell in the ninth inning. In the top of the ninth frame Church also showed signs of fatigue but Osborn stuck with the veteran anyway. Allowing Danny Kravitz to double, Eddie O'Brien came around to score what proved to be the difference maker. Miami went down quietly in the bottom of the same inning with all to show for their efforts another loss on five hits; two of those singles by Church. The final tally was Jets 2, Marlins 1.[18]

In the second game, twenty-two-year-old Blackburn—a highly regarded Pirates prospect—pitched a gem of a game, throwing seven innings of no-hit ball. The first Marlin base hit did not come until the eighth inning when third sacker Smith looped a single to centerfield, breaking up the no-no. The deciding run for the Marlins came in the ninth when Don Landrum led off the inning by coaxing a walk from the so far stingy Blackburn. Landrum then advanced to second on Herzog's sacrifice. R. C. Stevens tried to get the lead runner, but the throw was too late to catch the speedy Landrum, setting up what would ultimately be the winning run. With two outs, after Blaylock failed to lay down a sacrifice bunt, the next batter, Herrera, delivered the goods with his second hit of the evening, a ringing single through the infield, which brought in Landrum and gave the home town team a well-deserved and hard-earned 1–0 win.[19]

Steady rains continued to hamper play through the night and doused Miami Stadium the next evening, forcing cancellation and rescheduling of the doubleheader to be played the following day on August 29. Both teams arrived at the stadium early, but the way both clubs were swinging the bat one might have wondered if they hadn't left their bats out in the rain and allowed them to become waterlogged. Paige, despite allowing only three hits and not walking a single batter, dropped the opener 3–0. Unfortunately, two of the three hits came by the long ball as Roman Mejias and Stevens both homered. Jets starter George O'Donnell scattered four hits while walking three, frustrating the Marlins, whose only offensive producer was Pancho Herrera, who legged out a couple of singles.[20]

In the second game the Marlins received redemption in the form of Norwood's native son Dick Bunker, who pitched his best game since returning from Massachusetts. Going seven and two-thirds innings, the ex-Notre Dame Fighting Irish hurler masterly spaced out seven hits and two walks, allowing only a single tally as the Marlins came out ahead, 2–1. "Bunker had the life back in his fast ball and curve again," chimed Osborn. However, some late relief help from Saul Rogovin, who earned his third win of the season, was necessary to preserve the low-scoring affair. The big blow of the evening came off Marv Blaylock's bat in the ninth inning, when he crushed a 350-foot solo walk-off home run off of starter Dick Hall, the blast just clearing the wall. Blaylock's home run was the first by a Marlin to clear the right field fence all season. [21]

With thirteen games remaining, the sixth-place Marlins now trailed Rochester by only a game and a half for the fourth position, with Havana sandwiched in between. Osborn was especially concerned with the Sugar Kings, who had seemingly got their act together as of late by winning six out of their last nine contests. On the other side of the coin, Rochester was in the midst of their worst slump of the year, having lost seventeen of their last twenty-three games.

Next on the slate were Eddie Lopat's Vees. Thus far, Richmond had dominated Miami to the tune of taking eleven of the seventeen meetings between the two clubs. With only Havana waiting in the wings to close out the season in a home and away series, it was a matter of urgency for Osborn's crew to take charge of their own destiny. [22] Returning from the disabled list for the stretch was reliever Angelo LiPetri, which was tempered by some bad news when it was announced that Herzog would be taking his vanquished spot on the disabled list. Showing up at the club-house in a cast, he announced that he would be lost for the remainder of the season due to a torn shoulder cartilage suffered during the recent series with the Jets. [23]

The home opening doubleheader would prove to be a classic. Osborn chose Qualters (10–11) to face off versus Vees left-hander James Kite (9–11) in the early game. Despite the playoff atmosphere of the contest only 2,309 fans passed through the gates. No doubt distressing to Marlins' management, even the vendors in the stands anxious to peddle their wares voiced their dissatisfaction. The few fans who did come would get their money's worth, plus more than a little interest. "Money Bags" would have to work some overtime on this night. The customary seven innings ended in a 0–0 tie. [24]

Qualters, in one of his most determined performances of the season, hung tough and was up to the challenge, frustrating the Virginians at every turn with his low inside-outside curveballs and crisp fastballs. After a succession of tight games between the two squads, tensions were running high. It reached a fevered pitch during the ninth inning when Vees centerfielder Len Johnston, after riding umpire Bob Smith with a little too much gusto concerning his strike zone, drew some unwanted attention from the men in blue. Smith had had enough of Johnston's jockeying and, utilizing his thumb, he tossed him from the game. Johnston's teammates on the bench took exception and advised the angered umpire, in less than friendly terms, they wouldn't play without Johnston. In diplomatic fashion Smith agreed to their terms and, to skipper Lopat's chagrin, cleared the entire Vees bench for the remainder of the game. The only exceptions were a couple of Richmond players in the bullpen and a batboy. Finally, in the bottom of the tenth inning the game came to a merciful conclusion. With one out, reliever Sonny Dixon faced pinch-hitter Tompkins, batting for Micelotta, and promptly gave up a single to the Texan scoring Locklin from second base. Final score showed Miami 1, Richmond 0. The ejected Vees could at least take consolation in the fact that they weren't present to see the end.[25]

The second game of the twin bill featured Red Adams (1–2) squaring off against southpaw Bob Wiesler (11–11). Osborn was playing a hunch and not going with one his usual starting pitchers because Adams had been inconsistent since joining the team. On the other hand, Wiesler had been particularly adept at shutting down Marlins hitters all season and facing Adams, the Vees felt confident that they would salvage at least a split of the doubleheader.

However, the always-ready-for-action Bob Micelotta had other plans. Lifted for a pinch-hitter in the first game, the feisty shortstop found some redemption in his own brand of late-game heroics. With the score knotted again going into the bottom of the ninth inning, the scrappy shortstop played the hero, singling in the go-ahead run and leaving the finishing touches to Windy McCall to close the game and save the 3–2 win. Coach Eddie Miller was ecstatic after the game, proclaiming, "When you win two games by one run in a clutch doubleheader like this one, you've got a first division team." Osborn was a bit more reserved in his appraisal, and, not wanting to count his chickens before they'd hatched, he said, "It's been a long chase, but don't forget we've still got a piece to go."[26] Teamed with Rochester's 2–1 loss to Toronto, and Havana being shut out 4–0 by Columbus, the Marlins moved back into a fourth-place tie with the Red Wings. It marked the first time the Miamians had been in first division since June 9.

The Marlins were gaining momentum at just the right time. Although Osborn's crew was still lagging in the offensive department, the patchwork mixture of veterans and collection of youth on the hill had coalesced into the most impressive staff in the league. The next night Osborn stuck with his newfound ace, Semproch (11–4), to counter the right-handed control specialist Bill Bethel (13–6).

Semproch brought his "A-Game" to the table in another hand wringer, stymieing the Vees on five hits while allowing one base on balls. A credit to the efficiency of both Semproch and Bethel was the fact that the game only lasted one hour and forty-five minutes. Bucha's single following a Blaylock double accounted for the only RBI of the evening. The other Miami run came on a Bethel error and left the final score at Marlins 2, Vees 0. Combined with Rochester's 6–5 loss to Toronto and Columbus's 7–3 drubbing of Havana, Miami found themselves alone in fourth place with only ten games left until the finish line.[27] But there was more work yet to be done.

The Marlins, now aspiring to sweep the series—a feat they had not accomplished since June 23 when they took three games from Montreal in Miami Stadium—were eying the prize. But as experience had taught them, "Don't count those chickens before they're hatched." Tactician Lopat was optimistically planning on taking the last two games and would counter Miami's Church (6–5) with Marlins nemesis, and probably the league's most hated pitcher, Jim Coates (12–11) in the first game and Marty Kutyna (10–6) versus Judson (5–5) in the seven-inning late game. Coates continued to cement his unpopular reputation based on his head-hunting bean balls that were now becoming legendary around the IL.

Another sparse crowd of 2,633 welcomed the Marlins. But although small in number, the crowd was rabid. The early outlook was disillusioning after Richmond staked themselves to a 3–0 lead in the first frame. Micelotta cut the lead to 3–1 by driving in Smith in the second with a seeing-eye single restoring some hope to the hometown rooters.[28]

Despite appearing to be on the top of his game, Coates, the future Yankees star, continued to stymie the Marlins by mixing an exquisite repertoire of fastball, curves, and change-ups. Midway through the eighth inning, Miami had managed only five hits and a couple of runs, and were down 4–2. However, Coates was showing signs of fatigue and Lopat called on lefty Carlton Post to close out the game and preserve the win. Although Post had been inconsistent most of the year, this night the stars were in alignment as he retired the last five batters he faced, thus preventing the sweep. The workman-like starter Church had masterfully scattered thirteen hits, mixed in with three walks, allowing only four Richmond runs, but, as was so common all year, the offense continued its moribund ways and was the chief culprit in the loss.[29]

For the few loyal spectators who stuck around for the nightcap, there was better news. The Marlins staked Judson to a 6–0 lead in the first inning and they never looked back, cruising to an 8–1 victory. Judson earned the complete seven-inning win despite not striking out a single Virginian, allowing only seven hits and allowing one solitary free pass. In addition, he was the hitting star of the night, driving in three runs. Providing additional support were Herrera and Smith, purveyors of two RBIs apiece.[30]

The Marlins stood at 70–75, still fighting for the final playoff spot. On the same evening the Marlins split with Richmond, Havana was shutting out Columbus 2–0 in Havana behind the fine pitching of Pat Scantlebury, while in Rochester the Red Wings fought a hard-earned battle and earned two victories against the eventual IL champs, the Maple Leafs, sweeping a doubleheader by the score of 8–7 in twelve innings, and 3–1 in the late match-up. Rochester, by basis of percentage points at 71–76, was an ant's eyelash ahead of Miami and clinging onto fourth place, with Havana only a game and a half behind. As fate would have it, their archenemies the Sugar Kings were next up on the playbill. The rivalry was beginning to ratchet up, as evidenced by the fierceness of competition between the two teams each time they squared off. First, a four-game series in Miami would be played before both teams would travel 225 miles south to Havana for the close of the regular season. Rochester, on the other hand, would play their final seven games against Montreal and Buffalo on the road.

There was no need to explain to anyone why this was the most important series of the year for the Marlins. Playing the Sugar Kings, the Marlins carried their destiny in their own hands. However, Rochester could snatch the fourth spot while the two rivals battled it out, and could let both of the southern teams do their dirty work. Osborn wasn't taking any chances. Osborn, like many veteran skippers, had a tendency to depend on his veterans in key games. He would turn to this tried-and-true strategy once more in the opening contest. As of late Paige was used sparingly, but the importance of this doubleheader was vital as it would set the tone for the remainder of what was left of the season. No matter how frustrating Paige could be to Osborn, he was guaranteed to produce in the clutch. "MG," as Paige (8–8) liked to refer to Osborn, opted for his big-game pitcher to face long-limbed right-hander Orlando Pena (12–9) in the first game. For the nightcap Bunker (5–9) would be called on to face veteran righty Jose Santiago (4–7). Osborn must have been playing an especially strong hunch since Bunker had not won a game since June 26.

Osborn broke from his customary style. He chose Paige, who usually pitched the short game in the Labor Day doubleheader, and called on him to hurl in the long game. It was classic Paige. Mixing every pitch in his arsenal, he frustrated the Sugar Kings with hesitation pitches, nickel curveballs, and pinpoint placed fastballs. McCullough simply placed the target and Paige hit the mark. All of Miami's scoring came in the fifth inning when McCullough, Micelotta, and Landrum all drove in single runs off of Pena, who finally yielded to relief in the eighth inning with his Sugar Kings down 3–0. Paige was at his classic best, allowing only three singles and most importantly withholding a single walk. It was the twentieth time the Sugar Kings had been shut out, the most in the league.[31]

Little did anyone know, but the night game would prove to be one of the single greatest season performances by a Marlins pitcher in their short history. The contest started out innocently enough when Havana's Angel Scull hit a single and drove in the first run of the game in the top of the third inning, plating ex-Marlin Yo-Yo Davalillo. In the fourth inning the Marlins answered the bell and tied the score 1–1 when one of Smith's three hits on the night scored Herrera.[32]

These were the days before the prevalence of pitch counts, and Osborn was about to tax his man Bunker to the limit. By the end of the regulation seven innings both teams remained tied at a run apiece. Bunker and Santiago were locked in a nerve-wracking duel that continued through eleven innings. Sugar Kings skipper Nap Reyes, sensing his playoff aspirations fading, pulled his starter in favor of his young and up-and-coming star, Miguel Cuellar, later to be known more popularly in the States as Mike. Cuellar threw every pitch at enemy batters, using different angles and speeds that were designed to throw off their timing. He looked to play the perfect foil against the Marlins. Osborn refused to yield and, playing one of his famous hunches, stayed with the determined Bunker despite the oppressive humidity and heat bearing down on the youngster. In order to stay cool Bunker had been soaking his arm in a bucket of ice in spirit of ammonia between frames. With two outs in the bottom of the sixteenth inning, Osborn finally relented and pinch-hit for the bone-tired Bunker. With two outs, Tompkins stepped up to the plate and promptly rapped a single off of Cuellar, driving in Smith, who had previously doubled, ending the game with the Marlins coming out on top, 2–1.[33]

The performance would rate as one of the gutsiest performances ever for a Marlins hurler. Bunker had completed sixteen innings, stranding fourteen runners, allowing ten hits, and striking out ten while walking only three. More importantly, with the second win the Marlins stood two and a half games ahead of Havana and two games ahead of the idle Red Wings. The win over the Sugar Kings had driven a stake through the heart of their rival's postseason dreams and in the process uplifted the Marlins' own aspirations.

Bunker remembers his performance vividly. He recalled the game just like it was yesterday and the last pitch that proved to be the difference-maker in the win, along with a little sidelight—teaching his friend Paige the secret to throwing a spitball.

> *Dick Bunker*: Do I remember that? You know why I remember it? Because it was ninety degrees out and the flag was blowing straight down. I'm serious it was so hot. I know I pitched a long time and I was about ready to drop. And the next guy came up, and I never threw a spitter before in a game. I taught Satchel, this is the truth. I taught Satchel Paige how to throw a spitter. He used to show me and I said, "Satch, the idea of a spitter is you can't touch a seam. When you wet your hand and put it on the ball, it can't be on the seam. It's got to be below the seam. You know, off seam."
>
> So I remember I never threw a spitter in my life. But I called time out, and I don't remember who was catching that game, it could've been Johnny Bucha, but anyway he came out. They had their best hitter up, a third baseman [Patricio Quintana] I can't think, they called him the "White Rat" or something like that. He was a great hitter. And I said to Johnny, "Man, I mean I am tired," and he keeps fouling off pitches and I'm tired, and I said, "I'm going to load one up. I'm going to throw a spitter at him and see what happens and if it doesn't do anything I don't care." So he said, "Okay." He went back and I loaded this up and I threw a spitter and the ball broke about a foot, you know, and it struck him out, and I think that ended the game. I don't remember the score. [remembering] It was two to one. I pitched the whole sixteen innings? Oh my god, well that's a true story. I remember throwing that pitch and the guy turned around and looked at Bucha, or

whoever was catching, and said "That was a spitter." You know he
says, "He doesn't throw a spitter." And I think he [Bucha] wiped the
ball on the ground.[34]

The final two games in Miami Stadium turned out to be fairly un-
eventful. Forty-year-old ex-Brooklyn Dodger Joe Hatten won his ninth
game of the season, easily dispatching the Marlins 6–1. In the meantime,
Rochester split a doubleheader with Montreal, winning the first game 4–2
and dropping the second game 8–3.

The September 4 match was the final home game of the season before
one last road trip. Good feelings were in abundance for "Fan Appreciation Day" as the Marlins easily shut down the boys from Havana, 5–0,
behind their ace Semproch.[35] Among all the glad-handing, bad news
arrived from up north. Rochester, playing their second doubleheader in a
row, swept the Royals, winning the first game 4–3 and the second 5–2,
thus cutting the Marlins' fourth-place lead to one game with four games
left to play.

Being the last home appearance of the season, loyal fans, Marlins
ownership, and the press, in appreciation of their players' fine performances during the season, honored their heroes by awarding them with
various gifts as tokens of their appreciation. Beloved third sacker and
slick fielding glove man Woody Smith (.277, 14 HRs, 73 RBIs) was thrilled
when he received a tailored suit as the team's Most Valuable Player;
Frank "Pancho" Herrera (.306, 17 HRs, 93 RBIs) was voted the most valuable rookie and was presented luggage; Ray Semproch (12–4, 2.76 ERA)
received a twelve-gauge shotgun as the team's outstanding pitcher; and
Don Landrum (.294, 3 HRs, 70 runs) was given a television set as the
team's most popular player.[36]

With the season nearly wrapped up and the Red Wings still hot on
their heels, the weary Marlins departed on their chartered flight south.
Upon arriving at the Havana airport the visitors were greeted by the
warm Caribbean breezes wafting into Havana. Not as pleasant was the
usual hostile environment awaiting them in Gran Stadium. A small but
boisterous throng of *fanaticos* greeted the Marlins, besmirching them in
Spanish as they ground through the pregame ritual of stretching, running
wind sprints, and shagging flies. Although the crowd numbered just over
two thousand, it seemed like exponentially more as the loyal Sugar
Kings' rooters bellowed out cheers, banged their drums, and blew their
whistles. No team could brag of more passionate fans than those that
frequented Gran Stadium.

The unsympathetic crowds were the least of the Marlins' worries.
More than a few in the Miami contingent were apprehensive and always
a bit skittish when they arrived in Havana. The sound of gunfire and talk
of revolutionaries coming down from the mountains were disconcerting.

Stu Locklin remembers hearing from other players and coaches, warning him to stay alert when in Havana.

> *Stu Locklin*: But yeah, we got a lot of stories when we went there from Miami and played. You know they'd watch you. And you had to be cautious because there were a lot of things going on down there with the revolution and everything. But we only had to go there once or twice when things were getting rough. But it was a memorable experience that I had playing for Miami.[37]

The Sugar Kings' task was difficult at best. Reyes knew that only a sweep would give his team any chance of catching the Marlins and Red Wings. Taking three out of four in Miami seemed to take its toll as the Marlins dropped the series lid-lifter, 8–0. Judson continued to struggle and the usually anemic Sugar Kings' offense collected seventeen hits off of the combination of Judson, Mason, Rogovin, McCall, and Qualters. All the while, the Sugar Kings rode Pat Scantlebury's tireless iron arm to the end, securing the shutout win. The only consolation for the Marlins was that Toronto, motivated to capture their third pennant in four seasons, edged Rochester 3–2. Stan Jok drove in the winning run with a walk-off single, putting a blanket over the Red Wings' playoff hopes.

The Marlins received some bad news on September 5, but good news for Tom Qualters. It was the moment that all ballplayers, with aspirations and dreams of making it to the big leagues, pray for. The phone call came from Philadelphia for Qualters to catch the next flight out of Miami. Although Qualters had spent time with the Phillies in 1953 after signing a $40,000 contract out of high school, it was a bittersweet experience, since he was ill prepared to pitch at that level, not to mention being treated poorly by some of his teammates. His second call-up was more meaningful, especially since he had worked so hard proving to his doubters that he did indeed belong in the majors. After spending four years in the bush leagues, all his hard work was validated. As a token of respect and genuine friendship, his teammate "Satch" gave him a memento that was of special meaning that only a fellow ballplayer would appreciate. Along with that gift, an even more special memory, although not as rewarding, greeted him on his return to the big leagues on September 7 in Pittsburgh. The latter was peppered with a little razzing.

> *Tom Qualters*: We were in Havana, Cuba. We were only down for about three or four day trip and were then coming back to Miami. After we got in the first game, or so I can't remember for sure, but anyhow I was the short man out of the bullpen. And the manager [Osborn] come to me and says you're pitching tonight. And I thought, "Okay." I can't figure out why because our pitching staff was usually in pretty good shape. We had some really great arms. And so, I don't know, I pitched the game and after the game was over he said, "Hey, when you get

back to Miami, you're going to fly back from Miami, and you're going to fly back through Pittsburgh."

The next day, none of us had any equipment. It wasn't like we were on some big road trip and had a lot of gear with us. You know I had one glove, you know, just the basic stuff we needed for a couple of days. And I guess everybody would be in the same boat. But I was used to it.

Everybody used to kid Satch about his glove. It was an old flat glove, you know, and we played a game called Skidoodle, where you would throw balls at people's feet on bounces and stuff and you'd practice and practice and play the game all of the time. And somebody named it Skidoodle, and that was what Satch called his Skidoodle glove.

So, you know, we kidded him so much about that glove, and when they said that I had to go on the airplane that night and everyone said their goodbyes to me, Satch came over and gave me his glove. My God! A ballplayer doesn't give his glove away. He'd give his wife away before he'd do that. [laughing heartily] So I was just so flabbergasted that I gave him my glove.

The first thing, you know, I make it to Pittsburgh after missing a flight and sleeping in the airport. I go down to the bullpen and the first thing they want you to do is get up and start throwing. You know, I tried to get into the Miami ball field and get my equipment but I couldn't get in. All I had was what I had when I went to Havana. I had nothing except pretty much what I had on my back and no equipment. So I ended up, I warmed up, and I walked up on the mound.

Evidently, it was on a Sunday. [actually a Saturday] It was the Game of the Week with Dizzy Dean, and I forgot who the other announcer was, and they did their thing every week. You know when they started televising baseball. And of course, I'm a little used to what was going on, but I walked out there and threw a warm-up pitch out there and the catcher throws the ball back and the glove, when you rolled your hand over it, the fingers just kind of flipped over and it looked like a mushroom. [chuckling]

Oh, I can hear these guys over in the other dugout hooting and hollering and giving me a bunch of crap. I can't figure out what the hell is going on. I was over there throwing and I heard later that Dizzy Dean really made a big deal about the glove. And of course these guys didn't have any idea where the glove came from and what it was all about. That was some experience.[38]

Qualters received his well-earned slaps on the back, and although he would be missed in the playoffs, everyone was happy for his good fortune. Miami's pitching prevailed the next night behind the combined tossing of Paige and Semproch. An error by second baseman Jesus Mora proved costly, allowing Micelotta to score in the three-run Marlins sixth inning. Paige picked up his tenth and final win of the season. With the 3–2 victory over the Sugar Kings and Toronto's victory over Rochester in

Toronto by the final score of 3–2, the Marlins clinched fourth place in the IL.[39] You can be sure that the Marlins were out on the town celebrating the win. More than a few transistor radios were tuned in to Bill Durney and his sidekick Sonny Hirsch, as they excitedly trumpeted to the listeners in Miami the good news. Although the season had had its share of disappointments, in the end the Marlins had come out ahead and for the second straight year they would represent the city of Miami in the playoffs.

The rest of the season played out with the Marlins, despite a few hangovers, defeating the Sugar Kings 7–2 behind Church's fifth win, before losing the season finale the next night 8–3. Bunker showed that he was worse for the wear from his sixteen-inning outing, allowing eight runs in two and two-thirds innings. Humberto Robinson's eighteenth win was in dramatic fashion, providing an exciting finish to the IL season. The league-leading Leafs scratched out a 4–3 win over the Red Wings, winning the pennant by a sliver of one-half game over the Buffalo Bisons.[40] The Marlins' next opponent was now determined.

Final Standings:

	W	L	GB
Toronto	88	65	–
Buffalo	88	66	½
Richmond	81	73	7½
Miami	75	78	13
Rochester	74	80	14½
Havana	72	82	16½
Columbus	69	85	19½
Montreal	68	86	20½

NOTES

1. Baseball-reference.com.

2. Gary Gillette and Pete Palmer, *The ESPN Baseball Encyclopedia*, 5th ed. (New York: Sterling Publishing, 2008).

3. Jimmy Burns, "Leafs, Royals, Best Draws in Miami; Gate Off 57,000," *Sporting News*, August 7, 1957, 40.

4. *Sporting News*, August 14, 1957, 34–35.

5. *Sporting News*, August 21, 1957, 44–45.

6. *Sporting News*, August 14, 1957, 34–35.

7. *Sporting News*, August 28, 1957, 38.

8. Ibid.

9. Ibid.

10. "Osborn 'Blows Up,' Protests Game over Firing of Rocket," *Sporting News*, August 28, 1957, 38.

11. Norris Anderson, "Marlins Lose in 14, League Play Stops for All-Star Game," *Miami News*, August 19, 1957.

12. Norris Anderson, "Do-It-Yourself Home, Play Jets Double Bill Tonight," *Miami News*, August 27, 1957.

13. Tommy Fitzgerald, "One Mistake by Jets Allows Marlins Split," *Miami News*, August 28, 1957.

14. *Sporting News*, September 4, 1957, 36.

15. Norris Anderson, "Our Turn to Get Hot, Marlins against Vees," *Miami News*, August 30, 1957.

16. *Sporting News*, September 4, 1957, 36.

17. Ibid.

18. Ibid.

19. Anderson, "Our Turn to Get Hot, Marlins against Vees"; *Sporting News*, September 11, 1957, 42.

20. Norris Anderson, "Marlins Reach 4th and Put Semproch on Mound Tonight," *Miami News*, August 31, 1957.

21. Ibid.

22. Ibid.

23. *Sporting News*, September 11, 1957, 35.

24. Anderson, "Marlins Reach 4th and Put Semproch on Mound Tonight."

25. Ibid.

26. Ibid.

27. *Sporting News*, September 11, 1957, 35–36.

28. Ibid.

29. Ibid.

30. Ibid.

31. Ibid., 36, 42.

32. Ibid.

33. Ibid.

34. Richard Bunker, phone interview with author, January 15, 2011.

35. *Sporting News*, September 18, 1957, 43.

36. *Sporting News*, September 18, 1957, 44; baseball-reference.com.

37. Stu Locklin, phone interview with the author, March 7, 2010.

38. Tom Qualters, phone interview with the author, March 5, 2010.

39. Associated Press, "Buffalo Leading by Half over Leafs," *Miami Sunday News*, November 7, 2010; *Sporting News*, September 18, 1957, 44.

40. *Sporting News*, September 18, 1957, 44.

FOURTEEN

Making a Run in the Playoffs II

There were few, if any, sportswriters, fans, or pundits who would have predicted the Marlins would finish in first division with a losing record, much less being playoff bound. Nevertheless, the Marlins had scratched and clawed their way into the postseason for the second year in a row. It would be safe to say that few betting men would place good money on Miami's hopes of winning the International League title. Yet there was a precedent, albeit rare, of fourth-place teams finding success in the playoffs. Ironically, the last two IL teams to make the playoffs with losing records were the 1955 Rochester Red Wings (76–77) and the 1933 Buffalo Bisons (83–85), and both of them had swept through their perspective series to take home the Governor's Cup, the trophy given to the team that captures the IL playoffs.[1]

It had been a particularly frustrating season for Don Osborn, since his pitching staff had received an almost complete makeover over the course of the year. However, the emergence of some young arms, and the surprising late-season performances of the battle-hardened veterans, had given his team just enough push to land them in the postseason. Despite so many changes, Osborn had kept most of his everyday position players intact, though with mixed reviews. With the exception of Pancho Herrera, Don Landrum, and Woody Smith, most of the others had underperformed and were part of an offense that only generated 593 runs during the season, just ahead of Montreal (585 runs) and Havana (507 runs).[2]

On the other hand, Toronto, being Miami's scheduled opponent, featured the second best offense in the league. Their 686 runs scored placed them just barely behind league-leading Buffalo's squad that finished up leading the league, scoring 698 times. Toronto's offense featured a plethora of ex-major leaguers, including ex-Marlin Cal Abrams (.278, .386 OBP), Mike Goliat (.296, 28 HRs, 83 RBIs), Sam Jethroe (.277, 15 HRs, 83 runs),

Rocky Nelson (.294, 28 HRs, 102 RBIs), and Hector Rodriguez (.288, 2 HRs, 62 RBIs).[3]

Osborn was looking forward to his rotation performing in the playoffs and let it be known that he was not going to hold anyone back in their pursuit of the championship.[4] Despite losing a key reliever and spot starter in Tom Qualters to the parent Phillies, and John Anderson, Bob Conley, Earl Hunsinger, and Gene Snyder to demotion to Tulsa to allow room for the influx of veterans, he was quite confident going with his rookies Ray Semproch and Dick Bunker, combined with his veterans Satchel Paige, Howie Judson, and Bubba Church, to start against the pennant-winning Toronto Maple Leafs. If his starters faltered, Osborn was confident in his bullpen and newfound closer Hank Mason, dependable Windy McCall, and Saul Rogovin to stem any opponent's late-inning heroics.

The series would be in a 2–3–2 format with the series' opening two games played in Maple Leaf Stadium. It was the third pennant in four years for the Maple Leafs, but despite their past regular season successes they had yet to advance past the championship game to the Little World Series. It had been twenty-three years since Toronto last won the championship back in 1934. That year they finished in third place during the regular season yet steamrolled their way to the title.[5]

Fiery Skipper Dixie Walker was confident in his choice of thirty-year-old veteran James Madison "Jim" Pearce (15–8, 3.65) to face off against league percentage leader Ray Semproch (12–4, 2.76). Just like a caterpillar's transformation into a butterfly, Semproch's metamorphosis was complete. From a failed starter, to mop-up relief man, to ace, the Cleveland, Ohio, native had gone full circle, winning ten of his last eleven decisions, and was considered arguably the most masterful hurler in the IL. The anxious Maple Leaf hitters were hoping to play the role of entomologist and clip this butterfly's wings early.

The series started with immense fanfare. Inside Maple Leafs Stadium there was a near capacity full house, as both teams were announced. The Marlins were greeted with a chorus of boos and hisses, while the hometown boys received deafening, ringing cheers. Toronto supporters were certain that their starter Pearce would be up to the task and bring home victory. Pearce's name may have sounded presidential (although possessing slightly different spelling), but Marlins hitters nonetheless showed him little respect for his lofty office. In the top of the second inning, Smith sent an early message to the Leafs by planting a ball delivered right down the middle over the left field fence, giving the Marlins an early 2–0 edge. Pearce wasn't to serve in office long as Miami tacked on a couple of more scores on Herrera's single, Marv Blaylock's triple, and Smith's sacrifice fly in the top of the fourth inning, chasing the Leafs' veteran with two outs.[6]

While Miami was pasting runs on the board, Semproch — the hottest pitcher over the second half of the season in IL — was dominating the Leafs' batters. After pitching shutouts in his last two starts, Semproch once again baffled the Toronto lineup with his "drop off the table" sinkerball. Only a few scattered singles, none for extra bases, were the Leafs' batters able to muster. By the time the smoke had cleared, Miami had added a couple more runs, and the stingy Semproch had not allowed a single Leafs runner to touch home plate. To the surprise of the raucous 7,649 rooters in attendance, Miami had won handily, 6–0.[7] Much to their relief, Osborn's troops were spared the incessant fireworks that followed each Toronto score that Osborn had protested so vehemently against all season.

Semproch remembered how much he and the team wanted to make the playoffs and his memorable win against the Maple Leafs.

> *Ray Semproch*: Well, like I said, to me they were all great games because you're fighting for fourth place and then you know you want to get up there and you give it all you got. So every game you went into was important.
>
> [What was your highlight from the 1957 season?]
>
> Well, I would say the first of the playoffs with Toronto because I had just shut them out and you know shutting out that ball club was great. You know they had a lot of great players. They had the best record in the International League.[8]

In the other playoff match-up the Richmond Vees upset the Buffalo Bisons, 6–3, behind the pitching of Marlins' arch-villain Jim Coates. Despite a couple of monster home runs by Luke Easter, the cunning future Yankee tamed the rest of the Buffalo lineup and paved the way for the game one upset.

Although one game doesn't a series make, Miami had sent a clear message to Dixie Walker and his charges that they weren't about to lie down against his pennant winners. The Marlins had taken the regular season series by winning twelve out of the twenty-one meetings between the two clubs, and were confident coming in that they had the edge. The Maple Leafs' owner, Jack Kent Cooke, who spared no expense in building a winning team, was determined not to lose to a team that played sub-.500 baseball. Cooke was hungry to bring a Governor's Cup home to Toronto, but Osborn and his club had a different plan.

Cold northerly winds were blowing the next night in Toronto. The Maple Leafs' right-handed starter, Don Johnson (17–7, 2.96), was accustomed to the bitter weather and was employed by Walker to cool down the hot Marlins' bats. Osborn called upon Howie Judson (6–6, 3.42) to counter Johnson. But Judson wasn't around long enough to make much of an impression. The Leafs plated three runs in the first inning and another couple in the second inning, chasing Judson and sending him to the locker room with the consolation prize of a warm shower.

Bunker was called on with no outs in the second inning and pitched scoreless ball until the sixth inning when Toronto exploded for five more runs, increasing their lead to 10–1. The rest of the game was just a formality. Even though Smith's two-run home run and Bob Micelotta's solo shot off of reliever Jack Crimian narrowed the score to 10–4, the lead was too much to overcome and the series was tied at one apiece. Osborn summed it up best after the game when he said, "It was just one of those nights." [9]

Meanwhile, in Buffalo the Bisons evened their series at Offerman Stadium by edging the visiting Vees, 6–5. A potential double play ball, booted by Vees third baseman Dick Sanders, opened the floodgates to a five-run fourth inning. It proved to be the game breaker, sending the series back to Richmond's Parker Field knotted at one game apiece.

At the same time, Miami returned to their home digs. Although the Leafs were on the road it must have been a relief escaping the harsh northerly winds. Ominously, the next game would be played on Friday the 13th. Osborn was taking no chances and turned to his good-luck charm, Paige, to remove any chance of a hex that might be hovering over his team on this inauspicious day. Both teams were scheduled to fly back to Miami on the same flight. Paige, who was known to use any psychological advantage at his disposal to gain an edge, could be counted on to use his fluent Spanish against his next opponent, Panamanian Humberto Robinson, to try to get in his head and change his team's fortunes. Robinson's teammate and longtime ex-Negro League star Sam Jethroe warned, "Satch will have this boy all psychologized by the time we hit Miami." [10]

Paige was pitching on a week's rest and Osborn knew that when rested and called upon in a crucial game, the ancient one would be almost impossible to beat. The venerable Paige was up to the task early and after six innings the Marlins found themselves holding onto a 3–0 lead, spearheaded by Micelotta's two-run home run in the fifth inning. Toronto's offense was stifled, and adding to the frustration was Robinson's lack of command. As Jethroe predicted, Paige had gotten into Humberto's head. The slight-of-build hurler was pulled after six innings in favor of super reliever Bob Tiefenauer. The situation unraveled for the hometown Marlins in the seventh inning when an error, three singles, and a Loren Babe two-run double turned around the score, giving the Leafs a 4–3 lead. Although Paige closed out the inning, he would not return to finish the game. Instead, the honors would go to Windy McCall. [11]

The usually punchless Marlins offense wasn't caught sitting on their hands this time. They were quick to tie the score in the bottom of the seventh and pulled ahead for good, tagging the usually reliable reliever Bob Tiefenauer for three more runs in the eighth inning. In total Tiefenauer allowed four Miami runners to cross the plate, handing the Marlins a 7–4 win and a two-games-to-one series lead. Not only had Sam Jethroe's words proved prophetic, but Miami had also put a scare into a team that was already paranoid about their lack of success in postseason play. Instead of playing aggressively, they resembled a team playing not to lose.[12]

In Richmond, the Vees regained the series lead behind the combined pitching efforts of Bill Bethel and Marty Kutyna. The two Virginian right-handers limited the potent Bisons' attack to only six hits while striking out seven. The final score showed the Vees on top, 6–3.[13]

Game four, on September 14 in Miami Stadium, pitted Church (5–6, 3.69) against Blake (8–9, 5.54 ERA). Blake, the now thirty-one-year-old one-time St. Louis Cardinals and Cincinnati Reds prospect, was considered the weakest link in the Leafs' starting staff. Manager Walker was going out on a limb to depend on the struggling veteran, but was hoping that Blake would return to his 1956 form when he won seventeen games and posted a glossy 2.61 ERA for Toronto.

Ominous rain clouds were threatening as another less-than-spectacular crowd of 4,053 welcomed the Marlins with loud applause and cheers as they trotted out to their positions in the field. As skipper Walker had hoped, Blake regained his past form, relying on his trusty curveball, and after six innings of work he was holding the Marlins at bay, 2–0. Going into the top of the seventh and with bases loaded Church ran into trouble and was yanked in favor of Rogovin. The portentous drizzling rain began coming down as the crowd in the bleachers sought cover. Rogovin's uniform was soaked by the showers as he worked carefully on the Leafs' big slugger Rocky Nelson. Suddenly the crack of the bat; the sound reverberated like a clap of thunder as all eyes followed the flight of the soggy white sphere. It didn't take long for the ball to clear the outfield wall and the Leafs now found that they were holding a comfortable 6–0 lead. It was Nelson's second homer of the day, with the big guy accounting for five of the team's six RBIs. Miami tacked on their only run of the night in the bottom of the seventh before the weeping clouds mercifully opened up in full force, ending the day for the hapless home team. Rains forced the cancellation of the remaining two innings and the Leafs had tied the series at two games apiece.[14]

Meanwhile in Richmond, 7,962 raucous rooters came out to the old ball yard to cheer on their boys in hopes of taking a commanding 3–1 lead in the series. It was the largest crowd of the season, dating back to a spring training exhibition contest with the parent club Yankees. Bisons starter Cox was scheduled to face Virginians southpaw Bob Wiesler. It was to be Cox's day as he hurled a five-hit complete game shutout, blanking the Vees 5–0. To the consternation of the home crowd their series was now evened up at two games apiece.[15]

The next day torrential downpours continued, dampening the spirits of everyone. Being the time of year when hurricane season rears its ugly head, the rains continued all day and forced the cancellation of game five.

For one, Osborn was glad for the extra day because it gave his staff some much-needed rest. Osborn admitted, "Toronto has more depth in its pitching staff and certainly more front-line starters."[16] The extra day's rest was a godsend and it played an important role in the ultimate outcome of the series. The anxious Marlins, waiting to hear the results, finally received reports that Buffalo had regained the momentum by defeating Coates and the Vees 5–0 to take a crucial game and a commanding 3–2 series lead back to Offerman Stadium. Ray Herbert, who one day would win twenty games for the 1962 White Sox,[17] was masterful in allowing only four singles in the game.[18] More than a few of the Marlins were happy to see the headhunting Coates take the loss.

On September 16, the fair citizens of Miami woke up to one of those days that tourist brochures and picture postcards are made of. With mild breezes blowing in from the southeast and temperatures in the mid-eighties, by the time the evening game rolled around it was a perfect night for a game of baseball—albeit some humidity still loitering from the previous day.

Increasingly sunny were Miami's hopes of grabbing an important, if not must, win from the Leafs. Visiting manager Walker admitted to reporters before the game that a Miami win would give the Marlins an advantage in the series, despite the fact that the last two games would be played in Toronto.[19] Now more than ever, Miamians were pinning their fortunes on ace Semproch, who, for the second time in the series, was set to match up with the imposing six-foot-six Pearce.

The Miami squad was proving to be a surprise. Regrettably, a large part of the local fandom was failing to share their success. Although much larger turnouts were seen in Buffalo, Richmond, and Toronto, a small crowd of only 3,774 gathered in Miami Stadium for game five. Most were congregated under the aquiline roof, and though the fans were small in numbers, they were large in their support of their home team. The Marlins drew first blood in the bottom of the third frame when Semproch helped his own cause by singling sharply to centerfield, moved up to second base on Landrum's sacrifice bunt and to third on Pearce's wild pitch. Stu Locklin singled and Marlins were on top, 1–0.[20]

The fourth inning was the kind of inning that was few and far between for the Marlins all season long. Woody Smith got the party rolling by driving a 350-foot solo blast over the left field wall. Johnny Bucha, who had greeted Smith after his home-run trot, promptly singled to left field and moved to second when Micelotta singled behind him. After Semproch was retired, Landrum singled into center, scoring Bucha. Micelotta, aggressively trying to advance to third, scored when ex-Marlin Abrams's throw went awry at third base. The Marlins were now up by the score of 4–0. Bobby Young followed by receiving a free pass, then Locklin doubled, plating the speedy Landrum. Herrera kept the ball rolling, no pun intended, by driving another single toward left-fielder Sam Jethroe, who was playing in the place of the sidelined Charlie Wilson, out of action with an upset stomach. Thanks to Herrera's single, the Marlins built their lead to 7–0. Pearce was history and Semproch was cruising along, poised to capture his second win of the playoffs. [21]

Although Semproch had been virtually unhittable since rejoining the starting rotation in mid-July, the Maple Leafs began to figure out his sinkerball. The pesky Leafs tacked on two runs on a Lew Morton triple in the fifth inning and another pair in the sixth inning when they loaded the bases, tallying the scores on a Bob Roselli fielder's choice and on Babe's sacrifice fly. They had cut the Marlins' lead to 7–4. [22]

Osborn approached the mound and, sensing his ace's frustration, calmed him down by reassuring him to stick with his best stuff. Osborn's counseling paid instant dividends and restored Semproch's confidence. In the bottom of the sixth inning the Marlins tacked on their finally tally when Landrum doubled and later Locklin hit a sacrifice fly to end the scoring with the Marlins on top 8–4. A final rally by the Leafs was thwarted in the eighth inning when Marv Blaylock made a shoestring catch in right field, saving at least two runs and killing any hopes of a miraculous comeback. Despite surrendering ten hits, Semproch completed the game and earned the win. By sticking with Semproch, Osborn provided the Marlins' relievers a chance to take a breather before heading to chilly Toronto. "My sinker wasn't sinking low enough," a tired but happy Semproch said after the game as he added, "but it seemed to come around in the end." [23]

While the Marlins were taking out the Leafs, that same day the Buffalo Bisons exploded for twelve runs off of four Vees pitchers. Vees starter Kutyna was chased after only two and two-thirds innings after giving up six runs. The Bisons closed out their series with the Virginians in a 12–4 rout, taking the Cinderella Richmond club in six games. With their next opponents decided, the Marlins boarded a flight with their opponents to Toronto to decide who would play Buffalo. Everyone on the team was excited to go to Toronto, with the exception of Paige, who was already carping about the cold weather before he even landed. One thing was for sure—the Miamians were to receive a chilly reception in the great white north. [24]

For game six, Osborn chose Bunker to square off against Don Johnson. Despite going only 6–10 during the season, Osborn elected to go with left-handed curveball artist Bunker to force Walker to go with more right-handed batters in his lineup and to save the chilly-challenged Paige if necessary for a seventh and deciding game. Always disconcerting to the Marlins' staff was the short right field porch that lay only 302 feet from home plate in Maple Leaf Stadium. It favored left-handed sluggers like the Leafs' Nelson and Morton, who could do serious damage if not held in check. "I've got a lot of respect for Toronto's park," commented Bunker, and he further added, "You can't get careless with a single pitch here."[25]

Don Johnson, 17–7 during the regular season, was Walker's selection to try to stop a rejuvenated Marlins club that was flashing some new-found muscle. By season's end, Johnson would be named the IL's Most Valuable Pitcher and odds-on favorite to even the series. Many of the Marlins supporters were left scratching their heads wondering why Osborn hadn't elected to go with Paige, who thrived in these situations.

Most sportswriters—and fans—were expecting a high-scoring affair. Instead, from the beginning the game, the contest was quickly showing every sign of developing into a pitchers' duel. Miami seemed to have gained the upper hand in the third inning when Micelotta seemingly tagged up successfully and scored on the sacrifice fly. Landrum's scream-ing liner toward centerfield that Babe nabbed just above his shoestrings was hit long enough to allow Micelotta to easily score. However, umpire Frank Guzzetta signaled that Micelotta had not tagged up properly, and instead of scoring the run, it was ruled as a double play. Despite the vitriolic protestations by Osborn and his coach Eddie Miller, the umpir-ing crew remained unswayed and the score remained 0–0.[26]

In the seventh inning, Babe came through with his bat instead of his glove. With the bases empty, a Bunker offering caught just a little too much of the middle of the plate and within seconds the horsehide sphere found itself planted 345 feet over the fence, giving the Leafs the 1–0 lead. Osborn sensed Bunker's tiredness, but allowed him to finish the seventh inning before turning the ball over to Hank Mason. Mason's assignment was to hold the Leafs in check until his teammates could muster some offense.[27]

Tompkins entered the game as a pinch-hitter in the eighth inning. After losing his starting position to Bobby Young earlier in the season, Tompkins had become proficient in his new role of delivering key hits in the clutch. However, he failed in his assignment this time and hit into a double play, effectively ending the inning for the Marlins. With two outs, the speedy Landrum stepped up to the plate. Before the crowd could breathe a sigh of relief, Landrum—who had hit only three dingers during the regular season—caught hold of a Johnson pitch to his liking and sent it just over the right field fence to knot the score at one apiece. Although Johnson finished his eight innings of work, Walker had seen enough and called upon his ace reliever Tiefenauer to keep the Marlins from doing any further damage.[28]

Tiefenauer was the minor league's version of Hoyt Wilhelm. Relying on a tantalizing butterfly knuckleball and effective sinker, Tiefenauer[29] was the IL's most effective reliever with a 2.14 ERA in sixty-eight appear-ances.[30] Unlike the closers of today, he was usually called on to pitch more than one inning to save the day, and frequently did.

Nevertheless, on this day Tiefenauer would prove not to be Walker's knight riding in on his white horse in shining armor. Locklin's drive in the top of the ninth inning put the first kink in Tiefenauer's chain mail when his hard-hit liner to centerfield was good for a double. Herrera followed and did Locklin one better with a crushing drive to right centerfield that brought Locklin home for a 2–1 Marlins advantage. Blaylock then produced the third consecutive base hit, a single that scored Herrera to give Miami a 3–1 lead going into the bottom of the ninth inning before Tiefenauer finally stopped the bleeding.

Osborn was happy to see the kids who had come into spring training from Schenectady—Bunker, Herrera, Landrum, and Mason—so productive in such a critical game. Mason had been inconsistent and had struggled with injuries all year but on this night he was his old self as he put the Leafs down in order and earned the win to send the Marlins to the next round. The flummoxed Leafs stood in disbelief as the Marlins celebrated on their home turf. In the locker room the cocksure Osborn celebrated after the game by saying, "We're going to take it all now." He added, "After the determined job we did in Toronto this club is going all the way." The next day Paige was more staid in his appraisal and was already looking ahead to the next night's match-up in Buffalo. Being a time when newspapers were anything but racially sensitive, Norris Anderson quoted Paige as surmising, "Ah may move slow but ah'll be lightnin' out there tonight." [31] The Marlins' celebration went late into the night but there was little time to rest; Luke Easter and the Bisons were anxiously waiting to meet them. [32]

> *Ray Semproch*: What else can I say! We did battle because we were in the second part of the division. Like out of the playoffs, you know, and then all of the sudden we start playing baseball again and we made the playoffs and beat Toronto four times. [33]

Bisons manager Phil Cavarretta must have relished the fact that his longtime rival Dixie Walker was on the sidelines watching instead of playing. Cavarretta and Walker had a long-running feud dating back to May 23, 1946, when a fight broke out between his Cubs and the "People's Cherce's" Dodgers. The disagreement started when words between Cubs' Lennie Merullo and Walker were exchanged. Fisticuffs soon followed and Cavarretta intervened, adding more punches to the fracas. It took a squad of police to break up the brawl. [34] Although unclear whether Cavarretta or Merullo had the pleasure of knocking out a tooth and loosening another in Walker's mouth, it appeared in this case that the Cubs had come out ahead. Because of past bad blood and continued jawing between the two during the season, both managers received stern warnings from league president Frank Shaughnessy to cease and desist.

There was little time for either club to rest on their laurels. Both managers announced that for the September 19 opening game Cavarretta's choice would be Glenn Cox (12–5, 3.00) to oppose Osborn's expected selection of Paige (10–8, 2.42). Osborn had purposely avoided using Paige in relief against Buffalo and since Paige's last appearance was his seven-inning start on September 13 he was well rested.

Osborn's confidence in Paige had no boundaries and, knowing how important it was to win the first game, Osborn was certain that his team could pull off yet another upset: "Satch is the guy you can depend on. This is a hitters' ballpark and Satch can deal with the hitters." Just like Toronto, Buffalo had a short porch, except in this case it was in left field, only 297 feet away versus the reachable right field variety in Toronto.[35]

Buffalo, leaders of IL in attendance, drawing 385,620, once again received a strong show of support from their local fans as 10,028 filled Offerman Stadium. The Marlins carried on with their pregame workout and no doubt noticed that the proverbial "jet stream" was blowing toward left center field, ruffling the festive red, white, and blue banners haphazardly in the wind. Usually this meant the probability of a high-scoring affair was in the cards and the boisterous spectators were noisy in anticipation of seeing their hometown team take advantage of the breeze.

However, the fates had something else up their sleeves. Both Cox and Paige matched zeroes for the first four innings. Although Paige was bending, he wasn't breaking, and craftily worked his way out of three separate jams. Bucha almost decided the game in the fourth inning with a bases-loaded blast that fell just short of clearing the fence. It was the only real opportunity the Marlins had all night as Cox held the visitors to three measly singles and a walk. The Bisons scored their only two runs of the evening in the fifth inning when Rod Graber's single was followed by Dave Melton's one base hit and a hobbled Luke Easter's bloop doubles. The final score showed Bisons 2, Marlins 0. Surprisingly, the wind had proven to be a nonfactor in the outcome.

Paige and Easter's longtime verbal sparring match carried on after the game. It is what we affectionately call trash-talking today. Easter crowed, "Satch, I came off that hospital bed when I heard you was goin' to pitch. I was anxious to get at a sure thing even on one leg." To which Satch sourly replied, "I wouldn't be pitchin' today, man, if it wasn't for you. As long as I hear you're in baseball I'll keep pickin' up that pitcher's mitt and getting you out. I know a sure thing too."[36]

Game one may have had the Marlins suffering a bit of a hangover from their first round upset over Toronto, but the team was in a much more serious mood for game two. "Losing that first one really hurt us," exclaimed Osborn. "That means the pressure is on us whereas we won the first one and put the bead on Toronto." The veteran Church would be called upon to turn things around against the young upstart, five-foot-eleven, 185-pound right-hander Ray Herbert.[37]

Once again the Bisons, recipients of 149 home runs during the regular season, struck first with their all-too-familiar weapon—the long ball.

Cuban slugger and backstop Ray Noble launched a ball into the short left field porch, giving the Bisons an early 1–0 lead. Church battled gamely, keeping the Marlins in the game until the seventh inning. After third baseman Bill Serena doubled, Herbert attempted to sacrifice his teammate to third. Church fielded the ball cleanly but rushed an errant throw over the head of Herrera, allowing Serena to score and Herbert to advance to second base. Herbert later advanced to third base and scored on Easter's sacrifice fly. The way Herbert was pitching, the Bisons' 3–0 lead seemed insurmountable.[38]

Nevertheless, the Marlins were not giving up. In the eighth inning pinch-hitting for relief pitcher McCall, Tompkins smacked a double to centerfield. Landrum again proved that he was a clutch performer, following up with a double to left field and plating the first run of the night for Miami. Second baseman Bobby Young delivered the third consecutive hit off of Herbert and the Marlins had trimmed the lead to 3–2. Cavarretta, who tended to stick with his starters, remained confident that Herbert would regain his composure. Cavaretta's instincts were rewarded as Herbert closed out the inning and the game. The final tally showed Bisons 3, Marlins 2.

Although down two games to none in the series, Osborn remained confident in his assessment of the events: "They've got to beat us in our own ballpark." And based upon the two close games Cavarretta had just experienced he stated, "Any team that beat Toronto has got to be tough." He added, "We're not overconfident."[39] The series now headed back to Miami.

Both teams boarded the charter flight back to Miami to continue their battle. Upon landing they were greeted by eighty-six-degree temperatures, boiling gray threatening thunderclouds, and the all-too-familiar dense humidity hanging limply in the air. Marlins and Bisons players arrived on the field early to prepare for game three. Both squads went through their normal routines of stretching out tired limbs, shagging fly balls, taking infield practice, and swinging lumber in the batting cages to sharpen their eyes in anticipation of the upcoming game. It all seemed routine, because little did any of the participants know that what lay ahead would be a contest for the ages.

Buffalo's ace southpaw, Walt Craddock (18–8, 3.36), in the midst of the best season of his professional career, would take on his counterpart ace from the Marlins, Ray Semproch. So far, both hurlers were nearly perfect in the playoffs, going 2–0, and by all accounts this match-up was looking to be a low-scoring affair.

The night started rather ominously. An already fatigued Semproch, suffering from a bout of flu, was administered two shots of penicillin to fight off the effects of his nagging cold. It was a must-win game and Don Osborn was strategizing who he could count on to step up from the bullpen once his ace faltered. Instead, what he would witness would be one of the gutsiest pitching performances in the history of the Marlins—and possibly in his career in baseball.[40]

Semproch was perfect through the first two innings before allowing Bisons catcher Joe Astroth a lead-off single in the third inning. Craddock then sacrificed Astroth to second and later in the inning Astroth scored from third on shortstop Mike Baxes's fielder's choice, giving Buffalo the early 1–0 lead.[41]

Miami countered in the bottom of the fifth inning when the usually light-hitting Micelotta drove a double over the head of left fielder Dave Melton. Unexpectedly, Micelotta had been the Marlins' hottest hitter, carrying an almost .500 batting average. Semproch helped his own cause by sacrificing Micelotta to third base, and he later scored on Tompkins' sacrifice fly to knot the game at 1–1.[42]

A Canadian goose can lay as many as ten eggs in one nest,[43] but that's nothing compared to the goose eggs that the Bisons and Marlins laid over the next eleven innings. Although Cavarretta was taking no chances by overusing his pitchers, Osborn was stubbornly sticking to Semproch. So far Craddock, Fred Hahn, Mike Kume, and Steve Nagy had combined through sixteen innings to allow only one run. In defiance the Marlins refused to relent and, behind a determined Semproch, found themselves tied 1–1 after sixteen innings. Up to this point Semproch had allowed only five hits. Adding to the indignities of fighting the flu, Semproch was also dealing with a painful blister. Osborn was finally forced to concede, realizing he had pushed Semproch to the limit, and signaled for Clyde McCullough to pinch-hit.[44]

> *Ray Semproch*: I went sixteen innings in that game. And I was going to be sent home from Buffalo because I started to get the flu. And, oh well, there was doctoring. They weren't going to pitch me, but I insisted, and I went sixteen innings. We won the game, but they took me out in the sixteenth for a pinch-hitter.[45]

Both teams had missed several chances in extra innings to salt away the win. The Marlins alone missed eight opportunities to score with a runner or runners in scoring position. Osborn turned to veteran Howie Judson to hold the Bisons in check in hopes that his hitters could muster some kind of offense. To Osborn's distress, in the top of the seventeenth inning Astroth singled and after retiring the next two batters Judson promptly walked Melton and Baxes to load the bases. The always dangerous Luke Easter stepped up to the plate and when he sent a harmless grounder to second it appeared that the inning was over, but Tompkins misplayed the roller, allowing Astroth to score and the Bisons pulled ahead 2–1. Osborn was shaken, but thankful when Judson retired the next batter. It was now up to the Marlins to come from behind. Osborn was hoping for some divine intervention.[46]

In the opposite dugout Cavarretta was putting his faith in control artist Glenn Cox to bring home the win. Cox's aim may have been a little too fine on this night and Herrera caught an offering in his zone, sending the sphere toward left fielder Russ Sullivan, whose attempt at a shoe-string catch misfired and led instead to a double. Smith followed with an opposite field bloop single and the score again was tied — at 2–2. Osborn's prayers were answered.

In the top of the eighteenth inning, Judson settled down and quickly dispatched the Bisons, leaving it up to Cox to again save the day. Again, Micelotta delivered in the clutch with a single to left field with no outs. Osborn, running out of pinch-hitters, sent pitcher Windy McCall to the plate, who then uncharacteristically drew a walk. Landrum was then walked to load the bases, bringing up Tompkins. Tompkins, who earlier in the game came within inches of hitting a game-ending grand slam, was looking to redeem himself for an earlier mishap in the field. Instead, Tompkins hit a double play ground ball, forcing Micelotta at home and drawing a snap throw from catcher Astroth that nipped the former University of Texas quarterback just before arriving at first base. The next batter, Locklin, was walked, bringing up Herrera to face Cox. It looked as if the marathon was going to continue. However, the winds of fate changed their course and after over five hours of baseball the usually reliable Cox faltered and missed his target, walking Herrera with the bases full and giving the Marlins the run they needed to mercifully end the game in their favor, 3–2.[47] Although Semproch did not figure in the decision, his performance was widely regarded as the greatest pitching performance ever by a Marlin hurler. As it turned out, the match was the longest playoff game in the illustrious history of the IL.[48] "I've always said we do things the hard way," said a joyous Osborn after the game. And he was right.

A win in an eighteen-inning affair is usually the type of game that turns the momentum around in a series. And although Miami was down two games to one, they were in an ideal position at home and brimming with confidence, ready to even the ledger the next night.

Game four pitted Dick Bunker (6–10, 3.55) against Bisons southpaw Rip Coleman (7–5, 2.76). Coleman had spent the previous two seasons with the Yankees, compiling a 5–6 record as a swingman before being dealt in February of 1957. A throw-in player in one of the many Yankees/Athletics transactions of the 1950s, he found himself back in Triple-A after going 0–7 with a 5.93 ERA earlier in the year with the parent club Kansas City Athletics. Following his demotion, Coleman seemingly found his second wind in Buffalo and regained his lost form, developing into one of the anchors in Cavarretta's mound corps. Coleman's expectations were that a strong performance in the playoffs would buy him a quick ticket back to the major leagues.

With the all-too-familiar easterly winds blowing out and the ever-present thunderclouds threatening on the horizon, the Marlins confidently took the field. Bunker started off slowly and was quickly in trouble in the opening frame. In quick succession, he walked both Rod Graber and Dave Melton. Bunker regained his composure and retired the next two batters before being greeted by a sharp Lou Ortiz single that gave the visitors an early 1–0 lead. [49]

That small bout of early wildness proved to be Bunker's undoing, while at the same time Coleman was blowing through the Marlins' line-up like a September hurricane. Only one Miami batter reached as far as third base, and in total they could only muster two singles and one extra base hit—a Locklin double. The Bisons added a run in the ninth inning on pitcher McCall's throwing error that went awry of Herrera, but it was of little consequence as the Bisons registered a victory, 2–0. [50] After recovering from some early control issues Bunker's standout effort went to no avail. The loss left the Marlins one game shy of elimination.

Osborn turned to Paige in the must-win game five. Of concern to Osborn was Paige's lackadaisical attitude toward the postseason. He had already missed two flights, one during the Toronto series, and another September 19 flight that returned to Miami. In the matter of his defense, Paige explained, "I had to see about putting my kids into school." [51] The intense Osborn was hoping "Satch" would take a must-win situation a little more seriously.

Opposing Paige was Cox, the culprit who had cost the Bisons game three with his uncharacteristic bout of wildness. The 3,278 fans assembled at Miami Stadium were certain that Paige would work his usual magic and keep their hopes alive.

Whether it was the toll of a long season or other distractions, Paige was not his usual self. It would turn out to be a forgettable performance. Buffalo plated seven runs early and chased the "Satch" after five and two-thirds innings, staking Cox to a 7–1 lead. The only run the Marlins could muster was a solo home run by their hottest hitter, Micelotta, in the fourth inning. Cox went the distance, allowing eight hits and one walk while striking out three of the enemy, giving the Bisons the Governor's Cup and earning them a trip to play the Denver Bears in the Junior World Series. [52] The storybook ending that Miami supporters had hoped for was now nothing more than a broken glass slipper. A disheartened Osborn expressed it best while telling sportswriters and shaking his team's hands following the game, "This team never disgraced itself." He added, "These boys never gave up. They came from seventh to fourth place, won 10 of their last 13 regular season games and knocked Toronto, the champion, out of the playoffs. Can you ask for much more?" [53]

Despite the Marlins' overwhelming disappointment, there was a silver lining on the black cloud. News arrived from Philadelphia for two Marlins that relieved some of their pain. Both Blaylock and Landrum received word from General Manager Ryan that they would be joining their teammate Qualters soon. The two outfielders were to report to the parent Phillies for the remainder of the regular season.[54]

The remainder of the Marlins were left to their own devices to make plans for the off season. Bobby Young stated, "I'd like to stay in Miami during the winter and work at the race tracks." Ben Tompkins planned on going back and resuming studies toward his law degree. Pancho Herrera was committed to learn third base as a stepping-stone to make the Phillies roster in 1958. Church was putting his insurance business aside temporarily to play winter ball (he would return as the Marlins pitching coach in 1958 and appear in three games). And Satchel Paige, always the wanderer, was a little less sure, saying, "I may pitch winter ball or I may just tinker around my house in Kansas City."[55]

Despite the good times that abounded, as team members and staff separated for sundry places to spend the off season, a shadow of doubt and uncertainty hung over the Marlins. Osborn's status as the manager for the 1958 season was questionable. There were rumors flying that the team's status in Miami was no longer secure. Most of the worries centered on the team's inability to sign a favorable lease agreement for the use of Miami Stadium. Going forward into the winter and spring, all of these matters would come to a head.

NOTES

1. Bill O'Neal, *International League: A Baseball History 1884–1991* (Austin, TX: Eakin Press, 1992), 401–3.

2. Baseball-reference.com.

3. Ibid.

4. Morris McLemore, "Miami Marlins Leave for Playoff Round," *Miami News*, September 9, 1957.

5. O'Neal, *International League: A Baseball History 1884–1991*, 401, 403.

6. *Sporting News*, September 18, 1957, 44.

7. Ibid.

8. Ray Semproch, phone interview with the author, April 11, 2010.

9. Norris Anderson, "All Up to Satch Tonight in Marlins–Leafs Playoff," *Miami News*, September 13, 1957.

10. Ibid.

11. *Sporting News*, September 25, 1957, 36.

12. Ibid.

13. Ibid.

14. Ibid.

15. Ibid.

16. Norris Anderson, "Rain Affording Miami Pitchers Welcome Rest," *Miami News*, September 16, 1957.

17. Baseball-reference.com.

18. *Sporting News*, September 25, 1957, 36.

19. Norris Anderson, "Bunker Tries for Clincher Tonight," *Miami News*, September 17, 1957.

20. Ibid.

21. Ibid.
22. Ibid.
23. Ibid.
24. Ibid.
25. Ibid.
26. Norris Anderson, "Paige Pitches as Marlins Begin Series with Buffalo," *Miami News* September 18, 1957; *Sporting News*, September 25, 1957, 36.
27. Anderson, "Paige Pitches as Marlins Begin Series with Buffalo"; *Sporting News*, September 25, 1957, 36.
28. Anderson, "Paige Pitches as Marlins Begin Series with Buffalo"; *Sporting News*, September 25, 1957, 36.
29. Bill James, and Rob Neyer, *The Neyer/James Guide to Pitchers* (New York: Fireside, 2004).
30. Baseball-reference.com.
31. Anderson, "Paige Pitches as Marlins Begin Series with Buffalo."
32. Ibid.
33. Ray Semproch, phone interview with the author, April 11, 2010.
34. Baseball-reference.com.
35. Anderson, "Paige Pitches as Marlins Begin Series with Buffalo."
36. Norris Anderson, "Church Hurls for Miami against Taped-Up Buffalo," *Miami News*, September 19, 1957.
37. Ibid.
38. Ibid.
39. Norris Anderson, "Marlins Smell Money, 1-Down in I.L. Series," *Miami News*, September 21, 1957.
40. Ibid.
41. Anderson, "Marlins Smell Money, 1-Down in I.L. Series"; *Sporting News*, October 2, 1957, 54.
42. Anderson, "Marlins Smell Money, 1-Down in I.L. Series"; *Sporting News*, October 2, 1957, 54.
43. Iowa Department of Natural Resources, www.iowa.dnr.gov/wildlife/files/faqcago.html.
44. Anderson, "Marlins Smell Money, 1-Down in I.L. Series"; *Sporting News*, October 2, 1957, 54.
45. Semproch interview.
46. Anderson, "Marlins Smell Money, 1-Down in I.L. Series"; *Sporting News*, October 2, 1957, 54.
47. *Sporting News*, October 2, 1957, 54.
48. Ibid.
49. Ibid.
50. Ibid.
51. Ibid., 52.
52. Ibid., 54.
53. Norris Anderson, "Marlins Mapping Next Year's Plans," *Miami News*, September 23, 1957.
54. Ibid.
55. Ibid.

Part III

1958

FIFTEEN

Stadium Issues and the New Skipper

The off-season was proving to be full of uncertainties. The rumor mill was running rampant, asserting that the Marlins weren't returning for another season. As of December 1957, what ballpark the Marlins would call home was up in the air. Most of the indeterminateness surrounded the status of Miami Stadium. Continuing disagreements between the Dade County Commission, Jose Aleman Jr., and George Storer on a mutually acceptable lease agreement was making ongoing negotiations difficult, to say the least. Storer was hoping that the Dade County Commission would vote to buy the stadium, allowing him the leeway to work more comfortably with its new owners. On December 11, 1958, Storer was pleased to hear the Dade County Commission voted four to one toward purchasing Miami Stadium from Aleman Jr. for the price of $850,000. However, the caveat was that certain conditions were to be met, including (1) a free title to the property absent any liens and (2) a guarantee of an operation restricted by any contracts, licenses, or concession agreements. As part of the deal, the purchase would be secured with sale of revenue bonds.[1] Most of the concession agreements were tied with the Jacobs Brothers Sports Services, who were taking a percentage of concession sales at the stadium, and Storer was looking for a more complementary agreement that would benefit both parties when divvying up the pie.[2]

Negotiations continued at an impasse until mid-January before a change was seen. Because of the uncertainty swirling around the Marlins, IL president Frank Shaughnessy laid down an ultimatum and announced that he would give the team until January 22 to find a ballpark; otherwise, Storer would have to leave Miami.[3] Commissioner Otis Shiver, as an alternate plan, proposed that the Marlins could play at either the Orange Bowl or the abandoned Miami Field, which had previously served as the home of the Class B Miami Sun Sox back in 1949 and 1954. Storer found both options impractical and announced on January 19 that moving the club was imminent.[4] Rumors from various sources had cities as candidates for possible relocation in Jacksonville, Jersey City, and Norfolk.

Shortly after Storer's dire announcement, city commissioners, led by Shiver, called an emergency meeting. The previous year Shiver had fought to have the city surrender its option to buy Miami Stadium, but now he reversed his course. "I decided we couldn't afford to lose baseball," said Shiver. The commission, in an emergency session, agreed to lease the stadium with an option to buy, and although it left quite a bit of uncertainty—at least for the 1958 season—the impasse was resolved and the Marlins would be coming back.[5]

Despite all of the confusion surrounding whether or not the team would be staying, Storer and his trusted general manager Joe Ryan had come to a decision concerning a new manager, and together decided to part ways with Don Osborn. Although Osborn had done a magnificent job in the playoffs, taking his team to the brink of acquiring the Governor's Cup, his regular season performance, in the opinion of ownership, had not been up to par and they felt that a new direction was in order. With that verdict, on December 18, 1957, the Marlins named forty-five-year-old Kerby Farrell as their new skipper for the 1958 season.[6]

The pug-nosed and fidgety Farrell had been in the Cleveland Indians' minor league system since 1947. First as a player (first baseman), and later as a manager, Farrell had risen through the ranks and reached his pinnacle in 1957, taking over the reins as the Tribes manager from the legendary Hall-of-Famer skipper Al Lopez. However, Farrell's first season was a rocky one. Indians management was dissatisfied with the results from their demanding skipper. Farrell was unpopular with his some of his players for pushing them too hard. Cleveland was in the midst of a run of ten years as a perennial pennant contender and a losing record was unsatisfactory, especially to the fan base, who had become accustomed to winning. After trudging through a miserable 76–77 season Farrell was summarily dismissed and replaced by colorful longtime major league skipper Bobby Bragan.

It didn't take long before Storer reiterated his commitment to building a winning club, starting with its skipper. Farrell came highly recommended by Philadelphia Phillies general manager Roy Hamey, New York Yankees general manager George Weiss, and Cleveland Indians vice-president George Medinger, a close friend of Storer's. As a leader Farrell had established himself as one of the top minor league managers while guiding Indianapolis of the AA to two pennants in 1954 and 1956. To put the icing on the cake, he led his Indians to the 1956 Junior World Series title by sweeping the IL's champion Rochester Red Wings in four games. The decision was an easy one for the Marlins' owner to make.

Storer and Ryan liked the longtime skipper's style and stepped up to the plate to sign Farrell to a new one-year contract. Storer and Ryan were both counting on Farrell to inject some new fire into their club. They were convinced that the biggest problem the Marlins faced, at least financially, was lack of wins during the regular season. Farrell's track record was that of a proven a winner and the Marlins' brain trust was confident that they had fixed their main problem.[7]

With the stadium and new manager issues both resolved, the Marlins could now focus on the season ahead. "This is a great league and a real challenge," stated Farrell as he began to plan on setting the roster and preparing for spring training in Melbourne, Florida.[8] One of the first players to announce that he would be reporting early was Satchel Paige. However, there was a caveat. Paige admitted that his motivation wasn't so much to work his pitching arm into shape as it was to catch up on some fishing that the warm waters off the east coast of Florida offered, and to see the Ringling Brothers' and Barnum and Bailey circus that was scheduled to appear at Miami Stadium.[9] Still, Paige, true to his word, was one of the first players to report to Melbourne.

Also arriving in camp early was Phillies prospect Fred Hopke. It didn't take long before he crossed paths with Paige. A raw-boned stocky kid from New Jersey, Hopke had cut his teeth on the sandlots of Jersey, and now in his third year of professional baseball was poised to make the jump to Triple-A. Although he admitted to being naïve to the ways of veteran ballplayers, he warmly remembered his first rendezvous with the legendary Paige, and later sharing some quality time on the fishing pier with the baseball legend.

> *Fred Hopke*: I was very, very fortunate. In Melbourne, I was walking to go to batting practice. This was early in spring and a Cadillac comes riding right across the field. And I looked at the groundskeeper and said, "What's this?" He said, "That's Satchel Paige." That's how I met Satchel Paige. He drove a Cadillac right on the field.
>
> This is a funny story. He took me fishing. He says, "Do you fish?" I said, "I love fishing." [laughing heartily] I'd never fished in my life. So he took me and we went out to the causeway and he gave me a fishing pole. I threw it under the pier. You know, my first cast. He said, "Oh, let me outta here." What a man he was. Everything they said about that guy was true.[10]

"Satch," as his teammates loved to call him, was well known for his fishing expeditions. On more than one of his excursions he invited his teammates to join in on the fun. Often, on returning from a successful trip, he would hang the day's pungent catch in the shower for his *compadres* to admire. Other times, he simply stowed his trophies inside the custom installed refrigerator tucked in the trunk of his Cadillac that he used to keep the fish fresh while traveling.

As Paige got older, he seemed to be more inclined to settle down and spend more time at home with his wife Lahoma and their children. In *Maybe I'll Pitch Forever*, Paige recounts his feelings about Miami.

> Lahoma and the kids liked Miami just as good as me. They went swimming about every day and lived real high.
>
> "I love it here," Lahoma told me. "Everybody is so wonderful to us I almost feel like as a big celebrity as you. And we can be together the whole summer this way. I wish it could be this way always."
>
> I felt almost the same way about it that Lahoma did. A man can't run all his life. But as tired as I'd gotten over all that moving all those years, I was still hoping maybe I'd have to move once more. The way I was throwing for Miami, I figured I should be back in the majors for a spell in no time. And I'd have just about put off that settling down forever for one more crack at the majors.
>
> I was going so good with Miami that I even surprised me. Maybe it was because of all that relaxing I was getting there, just laying around in the sun and fishing and all between games.
>
> Whatever it was, I wasn't about to fuss with it. [11]

Unfortunately, history has a habit of repeating itself, and in Paige's case it would soon rear its ugly head. Without his allies to support him, unforeseen circumstances would ultimately lead to his departure from Miami. His situation began unraveling when Bill Veeck left town after the 1956 season. It further worsened when Don Osborn was fired in 1957. Osborn had dealt with Paige patiently, accommodating his star and making it easy for Paige to pursue baseball on his own terms. Now, with the stern Farrell coming on board and General Manager Ryan growing increasingly impatient with Paige's lack of discipline and ability to follow rules, the environment was becoming less comfortable for everyone involved. Although matters would come to a head before the season's conclusion, at least for now "Satch" was content to get on with the business of baseball and fishing.

Slowly, Paige's fellow Marlins began filtering into camp. Returning for another go-around were familiar frontliners such as Johnny Bucha, Dick Bunker, Pancho Herrera, Don Landrum, Hank Mason, Windy McCall, Bob Micelotta, Woody Smith, Ben Tompkins, and Bobby Young. Also joining the team for the third time was Wilbur "Moose" Johnson. The all-around good-natured utility infielder from Spokane, Washington, still with a chaw of chewing tobacco firmly planted in his cheek, was all smiles, seeing so many of his friends.

Every spring training brings with it a crop of new faces, while others move on. Two Marlins who were noticeably absent were hurlers Ray Semproch (12–4, 2.76) and Tom Qualters (11–12, 3.29), both stalwarts from the 1957 staff. Although Qualters would see little but spot duty with the Phillies during the 1958 season, Semproch went on to have one of the finest rookie seasons in all of baseball, winning thirteen games while losing eleven on a Phillies team that would finish at the tail-end of the standings. Semproch led both the American League and National League (NL) rookie pitchers in wins (13), games started (30), complete games (12), and innings pitched (204.1). In addition, Semproch led all NL rookie hurlers in win percentage (.543) and strikeouts (92), all the while posting a workman-like 3.93 ERA.[12] It is up for debate, but had Semproch pitched on a contending team he may have very well won the Rookie of the Year Award that was instead presented to San Francisco Giants' Willie McCovey.

Two rookies and a returning highly rated prospect made the biggest splash in spring training. They included the broad-shouldered and muscular first sacker up from the Class C Pioneer League, Fred Hopke; a Texas League Rookie of the Year catcher, Jimmie Coker; and a one-time Stanford University football star, Chuck Essegian. Hopke, viewed as a big-time prospect by the Phillies organization, was on the fast track after batting .337, driving in ninety runs, and slugging at an impressive .474 rate playing for the Salt Lake City Bees.[13] Coker, a Clemson graduate, batted .243 while bashing fourteen home runs and driving in sixty-one teammates in Tulsa (AA). What the parent Phillies found most tantalizing with Coker were his adept handling of pitchers and solid defensive work behind the plate. Essegian, recovering from an injured wing, was working himself back into shape with expectations of garnering an outfield job with the parent club in 1958.[14] Essegian was especially intriguing to the Phillies because of his ability to hit for power and average at each level of stops in Sacramento, Salem, Channel Cities, Visalia, Tulsa, and Little Rock. The ex-Stanford linebacker, who nearly signed to play professional football, slugged eighty-eight home runs over the previous three seasons (1954–1956), while combining to hit over .300. Although 1957 was a lost season due to a shoulder injury that shelved "Big Chuck" for the entire year, baseball prognosticators observed an increase in his arm strength in spring training. This was generally regarded as his only obstacle to making the big leagues. Conversely, there was no doubt in the minds of major league scouts that his batting eye was as sharp as an eagle's.[15]

Although Essegian was turning heads in camp with his mammoth home runs, the new recruit Hopke was busy impressing his coaches and teammates with his skill with the bat, and his desire to succeed. Although tabbed for a year at Class-A Williamsport, Farrell was so pleasantly surprised by his performance in camp that he named him his starting first baseman after Herrera was called up to the Phillies. "If desire has anything to do with it, Fred isn't too far away from playing first base for the Phillies," praised the optimistic Farrell.[16] Hopke proved his worth by crushing eight homers, batting .306—including a twelve-game hitting streak—and driving in twenty-one runs in twenty-one exhibition game appearances.[17] On the surface it appeared that the Hopke and Essegian duo would fill Farrell's biggest need of power in the middle of the lineup that had been so conspicuously absent the last two seasons.

> *Fred Hopke*: What happened was, I was supposed to report to Kissim-mee, Florida. I think I was with Williamsport. And what happened was Pancho Herrera stayed with the Phillies. And so everybody had to move up, I guess, in the minors. They told me to go down, and I went to Melbourne, and I had that kind of spring. And I had old-timers coming up to me, telling me, you better ask for $20,000. You know you are so in awe of everything. And they ripped up my contract and gave $100 more and I thought I was doing great.[18]

Once again the Marlins' staff featured a mixture of young live arms and battle-tested veterans. Farrell tabbed his starting rotation as Bob Conley, Don Cardwell, rookie Robert Frederick, Dallas Green, and Dick Bunker. Conley had split the previous season with the Marlins and AA Tulsa. Although somewhat effective in Miami, winning four games and losing three with a 3.91 ERA, in Tulsa Conley was more dominating, compiling a 7–3 record and a microscopic 2.19 ERA. Cardwell was back for his second turn. The six-foot-four native of North Carolina had starred as the ace for the 1956 Marlins club, but had struggled with the Phillies in 1957 and the parent club was hoping a little more seasoning in the land of palm trees may help the big right-hander regain his confidence and past form. Green, who ironically would lead the Phillies to a World Championship in 1983 as their manager, took an unexpected demotion in 1957 to Class-B High Point-Thomasville (Hi-Toms), but he made the best of the situation and put together a fine season with twelve wins against nine losses in 159 innings. Green was still on the Phillies' radar as a prospect destined to make the big leagues and Farrell was counting on the big right-hander to be one of his staff's mainstays. The new kid in the bunch was Robert Frederick. Frederick was another youngster from Schenectady (A) who benefited from the tutelage of manager Dick Carter. His 10–9 record in 1957, followed by an impressive spring training, had earned him a chance to make the Marlins' roster. Also turning heads was ex-Notre Dame star Dick Bunker. His work late in the previous year and in the playoffs created high expectations from Farrell, who was hoping his slight-of-build left-hander would dodge the injury bug that plagued him in 1957. Slotted to shore up the bullpen were John Anderson, Hank Mason, Windy McCall, and Bunky Stewart. Of course, the cherry on the top of the sundae was Paige, who resumed his role as the part-time starter and relief ace.

Returning for a second season in the broadcast booth for the Storer-owned WGBS would be play-by-play legend Bill Durney and color man Sonny Hirsch (sometimes Don Fischer would broadcast home games) from Miami Stadium. Probably as a money-saving measure, when the team traveled on the road Durney and his sidekick Hirsch would stay behind and huddle in a small box of a studio inside of WGBS, right above the Mayfair Theatre next to the Jordan-Marsh Department Store on Biscayne Boulevard and re-create games. Unbeknownst to most listeners, the two broadcasters read game accounts from a Western Union ticker tape, while using their imaginations to weave the account of the happenings on the field. Although a lost art today, re-creating baseball games was a staple of most teams, and was still in use in some minor league cities up until the mid-1970s.

Durney Jr. recalls watching his father and Hirsch work their magic at the cramped and bare studios in downtown Miami.

> *Bill Durney Jr.*: That was real interesting because they did it off a ticker or Western Union type setup and re-created the games. And every once in a while, the real interesting thing about it was, of course, they had sound effects along with everything else.
>
> Every once in a while the ticker would go down for a few minutes and they would have to have rain delays and everything to make up for when the ticker went down. So that was quite an art, and to watch them do that and re-create a ballgame, and make you feel like you were there. [pause] There were a great deal of people who had no clue that they weren't at the ballgame.
>
> They had recordings, you know on tape, and they would throw a switch for the crowd noise so they could simulate something happening. You know it just wasn't dead background noise. When there was something happening, the crowd noise would come up.
>
> So that it was basically what his duties were when he was up there. It was amazing because it was done in a dark, dank studio with no windows; it was nothing. Yeah, it was old building at that time. It wasn't by any means a modern studio. It was just a little radio booth. . . . . It was always amazing to me. Of course I was usually trying to sneak off somewhere so that I could watch the art films that were playing.[19]

Projected by the Marlins' front office, 1958 was a do-or-die season that would determine the viability of baseball in Miami. It was generally considered that barring a winning season, the future of AAA baseball's future in Miami was bleak. The general consensus by fans, sports writers, and most baseball experts was that a winning season would spur attendance and would motivate the city council to vote in favor of buying Miami Stadium. In turn, a more complementary lease agreement could be reached, freeing the team from the yearly pressures of dealing with Aleman Jr.

Shrinking attendance had resulted in mounting financial losses for Storer, a man who wasn't used to losing money. It was the old tale of a highly successful businessman who always made his fortune by using his wits, instincts, and head, but abandoned those traits when it came to owning a sports team and suddenly resorted to his heart. One's love of baseball only goes so far. Even a man like Storer, with affections for the national pastime as deep as he had pockets, had his limits. After all, business is business. Nevertheless, Storer had made it publicly known that he was committed to spending cash to bring home a winner. The Phillies were still filtering top-quality talent through their system and General Manager Ryan had some tricks up his sleeves to impress the apathetic fans. With a close eye on the ticket box and another on the purse strings, Storer was looking to General Manager Ryan and public relations and radio personality Durney to use their persuasive powers to lure the fickle Miami fans back into the ballpark just like the days of Salomon and Veeck.

NOTES

1. Jimmy Burns, "Farrell Took Miami Offer over Others," *Sporting News*, December 18, 1957; Tommy Fitzgerald, "Marlins Intend to Go to Court for Clear Field," *Miami News*, December 12, 1957.

2. Morris McLemore, "Sports of the News: Target Cleared," *Miami News*, December 12, 1957.

3. "Shag Gives Marlins until Jan. 22 to Find Ball Park," *Sporting News*, January 8, 1958, 16.

4. "Two Propositions on Parks May Save Marlins for Miami," *Sporting News*, January 22, 1958, 22.

5. Jimmy Burns, "City Official's Pride in Miami Saves Marlins," *Sporting News*, January 29, 1958, 9.

6. Norris Anderson, "Ex-Indian Kerby Farrell Named to Pilot Marlins," *Miami News*, December 8, 1957; Burns, "Farrell Took Miami Offer over Others."

7. Anderson, "Ex-Indian Kerby Farrell Named to Pilot Marlins"; Burns, "Farrell Took Miami Offer over Others."

8. Burns, "Farrell Took Miami Offer over Others."

9. Jimmy Burns, "Satch to Report to Marlins Early—Wants to See Circus," *Sporting News*, February 12, 1958, 28.

10. Fred Hopke, phone interview with the author, February 20, 2011.

11. David Lipman and Satchel Paige, *Maybe I'll Pitch Forever* (New York: Doubleday, 1962), 269.

12. David Nemec and Dave Zeman, *The Baseball Rookies Encyclopedia* (Washington, DC: Brassey's, 2004), 217–18.

13. Baseball-reference.com.

14. Ibid.

15. Baseball-reference.com; Allen Lewis, "Big Essegian Now Billed as Phil Sleeper," *Sporting News*, April 9, 1958, 23–24.

16. Jimmy Burns, "Hopke Makes Strong Bid for Phillies' Berth," *Sporting News*, April 30, 1958, 33.

17. "Hopke Wins Marlin Berth," *Sporting News*, April 23, 1958, 32.

18. Hopke interview.

19. Bill Durney Jr., phone interview with the author, December 21, 2010.

SIXTEEN

Tripping Out of the Gate

With so many IL teams huddled in the northern regions, it was customary to start the season in the warmer climes of the south. The vast majority of ballplayers yearned to escape the frosty weather and play in beautiful cities like Miami and Havana. Nevertheless, it was time to get down to the business of baseball, and for the 1958 season opener in Miami Stadium the Marlins were scheduled to meet the Rochester Red Wings.

Storer was tiring of the losing financial proposition he had jumped into. He envied the Marlins' Opening Day opponents, who were considered an elite organization with an extremely loyal fan base. Rochester was a city with deep baseball roots that went back to 1858 and continued to enjoy fan support that was the envy of the rest of the minor leagues. Rochester's first professional affiliation dated back to 1877 when a team with an unusual name—Hop Bitters—joined the International Association. The first year that Rochester appeared in the IL, as we know it today, was 1885.[1] Rochester eventually formed a longtime relationship with the St. Louis Cardinals and produced several winning seasons and titles in the IL. Essentially, the team became a perennial contender for the championship.

Both teams were very familiar with each other, and the season lid-lifter, always being special, was not lacking for incentive to start of the season right with a "W." Kerby Farrell's choice as the starter for Opening Night was hard-throwing righty Bob Conley versus the Red Wings' own right-hander, the towering six-foot-seven Dick Ricketts. Ricketts was more familiar as a hoopster than a ballplayer. Ricketts was a former number-one National Basketball Association (NBA) draft pick and one of few two-sport athletes. He had just finished a three-year NBA career, having played forward/center for the St. Louis Hawks, Rochester, and Cincinnati

Royals before deciding to focus exclusively on baseball for good following the 1958 hoops season.[2]

Opening Day Starting Lineups:

Rochester Red Wings	Miami Marlins
CF Donald Brown	CF Don Landrum
3B Tony Alomar	RF Bob Usher
RF Tom Burgess	1B Fred Hopke
LF Don Lassetter	LF Chuck Harmon
1B Ed Stevens	3B Woody Smith
C Gene Oliver	2B Bobby Young
2B Alex Cosmidis	C Jimmie Coker
SS Ruben Amaro	SS Bob Micelotta
P Dick Ricketts	P Bob Conley

On Wednesday, April 16, the Marlins opened their third season at
Miami Stadium to the delight of 5,191 onlookers. For the third straight
year predictions fell short of expected attendance, much to the dismay of
the Marlins' management.

The home-plate umpire yelled out his familiar refrain, "Play Ball,"
and the 1958 season was under way. Lead-off hitter Don Landrum
started the game with a ringing single off of Ricketts. Bob Usher followed, reaching base with another single, and Hopke wasted no time
collecting his first base knock and RBI that gave the Marlins an early 1–0
lead.[3]

After surrendering a run Ricketts settled down and began to dominate. What developed next was Miami's inability to hit with runners in
scoring position, and it would prove to be a recurring theme that haunted
the Marlins throughout the year. Miami failed to plate another run and in
the process left eleven runners stranded. Rochester fared better and
scratched together two runs on eight hits against Conley, eking out a
narrow win. Especially disconcerting to a manager like Farrell was getting beatEN by the opposing pitcher. Ricketts's own base hit proved to be
the difference maker, earning the Red Wings a 2–1 victory.[4]

Meanwhile, on the same night the Marlins were losing to Rochester,
bad news came from the Caribbean that left ownership and management
scratching their heads. It begged the question of what it was going to take
to fill seats in Miami Stadium. Reports from Havana of a packed house at
Gran Stadium and attendance to the tune of 12,143 paying enthusiasts,
most in the IL, were especially disconcerting. The fact was that the rival
Sugar Kings had not only filled their stadium, despite social and political

unrest, but planned promotions enticing Miami fans with extra entertainment had drawn little more than a sniff from locals.

In response to continued lagging interest in the club and in order to attract more spectators to the park, General Manager Ryan announced a new promotion. On Saturday home dates there would no longer be night games. Instead, afternoon games would take their place. To boost interest, all kids under the age of seventeen would be admitted free for the entire season. Ryan had stewed on his idea for weeks with his main concern being the reaction of fans to the change of time. Since the games were scheduled during the daylight hours, Major League Baseball's Game of the Week would be blacked out in the area, leaving some fans less than pleased with the Marlins' arrangement.[5] These were the days when Saturday's Game of the Week was still a big television draw, much like Monday Night Football is today.

Ryan's experiment paid quick dividends on the first Saturday home game of the year. An impressive crowd of 5,120 kids along with 3,332 paying customers crammed into Miami Stadium and cheered the Marlins to a 6–2 victory over the Red Wings, avoiding an embarrassing home sweep by Rochester.[6] Dallas Green earned the complete game victory, holding the enemy to four hits and giving his club a much-needed lift after three straight losses.

Playing early season games at home was supposed to offer the Marlins a good chance to get off to a strong start. Instead, Farrell's charges found themselves struggling to find their rhythm. A fourteen-game homestand against Rochester, Buffalo, Montreal, and Toronto amounted to a disappointing 5–9 start. Adding injury to insult was a rash of maladies, including veterans Bob Usher going on the disabled list with a sore right side and torn calf muscle,[7] Benny Tompkins chipping a knee bone, and Johnny Bucha with a leg problem. Despite Tompkins's and Bucha's difficulties, Miami's resourceful trainer Doc Ritter had given them the clearance to play.[8] Tompkins's prognosis would later change and shelve him for almost ten days.[9]

As if everything wasn't bad enough with all of the ailments the Marlins were suffering, their star pitcher Satchel Paige was called before Metropolitan Judge Charles H. Snowden for driving without a proper driver's license and speeding. It wasn't the first time—nor would it be the last time—that Paige would appear in court for traffic violations. Not to be discounted was the elder hurler's ability to work out of tight fixes, making him more proficient than Harry Houdini in escaping trouble.

Fortunately for Paige, Snowden, an ex-University of Miami football player, was a big sports fan. Sentencing was handed out for twenty days in the clink to be delayed until the conclusion of baseball season. The judge, who was aware of the rivalry between Paige and Luke Easter, also stipulated that the sentence would be reduced one day for each win collected, one for each hit delivered, and one for each time he recorded a strikeout against his arch-rival Easter.[10] It can be recorded that Paige ended up not serving a single day of his sentence.

Paige was but one of the cast of characters who were beginning to test the patience of Farrell and General Manager Ryan. Entering the picture was Freddie Van Dusen, picking up the mantle and taking over the starting right fielder's chores in place of Usher during his recovery from injury. Van Dusen, a one-time can't-miss prospect, was one of a gaggle of bonus babies that the Phillies signed during the 1950s that included the likes of Tom Casagrande, Paul Penson, and Tom Qualters, all of whom fell short of the grandiose expectations of the parent club. Major league baseball put into action a Bonus Rule in 1947 as a means of preventing the wealthiest teams from signing all the cream-of-the crop prospects. Although the rule was temporarily killed in 1952 through the efforts of Branch Rickey, the rule was again reinstated that a prospect signed under the Bonus Rule must remain on the major league team's roster for two calendar years from the time of signing. This led to many young hopefuls being rushed unnecessarily to the big leagues, arguably ruining the careers of some talented youths. Ill prepared for fame, and self-professed as being immature at the time, Van Dusen was one of those casualties. He was one of the most colorful personalities who passed through the clubhouse doors of Miami Stadium. The various hues of a rainbow paled in comparison to the colorful persona emanating from this young New Yorker and to say he kept his teammates in stitches was an understatement.[11]

At the tender age of eighteen, on September 11, 1955, after riding the bench for several weeks, Van Dusen made his long-awaited major league debut against the Milwaukee Braves. Generally shunned by most of his teammates, Van Dusen was more than ready to take his cuts. "I was numb," he recalled, "but I told myself to get up there and go down swinging." On a 1–2 pitch Braves starter Humberto Robinson threw a curveball that got away and plunked Van Dusen on the knee. After the next batter was retired in the ninth inning it was the end of his major league dream. Although Van Dusen would be a regular in many Phillies spring training camps thereafter, he would never make it back to the show and retired from baseball after the 1961 season.[12]

Fred Hopke remembers fondly his teammate Van Dusen and the antics he resorted to that kept his teammates rolling in the aisles.

> *Fred Hopke*: Wait a minute, I got to stop you right there. I got a baseball story and stop me if you heard it. If anyone talks about Freddie Van Dusen, they talk about this. He was in a very, very bad slump. I think he was oh for forty-five or something. And we got on the bus and we were going . . . I thought it was in. . . . It might have been that year, I don't know but, we got on the bus and Freddie misses the bus. So we're going down the highway and a state trooper pulls over the bus. And the trooper walks up and he comes in and says something to the driver.

The bus driver says, "What did I do wrong? I didn't do anything wrong."

The trooper says, "You're not going no further until you get that guy off the top of the bus." Freddie Van Dusen had climbed up and rode on the top of the bus. True story. Unbelievable!

He was a piece of work. One time, one day, he came to me and said, "We have to stage a fight on the bus."

And he had a little drinking problem, you know. And he took a swing at me and punched me right in the mouth. He said, "I meant to miss. I meant to miss."

I chased him off the bus. I was going to kill him. He was from the Queens, New York. He was, [pause] what a character. [13]

Wilbur Johnson remembered two incidents that pretty much encapsulated the comical side of his teammate, the first being when they teamed up in Miami and the next occasion when they played together for the Williamsport Grays in 1959.

Wilbur Johnson: Was he the one that said . . . oh yeah, I think we went to Miami and he was with us down there. And we were playing in Havana and he lost the ball in the air and he said, "The moon got in my way." Oh, he was a character.

[referring to Williamsport where he played with Van Dusen] He drove our manager Frank Lucchesi crazy. He drove all the managers in the minor leagues crazy. One day he was supposed to go to centerfield and he was up the flag pole. He was climbing the flagpole. And he was goofy, you know, he had goofy ideas and he was outspoken, and everyone knew that Freddie Van Dusen was around. [14]

The Marlins' early troubles were directly related to lack of offense. Van Dusen, although complimented for his defense, was struggling with the bat, hitting below .200. Among several Marlins in slumps was Micelotta, who was frequently finding himself replaced by Wilbur Johnson at shortstop in order to infuse some punch in the lineup. So ineffective was the team at scoring that in Don Cardwell's first two starts he went seventeen innings without giving up a run yet had failed to earn a single victory. [15]

Following a well-deserved day off the Marlins hit the road for the first time beginning on April 30, squaring off against the Montreal Royals. Mired in seventh place, the only team with a worse record was the Buffalo Bisons at 3–10. Circumstances didn't get any better at Delorimier Stadium as they dropped the opener, another one-run loss, 4–3. It was Miami's fourth one-run loss of the young season.

Showing signs of fatigue, Dallas Green took a 3–1 lead into the ninth inning. Farrell, confident in his big right-hander, stuck with him to face lefty batter Sandy Amoros and Bob Lennon. Green retired Amoros but promptly walked Lennon, setting up the tying run now standing at the plate. Instead of turning to a fresh arm out of the bullpen, Farrell left

Green in to face veteran right-handed hitter Jon "Clyde" Parris. The decision proved costly, as Parris went the opposite way, socking the horsehide sphere 340 feet, clearing the short right field fence, and knotting the score at three apiece. The blast was in the almost identical spot where Green had hit a homer during the seventh inning. A defiant Farrell still refused to turn the ball over to his bullpen and instead chose to stay with Green. The decision proved costly and Green let his manager down again by delivering up a two-bagger to the next hitter, Jim Koranda. Centerfielder Landrum made a gallant effort in an attempt to make a shoestring catch, but was unable to reach the ball. Farrell had seen enough and finally approached the mound, although just a little too late. He patted his right arm and called for rookie right-hander Earl Mossor, who came charging in from the bullpen. Mossor was supposed to intentionally walk pinch-hitter Fran Boniar to set up the force play. Although he carried out his assignment, unfortunately for Mossor, he uncorked a wild pitch in between, allowing Koranda to move to third base. Farrell grimaced in disgust when the next batter, catcher Dick Teed, hit a long fly ball toward right fielder Usher, who had no chance, pegging Koranda at the plate on the sacrifice fly. Scratching his head after the game Farrell lamented, "Why, of all things did a wrong field homer beat us?" Added the agitated and frustrated skipper, "Why did I have to depend on the batting of a pitcher to keep us in there? Why, of all people, did Montreal have a switch-hitter coming up with the winning run on third in the sudden death home portion of the ninth?"[16] Why oh why indeed.

When it rains it pours, and events continued to spiral downward on the road trip. More bad news from the injury front included Fred Hopke suffering a hand injury when umpire Joe Linsalata accidentally stepped on Hopke's right hand trying to get out of the way of a play at first base. The diagnosis was the big guy would be out for almost two weeks with a gash that required six stitches to close.[17]

Although Miami took two of three from Montreal, they regressed by losing two extra-inning games in Toronto in the process of dropping two out of three. The Marlins' problems were compounded in the next series, suffering a three-game sweep at the hand of Columbus that included another pair of one-run losses. And as if things couldn't get any worse, the Miamians followed up by losing two out of three to the Sugar Kings in Havana. Up to this point Miami had compiled a disappointing 5–9 record in one-run games and their 9–17 overall record left them mired in seventh place, only a game ahead the cellar-dwelling Buffalo Bisons.

Most of the staff was pitching well, despite picking the early-season losses. Paige was one of the few pitchers experiencing early-season struggles and blamed his woes on the unseasonably nasty weather conditions that had plagued the IL. On the team's first road trip, Paige came out on the short end of the stick during the opening game. The result at Maple Leaf Stadium was an extra-frame one-run loss to Toronto, 5–4 in ten innings. The *Miami News*, in a report that would be viewed as racially and politically incorrect today, quoted Paige as blaming his defeat on two factors, "both a cold in my head and another in mah' pitchin' arm."[18]

On the brighter side of the street the balmy weather of Havana provided some much-needed respite and was just what the doctor ordered to restore Paige. It was also good news for Farrell, who was growing weary of the losses piling up. Just in the nick of time the ageless wonder regained his form, hurling a classic Paige gem and beating the Sugar Kings 2–1 in the road finale with some unexpected offensive help from one of General Manager Ryan's latest pick-ups (and one of baseball's all-time flakiest characters)—Mickey McDermott.[19]

On May 9 the Marlins announced the signing of Mickey McDermott. The twenty-nine-year-old one-time pitching "wonder boy" was probably more famous for his all-nighters and club singing act than his chucking of the horsehide. He lived life just as fast as his legendary speed ball. The erstwhile class clown was now in the process of reinventing himself as a decent hitting first baseman/outfielder and filling in whenever he could on the mound.[20]

General Manager Joe Ryan was desperate to bolster the offense and felt McDermott could not only provide some pop but also still pitch a little. To say the Marlins weren't hitting was an understatement. So short on productive bats was Miami that even pitchers Dallas Green and Windy McCall had been called on for pinch-hitting duties. One of the walking wounded, outfielder Bob Usher, although back in the lineup, was trying to recover from various nagging ailments and was a further concern to Farrell. Making matters worse, first baseman Hopke and second baseman Tompkins, still on the disabled list, were joined by Wilbur "Moose" Johnson, who took an errant batted ball in the face on May 11, losing several teeth in the process. Incredibly, Johnson was able to play the next night. As a testament to his tough demeanor, Johnson let trainer Ritter know he could play on. Although limited to pinch-hitting duties, the scrappy hard-nosed Johnson recalls the ball to this day that nearly knocked him cold.[21]

> *Wilbur Johnson*: Yeah, the thing of it was I was going low for the ball, and the ball hit something on the rise and it hit me right square in the mouth. Yeah, I remember my mouth was bleeding and everything. But I told the trainer, "I'm all right, I'm all right." And I don't know, I was afraid to come out of the lineup for some reason. So the next day it got a lot better and it healed and I said, "I'm ready to play."
>
> Yeah, I remember that now because that was one the biggest jolts in my career. That thing really hit me square in the mouth. The ball hits you right square ... the ball probably fell right in front of my feet.[22]

At this point, Farrell was begging the Phillies' brass to send him reinforcements and requested Pancho Herrera and/or Chuck Essegian return from Philadelphia to bolster their sagging lineup.[23] Even the beleaguered McDermott, with his train-load of personal baggage and his crazy antics, seemed like a godsend to the Marlins. McDermott, refusing to report to Dallas-Fort Worth after Detroit general manager John McHale had sold his contract to the team, made the decision to forgo the season and go fishing instead. Soon after hearing about the dispute, Ryan, who was always looking for talent that could help his club, offered the out-of-work hurler a contract for $1,500 a month. Although the dollar figure was less than what he would have made playing in Dallas, McDermott was in no frame of mind to bend to McHale's whims and accepted Ryan's offer. Whether out of spite, or just because the climate was more appealing than the stifling heat of Texas, "Maury," as some of his teammates liked to call him, flew to Miami and signed on the dotted line.[24]

McDermott was one of a collection of several memorable characters who passed through the locker room doors of Miami Stadium. He was one of those personalities whose mold was broken soon after it was cast. A self-confessed alcoholic, he later reformed himself by getting sober in his declining years. Around that same time he became the recipient of a $7 million Arizona lottery prize win and then shortly after died in 2003 from an accidental fall. His rebel, devil-make-care personality sprang from a controlling, overbearing alcoholic father who ruled over him in his developing years. In his autobiography, *A Funny Thing Happened on the Way to Cooperstown*, he describes why he was the way he was:

> I'd been a rebel since I was a kid. I think I was born a Pancho Villa without sombrero. Part of it was because my father was so much into discipline. I hated being told what to do, and if we'd had a woodshed, I'd have spent a helluva lot more time in there than I did doing my homework.[25]

McDermott made himself at home in no time. In his second appearance in a Marlins uniform he hit his first and only home run of the season, a solo shot against Havana. In total McDermott drove in a pair of runs and accounted for Miami's total offensive support of Paige. "Satch," for his part, struck out only one Sugar King, choosing to let his defense do the yeoman's share of the work. Stingily, he allowed the Havana hitters three hits while not allowing a single base on balls. Paige, who didn't believe in expending any more energy than was necessary, completed the game in a miserly one hour, fifty minutes.

The Marlins' first homestand and road trip was just short of disastrous and definitely not what Farrell had foreseen. Getting out of the gate fast was what the jittery skipper wanted and starting out the season in a hole posed a new set of motivational obstacles that needed to be addressed immediately with his charges.

The team began their return on their charter flight to Miami. Flying over the Straits of Florida the view was beautiful, but the mood was subdued in the cabin. As a group they were discouraged, but still had the sense that things would get better. With some new faces in tow and other reinforcements on the way, the bleak picture was about to improve.

NOTES

1. Bill O'Neal, *International League: A Baseball History 1884–1991* (Austin, TX: Eakin Press , 1992), 341–42.

2. Basketball-reference.com.

3. *Sporting News*, April 23, 1958, 32.

4. Ibid.

5. Jimmy Burns, "Marlins Host Kid Matinees on Saturdays," *Sporting News*, April 30, 1958, 14.

6. Ibid.

7. *Sporting News*, April 30, 1958, 34; Norris Anderson, "First-Place Montreal Here for Three Games," *Miami News*, April 23, 1958.

8. Norris Anderson, "Rampaging Royals Fatten Averages, Flatten Marlins," *Miami News*, April 25, 1958.

9. Norris Anderson, "Marlins Bats Silent, Royals Win," *Miami News*, April 26, 1958.

10. "Satch Can Pitch Out of Jam," *Sporting News*, April 30, 1958, 41; Larry Tye, *Satchel: The Life and Times of an American Legend* (New York: Random House, 2007), 254.

11. Rich Westcott, "History of Phillies Spiced by Odd Characters, Events," *Baseball Digest* (July 1988): 57.

12. William Weinbaum, "Van Dusen Feels Greenberg's Pain," March 16, 2007, http://sports.espn.go.com/mlb/news/story?id=2800012.

13. Fred Hopke, phone interview with the author, February 20, 2011.

14. Wilbur Johnson, phone interview with the author, March 14, 2011.

15. Norris Anderson, "Vitamins Bolstering Toronto," *Miami News*, April 27, 1958.

16. Norris Anderson, "Farrell Desperate as Marlins Lose," *Miami News*, May 1, 1958.

17. *Sporting News*, May 14, 1958, 34.

18. Norris Anderson, "Marlins Seek 2 Victories," *Miami News*, May 5, 1958.

19. Norris Anderson, "Miami vs. Richmond at Stadium Tonight," *Miami News*, May 12, 1958; *Sporting News*, May 21, 1958, 32.

20. Norris Anderson, "Mickey's Lively Bat Welcomed," *Miami News*, May 10, 1958.

21. *Sporting News*, May 21, 1958, 32.

22. Wilbur Johnson, phone interview with the author, March 14, 2011.

23. Norris Anderson, "Reyes Tells Kerby: Leafs Are Loaded," *Miami News*, May 3, 1958.

24. Howard Eisenberg and Mickey McDermott, *A Funny Thing Happened on the Way to Cooperstown* (Chicago: Triumph Books, 2003).

25. Ibid., 80–81.

SEVENTEEN

The Lucky Sombrero Streak and Back to Bleak

Kerby Farrell was the type of personality that took to losing about as well as a cat takes to water. The highly strung skipper began his career as a field boss in 1941 at the youthful age of twenty-seven while playing first base and occasionally taking the mound for the Erie Sailors of the Class-C Middle Atlantic League. Serving as a player/manager most of his career in the bush leagues, the native Tennessean made stops in Erie, Spartansburg, Cedar Rapids, and Reading. As a player, Farrell played nineteen seasons in the minors, and even had a brief fling in the major leagues as a part-time first baseman with the Boston Braves in 1943 and the regular first sacker with the Chicago White Sox in 1945. His success as a manager in the minor leagues centered on developing players and winning clubs, and that was the reason he was named to the post for the Cleveland Indians in 1957. From 1947 until he took the helm for the Marlins, Farrell suffered through only four losing campaigns in twelve years. He garnered the *Sporting News* Minor League Manager of the Year award twice, in 1954 and 1956. He would later win a third award in 1961 with the IL's Buffalo Bisons.[1]

As a leader Farrell was temperamental, complicated, and suffered bouts of moodiness depending on how well his club was performing on the field. He was known to be a stickler at teaching the finer points of the game and his expectations were that his players know the minutest rudiments like the back of their hands. Much of his success was traced to his ability to develop within his players a clear understanding of the fundamentals that gave them an edge over their opponents. Demanding as a leader, and sometimes unpopular with his players, he had a tendency to be swayed by the press when criticized, sometimes to the point that when batting order changes were suggested by sportswriters, he would alter the lineup accordingly to please the scribes. Superstitious to a great degree, as most ballplayers and managers were at the time, he would sometimes wear the same suit or tie for days until whatever winning streak his team was on was broken.[2]

Bud Daley, who pitched for Farrell's pennant-winning teams in Indianapolis in 1954 and 1956, called him "the goofiest manager I've seen in my life." He remembered how Farrell once dove headfirst into the dugout and opened a gash on his head for no apparent reason.[3] Johnny Gray, a teammate of Daley's, was also a member of Farrell's pitching staff in Indianapolis in 1956 when he guided the club to the Junior World Series title. He would later reunite with his ex-skipper in Miami midway through the 1958 season. Gray shared one of his encounters with Farrell while with the Indians in 1957 and summarized his feelings about his old manager.

> *Johnny Gray*: I was on the mound pitching against him [Ted Williams] and I can't remember who was catching, but I got into it with the catcher because he called for fastballs, "You gotta great fastball, let's try to get out of here." We were so far behind he wanted to get out of the ballgame. And I just didn't want to give Ted a chance to hit my fastball. I know that Kerby Farrell had to be calling the pitch and he was the idiot of the world as far as I was concerned being a manager. If you called up and you were the press, and you talked to him on the phone, and if you told him something about that lineup, or so and so, and you thought that what was wrong the next day the lineup would be what the press said. And that was the God's truth when we were in Indianapolis. Whatever the press said that's what the lineup was. And there were reporters that told me that.[4]

On the other hand, Fred Hopke gave quite a bit of credit to his success that year to his manager and remembers him fondly.

> *Fred Hopke*: Our manager, I think, was Kerby Farrell that year. And that's probably the reason I had such a good spring. He really took a liking to me and worked with me in a lot of ways. . . . Kerby Farrell was a great one.[5]

George Storer had expected much better results from Farrell, but was also conscious that a baseball season is a marathon and was hopeful that his new skipper would right his team's ship soon. However, impatience was creeping in and sagging gate receipts were wearing on Storer's resolve like sandpaper on balsa wood.

Farrell was glad to see the first road trip come to an end and was looking forward to his team's return to the friendly confines of Miami Stadium. His ball club was less excited to leave than their frustrated manager, making the most of the night life in the glitzy nightclubs of *La Habana*; it's a safe bet that McDermott was part of the revelries. Showing up at the airport the next day several of the team members, including a member of the coach staff, arrived in the departure area wearing sombreros with ear-to-ear grins on their faces. Still partying from the night before, they possibly even stopped at the airport bar for a few rounds. Although the roisterers had a reason for their merriment, Farrell was less than pleased.[6]

Bill Durney Jr., son of broadcaster Bill Durney, shared many experiences with his dad while living in Miami and remembered hearing about the sombrero incident. Although unclear who the players were, he surmised the most likely suspects included pitching coach Bubba Church and pitchers Dallas Green, Windy McCall, and Mickey McDermott.

> *Bill Durney Jr.:* I remember stories about one trip over to Cuba, over to Havana, where they were ready to get on a plane and they can't find them [the players]. And I think it might have been the group, or was it a group of four pitchers they couldn't find when they board the plane and come back. And they are looking all over the airport and they found them sitting around a pillar on the floor with sombreros over their heads looking like Mexicans, and just sitting on the floor of the airport. I think they finally got them rounded up and got them on the plane.[7]

The opening game of the Marlins' second homestand was supposed to be a welcome relief from the road. Instead, the Marlins looked like they were still suffering from the aftereffects of Havana. Uninspired play resulted in a sound thrashing at the hands of visiting Richmond, 13–2. Although it was fireworks night at the park, the sparse crowd of 2,118 experienced more pyrotechnics from the Virginians' bats than from the evening's colorful display. Starter Bob Frederick was sent to the showers after working two and two-thirds innings, spotting the Vees a 4–0 lead. If it was any consolation, the rest of the group of pitchers that followed— including Windy McCall, Earl Mossor, John Anderson, and Bunky Stewart—wouldn't fare much better. Ex-Marlin Jim Command even joined in the Vees' feeding frenzy, bashing a two-run blast in the second inning.[8] This wasn't the way Farrell envisioned the homestand beginning, but nonetheless the outcome was still the same. On a brighter note, Fred Hopke returned to the lineup, collecting one of the Marlins' ten hits.

The following morning after the loss, Church, probably still recalling his exploits in Cuba, left his sombrero from Havana in General Manager Joe Ryan's office. Ryan was less than thrilled with the displaced tattered lid but, finding himself busy with more pressing issues, left the topper in its place, at least for the time being, in his office. That evening the Marlins' fortunes turned. In fact, the Marlins bounced back and restored some of Farrell's lost faith in his club. Uncharacteristically, the offense went into high gear and, after overcoming an early 6–0 deficit, exploded for ten runs to beat the Vees 10–7. Don Cardwell, who had been downright Ebeneezer Scrooge-ish in giving up runs in his past starts, was shelled early for six runs and removed in the third inning. It appeared to be a bad omen. However, relievers Stewart, Mason, and Anderson combined to pitch six and two-thirds innings of shutout ball to secure the victory and thus redeemed the bullpen from the previous night's macabre slaughter. Bob Usher contributed with a perfect night, his stick going five for five, playing a major role in securing a win.[9] It begged the question, could it be that the sombrero had something to do with the turn around?

After a rainout on May 14, Miami came back the next day and swept their doubleheader against the Vees by tallies of 4–0 and 5–3. In the first game, Bob Conley, the big right-hander from Kentucky, upped his record to 3–3 and dropped his ERA to a sparkling 1.93, earning his second consecutive shutout of the season. In the second game, Dick Bunker, fresh from his stint in the army, won his first appearance of the season, replacing Dallas Green in the fourth inning. Farrell gave Bunker a short rope, not wanting to overtax him, and pulled him after only four and two-thirds innings despite not allowing an earned run. Satchel Paige earned a save and preserved the win.[10] Miami had now won three in a row. Farrell, who was notoriously superstitious, ordered the sombrero to stay in place while, as they say, "the going was good."

Farrell received more good news the following day when it was announced that the Phillies were sending reinforcements in the person of slugger Pancho Herrera and diminutive relief pitcher Angelo LiPetri. "They are coming here as fast as possible," gushed an excited General Manager Ryan, who, along with Farrell, had been howling for help from the parent club all season. In addition, Ryan added some infield assistance, signing twenty-nine-year-old utility-infielder Jerry Snyder from the Washington Senators to help out the beleaguered Bob Micelotta, Wilbur Johnson, and struggling Bobby Young. A casualty of the move was Johnson, who was summarily dispatched to Williamsport after providing only one run batted in forty-nine plate appearances. Other than Woody Smith's eighteen ribbies, the aforementioned combination had only supplied eleven RBIs all season.[11] Sadly, after spending parts of three seasons in a Marlins uniform, Johnson would never return to the Magic City as a player again.

Next on the docket were the Columbus Jets. Cardwell took his scheduled turn and reestablished his dominating ways by shutting out the visitors, allowing only a solitary single by shortstop Leo Rodriguez in the first inning. Cardwell faced thirty-two batters in the game, striking out nine and walking four in the process of the 3–0 victory.[12] It was the Marlins' first one-hitter dating back to September 4, 1956, when Dick "Turk" Farrell shutout the Sugar Kings, 1–0.[13] With the good-luck sombrero apparently working its magic, and despite Ryan's dismay at having the tacky haberdashery loitering in his office, the team had now run off four victories in a row.

Miami pitching continued to be their forte as they completed a four-game sweep, their first of the season, against the Columbus Jets. Miami improved their record to 16–18, leaving them only two and a half games behind fourth place Toronto and Columbus, and seven and a half games behind the red-hot first-place Montreal Royals (23–10). In the four-game series Columbus's offense was throttled by dominating Marlins pitching and only notched four runs. Cardwell, Frederick, Green, and Paige all earned complete game wins. Also receiving a portion of the credit for their newfound success was the improved play of the defense anchored by Young at second, Micelotta at shortstop, and Smith at third. Ryan commented, "That hat, horrible as it is, will stay there until we lose." The winning streak now reached seven games, one game short of the record set by the 1956 team.[14]

Sadly, all good things must come to an end. On May 19, hard rains forced a cancellation of their match against hometown Richmond. The downpour seemed to have washed away the Marlins' luck and with the Mexican head topper residing back in Miami, the Vees turned back their visitors in the first game of a makeup doubleheader, 6–2. In the nightcap, Bob Conley was masterful, shutting down the home team and earning his second four-hit shutout of the season. Conley was nothing short of phenomenal in the 3–0 win, keeping his ERA under 2.00 for the season. Although Conley's 4–3 record wasn't remarkable, his dominance—including collecting five complete games—was.[15] Meanwhile, back in Miami, the sombrero was regrettably retired.

If you were authoring a book, an apropos title for the Marlins in the month of May would be *The Strange Case of Dr. Jekyll and Mr. Hyde*. After their successful home series, disaster struck again on the road. In Richmond, Miami dropped three of four to the Vees, three of four to Buffalo, and two of three to Rochester. The Marlins were now a pitiful 6–17 in road games. Even more disconcerting to Farrell was the fact that ten of the team's twenty-six losses on the season were by one run.

The usually dependable Paige faltered in his scheduled short start on May 26 against Buffalo. Facing his age-old antagonist Luke Easter, and hoping to reduce Judge Snowden's sentence, the irascible hurler failed to strike out Easter and instead gave up a double and two-run homer to the larger-than-life slugger. The always agreeable Easter later boasted, "If the judge wants to be fair about it, he should add on a day for each time I get a hit off of Paige."[16] Adding insult to injury, Paige garnered his second loss of the season.[17] Paige was uncharacteristically silent on the matter.

Two of the bright spots during the road swing were Cardwell's fourteen-strikeout performance and an 8–4 victory against Buffalo on May 24, breaking Earl Hunsinger's previous team record set back on April 29, 1957. Cardwell's performance was especially impressive, given that he rebounded from a tough first inning after giving up a grand-slam to Jack

Phillips. The lanky six-foot-four right-hander then shut out the Bisons to earn the complete game win.[18]

The other notable performance came from lefty curveball specialist Bunker, who was making his first start since being hit by a line drive on his shoulder May 23 against Buffalo. His May 28 blanking of Rochester was the Marlins' fourth team shutout of the season. Even more remarkable was the fact that Bunker went ten innings in the win, striking out ten Red Wings and only allowing three walks. The decisive RBI coming from a Herrera single in the extra frame was what Farrell was finally hoping for when he received the big Cuban from the Phillies. Herrera finished the night with four hits in all.[19]

The Marlins, residing in seventh place at 19–26, a distant twelve games behind Montreal, were reeling again. A dismayed Farrell openly opined, "We've got to start hitting with men on base and scoring after we get two out." He added, "When we won seven straight, we were getting those big runs after two were out."[20] Herrera, or "Pancho," as his teammates called him, back for his second go-around, had been the biggest disappointment since joining Miami, registering only one home run in forty-five at-bats. The only Marlin batting over .300 was Don Landrum, with a .306 average. Surprisingly, the most productive hitter of late had been McDermott, driving in eleven runs in his first fifty-three at-bats. Of all the regulars besides Landrum, only Smith and Bucha, the team's leading home run hitter with four, were hitting above .250. Newly acquired Jerry Snyder was the team's hottest hitter at .438 but had only come to bat forty-two times. Tompkins and utility man Chuck Harmon were on the injured list, forcing Farrell and General Manager Ryan to again call the Phillies for more reinforcements.

General Manager Ryan remained busy scouring the trade wires. Most recently he tried to trade a pitching prospect to acquire thirty-two-year-old slugger George Wilson from the New York Yankees' top farm club, the Denver Bears. Wilson was exactly the type of prospect that Ryan loved, preferring veterans over untried rookies.[21] With some major leagues experience—including limited time with the White Sox, Giants, and Yankees—Wilson would end up having a solid sixteen-year minor league career, hitting .311 and blasting thirty-four home runs for Minneapolis in 1953.[22] The parent-Phillies even found an unnamed pitcher to send to the Yankees' Double-A affiliate, the New Orleans Pelicans, but by the time the proposed offer was made, the deal was called off by the folks in pinstripes.[23] Much to Ryan's chagrin, he was still left without a viable power option on his team.

Turning the page to June, the Marlins welcomed their arch-rival Havana Sugar Kings to Miami Stadium. An uncharacteristically large crowd showed up for the Memorial Day holiday doubleheader. Some 5,519 anxious Marlins supporters turned out for what was billed as the largest fireworks display of the year only to see the Marlins split a twin bill, losing the first game 4–0 and coming back to win the nightcap 3–2. Both games featured numerous singles and crisp defense that were the hallmarks of both clubs.[24] Farrell would have liked nothing more than to light a fire under some of his slumping hitters. At least on this evening, only the fireworks technicians would handle those duties, and not a frustrated manager looking for answers.

NOTES

1. Baseball-reference.com.

2. Tom Clavin and Danny Peary, *Roger Maris* (New York: Touchstone, 2010).

3. Ibid.

4. Johnny Gray, phone interview with the author, February 28, 2010.

5. Fred Hopke, phone interview with the author, February 20, 2011.

6. Jimmy Burns, "McDermott Hopes to Bat Way Back to Majors with Miami," *Sporting News*, May 21, 1958, 32.

7. Bill Durney Jr., phone interview with the author, December 21, 2010.

8. Tommy Fitzgerald, "Farrell's Logical Strategy Backfired in 13–2 Fiasco" *Miami News*, May 13, 1958; *Sporting News*, May 21, 1958, 32.

9. Tommy Fitzgerald, "Marlins Win; Ryan Tries to Get Phillies' Herrera," *Miami News*, May 14, 1958; *Sporting News*, May 21, 1958, 32.

10. Norris Anderson, "'New Look' Marlins Out to Break Columbus Jinx," *Miami News*, May 16, 1958.

11. Norris Anderson, "Marlins Get Herrera, LiPetri," *Miami News*, May 15, 1958.

12. *Sporting News*, May 28, 1958, 31; "Hit in First Inning Deprives Don Cardwell of No-Hitter," *Sporting News*, May 28, 1958, 32.

13. Norris Anderson, "Miami Has 'Five-Day' New Look," *Miami News*, May 17, 1958.

14. "Marlins Win Seven in Row, One Short of Club Record," *Sporting News*, May 28, 1958, 31; Norris Anderson, "Marlins Seek Record of 8 Straight Wins," *Miami News*, May 19, 1958.

15. *Sporting News*, May 28, 1958, 32, 36.

16. Jimmy Burns, "Luke Batters Paige, Says," *Sporting News*, June 4, 1958.

17. Norris Anderson, "Marlins Visit Wings," *Miami News*, May 26, 1958.

18. "Cardwell Whiffs 14 Bisons for All-Time Marlin Record," *Sporting News*, June 4, 1958, 29; Norris Anderson, "Miami Bats Ring Out 8–4 Win," *Miami News*, May 25, 1958.

19. *Sporting News*, June 11, 1958, 51; Norris Anderson, "Marlins Win, Off for Day," *Miami News*, May 29, 1958.

20. Norris Anderson, "Marlins Face 'Kings' in Holiday Twin-Bill," *Miami News*, May 30, 1958.

21. Ibid.

22. Baseball-reference.com.

23. Anderson, "Marlins Face 'Kings' in Holiday Twin-Bill."

24. Norris Anderson, "Miami Divides Pair, Battles Havana Again," *Miami News*, May 31, 1958.

Sid Gordon inks his new contract with the Miami Marlins as Bill Veeck looks on. (Courtesy of AP Wirephoto)

New Marlins manager Don Osborn addresses the Optimist Club. Edwin F. Braun, president of the Optimist Club, is at his side taking in the proceedings. (Courtesy of *Miami News* Collection, HistoryMiami)

Left to right: Wilbur Johnson and Ben Tompkins practice turning the double play. (Courtesy of *Sporting News*)

Front to back: Woody Smith, Bob Micelotta, and Ben Tompkins—anchors of the Marlins' infield from 1956 to 1958. (Toby Massey, photographer; *Miami News* **Collection, HistoryMiami)**

Bob Bowman slides into third base ahead of the throw. (Courtesy of *Miami News* Collection, HistoryMiami)

Left to right: Jimmy Foxx (coach), Tim Anagnost (home team batboy), Don Osborn (manager), Jeffrey Green (visiting team batboy), Sid Gordon, and Eddie Storin (*Miami Herald* beat writer). Team batboys receive a reward for a job well done. (Courtesy of Tim Anagnost)

Pitcher Hank Mason contemplates his next delivery in the Miami Stadium bull-pen. (Courtesy of *Miami News* Collection, HistoryMiami)

Second baseman Ben Tompkins. (Courtesy of *Miami News* Collection, History Miami)

Pitcher Dick Bunker. (Courtesy of *Miami News* Collection, HistoryMiami)

Pitcher Gene Snyder. (Courtesy of *Miami News* Collection, HistoryMiami)

Catcher Johnny Bucha. (Courtesy of *Miami News* Collection, HistoryMiami)

Infielder Jerry Snyder. (Courtesy of *Miami News* Collection, HistoryMiami)

Left to right: Outfielders Chuck Essegian, Cal Abrams, and Jim Greengrass look forward to the 1957 season. (Toby Massey, photographer; *Miami News* Collection, HistoryMiami)

Don Landrum attempts to steal third base against Toronto but is thrown out by catcher Tim Thompson as Stan Jok makes the tag. (Charles Trainor, photographer; *Miami News* Collection, HistoryMiami)

**Manager Kerby Farrell contemplates his next move. (Bob Bailey, photographer;
Miami News Collection, HistoryMiami)**

Joe Ryan and Kerby Farrell (far right) admire a fine trophy fighting fish. (Courtesy of *Miami News* Collection, HistoryMiami)

Left to right: Woody Smith, W. A. Bird (assistant sales manager Rawlings), Jimmy Burns (sports editor of the *Miami Herald*), and George B. Storer (owner) presenting Smith with an award in April 1959. (Courtesy of *Sporting News*; photographer, Jay Spencer)

Pitcher Jack Fisher shown in his Marlins warm-up jacket. (Courtesy of *Sporting News*; photographer, Ray Fisher)

Pitcher George Zuverink. (Courtesy of *Miami News* Collection, HistoryMiami)

Baltimore Orioles manager Paul Richards and third club owner Bill MacDonald look on during spring training 1960. (Courtesy of *Sporting News*)

Left to right: Jimmy Burns (publisher of the *Sporting News*), J. G. Taylor Spink,
GM Joe Ryan, and manager Al Vincent chat before a game at Miami Stadium.
(Courtesy of *Sporting News*; photographer, Jay Spencer)

Satchel Paige, the most famous Marlin of all, lost in his thoughts in front of his locker. (Bill Tyler, photographer; *Miami News* Collection, HistoryMiami)

EIGHTEEN

Just Can't Seem to Win the Close Ones

June's arrival brought distressing news to the Marlins faithful, as if there wasn't enough of that already. The Red Cross might as well have hung its shingle over the Marlins' locker room, since their roster resembled the walking wounded more than a ball club. During the first part of June, Bob Usher, a key offensive weapon in the Marlins arsenal, suffered a hand injury and a broken blood vessel in his arm from colliding with the outfield wall;[1] Don Landrum was forced out of his starting position in centerfield because he had to have five teeth removed; Ben Tompkins was recovering from his knee cartilage injury; Johnny Bucha was playing with a badly bruised ankle; and Chuck Harmon was still on the injured reserve list from an unspecified previous injury.[2]

The situation got so desperate for Farrell that shortstop Bob Micelotta and catcher Jimmie Coker were forced into emergency duty as outfielders, and the bench was so depleted that during a June 2 game pitcher Dick Bunker was forced into pinch-hit duties against Buffalo. It might not have been a bad move, since Bunker was batting .400 at the time. Every time Farrell turned around he was finding the cupboard bare. General Manager Joe Ryan was working the phone so hard that his coke-bottle glasses were steaming up. So far he had contacted twelve major league teams for help, all to no avail. His hard work paid off on June 6 when he announced that the Marlins finally completed a deal, signing husky left-handed hitting outfielder Bert Hamric from the Baltimore Orioles.[3] The previous year with the Los Angeles Angels of the PCL, Hamric batted .291 with nineteen home runs and fifty-six batted in.[4] Ryan's hope was that Hamric would give the Marlins' batting order the jolt they had been looking for.

Despite the Marlins' woes on offense, the pitching staff was continuing to fire on all eight cylinders. Dick Bunker and Satchel Paige closed out the Havana series on June 1, as the locker-room neighbors each pitched four-hitters in both ends of the doubleheader. Bunker won the opener 6–1, supported by Bob Usher's only grand slam of the year, and Paige took the short second game 4–2 with the help of a long-awaited three-run homer by Pancho Herrera.[5]

Miami proceeded to drop three out of four to Buffalo before finishing up the homestand by coming back to take three of four from Rochester. Don Cardwell had another stellar performance against Buffalo on June 3, striking out thirteen and only walking two.

Miami hit the road for Canada to play the Maple Leafs first, followed by the Royals. The Marlins and hometown Leafs arrived to find the roof of Maple Leafs Stadium scorched and charred. Apparently while the Leafs were away some stacked furniture, as part of a huge sale being held at the stadium, somehow ignited and the overhang on the west side of stadium was touched by flames, leaving approximately $10,000 in damage.[6]

The stadium wasn't the only thing that had been on fire. The Maple Leafs had now closed the gap on Montreal and trailed by a mere half game in the standings, having won eleven of their last seventeen games. Led by perennial slugger Rocky Nelson, who would eventually win his third International League MVP (1953, 1955, and 1958) and third Home Run Crown (1954, 1955, and 1958),[7] he and his teammates would dominate the visiting Marlins by taking three out of four games and stay within striking distance of the Royals.

At least some encouraging news came in Toronto—studious Ben Tompkins traveled with the team to Toronto and made his first appearance since his injury on May 10. On the other hand, Paige stayed home on the disabled list temporarily to keep the roster down the minimum of twenty.[8]

The Marlins failed to do anything to help out Toronto in the Leafs' quest to catch the Royals, as they dropped another series and took only one of three games from Montreal. Uncharacteristically, Miami's pitchers gave up nineteen runs in one of their worst showings of the year. Dallas Green's troubles compounded as his record fell to 2–7. The imposing six-foot-five, 210-pound right-hander with the foghorn voice and intimidating demeanor lasted only four and two-thirds innings in the first game of a doubleheader, resulting in a 7–2 loss. He was followed by seldom-used lefty Bunky Stewart, who survived only three innings in the 9–4 loss in the nightcap. The Marlins failed to garner one extra base hit in any of the two games. To add insult to injury, their road record now stood at 8–21.[9]

For the year Miami stood at 28–37 in sixth place, eleven and a half games behind Montreal and six games behind fourth-place Columbus. Before leaving Montreal the weary-eyed Farrell exclaimed, "This is a day off and the Marlins can use it to dig in for the coming attack." And regroup the Marlins did in the next series of games.

With a chance to catch their collective breaths, the Marlins finally started to turn things around on their return to their home sweet home. To put it simply, they reversed the damage that occurred in Canada by taking two of three from Toronto and three of five from Montreal.

Farrell continued to complain that his hitters weren't stringing enough hits together to score runs, which solicited an agreeable response from Storer, "We get the hits, but we leave all the men on base." Undeniably there was many a game that the Marlins tabulated more hits than their opponents, but they still tallied a negative mark in the loss column. Farrell was at his boiling point and his equally frustrated club was repeatedly reminded of the unenviable statistic of having lost thirty-eight games on the year with exactly half of those being by one run.[10] With a little more luck, and/or just a little more consistent hitting, the Marlins would be in first division versus one rung up the ladder from the bottom.

The first game of the homestand started on an ominous note when rock-steady Conley failed to retire any of the batters he faced and left the game after giving up three hits and two walks. That was all that Toronto needed as they cruised to a 5–0 victory. Ironically, both teams netted nine hits but the Leafs proved more proficient at bunching their base knocks.[11]

Miami bounced back the next two nights, throttling Toronto's ace Pat Scantlebury and winning by the score of 7–2 and 6–1. Miami's own ace Cardwell continued to make a case for a return trip to the parent-Phillies. With Miami scoring all of their runs in the first two innings, highlighted by a Don Landrum rare home run blast in the first inning, they coasted the rest of the evening with nothing but a whimper from the Leafs' batters.[12]

Bunker, working his breaking ball to perfection, pulled off a *coup de grace* in the final game and shut down the Leafs 6–1, holding one of the league's top offensive units to just four singles. It was Bunker's sixth win against two losses and his performance lowered his ERA to a minuscule 1.69; tops on the team and second in the league. Tough-as-nails catcher Bucha, the only Marlins regular hitting over .300, and second baseman Tompkins were continuing to swing the hottest bats. Tompkins upped his average to .450, although he was only seeing limited action since returning from his injury.[13]

More good news came on June 20 when it was announced that Bobby Young would be recalled to the Phillies and replaced with Chuck Essegian. Farrell was confident that Tompkins could fill Young's shoes and in the process he was gaining that much-needed slugger that he had been asking for since the beginning of the season.[14]

That same day, Conley returned to start on three days' rest against Montreal and bounced back to his old form, putting the Royals away by tossing a five-hitter and squaring his record at 7–7. To Farrell's delight, Hamric's bat was finally starting to come around after a prolonged slump as he drove in a couple of runners to cement the 6–2 win. A sparse crowd of 1,951 were excited to see Tompkins, always a fan favorite, return to his regular position at second. It was like old times teaming up with his long-time keystone mate Micelotta again. [15]

On June 21, Youth Saturday, over four thousand fans—including 2,700 kids—watched as Montreal was temporarily knocked from their IL pedestal. Toronto regained the top spot, with a little help from Miami's hot bats and steady pitching from Dallas Green. Rangy right-hander Rene Valdes cruised through the first five innings, but gave up damaging singles to Smith and Bucha in the sixth inning in the midst of a four-run outburst that sent the native Havanan to the showers after five and two-thirds innings. Although Green had struggled for most of the season, he pitched well for eight and a third innings. However, the Marlins received a scare in the ninth inning after the big native from Delaware nearly gave up the 7–4 lead. With runners on base and one out, Farrell made the slow trip to the mound, and after signaling to the bullpen, turned the reins over to Windy McCall, who promptly slammed the door, procuring the last two outs and earning the save. [16]

Montreal regrouped the next day and split a rain-delayed, water-soaked Sunday doubleheader, winning the first game 3–1 and dropping the evening affair 4–1. Paige, making his first appearance in two weeks, was given the assignment of the seven-inning late game and proved up to the task despite his recent visit to the disabled list. Paige remained perfect through four innings, but he began to show signs of fatigue in the sweltering humidity starting in the fifth inning when Sandy Amoros doubled and later scored in the same inning. Paige received some much-needed support from his teammate Hank Mason, who closed out the game in the seventh inning. New arrival Chuck Essegian, who went 3–3 scoring twice in his first start since returning to the Marlins, was the game's MVP. Despite being a little rusty, Paige didn't walk any batters and allowed only three hits. "I hadn't pitched for 14 days," groused Paige as he added, "I wasn't real sharp. I got behind some batters but I'll come 'round with more work." [17] No doubt most of the staff wished they could pitch that well after sitting out for two weeks, but for the "pitchin' man" it was just another day in the office.

From June 17 up until the IL All-Star game on July 28 the Marlins won or tied every series, with the exception of a one-game stop in Rochester that saw the Marlins drop a 6–1 decision to their longtime nemesis Lynn Lovenguth. Despite an 8–21 road mark the Marlins reeled off an impressive record on their longest road trip of the year, taking ten of seventeen games, including manhandling Richmond and Rochester three out of four games.

Farrell's use of Paige provided just the contribution he was looking for to boost some of his younger pitchers, who had begun showing some signs of tiredness. From June 30 to the 4th of July Paige alone won three games in relief, shoring up Conley, Green, and Bunker. "Satch" threw a combined six and two-thirds innings over the stretch allowing no runs, six hits, and issuing one base on balls.[18]

In the midst of their success, the Marlins received disheartening news on July 9 when the Phillies announced Cardwell's promotion to the parent club. Following a brilliant 3–0 two-hit shutout against Havana on July 8, the long-anticipated promotion finally came, though not unexpectedly, to Farrell and General Manager Ryan. Taking with him his 12–5 record, Cardwell had completed twelve of his nineteen starts and was leading the league with 119 strikeouts.[19] His departure left the starting rotation perilously thin. Bunker was nursing a sore arm, and Green continued to struggle to find his pitches. Farrell had begun to work McDermott into the rotation, although he had been struggling as well and had no wins and three losses to show for all of his efforts before July 4.

Filling Cardwell's spot was right-handed side-armer Warren Hacker.[20] The eleven-year major league veteran was released to the Marlins by the Phillies. Only thirty-three years old, Hacker was seldom used by the big club, and had only pitched sixteen innings almost exclusively in relief, failing to earn a win. Hacker had spent most of his career in a Chicago Cubs uniform playing for poor teams and along the way collected an equally unimpressive 59–86 record.[21] However, to be fair, some of his lack of success can be blamed on the poor run support he received in Chicago.[22] Although Miami fans preferred Cardwell and were sorry to see him leave, Hacker was just the kind of veteran that General Manager Ryan loved and he was happy to see him join the flock.

On July 11 the Marlins were only four games behind the fourth-place Columbus Jets. With the upcoming four-game series ahead, a sweep of the Jets would lift the Marlins into fourth place and into the first division. They got off on the right foot in the opener behind the stalwart hurling of Bob Conley, the big guy who pushed his won-loss record over the .500 mark to nine wins and eight losses. Behind a seven-strikeout performance, and allowing not a single walk, Conley held the listless Jets to six hits. A key contributor on offense was Herrera, who cracked two doubles and drove in a run. Following the game, the Marlins' locker room reverberated with the battle cry, "Three more straight for fourth place."[23]

Over the course of a season a player's emotions run the gamut between highs and lows. Outfielder Bob Usher had been dealing all season long with a variety of nagging injuries, but it wasn't about to deter his competitiveness. Although a pretty even-keeled sort, Usher got caught up in the intensity of the game and had words with home plate umpire Hank Morgan that led to his early dismissal. At least he made the most of his time off, being the good father that he was.

> *Bob Usher*: Well, I was thrown out of a ballgame one night. And I was thrown out of a ballgame less than five times in my career. And I joined my family up in the stands behind the plate. And one of my children

said, "Daddy what did you say to that umpire?" I told him, "I wanted to go and have a hot dog with my family."[24]

On July 12, Farrell found himself in a quandary because of multiple players with injuries. Both the regular backstop Bucha and backup catcher Jimmie Coker found themselves incapacitated by maladies, leaving the team in a lurch. Since no one else on the roster had any experience at donning the tools of ignorance, regular right-fielder Bob Usher stepped up to the plate and volunteered his services. John Anderson, the knuckleball specialist, was scheduled to make the start, but to ease the burden on his inexperienced catcher Farrell instead opted for McDermott, who was essentially a fastball pitcher and easier for Usher to handle.[25]

Usher had several highlights, including an early season grand slam, while wearing a Marlins uniform, but listed his catching duties as one of the most memorable moments he had not only in the time he spent in Miami but also in his entire career.

> *Bob Usher*: I told Kerby I hadn't caught since I was in high school. That was seventeen years ago. "But if you want to gamble, I'm your man." So that's what happened. And the first ball that was hit to shortstop, the shortstop made the throw to first and I'm still sitting around home plate and then Kerby whistles at me and gives me the round figure to back up first base. I'd forgotten about that technique.
>
> And the second most memorable I guess was catching Mickey McDermott. I think I mentioned this to you the other day. Mickey McDermott was a left-handed pitcher and Johnny Anderson, we talked about this the other day, he was supposed to pitch that day, but the two catchers Johnny Bucha and Jim Coker were injured. So I volunteered. And so Mickey pitched against Columbus and we beat them 3–1 [actual final score, 4–2]. Satchel Paige pitched the next day and we beat Havana in Miami 5–1 [actual final score, 3–1].
>
> Kerby didn't want to have me getting the knuckles banged up. So he threw Mickey McDermott, a left-handed pitcher.[26]

McDermott earned his first win of the season, but the Marlins trailed the Jets by two games. After performing yeoman's duty behind the plate Usher received compliments from his pitcher. "Usher was a fine target and he moved around well back there," said the complimentary McDermott after the game. Herrera and Smith each collected three hits with Usher driving in a key RBI, earning McDermott his first Marlins win in a 4–2 decision.[27]

Usher performed so well that Farrell called on him again the next night. He started behind the plate catching the great Satchel Paige, who informed him what to expect. Jimmie Coker was forced into action the next night, mostly out of necessity, but Usher caught Paige for the first few innings before yielding to the more experienced backstop. Paige went five innings and then both he and Usher retired for the evening.

Mason and his battery mate Coker substituted and together they contributed to finishing out the 3–1 nightcap win.[28]

> Talk about fastballs. I asked Satch how many pitches he wanted to throw. He said, "Well, you can put down as many fingers as you want but I'm only going to throw my hummer." That was his fastball. I said, "OK, how about with a man at first base? What do you want to do in a switch?" And he gave me the same answer, "You can put down as many fingers as you want to decoy them but I'm going to throw my hummer." That's what he did we beat Havana, 5–1 [final score, 3–1].[29]

Miami completed the four-game sweep of Columbus the next day by taking both games of the twin bill. Eighty-five years' experience took the mound that night in the form of thirty-three-year old Hacker, drawing the starting assignment for the first game, and fifty-two-year-old Paige accepting the chore in the second short game. It was Hacker's debut, his first start in his new blue-and-orange-trimmed togs, and it was a dandy. He used his pinpoint control on his fastball, mixed with an occasional knuckleball and sinker; the astute veteran shut out the Jets 6–0, striking out seven enemy hitters without issuing a free pass. Hacker, who hadn't pitched for almost two weeks, later stated, "But I felt good out there today." He added, "I thought I had good stuff for six innings anyway."[30]

Helping out as key offensive contributors were Herrera and Smith, now dubbed "The Thump Twins" by the press. Each contributed by providing not only exemplary defense but also some much-needed punch, as Smith homered and drove in a pair of runs and Herrera singled and doubled, scoring twice. On the other side of the coin, lead-off hitter Landrum and middle-of-the-order Essegian had produced a 0–10 performance with runners in scoring position with the exception of a Landrum sacrifice fly.[31]

Sometimes offense comes from an unexpected source. Paige helped out his own cause by not only pitching five strong innings but also laying down a successful squeeze bunt in the middle of a three-run fifth inning that proved to be the difference in the triumph. It was Paige's first RBI dating back to the Orange Bowl game, ironically against the same club—Columbus.[32]

Paige, obviously not accustomed to being on base, was involved in a dispute when, in the same inning, Landrum lifted a sacrifice fly to right field. The wandering Paige had to scurry back to first base, drawing the ire of Jets' manager Clyde King to inquire if any one of the umpires had seen the play. After admitting missing the play, and vehemently arguing to no avail with home-plate umpire Hank Morgan, King was tossed and officially filed a protest after the game. All, of course, went to no avail and the Marlins' "W" stood up. Following the near mishap, Paige was lifted for a pinch-runner Green and watched from the dugout as once again Mason came in to pitch the last two innings and save his friend's eighth win. Paige now had reduced Judge Snowden's sentence to twelve days.[33]

For the first time since April 21 the Marlins (49–48) were over .500 and were now tied for fourth place. It was becoming evident that a three-team race was developing between Columbus, Rochester, and Miami for the third and fourth playoff positions. Montreal and Toronto had definitely established themselves as the front-runners and it was going to be another down-to-the-wire finish for a postseason berth.[34]

Looking forward to a final four-game home series with the sixth-place Richmond Vees, confidence in the Marlins camp was never more apparent. With a six-game win streak in hand, and despite slumps by Essegian and Landrum, Farrell confidently announced, "They'll come out of it."[35] It seemed that Hacker was proving to be a suitable replacement in the rotation for Cardwell, and the "Thump Twins" were smacking the ball. From now until the end of the season, it would prove to be a real dogfight.

NOTES

1. Norris Anderson, "Marlins Win Twice, Play Bisons Tonight," *Miami News*, June 2, 1958.

2. Norris Anderson, "Miami Out to Banish Deal's Jinx," *Miami News*, June 6, 1958.

3. Norris Anderson, "Woody's Steal His Own Idea," *Miami News*, June 7, 1958.

4. Baseball-reference.com.

5. Anderson, "Marlins Win Twice, Play Bisons Tonight"; *Sporting News*, June 11, 1958, 52.

6. "Fire Damages Roof at Leafs Park," *Sporting News*, June 18, 1958, 29.

7. Bill O'Neal, *International League: A Baseball History 1884–1991* (Austin, TX: Eakin Press, 1992), 413, 422.

8. "Irate Leafs Face Miami at Toronto," *Miami News*, June 10, 1958.

9. *Sporting News*, June 25, 1958, 34, 36; Morris McLemore, "Marlins Face More Trouble at Home," *Miami News*, June 16, 1958.

10. Norris Anderson, "Runless Club Discourages Storer, Kerby," *Miami News*, June 18, 1958.

11. *Sporting News*, June 25, 1958, 34, 36.

12. *Sporting News*, July 2, 1958, 31; Norris Anderson, "Miami in Morning Drill Despite Win over Leafs," *Miami News*, June 19, 1958.

13. *Sporting News*, July 2, 1958, 31, 32; Norris Anderson, "Miami Winning Games and Counting Blessings," *Miami News*, June 20, 1958.

14. *Sporting News*, July 2, 1958, 31, 32; Anderson, "Miami Winning Games and Counting Blessings."

15. *Sporting News*, July 2, 1958, 31.

16. Ibid., 31, 32.

17. *Sporting News*, July 2, 1958, 32; Norris Anderson, "Royals' Manager Claims Marlins Are a Better Club," *Miami News*, June 23, 1958.

18. *Sporting News*, July 9, 1958, 54; *Sporting News*, July 16, 1958, 33, 34.

19. "Two Straight Shutouts Speed Cardwell's Recall by Phils," *Sporting News*, July 16, 1958, 33.

20. Bill James and Rob Neyer, *The Neyer/James Guide to Pitchers* (New York: Fireside, 2004).

21. BaseballLibrary.com.

22. "Phils Summon Don Cardwell," *Palm Beach Post*, July 10, 1958, 19.

23. Norris Anderson, "'3 More For 4th Place,' Marlins Shout at Jets," *Miami News*, July 12, 1958.

24. Bob Usher, phone interview with the author, March 13, 2011.

25. "Miami Catchers Hurt, Usher Dons Mask, McDermott Wins," *Sporting News*, July 23, 1958, 35.

26. Usher interview.

27. *Sporting News*, July 23, 1958, 36.

28. Norris Anderson, "Bob Usher Catches as Marlins Win 4th Straight, 4–2," *Miami News*, July 13, 1958.

29. Usher interview.

30. Anderson, "Bob Usher Catches as Marlins Win 4th Straight, 4–2."

31. Norris Anderson, "Miami after 3rd Place, Faces Vees," *Miami News*, July 14, 1958.

32. Ibid.

33. Ibid.

34. Ibid.

35. Ibid.

NINETEEN

Turning It Around, But Trouble Ahead

The long-awaited magic that George Storer had been expecting was seemingly popping out of the magician's hat, the lid in question being Kerby Farrell's ball cap. The Tennessee Tactician was pushing all of the right buttons, having delivered fourteen wins in the last eighteen games to reverse the fortunes of his club. The recent success of the Marlins was attributed to their offense, which was producing just enough to support a stellar staff, arguably the best in the IL. And their air-tight defense, although performing quietly under the radar, was considered the best in the league. Ultimately the team would finish with best fielding percentage in the IL, only committing 123 errors by season's end and finishing second in double plays turned with 155.[1] Equally important, but not receiving much notice, was the play of Woody Smith, who was quietly putting together a fielding record unique in the annals of IL history.

Everyone around the IL knew of Smith's proficiency at the hot corner, but until it came to the notice of the IL's offices no one was sure who held the record for consecutive errorless games from that position. A search by league statisticians ensued and it was discovered that the previous record for errorless chances by a third baseman was fifty-six games, held by Irving Jeffries of the 1937 Montreal Club. Not only had Smith broken the record, but he had also smashed it in rather Brooks Robinson–like form.[2]

Finishing up their last home dates with Richmond, the Marlins split the four-game series and now were looking forward to playing against the tail-enders of the IL, the Havana Sugar Kings. The Marlins, who were patrons of the nightlife scene, were anxious to return to Havana, not only for the chance to improve their lot in the standings but also for ulterior motives that had nothing to do with baseball.

Miami's charter flight arrived late for the opening game and the team was not in their locker room until a mere thirty minutes before game time at Gran Stadium. Staying behind in Miami was Bob Conley with tonsil problems, which left Farrell in a dilemma on who should start.[3]

Warren Hacker was called on to face the lanky six-foot-two California boy, Gene "Lefty" Hayden. Miami wasted no time scoring in the first inning when Jerry Snyder singled, moved to second on a free pass, then scored on a Smith single. It was all the scoring Hacker and the Marlins would need for the night as Miami cruised to an easy 3–0 win. Hacker was causing Miami fans to forget Don Cardwell as he posted his second shutout in as many starts. "The way he pitches, it looks like nobody is ever going to score on him," chimed sombrero-less pitching coach Bubba Church. Hacker was so dominant that he held the Cubans to a mere four singles and issued his first base on balls in eighteen innings since joining the team.[4]

The following evening's scheduled game was supposed to be played in a town called Moron located farther inland on the island, but the deal was nixed by General Manager Joe Ryan, bringing on some major indignation from Sugar Kings' owner Bobby Maduro, who thought they had an arrangement. Ryan claimed that no such agreement was made and playing in Moron would cost the Marlins $10,000. Maduro was quick to respond, stating that on Buffalo's previous trip they had attracted over fifteen thousand enthusiasts despite heavy rains, proving it to be a profitable venture for both parties. Many advance tickets had been sold and a sellout crowd was expected. Needless to say, the next night's game returned to Havana when Ryan won out, but Maduro received some level of satisfaction as his *amigos* bounced back and edged the visiting Miamians, 3–2.[5]

Whether it was disgruntled Moron fans practicing voodoo hexes, or just the law of averages catching up, Smith finally did the unthinkable. In the eighth inning, with the score tied at two apiece, starter Dick Bunker returned to the hill in the eighth inning. Lead-off batter Nino Escalera dug in to face Bunker, who was showing signs of tiring in the Cuban heat and was looking to coax any kind of out from the rail-thin enemy batter who was facing him. Bunker was momentarily relieved after delivering his offering when Escalera popped the ball up toward third base and watched as Smith called off his mates to make the play. As the white sphere started its downward trajectory, it was a foregone conclusion that it would be the first out. Smith reached out as he had hundreds of times to squeeze the ball, but instead it popped out of his glove, allowing Escalera to reach first base. The streak was over; after 283 consecutive chances and eighty-six games (dating back to May 5), Smith had finally faltered.[6]

Farrell recognized that Bunker was too fatigued to continue. After a Rogelio Alvarez single, he called on his hottest hand out of the bullpen:

Hank Mason. After a balk, Al Grandacolas hit a sacrifice fly to score Escalera, providing the winning margin. Bunker was tagged with the defeat, which dropped his record to 7–5, and Smith lamented his error in the recesses of Gran Stadium.[7]

Before leaving Havana the Marlins continued their all-too-familiar trend of losing one-run games. They dropped both contests of the next day's doubleheader by identical scores of 2–1. Satchel Paige lost the short game to local favorite Raul Sanchez, who pitched a near perfect game, giving up only one base hit to Essegian on a solo home run. John Anderson followed with another strong performance, but dropped the nightcap to Vicente Amor, who limited the Marlins to five hits. The Marlins' batsmen produced a minuscule seven runs during the series.[8] Their pitiful offense was ruled by a court of opinion for being responsible for losing three of the four contests.

With the IL's All-Star break just a week away Miami hopped a quick flight back home in preparation for a three-game set against Montreal and four more against Toronto. Usually the Marlins returned from Havana suffering the ill effects of the nightlife. Instead, they came back to Miami Stadium as fresh as bread baked in the morning.

The Montreal Royals came out flat as day-old beer. Starter McDermott teamed with veteran McCall to hold Montreal to seven hits, garnering a 3–2 win. Essegian and the defense were the stars of the night. Essegian hit the difference maker, blasting a 350-foot shot. The bruised sphere wasn't the least bit bothered by the thick humidity in the air as it sailed over the bottled gas sign in left field. It was the eighth homer of the year for the big Armenian and plated both Tompkins and Bucha ahead of him. Aiding mightily in the Marlins' success was their interior defense that turned five double plays, highlighted by Smith, Snyder, and Herrera, who turned the 5–4–3 trick three times.[9]

Uncharacteristically, the next two contests saw the Marlins win two more one-run games by scores of 2–1 and 3–2, the latter game in extra frames. It would be the last time they would sweep an opponent that year. Green stayed strong and earned the complete game win and was a recipient of a gift better than a bow-tied birthday box of chocolates. In the ninth inning Micelotta hit an unexpected solo home run that provided the single tally difference. Micelotta was obviously trying to impress the females in the audience on Ladies Night.[10]

Mason was asserting himself as the Marlins' full-time closer and won the concluding contest in relief of Hacker. Hacker had another magic night, performing a yeoman's job lasting ten innings, allowing one earned run, five hits, and not a single free pass. Mason came on in the eleventh inning and benefited from the heroics of Smith. With two out and the twelfth inning coming down the pike, Royals shortstop Marty Devlin dashed toward second in an attempt to pick off Snyder on a surprise play at second base. Farrell, anticipating the move, flashed the hit-

and-run sign, and instead of drawing the throw from the anxious catcher
Dick Teed, Smith stuck his bat out and slapped the ball through the
infield right where Devlin had been standing, scoring Snyder and sending the Royals out of town empty-handed. Miami's recent surge left them
only one-half game behind Rochester for third place, and in sole possession of fourth place a one-half game ahead of Columbus, who had just
finished splitting a double dip with Rochester.[11]

Following the game it was announced that thirty-year-old right-
handed pitcher Johnny Gray would be joining the club from Philadelphia, reuniting him with his former manager. Gray had seen little action
for the Phillies, only making fifteen appearances while compiling a 4.15
ERA in seventeen and a third innings.[12] With a few of the pitchers beginning to show signs of fatigue, the veteran Gray was a welcome sight for
the sore-eyed Ryan and Farrell.

Toronto was greeted by a less-than-cordial welcome upon arriving in
the Magic City. Paige in particular was holding a grudge against Maple
Leafs' manager Dixie Walker. The bone of contention between the two
centered on another IL All-Star snub by Walker: the second time in the
last two years Paige had been left off the squad. Walker, as the previous
year's league champion manager, chose his roster, but had neglected to
select Paige, or, for that matter, any of his teammates from the league
ERA–leading Marlins. Paige was especially miffed and expressed his
frustration against Walker. Claiming a conspiracy, he stated, "They was
afraid I'd go up there and beat the Braves." Paige added, "That would be
bad publicity for the game—an old man like me beating them kids."
Walker, on the other hand, claimed there were other pitchers with better
records than Paige's 9–6 log.[13] This did little to comfort Paige, who
would later take out his frustrations the best way he knew.

After dropping two out of the first three games to Toronto, Farrell
called on the "Pitchin' Man" to make an example of the Leafs before the
All-Star break. It was vintage Paige as he painted the strike zone like
Picasso stroking a canvas, shutting down the Leafs by scattering seven
hits over nine innings and walking only one batter. The final tally
showed Marlins 3, Maple Leafs 0. "Guess I showed him [Dixie] whether
I'm too old to be on the All-Star staff." It must have been satisfying to
Paige to win, but equally frustrating to stay home while his teammates
Herrera and Smith made the trip to Toronto for the All-Star festivities.[14]

The Marlins had their eyes on more than third place; there was talk
around the league of them possibly catching Toronto for second place.
Having won twenty-nine out of their last forty-five games, many around
the league were reevaluating Farrell's club as the dark horse in the pennant race. Certainly they had proven that airtight defense and pitching
had been enough over the recent stretch, but was it adequate over the
course of an entire season? Unbeknownst to scribes—and fans—storm
clouds were brewing just over the horizon. As of late the Marlins hadn't

let distractions within the team alter their focus to the point of falling out of the race. The rumblings were growing louder regarding whether the team would maintain their focus on the prize as the dog days of summer approached.

Paige in particular was frustrated with the continuing demands by management of working within the club rules set down by Ryan and Farrell. Don Osborn had been tolerant of the veteran's alternate habits, including allowing "Satch" to live by his own rules. Farrell had been tolerant to an extent, but was growing weary of Paige's utter disregard of the simplest directives. Only his teammates, many who held him in awe, showed little, if any, concerns about his on and off the field activities.

Although it had been for the most part kept out of the newspaper, General Manager Ryan was especially growing increasingly tired of the double standard that allowed Paige so much freedom. The ornery bespectacled general manager was waiting for the right moment, lying in the weeds for the appropriate time to exercise his authority. It would not be long before the said opportunity came, and when it did, the confrontation had far-reaching consequences.

NOTES

1. Baseball-reference.com.

2. Norris Anderson, "Smith's I.L. Fielding Record Verified," *Miami News*, July 18, 1958.

3. Norris Anderson, "Miami 1 Game From 3rd," *Miami News*, July 19, 1958.

4. Anderson, "Smith's I.L. Fielding Record Verified."

5. Anderson, "Miami 1 Game From 3rd."

6. Norris Anderson, "Smith Makes Error, Marlins Beaten, 3–2," *Miami News*, July 20, 1958; "Boot Snaps Smith's Record Fielding Skein, Beats Miami," *Sporting News*, July 30, 1958, 30.

7. "Boot Snaps Smith's Record Fielding Skein, Beats Miami."

8. *Sporting News*, July 30, 1958, 29.

9. Tommy Fitzgerald, "Clutch Homer, 5 DP's Cheer Marlins, Crowd," *Miami News*, July 22, 1958; *Sporting News*, August 6, 1958, 33.

10. Tommy Fitzgerald, "Marlins Enjoying Fictional Finishes," *Miami News*, July 23, 1958.

11. Norris Anderson, "Leafs Invade Miami," *Miami News*, July 24, 1958.

12. Baseball-reference.com.

13. Jimmy Burns, "Snubbed by Walker, Paige Gets Revenge, Blanks Leafs," *Sporting News*, August 6, 1958, 34.

14. Ibid.

TWENTY

Falling Short and Paige's Last Hurrah

Kerby Farrell took advantage of the day off and sat in the crowd, joined by his boss George Storer, to view his two stars performing at the IL All-Star Game. "The best club in the league right now," gushed IL president Frank Shaughnessy. The superstitious Farrell cringed as if it was the kiss of death: "If we were the best we would be first, second, or third." It was almost as if Farrell was trying to reverse the hex.[1]

Herrera and Smith returned on July 29 from Toronto with little to show for their All-Star game appearances, going a combined oh for four in the 3–2 loss to the Milwaukee Braves. Prior to the IL bash Smith explained, "As bad as I've needed hits lately it would be awful to waste them when they didn't count."[2] Smith's concerns about using up his season allotment of hits failed to come to fruition. The "Thump Twins," anxious to get back with their teammates in Buffalo, were as optimistic as their mates on their chances for acquiring a championship. The exception: a fuming Satchel Paige. Paige was still smoldering over being left off the All-Star squad. Teamed with his disgust for being snubbed and continued anger that was being more compacted by increasing pressure to follow team rules by Joe Ryan, something was about to give. Getting ready for their push to stay in first division, the Marlins were happy to meet the Bisons (41–68), the worst team in the league. It was hoped that success in Buffalo would provide the needed springboard for the moving up in the standings.

Warren Hacker had been practically unhittable since joining the club and was called on to kick off the fourteen-game northern road swing. Hacker's confidence was quickly shattered when he failed to get out of four innings, giving up a bundle of runs before yielding to Hank Mason and leaving him with a 7–0 deficit. Buffalo had only scored fifteen runs in their previous seven games, but came out with renewed vigor and exploded for fourteen runs, highlighted by Luke Easter's twenty-third blast of the year.[3] By the time the smoke had cleared the Marlins had lost 14–6. The fourteen runs were the highest total allowed by the staff since their 14–5 loss to Richmond on May 22.

Those pesky one-run losses came back to haunt the Marlins in the final two games against Buffalo; Dick Bunker lost the next night 6–5, and John Anderson came up short in the series finale, 3–2. Especially baffling was Bunker's recent performance. On June 19 Bunker's record stood at an impressive 6–2 but with the loss to the Bisons he had dropped to a mediocre 7–7. The little left-hander was having trouble going into the late innings of games and there was concern over arm problems, which Bunker vehemently denied. A few unnamed teammates were blaming his lack of work regimen and recent experiments with new pitches for his troubles. A more likely explanation was simply that the wear and tear of a long season was taking its toll.[4]

The August 1 game started off innocently enough in Rochester when the Marlins astonishingly put eleven runs on the board, chasing Red Wings starter Cal Browning after six innings. Smith cashed in some of those hits he had not used at the All-Star bash, going 4–4 including a home run. Jimmie Coker crushed a grand slam, and Bob Usher chipped in with three ribbies in the 11–6 victory.[5]

Prior to the series curtain-raiser against Rochester, several members of the team noticed Paige was conspicuously missing. Paige had last pitched on July 27 and was not scheduled to pitch until August 3. It was not unusual for him to take one of his usual leaves of absence from the team so no one found it strange that he hadn't joined his teammates. Part of the reason that Paige had not traveled with the team was his continued brooding over being left off the All-Star team and Miami's lack of effort to plead his case to IL to add him to the roster. Instead of being at the ballpark, Paige was waiting outside the hotel in Rochester, pacing back and forth in anticipation of confronting Ryan about meal money he had not received. George Weaver, a team employee, had previously told Paige that he had already been advanced money by the club and was not entitled to receiving his usual allowance of $65.00.[6] "This has been goin' on a long time and I'm tired of being pushed around," said Paige. Ryan stated that the disagreement centered on Paige not being with the team when they left on the current road trip and so he was absent when the meal money was passed out. Paige and Ryan were about to come to loggerheads, and Paige in his frustration decided to bolt the club. As far as Paige was concerned, he was done being a Marlin.

Airplanes were not Paige's favorite mode of transportation but it was the quickest way to get back to Miami. The dissolving relationship between Ryan and Paige that had been brewing for three years had finally reached its zenith. Although Paige had been a happy man for most of his time in Miami, he was unwilling to continue to work under any conditions except those that were of his preference. Paige gathered up his bags and made his way to the airport to catch the earliest flight available.[7]

At six o'clock that evening, the airplane carrying Paige was preparing for takeoff when Ryan hastily called the airport, may have even attempted to invalidate Paige's ticket, and asked to speak with the fuming veteran. It took some smooth talking, but Ryan, through an employee with the airline and under the guise of a possible bookkeeping mistake, managed to persuade the temperamental veteran to return to the ball-park to try to work things out. Paige disembarked and by the third inning he was back at Red Wing Stadium. At least temporarily, the misunderstanding had been worked out. Paige explained, "Ryan promised he would look at the books again and see if I had anything comin' to me. He got me just by a hair. They had to hold up the plane's takin' off so they could get my bags off." He added, "I love Miami and the people there. It's just that the ball club has gotta quit treatin' me like some kid who didn't know better."[8]

No doubt Ryan was aware that Paige was scheduled to pitch in the third game of the series and, realizing the importance of the games between the two teams, made some concessions. Miami and Rochester were locked up in a tooth-and-nail fight for a postseason spot, with Columbus hot on their heels. Given the fact that the Marlins trailed Rochester by only one game for third place, Ryan was more than willing to put a patch on any differences—that is, at least in the very short term.

Paige, as scheduled, was set to go for his August 3 start against the Red Wings. He had reason to be hopeful, as the Marlins had been impressive in the first two games, winning 11–6 and 9–4, but from the outset Paige seemed out of focus. The Red Wings jumped on him for four runs in six innings of work, while future St. Louis Cardinals standout Bob Gibson in relief of Lynn Lovenguth, who was pulled after one inning because of his own disagreement with manager Cot Deal, was exemplary pitching eight innings of shutout ball. Paige lamented afterward, "I just wasn't tops today." He further complained, "Bothered with a little gas on my stomach last night. Just wasn't sharp at all."[9] Paige was famously credited for saying, "If your stomach disputes you, lie down and pacify it with cool thoughts." On this night he failed to heed his own sage advice.

The next day, Joe Ryan announced that Paige was to be placed on the inactive list and replaced by recently acquired Johnny Gray. Paige was beside himself, and promptly requested his unconditional release from the Marlins: "All I want them to do is just pay me what they think they owe me and let me go free."[10] Ryan, not in the mood to give in to anyone's demands—especially Paige's—refused to offer him his release and placed him on inactive status, which constituted a minimum of ten days without pay before being able to return to the club. With that Paige returned to Miami on the next flight out of town on the Marlins' dime.

When the Miami press approached Ryan, the tight-lipped general manager simply stated, "No comment."[11]

The release couldn't have happened at a worse time. The Marlins were playing teams that they needed to make up ground against and distractions were the last thing Farrell's troops needed. Although Farrell had talked to Ryan about the suspension, he was none too happy to be without Paige at this critical juncture. Farrell tried to smooth the situation over with the press, saying that Paige usually wasn't used much on northern swings, but this wasn't the time of year when cold weather was a factor keeping Paige on the sidelines and obviously Farrell was trying to toe the company line.

The next stop was against front-running Montreal where Paige's replacement, Gray, dropped the first game, in relief of McDermott, 3–1. The Marlins promptly dropped three of the next four games, and four of the five games total, winning only the second game of the series, 7–4, behind the twirling of knuckleball specialist Anderson. The Marlins were outscored 24–13 and held to a single run in three of the five contests.

The Marlins regained their confidence by taking two of three from Toronto at Maple Leaf Stadium before returning to Miami. The series could best be categorized as "I went to a boxing match and a baseball game broke out." The three-game set started quietly enough with the Marlins matching the Leafs hit for hit, but still failing to come through consistently with runners in scoring position. Miami was also a victim of their own poor defense and, combined with some base-running gaffes, they were proving to be their own worst enemy. In the second inning of the series opener, Pancho Herrera fielded a ground ball cleanly for an easy out at first, but instead threw wildly to home, allowing a runner to score. On the same play, Johnny Bucha recovered the ball and threw it away, allowing two more runs to score and handing Toronto a 3–0 advantage.[12]

In the sixth inning frustrations came to a head. Toronto's Milt "Smoky" Smith tried to score on a sacrifice fly and in the process of crossing the plate pushed Bucha. Both players started jawing and came close to blows and the two benches emptied in response. The Marlins' frustrations were reaching a boiling point. Smith's reaction was likely a result of a plunking that starting pitcher Gray put on the Leafs shortstop Bob Johnson earlier in the inning. Although manager Dixie Walker demanded that umpire Augie Guglielmo put Gray out of the game, his hysterics all went to no avail. Farrell pulled Gray after six innings anyway, based on his ineffectiveness, and the Leafs finished up the evening with an easy 5–1 victory.[13]

Following the game, Farrell held a closed door meeting to air things out. The one player missing from the gathering was Paige. There were more than a few loud voices heard and even some laughter coming from the locker room, but the moody skipper got his message across with the intention of shaking his boys out of their doldrums.

If the Marlins didn't have enough excitement swirling around them, rumors were flying that the Maple Leafs were interested in signing Paige as insurance to improve their chances for procuring their third pennant in a row. Paige announced that he had received several offers, including a sweet deal from Leo Leavitt's Western Promotions to tour Hawaii, Japan, and the Philippines, as well as feelers from as far away as Chicago and Kansas City. General Manager Ryan had no comment on the matter.[14]

In a two-hour interview with the Miami press, Paige expressed his concern about taking care of his wife, Lahoma, and their five children, who were currently in Kansas City. Although the offers to barnstorm may have been substantially better financially for Paige, he seemed to be more interested in returning to the Marlins, at least for the conclusion of the season. Paige succinctly stated, "I know I can help this club, but I can't do anything when I'm on that list. I want to be ready to pitch when they need me." He added that he didn't hold any malice toward the club and stated, "I don't want to say anything against anyone up there. I think we can get together." Paige concluded by denying that he was interested in signing with Toronto. Not much of a surprise, since Paige had a near hatred toward playing there. He concluded the meeting by telling the press, "If they don't want me, just turn me loose. That's all I want."[15] "Satch" had the itch to come back to play and he needed to satisfy his need to pitch with the scratch.

Bad feelings from the previous game and the Gray incident carried over to the next day when the Marlins took the field for the second game of the set. The rejuvenated Marlins came out aggressively. In the third inning Herrera hit a solo home run to increase the Marlins' lead to 3–0. The Maple Leafs' Pat "The Lord" Scantlebury, a forty-year-old minor league journeyman in the twilight of his career, had pitched several years in the Negro Leagues and spent some time in the Caribbean, and even had a brief fling with the Cincinnati Reds in 1956.[16] He was in no mood to be shown up and was more than happy to send a message to that effect. The next batter, Woody Smith, strolled to the plate expecting some retribution and was promptly greeted by a little chin music. Smith was livid and on the next delivery, always the intense competitor, let his emotions get the best of him, letting his bat fly in the direction of Scantlebury. The bat landed at the six-foot-one left-hander's feet and he instantly picked up the projectile and started heading in Smith's direction at home plate with fire in his eyes. Bob Usher, at the time sitting on the bench, immediately charged from where he was in the dugout to the field. He was followed closely by Chuck Essegian, both of them rushing toward the area between home plate and the mound to intercept Scantlebury. The fracas was on.[17]

Scantlebury started swinging the discarded bat back and forth to clear the charging Marlins away as both benches emptied. Essegian, the ex-Stanford linebacker and one-time NFL prospect, in defense of Usher utilized his experience and tackled Scantlebury to the ground, saving his teammates from serious injury. For seventeen minutes both clubs went at it. Many scribes considered it the worst bench-clearing incident of the season in the IL. Essegian and Scantlebury were involved in the worst of it, exchanging punches and rolling on the ground, with Essegian gaining the upper hand, getting on top of the Leafs' pitcher and flailing away with a flurry of blows before police were able to pull the two apart. Like most baseball fights, there were sidelight pushing and shoving incidents around the perimeter of the action, including Marlins' catcher Bucha getting into the act and taking a swing at Leafs' manager Dixie Walker, only to be separated by other players. By the time the smoke had cleared, and with the assistance of local police, Scantlebury, his battery mate Joe Hannah, fellow pitcher Ernie Broglio, Essegian, and Smith had all been ejected. Surprisingly, Usher stayed in the game and only minor injuries were suffered by the combatants.[18]

In the locker room after the game, Smith claimed that the bat slipped out of his hands. Scantlebury's assessment was a bit more severe, claiming the incident was intentional as he angrily opined, "If I had gotten to Woody Smith, his career would have been done." He added, "I'd have broken his arm with that bat." Dixie Walker placed some of the blame on umpire Angelo "Augie" Guglielmo for ignoring league rules the night before and allowing Gray to stay in the game despite his obvious intent to hit Johnson in the head intentionally. According to IL rules, a pitcher is automatically ejected if he hits the next batter between the waist and head or if, in his judgment, the pitcher deliberately throws at the batter without actually hitting him.[19]

The following evening, the series finale, found a larger than normal crowd. Over seven thousand were on hand with many, no doubt, eager for some ringside action. Once again the Marlins came out swinging, not with their fists, but with their bats. Aided by Essegian and Herrera home runs, and a four-hit night by Jerry Snyder, starter Conley coasted to his tenth win of the season, putting down the Maple Leafs 8–2. "It woke us up. We were a dead club." Shortstop Bob Micelotta commented, "The fight is the thing that will win fourth place for us and a playoff spot." With that the Marlins boarded their flight to Miami with a 62–64 record, looking forward to hooking up again with Rochester. The Marlins were now five games behind the third-place Red Wings, residing in fourth place and only a couple games ahead of the heel-nipping Columbus Jets. Quietly, Paige's teammates were hoping for his quick return.[20]

Miami was in a perfect position to maintain, or at the very least make up ground against, third-place Rochester. Opening up a thirteen-game home stand on August 12, the Marlins would face Rochester, Buffalo,

Columbus, and Richmond. Things got off to a rocky start in Miami Stadium when the Marlins were shut out by, as Red Wings manager Cot Deal labeled him, "Money Pitcher" Gary Blaylock, 2–0. Blaylock struck out eleven Marlins while scattering eight hits.[21]

To make matters worse, the Marlins received three pieces of terrible news. First, the Phillies announced that they were recalling John Anderson to join the parent club and were sending down thirty-two-year-old right-handed veteran Bob J. Miller to take his spot. The one-time Phillies "Whiz Kid" had since fallen on hard times and had been used sparingly by the parent club, appearing in only seventeen games with an astronomical 11.69 ERA, all in mop-up duty, while tossing a mere 22.1 innings.[22] Anderson would be sorely missed down the stretch. Second, Woody Smith began serving the first of his two-game suspension for the Toronto incident, breaking a skein of 327 consecutive games dating back to when he was acquired from Havana in 1956. Taking his place in the lineup, for the short term, was hot-hitting infielder Jerry Snyder. And lastly, and of most concern to Farrell, was the acquisition of Lynn Lovenguth by their closest competitor Columbus. Rochester's Lovenguth, under suspension, was in Manager Deal's doghouse off and on all season. By acquiring the Red Wings' ornery hurler, the transaction was the boost the Jets' management felt they needed to push them over the top and gain the coveted final playoff spot. Deal was more than happy to part ways with the surly veteran and accepted another pitcher, Hugh Pepper, in an even exchange.[23] With the Marlins suddenly finding their pitching cupboard bare, it was increasingly urgent that Paige return to action to fill the void.

On August 14 the Marlins' team officials announced that Paige would be returning and available to pitch. Ryan stated, "Paige wants to pitch and we think everything will be okay."[24] Paige made his first appearance in uniform since being placed on suspension the night before Ryan's announcement, although he was not called on to pitch in the game. Arriving for duty at 6:30 pm, when the crowd of 3,252 spotted Paige warming up in the bullpen a slow swelling chant began to rise in the crowd: "We want Satch. We want Satch." Paige's exile was over and it was time for him to return. The fences between Ryan and Paige were temporarily patched. Manager Farrell was especially anxious and hinted to the press that his erstwhile prodigal son would be heavily counted down the stretch. Farrell chimed, "Well, we have only seven games left up north [three in Richmond and four in Columbus] and 17 games here and in Havana." He added, "You know Paige pitches best in Miami and against the Cubans."[25]

During Paige's absence the Marlins dropped six of ten games. In celebration of the expected return of their dispatched teammate the team reeled off an impressive 9–7 victory against Rochester. Gray reveled in his first win as a Marlin although it took some impressive relief effort by Windy McCall, pitching three and a third innings of scoreless work, to secure the win. The Marlins (63–65) now trailed the Red Wings by five games for third place and despite their poor play had been successful at keeping Columbus at bay for the fourth spot.[26]

Buffalo was next on tap. Since the All-Star break the last-place Bisons had been the hottest team in the IL. Paige was especially looking forward to the series and catching up with his old friend Luke Easter. And besides, "Satch" was looking to trim some more time off Snowden's sentence.

After losing two heartbreakers to the Bisons, 3–2, and 4–3, Farrell's charges bounced back by taking the final two games to sweep the double-header. Especially gratifying to Paige was winning the short game of the series-closing twin bill 6–1. Although most of the sports talk in town centered on the Floyd Patterson vs. Roy Harris heavyweight title defense at Wrigley Field, it was Paige who delivered a knockout blow when he held the Bisons to a pair of base hits.[27] Paige, who had recently switched to a lighter bat—one of Bob Usher's clubs—equaled his opponents' hit total by singling twice himself.[28] The only disappointment for Paige was his failure to strike out Easter.

Paige wasn't the only Marlin making headlines. Twenty-nine-year-old infielder Jerry Snyder was in the midst of a fourteen-game hitting streak and was playing a major role in helping the Marlins at least tread water in the standings. Over the course of the skein Snyder had collected thirty hits in fifty-six at-bats, all the while increasing his batting average fifty-six points from .257 to .313.[29]

With a critical series against visiting Columbus next on the board, the Marlins were looking forward to taking steps to secure a playoff position. There was loads of optimism since the Jets had failed in their previous eight attempts to win in Miami Stadium. Columbus (62–69) had narrowed the gap between themselves and Miami to only two games. Hacker, three wins and three losses on the season, was poised to start the August 19 opener. Columbus countered with one-eyed Charles "Whammy" Douglas. Douglas, who sported a glass eyeball, had lost his right eye as a result of a fight when he was eleven years old.[30] He had his sights set on spoiling the Marlins' hopes.

Although Douglas was prone to bouts of wildness he was right on the target this night. After allowing a solo run in the second inning, the right-hander proceeded to mow down the Marlins through eight innings. Douglas averaged 3.6 walks per nine innings during the course of the season, but on this night he seemed to have zeroed in on the strike zone. His only mistake was a pitch to Woody Smith that resulted in a solo home run. Hacker, who had started the season so well, had since fallen on hard times. Before exiting he allowed nine hits and four runs, heading to the showers after seven and two-thirds innings, the owner of the loss. New arrival Bob Miller fared even worse after replacing Hacker, allowing two runs in the ninth inning as the Marlins fell short of the Jets, 6–2.[31]

Hoping to turn their fortunes around, Farrell was confident that veteran McDermott would even the night's ledger. McDermott, who was known to imbibe more than a few adult beverages, was conspicuously absent as the game approached. Farrell was not amused. This was the third time in the same season that one of his players had come up absent. The first was Essegian, when earlier in the season he became upset when he was pulled for a pinch-hitter and temporarily walked out on the club. The second incident was the Paige–Ryan disagreement, and now McDermott going AWOL.[32] The third time wasn't a charm.

Forced to make a last-minute change, Farrell decided to turn to Conley, his most reliable starter, to face the Jets' best starter, Bennie Daniels. Whether out of sync or just plain mystified by McDermott's failure to appear for such a critical game, the Marlins came out flat. Backed by Daniels's own two sacrifice flies and timely hitting by Jets third sacker Leo Rodriguez, the Jets cruised to an easy 5–0 win. Things were so bad that Jerry Snyder, who had been on a recent tear, failed to collect a hit, ending his batting streak at fifteen games. Bennie Daniels stingily held Miami to just four hits. The Jets had managed to pull themselves into a virtual tie for fourth place with their opponents.[33]

Farrell and General Manager Ryan were beside themselves during and after the game. With little to say to the press the frustrated skipper's only comments were "All I know is that he [McDermott] knew he was going to pitch and he didn't show up."[34] The following morning *Miami News* sportswriter Norris Anderson was able to finally reach McDermott's wife, who had no comment except that her husband was sick in bed. Although there was some truth to the fact he was not feeling well, it was most likely related to his late-night antics rather than being under the weather. According to Miami police reports, McDermott had been ejected from two night spots that same night of the game and was arrested later. He posted bond for $100 and was given a court date of August 25 to appear before the judge.[35] McDermott was no stranger to the law or shirker of his own responsibilities. In his autobiography, *A Funny Thing Happened on the Way to Cooperstown*, he recounts his experience from the 1957 season:

> Having the lowest ERA in the league excused a multitude of my sins. Like the time Larry King, then a Florida DJ, was interviewing me on his show. We were both having such a good time that I forgot what time it was. Finally, Larry asked, "Aren't you supposed to be at the ballpark?" I looked at the studio clock, "Oops!" I said. "Oh well, if they've got the radio on they know where to find me." P.S. I missed the game. But that wasn't as bad as the time I missed two games. I lost track of time for an entirely different reason in a bar across the street and blew a doubleheader.[36]

McDermott was known as one of the most fun-loving guys who ever walked on the diamond. He was just as comfortable on a baseball field as he was in a nightclub singing and entertaining the crowd, but to his bosses he was a nightmare. The press loved him for always being quotable and cooperative and his teammates found him humorous, although after a few drinks he could be quite confrontational. No one doubted his work ethic, being the fierce competitor that he was. However, he could never escape his battle with his personal demons that derailed what might have been a record-setting career.[37]

The Marlins' officials were swift in handing down punishment, suspending McDermott for two days.[38] The punishment seemed light under the circumstances, but being short-handed on pitching, the team was more than anxious for "Maury," as his teammates liked to call him, to return.

For the second night in a row the Marlins fell to the Jets, 5–0. This time they were the victim of the Jets' newly acquired hurler Lynn Lovenguth. As Farrell had predicted earlier, when the trade between Rochester and Columbus was made it would have implications in the Marlins' quest for a postseason berth—and it did. As Yogi Berra once said, "It was *déjà vu* all over again." The Marlins again were held to four hits and Lovenguth was on top of his game, striking out five and handing out nary a free pass. The Jets scored all of their runs in the first two innings and made short work of Dallas Green, sending him to the bench with not a single batter retired for his efforts. The Miami staff had become so thin that pitching coach Bubba Church was activated and pitched the ninth inning of the game in mop-up duty. By breaking their eight-game losing streak at Miami Stadium, the Jets left town with renewed vigor, confident of taking the final postseason spot.[39]

Richmond was coming into town and the Marlins had now dropped five games in a row. Matters worsened when the Vees captured two of three games in the set, further putting a damper on the Marlins' playoff aspirations. Richmond won the first two games by scores of 4–1 and 7–1. Paige, now 10–8, was the victim of the 4–1 loss; despite pitching well "Satch" was sabotaged by four unaccountable errors, three alone by the usually sure-handed second baseman Jerry Snyder. Miami did salvage the series closer behind Conley, who evened his record at 11–11. Although among the league leaders with a 2.95 ERA, Conley had been beset by poor run support. It was thankfully the end of the worst homestand of the season, the hometown lads winning only four of the thirteen games.[40] Instead of making a run for third place, the Marlins were hanging on to their playoff hopes by a proverbial thread. Not only did the team play seem indifferent, but fan apathy had also set in. Concerns voiced by devotees were crying that Farrell had lost control of the club, that the proper talent wasn't in place, and that the team wasn't focused were being expressed openly by the local citizenry of Miami. William Styron, a loyal follower and member of the Coast Guard, summed up his feelings in a *Miami News* poll held at a local barber shop. He complained, "First of all good players move up to the majors. Second, they need a better manager. Third, I don't go for this suspension stuff they've been pulling." The local barber quickly piped in, "I'll tell you the real trouble. There's dissension on that ball club."[41]

Dissension or not, McDermott's return to the team renewed hopes that he could provide a shot in the arm that the team needed as they headed south to Havana for a four-game set. Traditionally Miami fared well against their rivals in Cuba, and with thirteen critical games left in the season, the Marlins were hoping for positive results. Farrell placed his faith in two of his most seasoned veterans, McDermott and Hacker, to face the Sugar Kings in the series opening doubleheader.

The series opening twilight contest saw the Sugar Kings sending to the hill their young phenom Mike Cuellar to do battle with the big Irishman McDermott. It was the promising upstart against the former promising upstart. Like the young McDermott, Cuellar was a bundle of talent looking for the right person to harness its enormous potential and focus it. Later in Cuellar's career the Baltimore Orioles, under the tutelage of Earl Weaver, would finally help Cuellar realize the potential that would culminate in four twenty-win or more seasons, a 1969 Cy Young Award, and 185 major league wins.

Both clubs tacked zeroes on the board until the bottom of the eighth inning when Raul Sanchez, a pitcher pinch-hitting for Hank Izquierdo, surprised McDermott by doubling toward Essegian in left. Elio Chacon replaced Sanchez on second as a pinch runner and moved to third after Cuellar sacrificed. McDermott then retired Yo-Yo Davalillo, only to give up a single to the next batter, Nino Escalera, plating the first and only run of the game. Despite pitching his heart out and allowing four hits while striking out seven enemy hitters, McDermott was hung with another loss.[42]

Miami bounced back in the nightcap. Hacker seemed to have regained his original form that he had when he first arrived in Miami. The former Cubbie shut down the Sugar Kings by scattering seven hits, striking out four, and not issuing a free pass the entire evening. Havana starter Rudy Arias, the proud bearer of a no-hitter against Rochester only a week ago, struggled the majority of the game, but successfully managed to keep the damage to a minimum. The Sugar Kings were trailing only 2–1 after eight innings. In the ninth inning came what proved to be the game breaker. Back-up catcher Jimmie Coker hit a 365-foot blast off Arias that left fielder Jack Daniels could only watch helplessly as it cleared the wall. The Marlins had gained the 3–1 edge. Bob Miller was called on to save the day in the bottom of the ninth, but promptly gave up hits to the first two batters he faced. Impatiently, Farrell, fearing that the game might get away, signaled to the bullpen for Hank Mason to get the final three outs.

Mason wasn't derelict in his duties and earned the save, giving the Marlins a hard-fought 3–2 victory.[43]

In the morning, rising from a much-needed rest from the previous night's contests, the Marlins, smarting for a disappointing split in the doubleheader, were relieved to hear the good news that the fast-approaching Hurricane Daisy, targeted to hit South Florida, was instead turning north. Dallas Green was scheduled to start the third game of the series. Green had struggled mightily all season, exhibiting a 4–10 record for all his efforts. Havana would counter with the right-handed string bean Manny Montejo. The summer weather, more humid and sweltering than usual, seemed to sap the energy from Montejo, who was lifted after five innings with the Marlins ahead, 4–1. Snyder, starting a new streak, continued his hitting rampage and poked two singles, a double, and a triple. Don Landrum and Woody Smith contributed three hits apiece to go along with Snyder's three-RBI performance, giving the Marlins an easy 7–3 win. The six-foot-five 210-pound Green fared slightly better than his opponent, but also folded under the intense humidity. Green lasted an inning longer than his opponent and stayed around long enough to gut out his fifth win of the season. He received some welcome help from Mason, who closed out the last three innings, earning his second save in two days. Combined with Columbus's 7–3 loss against Richmond, the Marlins (68–74) were now a scant one game behind the Jets (68–72) for the fourth spot, and they had Paige appointed to pitch the next night. Rochester (72–64) had pulled away from Miami, Columbus, and Richmond, pretty much securing third place.[44]

Paige's history against Havana was one of domination, having won eight times and losing only once in his three years with the Marlins. "Satchel Paige will pitch the series windup [tonight] and I think the old man can pull us up there," announced a confident and smiling Farrell.[45] Although his manager outwardly seemed optimistic, many had noted that since returning from the inactive list Paige seemed to have lost his focus and had been somewhat lackluster in his recent performances. Havana, the lowest-scoring team in the IL, wasted no time against the senior hurler and exploded for six runs, sending Paige to an early shower; he survived only three and a third innings. Gray quickly got warm and came in for relief to finish the inning, but faring little better than his predecessor as the Sugar Kings tacked on two more runs. After four innings the score was 8–1. Starter Emilio Cueche coasted the rest of the way, striking out twelve Marlins and earning the 9–2 win. The loss, combined with Richmond's 9–6 victory over Columbus, kept the Marlins one game behind the Jets with ten games left to play, and only one game ahead of the now fast-charging Vees for fifth place.[46]

The Marlins had a day off on August 28 but lost ground when Columbus beat the Vees 5–2. Bennie Daniels logged a strong outing by holding the visitors to six hits, pitching the complete game.[47] With Richmond on the ledger next, the Marlins were in no mood to drop down further in the standings. Columbus boarded their charter flight to Havana feeling good about their chances. On the other hand, the Marlins were staring over the cliff looking at elimination; although down, they were not out.

The next night Bob Conley was slated to face off against struggling right-sider Johnny James. For Conley, ninth in the league in ERA, this should have been an easy night. But, as experience had taught the Marlins all year long, nothing comes easy. Instead of James, it was Conley who played the part of the struggling pitcher. Richmond scored in the first inning but the lead was short-lived. The Marlins countered in the fifth inning when Bert Hamric hit a solo home run. The Marlins added two more in the sixth inning when Essegian blasted a triple, scoring both Snyder and Herrera, putting the Marlins on top, 3–1. The Vees knotted the score in the bottom of the sixth when Bobby Del Greco homered and Jerry Thomas worked his way around the bases and scored on a sacrifice fly, knotting the score at three apiece. Farrell, facing a near must-win situation, pulled his starter Conley after only five and a third innings of work and then both clubs traded zeroes until the fifteenth inning. With Hacker on in relief, he had been able to keep the Vees in check. Hacker finally weakened, allowing three singles in the bottom of fifteenth, the big hit coming off the bat of Deron Johnson, who drove in the winning tally. The loss was devastating and sent the Marlins spinning down into a fifth-place tie with Richmond two and a half games behind Columbus.[48] The "fat lady" was warming up, but the Marlins weren't ready yet to let her croon just yet.

Farrell's assessment for the rest of the season was to the point: "Let's face it. We have to win every game," said the urgent skipper with frank matter-of-factness. Farrell's next move was a surprise when Bunker was named as the starter to face the Virginians in the series finale. Back from his exile in the bullpen, Bunker had not won a game since July 10 and was drawing a tough opponent in Vees rookie right-hander Jim Bronstad, now carrying a 13–11 record. Bunker had been used sparingly by Farrell as of late, but his recent successes in a relief role had restored his manager's faith in him. Farrell's evaluation was that his southpaw was ready to recapture his early season magic.[49]

Whether Farrell called on one of the local fortune tellers or had his crystal ball fine-tuned, Bunker proved his mettle in a must-win situation. The Massachusetts native pitched a strong seven and a third innings, allowing only three hits and a solitary run. Bunker remained strong until the eighth inning. Johnny Gray was called in to put the icing on the cake and pitched scoreless ball the last one and two-thirds innings as the Marlins coasted to an easy 7–1 victory. The Marlins' victory, combined with Columbus's sweep of a doubleheader over the Sugar Kings in Havana, left Farrell's troops three games behind the Jets for the fourth spot.[50]

Upon returning to Miami and hearing the news that Columbus had finished off their series against Havana sweeping all four games, a disgusted Farrell launched a diatribe that was picked up by the press. Whether it was the heat of the moment that got the best of him, or the use of a clever ruse to motivate his players, nonetheless Farrell accused their biggest rivals, the Sugar Kings, of laying down in the series in order to ensure that Miami would be left out of the playoff picture.[51] Tom Keys, the executive editor of the *Citizen*, a Columbus newspaper, quoted Farrell as saying:

> That Havana club blew four straight to Columbus. They handed you four games . . . just handed them to you. I heard all about it from some pretty good baseball people when I arrived at the Washington airport, and I got the same story when I reached Columbus.[52]

Keys's story was page one fodder in the local Columbus papers. Farrell later claimed the comments were accompanied by a wink but George Trautman saw little humor in the remarks and set up a meeting with Farrell to discuss the matter. Farrell's claim was that he was just trying to jack up his ball club. Trautman listened intently but the outcome was predictable. Farrell was fined $300 for his remarks.[53]

With Columbus coming into town to start off a four-game set against the Marlins, Farrell stated that nothing less than a sweep was needed if the Marlins were to catch the Jets. To Farrell's consternation, Columbus was coming into town fired up and determined to put the pesky Marlins behind them. For the Monday doubleheader, Farrell put all his poker chips on Paige against Bennie Daniels in the first short contest, and Green versus Joe in the nightcap.

Perhaps sensing a bit of history was in the making, mixed with a touch of the playoff run fever, 7,882 crowded into Harold Cooper Stadium on an unseasonably cool Labor Day evening.[54] Ever since his suspension the rumors of Paige's departure from Miami had been running rampant. A local sportscaster had reported that Paige would definitely not be back in a Marlins uniform, to which Paige responded by denying the report.[55] Paige had pitched poorly in his last few outings, but there was always a high degree of confidence that in a do-or-die game there was no better man than the future Hall-of-Famer to get a must-win.

Farrell paced the dugout as Paige got off to a shaky start, giving up a quick first inning run. Both teams were quiet until the Marlins' half of the sixth inning. With Tompkins hugging second base and two outs, Daniels offered up a hanging curveball that Herrera couldn't resist. It looked as if the Marlins were going to take the lead as the ball sailed high and deep toward the left field fence. At the last moment the baseball took a bit of a turn just inches on the wrong side of the foul pole and the Marlins' hopes were dashed. Daniels didn't make the same mistake twice and retired Herrera to end the inning. Columbus added an insurance run in the bottom of the sixth after Herrera, adding insult to injury, booted a Paul Pettit groundball. Speedy Tony Bartirome was sent in to pinch run and later scored after a sacrifice and a Leo Rodriguez two-out single. The discouraged Marlins went down quietly, dropping the first game 2–0. It was Paige's tenth loss of the year against ten wins. It was also Paige's last starting assignment in a Marlins uniform.[56]

With their backs against the wall the Marlins turned to the "you never know what you're going to get" Green in the night game. Green seemed to have gained a second wind late in the season and was up to the task, pitching a complete game to hold the Jets to four hits and striking out eleven. Tompkins, with three hits and two RBIs, was the hitting star of the night. Shortstop Ken Hamlin wore the goat horns for the Jets, as his error in the five-run second inning led to a basketful of unearned runs.[57] The Marlins were still clinging to dim hopes as they remained three games behind Columbus with five games left to play and the Jets still with six contests on their schedule.

Conley drew the next night's assignment to face off against the always troublesome Lynn Lovenguth. Lovenguth had given the Jets a shot in the arm since being acquired in August, winning three and losing one, and Farrell was experiencing flashbacks, remembering how he had predicted that the right-hander would have an adverse effect on the Marlins' chances of making the postseason.

Clutch hitting proved the difference in the third game between the combatants. With the Jets leading 3–1 after five innings, the Marlins dropped their own three spot in the sixth. The key hit of the night was an Essegian double that scored a pair of runs. Getting in trouble in the seventh, Lovenguth was yanked with one out in favor of "Whammy" Douglas, who in quick order snuffed the Marlins' rally. However, Conley, who seemed to strengthen as the night progressed, shut down the Jets the rest of the way and earned his twelfth win of the season while holding onto the 4–3 lead. The victory narrowed the gap between the Marlins and the Jets to two games.

With renewed vigor in their step, the Marlins' bats came out with a vengeance in the final game of Columbus's last homestand, utterly destroying the Jets 11–2. Warren Hacker and Hank Mason combined to hold the hometown team to only six hits. Hamric and Essegian both homered and Landrum garnered three hits, igniting two Marlin big innings—a six-run seventh and a four-run ninth.[58] As improbable as it seemed, the Marlins were still alive and trailing Columbus by only a single game. Miami would travel to Havana for three games, while Columbus had the unenviable task of playing four in Richmond. Miami was counting on Richmond to help them out, all the while counting on Bunker, Green, and Hacker to sweep the Sugar Kings in Gran Stadium.

McDermott was originally scheduled to start the opening game against Havana, but had suddenly come down with a virus attack, leav-

ing him unable to pitch. Farrell adjusted his plans and named a reinvigorated Bunker to take the hill against Havana's fourteen-game winner,
Cueche. Every game was critical, and with Columbus playing a twin bill
in Richmond, the Marlins could conceivably move into fourth place with
a win and a Vees' loss.

Whether sensing the viability of a postseason paycheck or just an
increase in those flowing competitive juices, Paige stated to the local
press, "I wants to pitch relief wherever and whenever I is needed from
here on out." [59] Farrell had actually considered starting Paige in the opener against Havana, but instead played a hunch and went with Bunker,
feeling that he had returned to his early season form.

A larger-than-anticipated Friday night crowd of 3,133 pressed their
way through the gates. Many in the crowd were tuned into Bill Durney
and Sonny Hirsch on their transistor radios. Both broadcasters had a little
more giddy-up in their voices, perhaps sensing that there may be an
extension to the season. Miami got off on the right foot, plating a first-
inning run. What soon followed was the sound of the wheels coming off
Havana's chances. In the third inning, Coker singled off Cueche toward
left fielder Ultus Alvarez and Hamric raced around the base path with
Herrera following close behind. It looked to be a close play at the plate as
Alvarez's throw was on target. Hamric slid into home plate hard, jarring
catcher Alberto Alvarez, who mishandled the ball and dropped the
throw. Herrera then dashed in from third base to score and spot the
Marlins a 3–0 lead. After that the Sugar Kings came unhinged and by the
end of the inning the Marlins had built a 7–0 lead. The Sugar Kings' Al
Grandcolas tried to spark a rally in the sixth inning when he blasted a
Bunker mistake pitch over the left field wall, but it would prove the only
offense of the night of any consequence for Havana as the Marlins easily
prevailed, 7–2. Farrell's hunch had paid off. It was Bunker's first complete game since June 19 and his ninth win of the season. [60]

In the meantime, farther north, Richmond won the opening game of
their double dip 10–6, but dropped the second game 7–6. It took a Jets
miracle to avoid disaster. Columbus, trailing 4–2, scored five runs in the
top of the ninth inning, triggered by a Gair Allie pinch-hit double, giving
the Jets a 7–4 lead. Richmond mounted a comeback in the bottom of the
final frame and scored a couple of quick runs off of reliever George
O'Donnell before he finally settled down and closed out the win. Miami
now stood only a half game behind the Jets with both teams having only
two games left to play.

Saturday Night Youth Day promised to bring out the usual large
crowd. Although only 1,920 paying adults purchased tickets, over 4,700
kids crashed the gates in anticipation of the Marlins moving back to the
top half of the IL. Havana was still smarting from Farrell's accusations of
throwing a series and manager Tony Pacheco was hoping to play the role
of the spoiler. He named his ace Cuellar to oppose Miami's own Dallas

Green. Farrell had rolled over in his mind many times whether he should start Paige or not, but again decided to play another hunch and opted for Green in order to save Paige for emergency relief duty.

For the second night in a row, Miami scored in the first inning when Herrera singled and scored Tompkins. Miami added to their lead in the fourth inning when Herrera and Essegian both homered off of Cuellar, increasing the lead to 3–0. Until the sixth inning Green was cruising along like a '57 Chevy, before running into trouble and loading the bases. Farrell, not wanting to take any chances this early in the game, called on veteran McCall instead of Paige to squelch the rally. Farrell was still keeping Paige as his ace up the sleeve for an emergency. After McCall retired the first batter, with one out and ducks on the pond, he followed by coaxing an infield roller. McCall fielded the ball cleanly and forced the runner at home. Coker finished off the double play by nipping the runner at first base on a bullet throw to Herrera, escaping the inning unscathed. From there on out, Paige watched from the sidelines as the ex-Marine dominated and held the Sugar Kings to two base hits in the final four innings, preserving the win for the Marlins. Meanwhile, in Richmond, Columbus snatched another come-from-behind win, overtaking the Vees, 7–4.[61] With both teams having one game left on their schedules, everything was up for grabs. In order for the Marlins to make the playoffs, Columbus would have to lose to Richmond and Miami had to beat Havana. The Marlins could still slip in through the back door.

Scattered showers pelted the Miami area intermittently all day. For the crowd of 4,915 huddled beneath the cantilever overhang of Miami Stadium, there was no way a few raindrops were going to dampen their spirits for what would prove to be an exciting season finale. The Marlins were placing all of their marbles in the hands of Hacker to face an unknown string bean pitcher from Havana, Candido Andrade.[62]

Andrade was an unknown commodity to the Marlins hitters. The six-foot-five, 170-pound right-hander was making his first appearance in a Sugar Kings uniform. It seemed rather an odd choice for the skipper Pacheco to pick a rookie in such an important game, but he had seen Andrade pitch in Winter League ball and was very familiar with his skills. Perhaps the shrewd Havana manager was playing a hunch and had one up on his rival across the field. Although a mystery man to the Marlins, Andrade was a pitcher who had enjoyed some measure of success already. During his first season of minor league ball he recorded twenty wins for Class-C Tucson in 1957, and had pitched the majority of the 1958 season at Class-A Savannah, going 15–12 with a glossy 2.96 ERA before joining the Sugar Kings late in the season.[63]

Prior to the game the fans and press showed their appreciation to all the players. Especially honored in the pregame festivities was Woody Smith, garnering the team MVP award and Most Valuable Player as voted by the Miami press corps. Pancho Herrera was also honored for his twenty home runs, which broke the team's previous record of nineteen set by Bob Bowman back in 1956. It was the second consecutive year that Smith was voted the MVP. For Smith the award was bittersweet. Although he had enjoyed an All-Star season, it was another year passed that the Phillies failed to bring him up to the parent club for a September call-up. At age thirty-one, his window of opportunity seemed to have closed. Many of his teammates were scratching their heads, wondering why year after year the Phillies continued to look the other way, especially since the parent club was less than spectacular at the third sack position.[64] It was a sad commentary that, even though some players of lesser skills enjoyed a cup of coffee in the big leagues, a quality gentleman like Smith didn't even draw a look-see.

The reason for Smith's being overlooked by the parent club can be traced to an incident that took place a couple of years before involving a dispute between Smith and Phillies general manager Roy Hamey. Tom Qualters, a teammate with Smith on the 1956 and 1957 squad, remembered an incident during one spring that had repercussions later. Hamey, who was known to hold a grudge, probably was the chief hurdle in Smith's never receiving his call to the big leagues.

> *Tom Qualters*: Yeah, Woody Smith, I'll tell you a little story about him. He was probably the best defensive third baseman you could ever see. He was unbelievable, but he had a weak bat. So he had come to spring training, while down there, and it was in Florida. We just needed a body and there was no chance he was going to make the team and it was just obvious, I don't know what the hell they were thinking. They just didn't treat him right. They just didn't show him any interest in him at all. And he just packed his stuff and went home. Well, Roy Hamey was the general manager and he blackballed Woody.[65]

Smith later returned to the team, but Hamey never forgot how Smith walked out of camp. Hamey was the type that didn't forgive easily.

With all the accolades handed out, it was time for the combatants, including Smith, to get down to business and play ball. After two scoreless innings, Havana put the first score on the board when first baseman Rogelio Alvarez's liner skipped by right fielder Hamric for a triple. Grandcolas followed up by hitting a sacrifice fly and the Sugar Kings led 1–0. Hacker got in trouble in the fourth inning. After Escalera hit a shot to right field that was mishandled by Hamric for an error, Rogelio Alvarez followed and made Hacker pay by driving an offering 350 feet over the left field wall. With one out and trailing 3–0, Farrell, who was not in the mood for taking chances, quickly called upon his latest hot hand out of the pen, Mason. Hacker took his slow stroll toward the bench.[66]

Throughout the game, the PA announcer—and Durney and Hirsch on the radio in the press box—were keeping the fans abreast of the score in Richmond. The crowd noise rose sharply after the announcement, "Richmond 3, Columbus 2, after three innings." Cheering from the hometown crowd gave the Marlins a measure of inspiration. In the bottom of the fourth Herrera doubled, and making up for his earlier miscue, Hamric singled to center, scoring Herrera for the first run of the game. Miami was pounding Andrade all night and were again failing to hit with runners in scoring position, not to mention hard-hit balls that found enemy fielders' gloves. Paige made his final appearance as a Marlin, relieving Mason and sending the Sugar Kings down in order in the sixth inning. In the seventh inning the Marlins came to life. Rudy Arias relieved Andrade and promptly allowed Tompkins to single. Tompkins moved up on Smith's fielder's choice, and with two out Usher drove a single to left field, scoring Tompkins and closing the gap to 3–2. Arias settled down and big Bob Conley was called on to hold Havana at bay, hoping for his teammates to mount a comeback. Both clubs matched goose eggs the rest of the way. The Marlins had failed to rally and fell short, losing to the Sugar Kings by the score of 3–2. When the news came across the PA that Columbus had rallied late and beaten the Vees 9–4, the death dirge began.[67] The Marlins had fallen short.

A dejected Marlins team, some with sloped shoulders and others with towels on their heads, slowly made their way to the locker room, no doubt contemplating what might have been. Owner Storer met with the team after the game to express his appreciation for their efforts and wishing everyone well. It was little consolation to the club and its manager, who were about to scatter to the four winds.

Final Standings:

	W	L	GB
Montreal	90	63	–
Toronto	87	65	2½
Rochester	77	75	12½
Columbus	77	77	13½
Miami	75	78	15
Richmond	71	82	19
Buffalo	69	83	20½
Havana	65	88	25

The old cliché "too little, too late" was a fitting epitaph for the entire Marlins season. Looking back over the course of the year, it was the little things that came back to haunt the Marlins before they reached the finish line. Hard to ignore was Miami's failure in one-run games, posting a disappointing 20–33 record, teamed with their failures on the road, win-

ning only thirty-two of seventy-six games; it all added up to what otherwise may have been a promising season. One has to wonder whether
Paige's suspension at such an important juncture of the season cost the
team a game or two and a playoff spot to boot. If so, the blame rests
squarely on the shoulders of Ryan, who issued the suspension.

Farrell's dissatisfaction of a rare losing season must have weighed
heavily on him. Despite failing to make the playoffs, Farrell did express
his interest in returning. At the same time the skipper accepted little of
the blame for the team's misfortune. Instead, in his own words, he laid
much of the blame on his team's lack of fleet-footedness: "With more
speed we could have won some of those 33 games we lost by one run." [68]

An emotional and somewhat crestfallen Storer, in his appraisal of the
future of baseball in Miami, was a recipe of dourness mixed with a dash
of some hope. He forlornly stated to the press following the season-ending loss:

> I am hopeful we can work something out. . . . I feel we can generate
> enough interest to make Miami a good baseball town in years to come.
> It is a matter of whether I can keep taking these substantial losses until
> then. . . . We have some problems to eliminate, such as getting our own
> lease on concessions and keeping major league television out of the
> area. . . . Right now I am making no commitment for next year. [69]

For the second year in a row Storer reported losses of over $100,000.
By season's end the final tally in the Marlins' books showed the ledger in
the red for $125,000. Storer was staying in the game at least for now,
probably tantalized by the possibility of a third major league known as
the Continental League. The communication giant was willing to hang in
a little longer to see if baseball was indeed still viable in Miami. "I would
like to become a major league magnate," said Storer, all the while still
indicating that he was weighing his options on a year-to-year basis. [70]

With that the books closed on the 1958 season and the majority of the
ballplayers scattered in all directions. Montreal, who had finished in the
cellar the season before, cruised through the IL playoffs only to be swept
by Minneapolis (4–0) in the Junior World Series. Miami's affiliation with
the Phillies was in doubt and most of the departing players were not
expected to return. At the conclusion of the season Kerby Farrell hit the
road for Venezuela, having already signed to manage the Oriente team in
the Venezuelan Winter League. He didn't know whether he would be
asked by Ryan to return for a second term or not. [71] Ultimately, Farrell
would not be asked to return and instead landed on his feet managing
Buffalo for the 1959 season, the new Philadelphia Phillies affiliate. Both
Jimmie Coker and Don Landrum were called to report to Lackland Air
Base in San Antonio, Texas to serve a six-month hitch in the Air Force
Reserve. [72] Mickey McDermott had resigned himself to stay in Miami,
nursing his sore elbow and showcasing his velvet singing voice in clubs,

all the while keeping his hopes up that a major league team would call him. And Satchel Paige, disgusted with the treatment he had received at the hands of Joe Ryan, was now setting his sights on Hollywood. Shortly after announcing he would not return to the Marlins for another season, he was approached in late September to appear in the production of the movie *The Wonderful Country*, starring Hollywood heavyweights Robert Mitchum and Julie London. Miami had lost its greatest star. The loss of Paige was mourned by the fans not only in Miami but also around the whole IL. Baseball at Miami Stadium would never be the same.

NOTES

1. Tommy Fitzgerald, "Hacker Will Open Series for Miami at Buffalo Tonight," *Miami News*, July 29, 1958.

2. Ibid.

3. *Sporting News*, August 6, 1958, 34.

4. *Sporting News*, August 13, 1958, 35–36.

5. Tommy Fitzgerald, "Ryan Coaxes Satch off Plane after Paige Indicts Marlins for 'Cheating' on Money," *Miami News*, August 3, 1958.

6. Fitzgerald, "Ryan Coaxes Satch off Plane after Paige Indicts Marlins for 'Cheating' on Money"; Jimmy Burns, "Paige Suspended by Miami to Climax a Hectic Interlude," *Sporting News*, August 13, 1958.

7. Fitzgerald, "Ryan Coaxes Satch off Plane after Paige Indicts Marlins for 'Cheating' on Money."

8. Fitzgerald, "Ryan Coaxes Satch off Plane after Paige Indicts Marlins for 'Cheating' on Money"; Tommy Fitzgerald, "Paige Lost on Runout," *Miami News*, August 4, 1958.

9. Fitzgerald, "Paige Lost on Runout."

10. Tommy Fitzgerald, "Paige Asks Release," *Miami News*, August 5, 1958.

11. Tommy Fitzgerald, "Deal-Lovenguth 'Trial' Key to Marlins Loss," *Miami News*, August 4, 1958.

12. Tommy Fitzgerald, "Marlins in Private Meet," *Miami News*, August 9, 1958.

13. Ibid.

14. Norris Anderson, "Paige Offered Barnstorming Trip through the Orient," *Miami News*, August 10, 1958; Norris Anderson, "Paige Eager for Reinstatement," *Miami News*, August 10, 1958.

15. Anderson, "Paige Eager for Reinstatement."

16. Baseball-reference.com.

17. Tommy Fitzgerald, "Marlin–Leaf Riot Lasts 17 Minutes," *Miami News*, August 10, 1958.

18. Ibid.

19. Ibid.

20. Norris Anderson, "Blaylock August 'Money Pitcher,' Hexes Marlins," *Miami News*, August 13, 1958.

21. Ibid.

22. Anderson, "Blaylock August 'Money Pitcher,' Hexes Marlins"; baseball-reference.com.

23. "Jets Buy Lovenguth, Wings Get Pepper," *Sporting News*, August 20, 1958, 30.

24. Jimmy Burns, "Paige's Suspension Lifted, Old Satch Rejoins Marlins," *Sporting News*, August 20, 1958, 36.

25. Norris Anderson, "Satch Has 'Great Chance' of Returning Tonight — Ryan," *Miami News*, August 14, 1958.

26. Ibid.

27. Norris Anderson, "Miami Has Advantage in Battle of 'Homers,'" *Miami News*, August 18, 1958.

28. Anderson, "Miami Has Advantage in Battle of 'Homers'"; Jimmy Burns, "Paige in Form, Wins No. 10; Gets First Hits Since Mid '57," *Sporting News*, August 27, 1958.

29. Norris Anderson, "Snyder 30 for 56," *Miami News*, August 18, 1958.

30. Minorleaguebaseball.com.

31. *Sporting News*, August 27, 1958, 38.

32. Norris Anderson, "Farrell Pulls in Empty Line as Third Marlins Gets Off the Hook," *Miami News*, August 21, 1958.

33. Ibid.

34. Ibid.

35. Jimmy Burns, "McDermott's Night on Town Brings Two-Day Suspension," *Sporting News*, September 3, 1958, 32.

36. Howard Eisenberg and Mickey McDermott, *A Funny Thing Happened on the Way to Cooperstown* (Chicago: Triumph Books, 2003), 153.

37. "Mickey McDermott and Mr. Hyde," *Miami News*, September 22, 1958.

38. Burns, "McDermott's Night on Town Brings Two-Day Suspension."

39. *Sporting News*, September 3, 1958, 31–32.

40. Ibid.

41. Ray Biagiotti, "Man in the Barber Shop Solves Riddle of Tailspinning Marlins," *Miami News*, August 26, 2011.

42. Norris Anderson, "Marlins, Kings Swap Shaves, but Virginians Gain Ground," *Miami News*, August 26, 2011; *Sporting News*, September 3, 1958, 3.

43. Anderson, "Marlins, Kings Swap Shaves, but Virginians Gain Ground"; *Sporting News*, September 3, 1958, 3.

44. Norris Anderson, "Is Playoff Payoff Spurring Marlins to Better Things?" *Miami News*, August 27, 1958.

45. Ibid.

46. *Sporting News*, September 10, 1958, 29.

47. Ibid.

48. Special to the *Miami News*, "Marlins Fall Back into Tie for Fifth," August 29, 1958.

49. Special to the *Miami News*, "Can Miami Pull Small Miracle in Jets' Series?" September 1, 1958.

50. Ibid.

51. Earl Flora, "Farrell Fined $300 by Trautman for Saying Kings 'Tossed' Series," *Citizen*, September 10, 1958, 29.

52. Ibid.

53. Flora, "Farrell Fined $300 by Trautman for Saying Kings 'Tossed' Series."

54. Special to the *Miami News*, "Jets Hoping to Finish Miami Soon," September 2, 1958.

55. *Sporting News*, September 10, 1958, 30.

56. Special to *the Miami News*, "Jets Hoping to Finish Miami Soon."

57. Ibid.

58. *Sporting News*, September 10, 1958, 30; special to the *Miami News*, "Marlins Still Alive," September 4, 1958.

59. Norris Anderson, "Marlins in 'Must' Games," *Miami News*, September 6, 1958.

60. Norris Anderson, "Who Said Marlins Are Dead? Pressure's on Columbus Now!" *Miami News*, September 7, 1958.

61. *Sporting News*, September 17, 1958, 38.

62. Norris Anderson, "Marlins Drop $100,000 Second Season in Row," *Miami News*, September 8, 1958.

63. Minorleaguebaseball.com.

64. *Sporting News*, September 17, 1958, 38.

65. Tom Qualters, phone interview with the author, March 5, 2010.

66. Anderson, "Marlins Drop $100,000 Second Season in Row."

67. Ibid.

68. Ibid.

69. Jimmy Burns, "Storer, Marlins Boss, Wants Club in Third Major," *Sporting News*, September 17, 1958, 40.

70. Ibid.

71. Anderson, "Marlins Drop $100,000 Second Season in Row."

72. *Sporting News*, September 17, 1958, 38.

TWENTY-ONE

A Farewell Ode to "Satch"

Perhaps it was a wise sage, whom I don't recall right now, who once said, "We all have in us a book waiting to be written." If that's the case, then Leroy "Satchel" Paige would be a library with an extra wing attached. For three years, Paige toiled in Miami, much to the delight of not only the hometown fans but all those who idolized him throughout the IL, the United States, and the world for that matter. When Paige made an appearance, the turnstiles clicked and team owners loved it. Never before, or since, would a bigger star shine so brightly on the green grassy fields of Miami than the man with the rubber arm made of gold.

During his tenure in the IL fans became familiar with his recognizable trademark big, comfortable easychair in the bullpen. His late arrivals to games were legendary around the league, but the fans and his teammates held no ill feelings toward him for living by his own set of rules. However, the team owners, general managers, and managers for whom he performed sprouted more than a few gray hairs dealing with a man who refused to live by their constraints. He was a burr in their saddles, and it was this continuing cycle of Paige's that kept him moving his whole career. His utter disregard for team rules, endless disagreements over financial matters, and penchant for showing up for games at his convenience eventually would wear out his welcome. Ultimately the end was always the same: when he faced discipline he would start to plot his next move and thus the cycle would begin again.

Seemingly, Paige had found some level of contentment in Miami and was even contemplating retirement. He had become more of a homebody and was spending more time at home enjoying his kids and wife Lahoma, where she was now managing most of his affairs. Still, it was also not unusual to find him hobnobbing with his old friends like Duke Ellington or Fats Domino, occasionally taking the stage to sing a few notes when they were performing in Miami.[1]

However, he admitted in his autobiography, *Maybe I'll Pitch Forever*, that going back on the road was an option.[2]

Although Paige was enjoying his private time at home and cavorting with his friends, he was considerably dissatisfied with his baseball life. The handwriting on the wall was when Bill Veeck left after that first season; anyone who knew Paige knew it was just a matter of time before he'd get the itch to move on to the next opportunity. By his third season his continued run-ins with team officials—most notably General Manager Joe Ryan—over money matters and his continued utter disregard of team rules had accelerated to the point that it had reached a head, and Paige was insinuating he was ready to part ways. Strangely enough it wasn't baseball that called, but Hollywood and the silver screen. Late in September 1958 he was approached to be in the movies and signed on the dotted line to appear with Robert Mitchum and Julie London in *The Wonderful Country*.[3] With little hesitation Paige left the sandy beaches of Miami for the bright lights of Los Angeles.

Theatrics were no stranger to Paige and whatever performance he projected on the big screen paled in comparison to his exploits on the playing field. Many of his teammates remember fondly some of those feats, including a throw that left everyone speechless.

> *Tom Qualters*: Bases are loaded. Yeah, bases are loaded and this guy hits a one-hopper right back at Satch. He catches it, and our dugout of course is on the third base side, and Satch starts walking to the dugout. And he didn't even look at first base, and if anything he caught the ball and started walking to the dugout. And he keeps walking, my first thinking is "Oh hell, he thought he caught it on the fly." And he kept going, and all of the sudden the people start screaming and he never turned around or anything and he's walking toward the dugout and he lifts up his arm, left arm, he throws the ball under his arm a perfect strike to first base, and I think Frank Herrera was playing first base then, and beats the runner by a step and a half. And I thought, "Holy hell, what is this?"[4]

> *Mel Clark*: It might have been another game. It was opening game that I remember. They had a runner on third with two outs and the manager asked Satchel if he could get the last man out. He said, "You better believe it." And he went out on the mound and threw five or six warm-up pitches. And the first ball, I remember, was hit right back to him on a hop and the guy was scoring from third and he made a couple of strides toward third base and threw the ball back under his arm to first base. I followed him into the dugout and he said, "I had him by a step and a half." Oh boy![5]

> *Jack Spring*: Anybody tell you about one of the first times he ever pitched? That was quite a story, too. I think it was maybe his first

appearance and he came in relief in the ninth inning and there must have been two outs, I'm sure there was, and I don't remember the score or who we were playing. But anyway, he came in and the hitter hit a one-hopper right back at him. You know not real hard or just nice easy one or two bouncer. He caught the ball. Our dugout was on third base side, but he turned and started walking off the field like he was leaving, like he caught it in the air or something. He lifted his left arm and whipped the ball underneath his left arm with his right and threw a perfect strike to first base and just nipped the runner at the end of the game. And Don Osborn was almost passed out in the dugout; he was having a heart attack.

But we found out later he practiced that. I used to every once in a while see him out in the corner of the outfield with a batboy, or something, and he would be practicing throwing without looking. And that's the first game he pitched in and I'm not positive that but I'll never forget it. We all 'bout had a heart attack. He's got the last out of the game with a throw to first base without even looking.[6]

Paige's confidence in his abilities was legendary. He never hesitated to take the ball in any situation, especially in critical scenarios. Although his nerves were jangling a bit when he pitched in the famous Orange Bowl game, no one playing behind him had any inkling of his nervousness and every last one of his teammates had the utmost confidence in his abilities.

Listed as six feet, three inches and his weight at 180 pounds, Paige was still intimidating on the mound. Whip-thin, he appeared to be all arms and legs. One can imagine the team trainer must have weighed Paige in his wool uniform soaking wet to arrive at that generous scale reading. "Satch" was a master of psychology and used everything in his arsenal, including getting into his opponents' heads to upset their timing with his endless trash talk, and an endless assortment of pitches. Although he had lost some of his legendary speed by the time he arrived in Miami, opponents were still in awe of his skill and ability to place the ball wherever he pleased, often befuddling even the most confident hitter.

> *Bill Durney Jr.*: He was a big man. And Satch, as skinny as he was, was just an opposing looking figure on the mound. You know he wasn't a bulky man at all. He was just imposing looking on the mound.[7]

A naïve but quizzical rookie remembers approaching Paige during an early appearance in 1958. Paige, ever so certain in his abilities on the mound, was somewhat perplexed when the raw rookie first baseman approached him on his pedestal to make an inquiry.

> *Fred Hopke*: The first time he came into pitch I went over to the mound and I said, "Satchel, what kind of move do you have to first base?" He kind of had a nickname for me. He called me "Fatboy." He said, "Fatboy, when I have to throw to first base I'm getting out of the game."[8]

No one loved a challenge more than Paige, and during his stay in the IL his biggest rivalry was when he was pitted against his old friend and nemesis from the Negro League, Luke Easter. Easter and Paige developed a close relationship and even shared their Cadillacs when travel necessitated the use of wheels. On the field it was all business but good-natured when the two jawed back and forth, and the fans loved it.

> *Bob Bowman*: In fact, Luke Easter and Satchel had quite a thing going on. When Satch pitched against him they talked to one another; yelled back and forth. I remember one night in Miami Easter hit a home run over the centerfield fence off of Satch. That was really a blast. And Satch followed him around the bases, yelling at him all around the bases, but good naturedly.[9]

> *Ray Semproch*: I'll tell you one thing, he and Luke Easter used to go at it. I'll tell you, that was funny. The people used to love it because he would holler to Luke, "Here comes a curveball. Hit it Luke." We had a lot of fun.
>
> Oh yeah, those two, I'll tell you, it was like Laurel and Hardy.[10]

> *Jack Spring*: Like I say, I didn't have a great season myself personally as far as individual games. It seems like most of memories about that team around revolve around Satch. I remember one game he pitched against, I think it was Columbus [actually Buffalo], but I can't remember for sure. They had a guy named Luke Easter. A big guy. I think he and Satch had played together in the Negro Leagues, or something, I can't remember for sure. But anyway, Satch pitched every Sunday. We used play those nine- and seven-inning games, doubleheader, but one of them was seven innings and Satch would pitch the seven-inning game which as I recall was the second game. But anyway, we were playing, I'm pretty sure it was Columbus [Buffalo], Luke Easter came up, he was a left-handed hitter. . . . Anyway, he hit a home run off of Satch in the first inning and Satch kind of walked around the infield, shook his finger at him, and yelled at him as he went around the bases, "That's all you're getting big boy. That's it. That's all you're getting."
>
> And by god he struck him out as I recall the next two times, or three, whatever and he didn't get another smell out of it. We were dying in the dugout laughing. He kind of walked around the edge of the grass and followed him around and said, "You ain't getting no more."[11]

> *Tim Anagnost*: There was a great confrontation that I saw between Satchel Paige and Luke Easter. Luke Easter, I think, played for Buffalo, and he was a left-handed hitter. At the time I was at Miami Stadium, which was a really neat stadium because it was symmetrical. It was like 330 down the lines, 375 in the power alleys, and I think it was 400 in straight away center.
>
> And of all of the time I was the batboy I saw very, very few home runs go out of right field. Somebody told me much later that because of

the wind currents or something the wind would hold up the ball in right field.

Well, 330 wasn't too bad, but for some reason there weren't a lot of home runs but particularly in right field. In right field they had the scoreboard also over there.

I remember Luke Easter getting up against Satchel Paige. And they would talk to each other. You know you could see them, I couldn't actually hear everything they were saying, but I know they were talking to each other. Satchel Paige apparently liked to talk to people and Luke Easter was talking back. And I'm watching this and then I see the longest home run I've ever seen in right field hit by Luke Easter off of Satchel Paige.

And my friend told me that he saw that game as well and he said that he remembered before that or after that on the next at-bat that Satchel Paige struck out Luke Easter. And he remembered them talking back and forth talking all the way back to the dugout.

So these guys had a thing going and we got to watch that, you know. So it was fun. But Luke Easter hit the longest home run that I saw in right field in Miami Stadium.[12]

Easter aside, Paige also had numerous pitching rivals across the diamond over the years. One of the most unique games he pitched was against the Sugar Kings in Havana on July 11, 1956. Paige, then fifty years old, faced off against another senior citizen, forty-five-years-young Connie Marrero, in a classic duel under the stars. Combined ages of the two were nearly one hundred years, but you could never tell by the way they mowed down their much younger competition.[13]

Mel Clark: I enjoyed playing with Satchel Paige. He was quite a guy you know. I enjoyed him very much. But I remember one day we were playing in Cuba. He, Satchel, was pitching and starting. And there was a pitcher, Connie Marrero, who had pitched for the Washington Senators. He was starting for Havana and [chuckling] Satchel had him 1–0. And the bases were loaded in the fifth, and I can remember this very well, and he worked the count 3 and 2 and struck the guy out. We won the game 1–0 and he walked off the mound and told the manager to take him out and said, "That's all I had left."[14]

Paige worked six innings, allowing five hits and striking out eight. Marrero also logged six frames before leaving the game. Paige, however, had the satisfaction of earning the win, thanks to Ray Holton's single in the top of the seventh that plated Larry Novak. It would be the last time the two baseball-lifers would meet head to head.

As legendary as his numerous deeds on the field were, his exploits off the diamond were equally so. Over the course of interviewing several of Paige's teammates and others who knew him, the stories they told were so vivid that if you didn't know any better, you would swear they happened yesterday. Besides the never-ending hijinks with the "Dalton

Gang" and other teammates, they told of the leisurely fishing trips, mixing with his celebrity friends, and nights on the town; without exception, everyone whose path crossed his was touched in a positive and profound way.

Qualters, who credits Paige for saving his pitching career with the sage advice of "the sons-of-a-bitches can beat ya, but they can't eat ya," remembers fishing excursions that he and some of his teammates enjoyed with "Satch" on their days off. Miami was very much a city of the Old South and in turn a city where segregation and accompanying Jim Crow laws were still in force. Qualters and his teammates were perplexed by the unfair standards that would not allow their black teammates to travel back and forth and move freely around the marina area on the east side of town. In order to share fishing excursions with Paige and Mason, Qualters and his fellow players had to acquire special work permits for their black teammates that allowed them access to the docks to charter a boat for their expedition.

> *Tom Qualters*: I organized a couple of trips where we would get one of those boats and they would take you out. One of the problems was you had to get out there on the island, to around the beach area to get to the marina where the boats where actually at. In those days, they didn't let black people on the beach. And they didn't allow them across the Causeway, they would stop them, unless you had a work permit.
>
> You know, we got Satch out there, Henry Mason another black guy; they went along. What I can remember about Henry he would get seasick every time we'd go. Henry must have been a city boy. . . . And Satch would always bring the day's catch to the locker room.[15]

Qualters enjoyed a close relationship with his father. As a youngster his dad shared stories about seeing the great Satchel Paige pitch in the Negro Leagues. Qualters was taken aback when he came across segregation Southern-style for the first time and was appalled by the treatment that Paige, Mason, and Herrera received while traveling south of the Mason-Dixon line.

> *Tom Qualters*: I came from an area where Satch played baseball for a number of years here for the Homestead Grays and Pittsburgh Crawfords. And I was too young to see any of that at the time, but my dad did. My dad would tell me stories about how great these players were and everything. So one of the early conversations I had with Satch was just about that.
>
> We struck up a very close relationship. . . . In the South he couldn't stay in hotels with us and all of that stuff. That was shocking to me, you know. Of course my friends up here knew I played sports in school with black kids and hell, we were best of friends. . . . Here Satch wasn't allowed to even stay in the same hotel with us.[16]

Over the course of the two years that Qualters was a member of the Marlins, he developed a close relationship with Paige. One of his great regrets surrounded a special party. Qualters, who, like many at the time, was unsure of Paige's age (fifty years old), was left to wonder what good times would have been had if he gone to the gathering.

> *Tom Qualters*: I know that Satch had his 55th, he was going to be fifty-five, or fifty-six. Anyway, he was going to have a birthday party and I was invited to his birthday party at the Sir John Club, a night club down in Miami. I was danged if I could find it and I said, "I'll never find that place and get lost." I said, "I've got a wife and three kids." And he said, "We'll get you there, we'll get you there." I regret to this day I didn't go; I'll bet that was a circus.[17]

Paige loved life and lived it to its fullest extent. However, on a minor league salary he frequently found himself short of money and was constantly seeking pay advances to supplement his lifestyle. When Bill Veeck ran the club this wasn't a problem, but following his departure from Miami it soon became a constant source of disagreements between General Manager Joe Ryan and Paige. Dick Bunker remembers an evening when Paige woke him from a sleep to borrow some cash. Bunker used the moment to advantage to satisfy his curiosity.

> *Dick Bunker*: Oh God, I have some great stories about Satch. Jesus! I think I'm the only one that ever knew exactly how old he was and I'll tell you why. In 1957 or '58, I think it was '58. I think I told you before that we were in Richmond and he couldn't stay with us, you know. He couldn't stay at the hotel. At 2:30 in the morning the phone rang. And I picked it up and I said,
> "Hello."
> And he said, "Youngblood."
> I said, "Aw, Satch what are you doing? What time is it?"
> He says, "Two-thirty."
> "What the hell do you want?"
> He said, "I need some money."
> Oh, I says, "How much do you want?"
> I think it was $50. Holy Christ, I think that was the most. We didn't even get that much meal money back then, I don't think.
> But I said, "Oh, $50. I can't give you $50, Satch."
> He said, "So, I need $50, Youngblood."
> "Okay."
> So he said, "I'll meet you down at the side door in about ten minutes."
> So I got dressed and snuck down the back there. He pulled up with some lady he was with in a Pink Cadillac. I met him at the side door.
> So, he said, "Give me the money."
> "Tell me how old you are and I'll give you the money."
> He says, "I'm fifty, add a couple and now give me the damn money."

So I figured it out, [this was in 1958] fifty and add a couple would have been fifty-two and his mother, his mother who would swear that he was born in 1906. So July 6, 1906. So she said he was born then. She kept all the records. She had fourteen children and she kept all the records in a family Bible. And one day the husband, Satch's father, went under the cherry tree and was reading the Bible and he fell asleep and the family goat ate the Bible. That's the truth. And so that she never really knew but she said that he was born in 1906 so that would figure out to exactly how old he was.[18]

Paige was quite the chap about town, not to mention a ladies' man. Many of his teammates recall how in each city tickets would be left at the gate for Mrs. Paige, but inexplicably it was a different woman each time. In Larry Tye's biography, *Satchel: The Life and Times of an American Legend,* Spring remembers Paige introducing him to two women, both as Mrs. Paige. "I'm not sure which was, but both were quite pretty ladies. Satch seemed to be a bit of a ladies' man but he didn't flaunt it," recalled Spring.[19]

Wilbur Johnson remembers Paige's charms with the ladies and his manager Don Osborn sending him and trainer Doc Ritter on a mission to find Paige to have him ready to pitch for an upcoming game.

Wilbur Johnson: Oh well, he didn't even have to look for them, they were waiting for him as soon as we got off the airplane. When we got to the airport they were waiting, beautiful black women.[20]

Wilbur Johnson: And then another thing about him . . . we would see Satchel Paige save the game that night and we wouldn't see him for five days or a week. Either he went out with these girls or he went out on benders. We would never see him until he showed up at the ball-park. He paid his own way and one day he had a bout of gout.

Doc Ritter was our trainer and Don Osborn went up to Doc and he said, "I want you to take the rookie." That was me. "Take the rook, and go see where Satchel Paige is and tell him I need him. We needed him to pitch. I'm short on pitching."

So Doc Ritter and I went out and we looked at a couple of address-es. Finally we knocked on this one door in a motel and there's Satchel Paige in there with two beautiful women stripped naked. Either I opened it or Doc opened the door, and he says, "Satchel, it's Doc."

He opened the door and says, "Doc, and Shorty, what are you doing here?" He says, "Come on in."

He was stripped naked.[21]

Paige sure loved the ladies and one is left to wonder what he must have been like in his heyday. Paige had a complex personality and had his eccentricities. He disliked flying, cold weather, and driving slow. On many road trips he opted to drive himself to wherever the Marlins were scheduled to play, or in some cases board a train, rather than taking the team's charter flight. "Airplanes may kill you, but they ain't likely to hurt you," said Paige.[22] Probably because he grew up in the South, he was accustomed to pitching in the hot weather and thus acquired an aversion to chilly temperatures. Although his stroll to the mound was slower than molasses pouring in Michigan in December, he loved to drive fast and amassed quite a collection of speeding tickets, which he was as skilled at eluding as he was slipping a fastball by an enemy hitter.

> *Bob Bowman*: He didn't like to fly that much and whenever he could he took the train or some other way to go.[23]

> *Tom Qualters*: We were in the clubhouse one spring, it was colder than hell, horribly cold, and I was going to pitch the second game of a doubleheader. And Satch if it was cold on the field he would stay in the clubhouse and if they needed him he would come.[24]

> *Jack Spring*: Another thing he did when it was real cold and he wasn't pitching, or he wasn't starting, he would just stay in the clubhouse where it was warm. He wouldn't sit out on the bench. Yeah, he didn't like that cold weather.[25]

One idiosyncrasy that Paige possessed was carrying quite a collection of luggage wherever he went. He always carried a special suitcase that he filled full of gifts that people would bestow upon him as he traipsed from city to city. Johnny Gray recalls one of the many times he saw Paige toting his array of baggage, this time at the airport.

> *Johnny Gray*: Satchel Paige showed up there too. And you know when he showed up I got the biggest kick out of seeing him. Because Satchel Paige was actually called Satchel Paige, I think because he carried so many satchels with him. I mean he had three or four suitcases. He had, I want to call it a Victrola. He took everything with him. He was a piece of work. He just loaded up. I can't believe he carried that much stuff.[26]

Paige frequently let bellboys at the hotel, or the porters on the railroad, assist him carrying his various bags. But he was known to carry one particular satchel that only he was allowed to touch that carried his famous snake oil and other assorted potions. It was all part of his own remedies held to keep his arm in shape, not to mention calm his stomach and ease the throbbing bunions that occasionally plagued him. Based upon the results, whatever Paige and the witch doctor he consulted had concocted proved effective.

> *Bob Usher*: After he pitched he would take a shower and he had a bottle, and I said, "What do you got in there?" He said, "That's my lucky potion." I said, "What do you put in it?" He said, "I can't tell ya."[27]

Besides his magic potion Paige had other remedies that kept his ageless arm loose and comforted his assortment of ails. He was renowned for keeping physical exertion to a minimum, although he loved a good game of Skidoodle on the sidelines. Two of the most famous quotes credited to

Paige were "Avoid running at all times" and "I don't generally like running. I believe in training by rising gently up and down from the bench." He certainly lived by his own sage advice.

> *Tom Qualters*: Satch would unscrew the nozzle on the shower head so that there was one heavy strong bead that would come down and he would turn that thing on and gradually make it hotter, and hotter. He did that all his life and got back out there. I sometimes wonder about this icing thing. You couldn't stick your hand under there, it was burning. . . . I'm telling you, the steam would come out of there.[28]

> *Wilbur Johnson*: He never had a sore arm. And then he'd put some kind of oil juice on his arm and rub it around awhile. And then he never ran. He never took a wind sprint in his life. What he would do for exercise, he would go the days he wasn't pitching, he would go to shortstop and he'd have the guys hit ground balls to him. And then he would flip them underhand all the way to first. And he'd flip the ball and he say, "Help me. Help me." He would just lazily go over there and that was his training.
>
> [Mentioning that it didn't take long to loosen up his arm] That's right. And he could be loose, and loose by three pitches. That is very true. And he threw every day. He never had a bad arm in all those years he was barnstorming. You know he'd throw three innings a day and throw the rest of the week three innings and never come up with a sore arm. He was tall and skinny. He was all bone.[29]

> *Johnny Gray*: But he was a funny, funny man. He'd come up there and we'd be running our ass off and Satchel would turn around and he says, "Son." And someone says to him why don't you run? And he says, "Son, I need all the energy I got."[30]

Paige had his humorous side and part of his value was his ability to relate to all of his teammates. He kept things loose in the clubhouse and despite his status as a legend he considered himself to be on equal ground with his fellow players, whom he loved to banter back and forth with all the time. One of the most famous stories involving Paige is him playing the game GHOST with his teammates. (GHOST is a word game that is a spelling version of the basketball shoot-around game HORSE.)

> *Dick Bunker*: I told this story maybe a thousand times. You know I used to give talks and stuff when I got out of baseball. And I always said I played with the great Satchel Paige. And I had this story. And anyway, it's a story about we're on a bus and we're going from Toronto to Montreal, or Montreal to Toronto. We would just take a bus, you wouldn't fly. So we're on the bus and we played this game called, oh what was it called, Ghost. It was called Ghost. And the reason it is called Ghost is that it was a word game. So in other words somebody started with "A," and the next guy said "B," and you'd have to keep adding on to this word without making it a word. Get me. Okay, so

you had to keep adding on so that you don't end up with a word then you get like G,H,O,S,T and the first one that gets Ghost loses.

So anyway, we were playing one night and the guy starts out with "Q." So we all go, the only thing that follows "Q" is "U." So the next guy says "U." So Satch was next and then I was after Satch. So you have about two minutes and then you challenge the guy.

So Satch goes, "Q. U. C. Q. U. C."

God, I thought and I thought and I thought and said, "Jesus, Satch, I don't know, I got to challenge it."

He says, "I got you this time, you hot dog; cucumber."

That's a true story. I told this doctor friend of mine and he's told it a hundred times and gets so many laughs out of it. That's a true story—cucumber.[31]

Jack Spring: You hear the cucumber story. Well we had this little game we played. They, we were waiting around at airports for buses or the bus to the ballpark or something. We had this little game and we'd start this spelling game. I guess somebody started with a letter and say it and a guy after would make a letter and keep going until somebody made a word. And then of course they were out of the game if they made a word. So Satch loved to play it. Satch was pretty good. So one day they were playing it and the guy next to him started it and said, "Q." No, I'm sorry, Satch started the game, and that was it—Satch gave the first letter. He said, "Q" and the guy next to him said, "Satch, I challenge that." And he said "Cucumber." Just as fast with no hesitation. He was ready.[32]

Paige was a man with a multidimensional personality. Along with having fun he also had his serious side. Somehow he found the time to develop other skills besides painting the corners of a strike zone. As his teammates would soon come to find out, his talents were not confined to the baseball diamond. He was a skilled musician, a crooner and a writer of sorts. One of his favorite performers to sing along with was Al Hibbler. He was known to frequently join the singer on stage.[33] During his time in Miami he had already begun writing his memoirs, and he was known to haul a typewriter with him wherever he went. In 1962 Paige released his autobiography, *Maybe I'll Pitch Forever*, which was a great success. Paige was truly a Renaissance man. Qualters remembers an especially enlightening encounter with Paige.

Tom Qualters: Yeah, I can tell a story. We were up in Buffalo, New York. This was when it was very early in the season. And I didn't know what to do with myself. So, it was night. I went down the elevator and I stepped out and there was hardly anybody on the streets. And here's Satch standing there leaning against the building. So, we spent quite a bit of time talking stuff and me asking him a bunch of crazy questions.

Anyhow, we walked back inside this motel, or hotel, and he looked over. And there had to be a room in the lobby. And there was a piano in there. And he says, "Let's go in there."

And we went and I sit down beside him on the bench. And he starts playing this piano. And I'm telling you, just real soft, slow, beautiful music. He would just play and play. I'm telling you, he could flat out play the piano. That shocked me, and I'm sitting there thinking in mind sitting there, how in the hell did he have the time to learn to do that.

So then I come to find out he was an avid guitar player. And there was a group of singers. I think it was three brothers, and their dad. I don't know what the heck their name was, but they were popular, and they were on television back in the day. And I hear something happened to the dad. He had a heart attack or something, either died or couldn't perform anymore, and here these brothers called "Satch." They wanted him to join their band, him being one of the singers. And he also played the guitar and was going to take the place of the dad. That was pretty interesting.

He could sure sing. We would be down in the bullpen and he would have all the guys sing all the time. Some were terrible. Some were pretty good. You'd go down there and get singing, you know, and Satch would stop everybody and then he'd teach each guy his part, you know, in different harmony, which was pretty hard to do with our guys. He had a great voice and he could harmonize and he could tell you how you were supposed to harmonize with the music and everything.

So he wasn't just a baseball player; the guy had a lot of talent.[34]

Bob Bowman: He was writing his memoirs then. I could remember, let's see in Montreal I think it was. I got a phone call couple of times from him wanting to know how to spell this, or how to spell that. And I said Satch, you got to get yourself a dictionary. I wasn't much of a speller either really. Satchel really was a character and a great guy.[35]

It has been over fifty years since his teammates shared the field with Paige, yet the impressions he left were long-lasting. Some, like Tom Qualters, credit him with saving their careers and others just remember him in awe and recount stories of glories long past, a few life lessons they learned, and good times that will remain with them forever. Others simply idolized him. And whether they were a teammate, the batboy, or the son of the team's broadcaster none had a disparaging word for the greatest pitcher that ever lived.

Ray Semproch: Satch, that was a great guy. Hey, he was somebody that kept the team laughing and kept us loose, let's put it that way.[36]

Jack Spring: But of course, one of the neat parts, or one of the things that I'm most, remember the greatest was about Miami was Satchel Paige was on that team. And he, it was an honor and looking back what a thrill it was to play with him and get to know him and be around him that summer it was quite an enjoyable time.[37]

Tom Qualters: When we went north, you know Satch would come down to the room and he wanted to go outside and walk around and wanted one of us to go with him because he wanted to go shopping or whatever. So, we spent a lot of hours off the field and he was just one of the greatest people I have ever been around. . . . We would sit side by side by each other in the bullpen and I don't know you just, I don't know, I think he was just the most interesting person that I ever met in my life. I drove him crazy; I asked him so many questions. It was funny, in fact the last time I seen Satch, I might have been with the Chicago White Sox, I'm not sure who I was with then, and he came to Miami in spring training before we were heading north and you know we started kind of barnstorming north. Or no, I was still with Philadelphia, that's the year that I got traded to the Chicago White Sox. And so here we were sitting in the bullpen and it was still when they had white sections and black sections and then all of the sudden I'm sitting there and I hear Satch hollering at me. I turn around and here he had walked down into the white section and we shook hands and talked for a while. And I said, "What are you going to do?"

He says, "I'm going to try to help out the NAACP and doing that kind of stuff."

I said, "Well good luck."

And then we parted and he goes up the steps and I holler at him, "Hey Satch, be careful."

It startled him and with "Satch" things got pretty wild. And that was the last time I got to see him. [38]

Tom Qualters: The thing about it, and I have pitched baseball to this day, and one of the things that impressed me was we would play, go down to third base and have some pitcher with a fungo bat hit ground-balls to us. And our third baseman, and maybe Satch and I, we would play for a Coke, or money, or whatever. And if you booted a ball that was a point against you, and whoever ended up with the fewest points won. And they hit balls down there, and I'm telling you, Satch, he'd get those balls. But the thing that impressed me most was, and we threw the ball to first base, every time he'd throw the ball, I don't care where he was at, or what the situation was, every time he threw the ball it was a strike. And it was just a focusing mechanism, I think, and where you just don't pick it up and throw it in the general direction, you know you throw a strike. And I teach that to my kids to this day because I know it benefited me.

You know when you're in a pressure situation and the ball is hit back at you and you just don't turn and throw it. I've made some bad throws and I, because of Satch, learned to catch the ball and throw a strike. You know it works. [39]

Fred Hopke: Oh, I loved him. I followed the guy; I followed him around like a puppy dog. You should've seen it. It was really something. And we really hit it off. And he took good care of me the short time I was there. As a matter of fact, he went to the general manager Joe Ryan, I think his name was, and pleaded for him to keep me. But they sent me down to A-ball. [40]

Tim Anagnost: He was always nice to me. I mean, like everybody was equal, and it wasn't like he was terrible to the people that didn't treat him right. Nobody ever treated him like a superstar that I saw, they just liked him and everybody kind of got along. [41]

There are too many accolades to fit in this book to describe what a great man Satchel Paige was. In Wilbur Johnson's fifty-plus years in baseball as a minor league infielder, minor league manager, and scout beating the bushes of America, he crossed paths with Paige several times. He saw him still barnstorming into the 1960s and visited with Paige on several occasions in clubhouses in the lower minor leagues. In Kansas City, sharing memories with his old friend Buck O'Neil, Johnson cherished hearing the stories of past triumphs, no doubt seasoned with a little embellishment to add flavor to the tale. Although simple and to the point, "Moose" may have said it best: "The most amazing man I ever saw in my life." [42]

NOTES

1. Larry Tye, *Satchel: The Life and Times of an American Legend* (New York: Random House, 2007), 235.

2. David Lipman and Satchel Paige, *Maybe I'll Pitch Forever* (Garden City, NY: Doubleday, 1962), 269.

3. Ibid., 279.

4. Tom Qualters, phone interview with the author, March 5, 2010.

5. Mel Clark, phone interview with the author, March 15, 2010.

6. Jack Spring, phone interview with the author, March 16, 2010.

7. Bill Durney Jr., phone interview with the author, December 21, 2010.

8. Fred Hopke, phone interview with the author, February 20, 2011.

9. Bob Bowman, phone interview with the author, February 22, 2010.

10. Ray Semproch, phone interview with the author, April 11, 2010.

11. Spring interview.

12. Tim Anagnost, interview with the author, May 9, 2010.

13. "Paige, 48, Beats Marrero, 41, in Pitching Duel, 1–0," *Sporting News*, July 18, 1956, 34.

14. Clark interview.

15. Qualters interview.

16. Ibid.

17. Ibid.

18. Richard Bunker, phone interview with the author, May 26, 2011.

19. Tye, *Satchel: The Life and Times of an American Legend*, 221.

20. Wilbur Johnson, phone interview with the author, March 11, 2010.

21. Ibid.

22. Brainyquote.com.

23. Bowman interview.

24. Qualters interview.

25. Spring interview.

26. Johnny Gray, phone interview with the author, February 28, 2010.

27. Bob Usher, phone interview with the author, March 13, 2011.

28. Qualters interview.

29. Johnson interview.

30. Gray interview.

31. Bunker interview.

32. Spring interview.

33. Mark Ribowsky, *Don't Look Back: Satchel Paige in the Shadows of Baseball* (New York: Simon & Schuster, 1994), 314.

34. Qualters interview.

35. Bowman interview.

36. Semproch interview.

37. Spring interview.

38. Qualters interview.

39. Ibid.

40. Hopke interview.

41. Anagnost interview.

42. Johnson interview.

Part IV

1959

TWENTY-TWO

Storer's Ultimatum and New Birds in Town

"I will get out of baseball after the 1959 season," announced Marlins owner George Storer. The communications magnate gave his final ultimatum that after two seasons of losing stacks of cash, enough was enough. He added, "The only way I would think of continuing would be for the club to break even this next season."[1] The Marlins' fourth season in Miami was again plagued by the question of whether or not professional baseball would survive.

Fan interest was steadily declining each year despite the close race to the finish line that had the Marlins in the playoff hunt until the last day of the season. Although a policy instituted by General Manager Joe Ryan allowed youngsters (seventeen years and under) free admission on Saturdays, including a few specially designated dates, there were several theories bandied about why fans were staying away from the ballpark. The encroachment of major league baseball's television and radio broadcasts, the distractions of the South Florida sun and sand, and even betting on the horses and jai alai were all mentioned as the reason for fan apathy. Although not counted in the final attendance numbers, the kids' promotional days accounted for 74,934 extra customers, making it a success in terms of drawing interest to the club.[2] But, despite the valiant efforts of Ryan and his promotion team, overall attendance suffered as the Marlins finished the season with 183,681 paid admissions, down 22,075 from the year before.[3] Just to show how terrible the situation was, in comparison the seventh-place Buffalo Bisons, cellar dwellers for the majority of the season, drew 287,814.[4]

Along with the dreadful attendance figures was the fact that Storer was still working under an unsatisfactory lease with Miami Stadium that was costing him $40,000 a year along with a less-than-ideal concessionary contract with the Jacobs Brothers Sports Services that further sliced into the team's potential profits. Ultimately, revenues generated from ticket sales were not enough, and unless there was a radical turnaround in fortunes, Miami would be left without professional baseball.

In hopes of turning their fortunes around the Marlins reached a mutual agreement with the Philadelphia Phillies to break their ties with the club, thus allowing them to become independent. However, the funds available to sign players was restricted by a tight budget and in order to supply the team with quality players, Ryan would ultimately sign on with the American League's Baltimore Orioles under a limited working agreement that essentially made them a second Triple-A affiliate, along with Vancouver of the PCL, of the parent club. Ryan would even go a step further, accepting some players on loan from the Detroit Tigers' and Washington Senators' minor leagues to fill roster spots.

Ryan was sticking to his familiar plan of mixing veteran players, many of whom were nearing the end of their major league careers, with the upcoming prospects supplied by the Orioles. Ryan, a shrewd evaluator of talent, knew that he needed a skipper who could teach the young guys as well as placate the veterans, who oftentimes could be difficult for rookie managers to handle. Storer and Ryan, perhaps hoping to bring back past glories, turned to a face that was very familiar to Miami supporters. The decision was made to hire fifty-five-years-young Johnny Leonard Roosevelt "Pepper" Martin.

Miamians were very familiar with Martin, dating back to his early managerial days when he skippered the local Sun Sox (1949–1951), the Fort Lauderdale Lions (1953), and the Miami Beach Flamingos (1954), all members of the Class-B Florida International League. His inspiring leadership culminated with five successful seasons, compiling a glossy 417–263 record. Martin also brought along his longtime assistant coach Bill Cates to help with his new club.[5]

The energetic, piss-and-vinegar Martin may have looked older than his years, wearing his craggily sun-weathered face like a badge of honor, but he was still spry enough to swing a bat and had made a plate appearance for Double-A Tulsa the previous season. Martin was a dry cleaner's dream. For those who fondly remembered his playing days with the Cardinals, his uniform was perpetually soiled and in disarray as if he had just rolled out of bed ten minutes before. Sometimes he would show up just before a game with oil and grease smeared on his uniform, a result of working on and racing midget automobiles—one of his many hobbies outside the diamond. As a ballplayer he was remembered for performing in each game as if it was his last. Although short on natural ability, he used every bit of his heart and soul combined with hustle to make up for his athletic shortcomings, establishing himself as the leader of the 1930s famous Cardinals "Gashouse Gang."[6]

With Martin in tow, the Marlins announced a change of venue for their 1959 spring training site. This year's workouts and scheduled games would be held in Miami Beach's Flamingo Park at the corner of 14th and Michigan Avenue in Miami. Located in an area known as South Beach, it was a ballplayer's dream. As part of the spring training schedule the Marlins slated jaunts to Puerto Rico and Cuba as part of their warm-up for the regular season.[7] Martin, not known for his book knowledge but long on street smarts, sounded downright scholarly when he spoke with *Miami Herald* writer Jimmy Burns: "We plan to use some psychology to instill certain resolutions into our players," said Martin. He added, "Sometimes our practices will be drab and colorless, but we'll always have a purpose in mind. We hope to plant the seed of expectancy in the sub-conscious mind by working on the little things and the fundamentals."[8]

Some early reportees made their way into camp, including major league veterans Foster Castleman and Harry Byrd. There were also familiar faces from the year before filtering into Flamingo Park to burn off some winter fat—the likes of catcher Johnny Bucha, infielders Woody Smith and Jerry Snyder, outfielder Bert Hamric, and pitchers Windy McCall and Bunky Stewart all reported ready for duty. And then there was Mickey McDermott, who of course showed up late.[9]

Along with the veteran presence, there were some fresh faces that would have an impact on the team during the year. The Orioles were especially excited about two prospects from Class-B Wilson: speedy twenty-four-year-old outfielder Fred Valentine and twenty-year-old peach-fuzz-faced pitcher Jack Fisher. Valentine was coming off a big year in which he hit a blistering .319 along with sixteen homers, and Fisher had also caught the eye of the Orioles' brass, notching an impressive 14–13, 3.62 ERA record during his first full year of pro ball.[10]

Some other rookies in camp making positive impressions on their new field general Martin were outfielder Leo Burke, whom Martin would convert to a second baseman, and hurler Jim Archer. Burke was coming off his first productive season in the minors, where he hit an impressive .307—combined with seventeen taters—in Knoxville of the Class-A Sally League. Archer, on the other hand, had kicked around the minor leagues for seven years. He lost three valuable seasons early in his career due to active military duty starting in 1952. Archer returned for the 1955 season and pitched in the Class-B Piedmont League, where he put together solid numbers, winning nine and losing ten with a 2.88 ERA. In 1957, Archer appeared to have put it all together in Class-A Knoxville, dominating enemy hitters and putting together an impressive record (17 GS, 11–6, 1.89 ERA).[11] It seemed as if the hard-throwing left-hander was finally getting his shot at the big leagues when he was called on to meet with Paul Richards in his office.

Jim Archer: He [Richards] called me in the next day and he said, "You just didn't make it just now. We've got pitchers here established and we're going to send you down to San Antonio in the Texas League. It's a good league, one of the best classifications for AA ball."

And so I said, "Do I have a choice?" to Paul Richards.

"Yes, you have a choice. You can bust your ass and hope that someone picks you up, if we don't pick you up, or you can go home."

Guess what I did? I picked up my bags and flew to San Antonio. [12]

As is so often the case in life, adversity proves to be the very springboard that vaults an individual toward his ultimate goal. At a crossroads in his career, Archer, instead of hanging up his cleats, chose to stay in the game. With renewed focus on attaining his goal of pitching in the big leagues, he reported to San Antonio in 1958 and completed the season. He would spend the next couple of seasons in a Marlins uniform, and later land a job in the major leagues in 1961 as part of the Kansas City Athletics starting rotation.

With most of the roster spots filled, General Manager Ryan continued working feverishly on the phones, fine-tuning the roster and seeking to make last-minute deals. One area of concern was catching. Bucha, who had rotated the season before with Jimmie Coker, was the only backstop returning with extensive experience. Ryan spent considerable time negotiating with Senators owner Calvin Griffith and the Marlins were able to secure the services of major league veteran Steve "Hoss" Korcheck. [13] During the 1958 season he served as the Senators' third-string catcher, batting .078 in fifty-one at-bats. His best season in the professional ranks was in 1955 when he split time between Charlotte of the Sally League and Chattanooga of the Southern Association, hitting a combined .270 in 103 games. [14] The former football star center from George Washington University added much-needed depth to a position the Marlins were most lacking in coming into the season. Known for his excellent handling of pitchers, he was a welcome addition to Martin's roster. [15]

Korcheck, who spent time in the big leagues with the Senators in 1954, 1955, and 1958, [16] reminisced about his time in Miami, one of his favorite stops during his career.

> *Steve Korcheck*: It was the Baltimore club, and they needed a catcher, and so I went to Miami. In fact, my son ended up being born in Miami, Jackson Memorial Hospital. And I had a good time there, Sam. You know, Pepper Martin was our manager and he was just a great guy to play for. And it was great.
>
> I told somebody, if I had to play in the minors, the greatest was the International League to play because you went to Montreal, Toronto, and Havana. You can't get it better than that. [17]

To bolster the pitching staff, Ryan made a couple of last-minute deals and signed two veterans: John Anderson from the Phillies [18] and forty-one-year-old Virgil Trucks, recently released by the Yankees.[19] Twenty-six-year-old Anderson, a fixture in Miami, was enjoying his fourth season in a Marlins uniform. Anderson (4–5, 3.23 ERA)[20] had performed admirably during the 1958 season in the role of a swingman. Anderson would hold a distinction of being one of only two players to wear the blue and orange each season the team was in Miami. The only other was Woody Smith.

Trucks was an especially intriguing signing because of his advanced age. The Miami newspapers and the *Sporting News* made light of the fact that the Marlins had trimmed twelve years off their payroll by signing the veteran after the release of Satchel Paige.[21] In 1938 Trucks, a minor league sensation, struck out 420 batters in the Alabama-Florida League. The ex-Tiger was finishing up his stellar major league career (177–135, 3.39 ERA) and hoping for one more shot at the big leagues. Trucks had spent the majority of his playing time in a Detroit Tigers uniform, joining their starting rotation in 1942. Among Trucks's highlights were two starts in the 1945 World Series, winning one decision; a 1949 All-Star game victory, twirling two no-hitters during the 1952 season with Detroit; and a twenty-win season in 1953 while splitting time between the St. Louis Browns and the Chicago White Sox.[22]

With Trucks in tow and the rest of his roster intact, Martin, along with his coaches Bill Cates and newly signed pitching coach Lloyd Brown, and the Marlins were ready to kick off their fourth season with an April 14 opener against the defending champion Montreal Royals.

Gone but not forgotten, Paige was still ranting and raving over the fact that the Marlins had yet to fulfill their financial obligation to him. "They owe me the money and I got it in black and white to prove it," complained the ornery veteran.[23] Despite Paige's grumblings, Storer, Ryan, Martin, and their new charges were optimistic, paying little attention to the once-popular veteran. After all, there was work to be done, and just like every season's Opening Day, the always optimistic players had the comfort of knowing, at least briefly, they were tied for first place.

NOTES

1. "Miami's Storer Seeking Exit in Red Ink Deluge," *Sporting News*, December 17, 1958.

2. Jimmy Burns, "Marlins Hosts to 74,934 Kids at Games This Year," *Sporting News*, September 10, 1958, 29.

3. Jimmy Burns, "Storer, Marlins Boss, Wants Club in Third Major," *Sporting News*, September 17, 1958, 40.

4. Cy Kritzer, "9,240 Fans See 7th Place Bisons in Closing Game," *Sporting News*, September 17, 1958, 37.

5. Jorge Figueredo, *Cuban Baseball: A Statistical History, 1878–1961* (Jefferson, NC: McFarland, 2003); baseball-reference.com.

6. John Heidenry, *The Gashouse Gang* (New York: Public Affairs, 2007).

7. "Miami Marlins Book Spring Visits to Puerto Rico, Cuba," *Sporting News*, March 11, 1959, 17.

8. Jimmy Burns, "Pepper's Spiel of Training Keeps Marlins and Fans Spellbound," *Sporting News*, March 25, 1959, 24.

9. Baseball-reference.com.

10. Ibid.

11. Ibid.

12. Jim Archer, phone interview with the author, February 21, 2010.

13. "Marlins Snag Korcheck," *Miami News*, April 4, 1959.

14. Baseball-reference.com.

15. "Marlins Snag Korcheck," *Miami News*, April 4, 1959.

16. Baseball-reference.com.

17. Steve Korcheck, phone interview with the author, April 11, 2010.

18. "Bingo! Marlins Hit Player Jackpot," *Miami News*, April 5, 1959.

19. "Marlins Go for Youth, Cut Paige 52, Sign Trucks 40," *Sporting News*, April 22, 1959.

20. "Bingo! Marlins Hit Player Jackpot," *Miami News*, April 5, 1959.

21. "Marlins Go for Youth, Cut Paige 52, Sign Trucks 40," *Sporting News*, April 22, 1959.

22. Baseball-reference.com; John Brattain, "Blast from the Past: Virgil Trucks," January 4, 2005, www.hardballtimes.com.

23. "Marlins Go for Youth, Cut Paige 52, Sign Trucks 40," *Sporting News*, April 22, 1959.

TWENTY-THREE

Pepper Off to Good Start

Painted clouds on the blue sky canvas hovered lazily in the distance as Miamians stepped briskly up to the turnstiles of Miami Stadium. Program hawkers, ticket takers, and a bit of a cool nip in the air greeted the spectators as they filed through the runways. The familiar palm trees standing like soldiers just beyond the centerfield wall swayed a "hello" greeting for the onlookers strolling to their seats for the curtain-raising Opening Day.

Marlins owner George Storer sat in his usual seat, scanning the sparse crowd taking their places throughout the ballpark. Bill Durney and Sonny Hirsch were anxiously filling the airways with greetings and introductions for another new season, while Storer was no doubt contemplating his next move as his third season as owner began to unfold with the usual disappointing fan turnout.

IL president Frank Shaughnessy was projecting league record attendance and based on Opening Day crowds he had to be encouraged—the exception being Miami. In Columbus, 14,138 Jets fans turned out to see their hometown boys. Farther south Bobby Maduro's Sugar Kings were close behind with 14,106 customers, perhaps many in the crowd drawn to the game to see Fidel Castro throw out the first ball. And in Richmond, despite an inhospitable forty-six-degree chilling blast, the Virginians drew a respectable crowd of 7,116 into Parker Field. Meanwhile, in Miami, where the climate-friendly temperatures dipped down into the low sixties, the numbers belied reasonable comprehension as a mere 3,504 loyal rooters were chaperones to several empty seats.[1]

Opening Day Starting Lineups:

Montreal Royals	Miami Marlins
CF Thomas Humber	CF Fred Valentine
LF Sandy Amoros	LF Chuck Oertel
3B Clyde Parris	SS Foster Castleman
RF Bob Lennon	C Johnny Bucha
SS Harry Schwegman	RF Bert Hamric
1B Tim Harkness	2B Leo Burke
C Mike Brumley	3B Woody Smith
2B Don Domenichelli	1B Bill Lajoie
P Rene Valdes	P Harry Byrd
Manager: Clay Bryant	Manager: Pepper Martin

Strolling out to the mound for his warm-up tosses was six-foot-one right-hander Harry Byrd. The thirty-four-year-old veteran was no stranger to ups and downs. Earning a cup of coffee with the Philadelphia Athletics in 1950, he was less than impressive, making six appearances in ten and two-thirds innings with a 16.88 ERA. In 1952 he returned to the A's and at the age of twenty-seven reached the pinnacle in his career when he won the American League (AL) Rookie of the Year Award, finishing with a 15–15 record along with a sparkling 3.31 ERA. The following season the bottom fell out and Byrd led the AL in losses (11–20, 5.51 ERA). Although he hung around the big leagues until 1957, and even pitched for a short time with the Yankees, he never again attained the success that he enjoyed in 1952.[2] Byrd, like many veterans in the IL, was hoping for one more shot at the big time.

On the opposite side of the diamond Montreal Royals' field general Clay Bryant chose six-foot-three Cuban right-hander Rene Valdes to oppose Byrd and with any luck thwart Miami's hopes of bringing home an Opening Day victory.

The experienced Byrd started off sluggishly. In the first inning he allowed the first three batters he faced to reach base. Tom Humber walked, Sandy Amoros singled, and Clyde Parris reached on a free pass putting "ducks on the pond." Byrd settled down and retired the next two batters without incident before Tim Harkness doubled, scoring the trio and spotting the Royals a 3–0 lead. Miami was not able to counter until the third inning when Chuck Oertel singled and advanced to second after catcher Mike Brumley mishandled a Valdes offering. Foster Castleman then singled, advancing Oertel to third. Valdes, seeming rattled, allowed Johnny Bucha to single and the Marlins scored their first run of the season. Bert Hamric followed with the Marlins' fourth consecutive base hit, moving Castleman to third. Valdes became further unglued and un-leashed a wild pitch. Castleman raced home and cut the Royals' lead to 3–2. Smith followed by smacking a long sacrifice fly that scored Bucha, evening the score at three apiece.

The Marlins tallied single runs in the seventh and eighth innings. The Royals also added one of their own runs in the eighth to keep the score close; going into the top of the ninth inning the Marlins held a 5–4 advantage. Byrd regained his composure and settled down after a shaky start, but ran into further trouble in the ninth inning. With one out, Brumley singled and then advanced to second when Don Domenichelli sacrificed. Pinch-hitting for relief pitcher Ron Negray, Bob Wilson was hit by an errant pitch. Martin, seeing that Byrd was cooked, turned to the bullpen and called on Windy McCall to retire the next batter, Amoros. The one-time Brooklyn Dodger left fielder was having none of that and tapped an infield roller and through sheer hustle Amoros legged out a single, load-ing the bases.

In what must have looked like old folks' night at the park, Martin went to his bullpen again and called on another one of his graybeards. Known for his sour disposition, crusty thirty-nine-year-old left-hander Karl Drews strolled to the mound to face the right-handed-hitting Clyde Parris. Why Martin chose a lefty instead of sticking with the right-hander McCall is unknown, but the results didn't justify the strategy, as Drews promptly walked Parris to tie the score. Drews redeemed himself when he retired the next batter, Harkness, to send the game into extra frames, but the damage had been done.

Both teams exchanged scores in the twelfth inning. Fred Valentine, utilizing his best weapon—speed—delivered in the clutch in the same inning with a single, advanced to third base on an Oertel single and then scored on Bucha's sacrifice fly. After twelve innings the score was knot-ted at 6–6.

Mickey McDermott replaced Drews in the twelfth inning and had his best fastball working. He continued to mow down the Royals through the fourteenth inning. By this time only a few souls were left in the stadium. Facing Royals' reliever Babe Birrer, the Marlins finally broke through. In the bottom of the fourteenth frame McDermott helped his own cause by ripping a single. Valentine followed with a double, but the slow-footed McDermott was unable to score. Hoping for the force at home or a double play, Oertel was walked, leaving Birrer to face Bill Davidson. Martin, perhaps anxious to get home to a warm stove, sent in pitcher Rolf Scheel to pinch-run for McDermott. Davidson, an ex-Yankee shortstop prospect who had been inserted earlier in the game for Castleman, stepped up to the plate. With one out and the bases full Davidson lofted a soft fly on a mistake swing to right fielder Bob Lennon. Although the lazy fly ball didn't appear to be hit deep enough to score the runner, as soon as the ball landed in Lennon's glove Scheel broke for home. Martin yelled out,

"Hold it," but to no avail. Lennon threw a laser home, but his throw was wide right of catcher Brumley and Scheel crossed home plate with the winning run, all thanks to Davidson's sacrifice fly. The final tally showed the Marlins as winners, 7–6, to the delight of the few spectators sprinkled throughout a near-empty Miami Stadium. "I already had gotten too good a start and I was afraid of being thrown out at third if I went back," said Scheel after the game. Ironically, the two unlikely heroes Scheel (3 G's, 1 GP) and Davidson (9 G's, 6 AB) would have rather brief stays in Miami and Davidson's RBI would be his first and last as a Marlin.

With his team starting the season off on a positive note Martin was looking forward to the rest of the club's sixteen-game homestand. Following a day off the Marlins continued their series with Montreal, splitting a doubleheader. Newcomer Jim Archer dropped the opening game 3–2, losing the seven-inning affair in extra innings after allowing an eighth-inning RBI single to spoil his debut.[3]

In the aptly named nightcap, something Marlins rooters would find as appropriate attire, for the third straight game the contest went into extra frames. Starter John Anderson pitched well into the eighth inning before his knuckleball failed him, allowing the Royals to tie the score at five in the eighth inning. Windy McCall finished out the eighth frame and remained strong for the next one and two-thirds innings before being removed for a pinch-hitter. Martin, not wanting the game to slip away, beckoned Opening Day starter Byrd to start the tenth inning. Although he walked three batters in two innings, Byrd kept the Royals' batters in check through the eleventh inning. Woody Smith, obviously tired of working overtime, put on the hero's cape and with two outs hit a walk-off single, upending the Royals 6–5.[4]

Montreal finished the series the next day by thumping the Marlins, 8–3, as right-hander Mel Held, in the throes of his last season in organized ball, took the loss. Martin once again turned to his veteran trio of Drews, McCall, and McDermott to save the day, but for the first time in the young season they faltered. Some ominous notes were sounded by veterans McCall and McDermott, both complaining of sore arms. McCall actually asked to be removed from the game and clarified in the clubhouse later, "I asked to be taken out because my arm didn't feel right." McDermott also fretted, "My arm isn't strong enough for that much work."[5] Martin had been depending heavily on his veterans early, but was coming to the realization that he might need to work his younger arms more often. Ultimately, this would open the door to little five-foot-nine, twenty-four-year-old reliever Artie Kay to establish himself as the Marlins' chief arm out of the bullpen.

Next came one of the more peculiar contests of the season: Martin would turn to his batting practice pitcher to secure a win. The Toronto Maple Leafs were next on tap and Martin decided to go with his fifth different starting pitcher in as many games. Although Artie Kay would be used primarily in a relief role during the season, he was called on to serve as the starter against Toronto in the series lid-lifter. Miami led off the scoring in the first inning on three consecutive singles by Oertel, Castleman, and Bucha, the hard-nosed catcher the recipient of the game's first RBI. Bert Hamric contributed a fourth straight base knock by tripling and driving in two more runs and the Marlins lead stood at 3–0. Miami tacked on another run in the second inning to pull ahead, 4–0. Kay, who had never pitched more than seven innings in any single appearance in more than three years, struggled in the third inning and surrendered a couple of runs. Sensing that Kay didn't have his best stuff, Martin made a pitching change. To everyone's surprise, Martin hailed Charles Parsons from the bullpen. Parsons, a native of Nova Scotia, had spent the previous season with the Yankees farm team in Richmond and had only been used in spot duty. With the Vees, he accumulated an unimpressive 2–6 mark and utilitarian 3.62 ERA.[6] With no one out and the Leafs threatening the right-sider, Parsons, who hadn't pitched a single inning in spring training, calmed down the mighty Leafs bats and escaped the rest of the inning unscathed, holding the Marlins' 4–2 lead. Impressed by his performance, Martin stuck with his batting-practice pitcher, who promptly shut down Toronto the rest of way, allowing one run on four hits and earning the well-deserved 5–3 victory.[7] Parsons, like Davidson and Scheel, would appear only ever so briefly in a Marlins uniform, appearing in just three more games before disappearing into baseball obscurity. Before exiting Miami Stadium for good, though, he would add one more decision to his record, closing his ledger with a perfect 2–0 record.

Postseason prognosticators had envisioned the Marlins as a team doomed to finish at or near the bottom of the IL. Nevertheless, early season results were giving rise to higher expectations. After splitting their first series with Montreal, the Marlins took three out of four from Toronto, split four games with Buffalo, then closed out their homestand by taking three of four from Rochester. The only loss to Rochester came on a night that found senior statesman Trucks making his first start of the season. Celebrating his forty-second birthday, the cagey old-timer did little to lift his own spirits as he struggled with control all night, walking eight Red Wings and surrendering the mound after only three innings of work.[8] Despite all the bluster by the press surrounding the one-time Tigers star, his career in Miami would be short-lived, as he would only appear in four games before calling it quits.

The good news for the Marlins and their supporters was that early returns showed the Marlins in first place. Much of the Marlins' start was attributed to the hot hitting of shortstop Foster Castleman and outfielder Fred Valentine. Castleman's club-leading twenty-four hits, along with a sparkling .429 batting average, and Valentine's twenty-three hits and a .329 average from the lead-off spot were setting the table for success. On the mound, Jack Fisher (2–0, 1.50 ERA) and John Anderson (1–1, 2.25

ERA) were among the league leaders in ERA as part of a solid rotation that also featured Byrd (3–0) and Archer. The one major weakness thus far in the starting corps was Held, currently holding down the fifth spot.

Miami's first true test of the season was the upcoming thirteen-game road trip beginning in Montreal, followed by Toronto, then Richmond before finishing off by flying south to Havana.

Arriving at Delorimier Stadium, the Marlins were greeted by a sight that they were unaccustomed to seeing. Some 5,864 Royals rooters filled the park with almost triple the crowd that Miami Stadium had been drawing on most nights. Skipper Martin was especially happy to return to Montreal, where he once made quite an impression on the local sports enthusiasts as a member of the Brooklyn Dodgers and all without the use of a bat or glove. The Brooklyn Dodgers? No, not the baseball Dodgers but the football Dodgers. In an exhibition game against the local football Alouettes, Martin made a special appearance and much to the surprise of locals booted five field goals. Martin admitted, "I kicked so hard that day that I tore some muscles in my thigh and had to give up professional football for good."[9] Fortunately for everyone, Martin stuck with hardball. Not to be deterred, the Marlins kicked off the first game away from home by displaying some rare offensive muscle.[10]

Royals starter Birrer was chased with no outs in the second inning after giving up five runs. First baseman Bill Lajoie coming into the game, and batting only .133, hit his first home run of the season, spotting the Marlins a 1–0 lead. Leo Burke followed with a double and then pitcher Jack Fisher singled his teammate home. When Fred Valentine followed with the inning's fourth consecutive hit, manager Clay Bryant had seen enough and called on Roberto Vargas. Vargas walked the bases full, allowing Oertel to reach first base, and then Castleman plated Fisher on a force play. With only one out, Hamric singled in another run and the Marlins were up 4–0. Before the inning ended Woody Smith singled in yet another run, putting Miami in the driver's seat, 5–0.[11]

Vargas had failed to get out of the second inning. The Royals' bats were, for the most part, silenced as Fisher earned the complete 11–2 win, striking out eight while allowing seven hits. The victory put the Marlins (11–6) in first place, one game ahead of Columbus (8–5). On the other hand, the Royals (6–9), who had gone from last place in 1957 to first place in 1958, had once again slipped into the IL cellar.[12]

Getting off on the right foot, the Marlins completed the series, taking two of three in Montreal. However, following a rainout, the Miamians temporarily came back down to earth, dropping the first game of a doubleheader to Toronto by a score of 7–4, and escaping an almost certain loss trailing 4–0 in a game called because of curfew. Bouncing back, the Marlins swept a three-game affair in Richmond and split the last four games in Havana. Returning home to Miami with an impressive 18–9 record and in first place—three games ahead of Buffalo—the Marlins were brimming with confidence.

Storer was so encouraged by his club's early season performance that he approved the purchase of two veterans to address a couple of weaknesses on the team: Lajoie's poor performance with the bat and the lack of depth in the pitching staff. In a deal with the Washington Senators, General Manager Ryan engineered the purchase of first baseman Norm Zauchin and thirty-year-old veteran hurler Vito Valentinetti for a reported amount in the excess of $35,000.[13] Zauchin had spent time in the big leagues with the Boston Red Sox in 1951, 1955, and 1956 before landing with the Senators in 1958. Zauchin had one memorable season in Boston, smashing twenty-seven homers and driving in ninety-three runs in 1955 before being displaced by Mickey Vernon during the "56" campaign.[14] Ryan saw Zauchin as the big bopper the Marlins were perennially seeking since their inception. In addition, Ryan was further hoping that Valentinetti would bring the much-needed veteran experience the club lacked, since both McCall and McDermott were still residing on the injured reserve list. Valentinetti arrived in the big leagues in 1954 with the Chicago White Sox. His second stint in the majors came in 1956, pitching for the crosstown Cubs for two seasons before bouncing around the American League with the Cleveland Indians, Tigers, and finally the Senators.[15]

Kicking off the homestand, the Marlins matched up, for the first time, against the Columbus Jets. Longtime IL star Lynn Lovenguth was set to face Miami's upcoming star twirler Archer. The Jets were currently standing in seventh place and eager to spoil the Marlins' party. A surprisingly large crowd of 5,064 turned out for Ladies Night only to see the first six innings produce nothing but zeroes. In the seventh inning the stalemate was broken when Jets shortstop Ken Hamlin singled and, with one out, scored on speedy Joe Christopher's triple. Archer worked carefully to Jets outfielder Jim McDaniel. Looking to put wood on the ball, McDaniel hit a shot toward Smith at third. Smith fielded the ball flawlessly, looked Christopher back to third base, and then heaved the ball across the diamond to Lajoie. As soon as the ball left Smith's hands, Christopher broke for home plate. Lajoie caught the throw, but was off target on his exchange to home plate, allowing Christopher to score and hand the Jets a 2–0 lead.

In the bottom of the seventh inning, Castleman singled, extending his hit streak to seventeen games and later reaching third base scored on Lovenguth's wild pitch. It proved to be the only run for Miami as they dropped a heartbreaker to Columbus, 2–1. Archer pitched valiantly for eight innings, but nonetheless was tagged with his second loss—against three wins—for the season.[16]

John Anderson followed up the May 11 loss, tossing a gem on "Dollar Day." For the price of a "George Washington," a crowd of 3,145 were treated to some mighty fine glove work and strong pitching. In the fourth inning, Smith made a diving catch into the stands, squelching a Jets rally. In the seventh inning shortstop Castleman made a highlight stab that would have been a Sports Center moment today. Snagging a certain base hit line drive, the veteran then threw a bullet to Bucha at home plate, nipping Jim McDaniel with what might have been the deciding run. The biggest play of the night was by little five-foot-eight left fielder Chuck Oertel, who made a wall-jarring grab and save on an Elmo Plaskett line drive, dousing the Jets' rally. In the bottom of the tenth inning, Valentine singled off Red Swanson and Oertel followed with a bunting perfectly for his second base knock of the night. Castleman, facing George O'Donnell, who had replaced Swanson, then singled home the lightning-fast Valentine with the deciding run. "The Quiet Man" did the rest, pitching ten innings while allowing only four hits, walking one, and striking out seven. The final score on Miami Stadium's electronic scoreboard showed Marlins 3, Visitors 2.[17]

The Marlins dropped the next two games to Columbus 7–1 and 7–2. Salvaging the remainder of the homestand, the Marlins took three out of four from Richmond and were still holding fast to first place with a 22–13 record. Making headlines around the IL was rookie Jack Fisher, who had upped his record to 5–0, and Fred Valentine, with twelve stolen bases and a batting average hovering around the .300 mark. The Marlins received bad news when it was announced that Castleman would be lost for at least two weeks due to a wrenched knee he suffered after slipping on the outfield grass during the May 17 doubleheader.[18] It couldn't have come at a worse time, as the Marlins were facing a long road trip ahead.

And sure enough the Marlins started off their second road swing by dropping three of four to Columbus. Prompted by the loss of Castleman, career third baseman Smith was moved to shortstop and left fielder Chuck Oertel was shifted to the hot corner. Martin, not wanting to lose any offensive punch, moved recently acquired Frank Kellert in left field to take Oertel's place. Thinking he had settled on a lineup, at least until Castleman's return, the Marlins were dealt yet another injury blow in the series opening game when Burke was taken out by the runner trying to turn a double play in the sixth inning. He hit the ground hard and suffered a severe self-inflicted spike wound above the knee. It would take twenty-four stitches to close the nasty gash. Adding insult to injury, starter Byrd was roughed up for eight runs—six earned—in six-plus innings in the 13–8 defeat. Byrd's only consolation was that reliever Artie Kay was hung with the loss after giving up the difference-making runs in the seventh inning. The hardest part for Martin to swallow was blowing a seven-run lead that the Marlins had built early in the game, some of the damage a result of errors by Smith and Kellert playing out of position.[19]

The Marlins were missing their two best middle infielders in Castleman and Burke. Jerry Snyder, Burke's replacement, was forced back into duty despite his own nagging injuries to fill the void. Also, pitchers Jim Archer and Virgil Trucks came up missing in action. Ultimately, Trucks was suspended ten days for missing the team's flight and Archer, one of the team's big three starters, was AWOL after refusing to board a flight from Tampa.[20]

Leo Burke recalled Archer missing the flight and the extenuating circumstances that led to his absence and the reason for the Miami newspapers reporting him AWOL.

Leo Burke: Well that was the reason. I can verify that. He was a roommate of mine and a very close friend of mine and every time, and of course being in Miami you know we had to fly everywhere. The closest place was Cuba and you couldn't swim that far. But anyhow every time that we would go on a road trip, every single time, he'd have to go into a bar and have a shot of scotch before getting on the plane. "Come on, roomie, let's go," and then we went.

One time I think we were going to Montreal. We usually went to Montreal and Toronto and then came down and hit Buffalo and Rochester. I think we were going on that trip, either Montreal or Toronto, and then came down to Richmond. I can't remember. But I know that we got on the plane in Miami. We left and for some reason we landed in Tampa. And they said that they were having some trouble and they'd have to, they'd have to check the plane out, and take it up for repairs to test it, and then we would continue on the trip. And he [Archer] looked at me and he said, "Roomie, I'm outta here" and that was the last we heard of him — of Jim. And what happened actually, is he had a, I don't know if it was a half-brother or a brother or a brother-in-law, had a car dealership in Dunedin, Florida. And he went with him. Nobody knew where he was. And, of course, our manager didn't know.

It got back to the parent organization. Richards was calling and he didn't know where he was. And finally when we found out what happened, and why it happened, I don't think he was reprimanded. He may have gotten a tongue chewing, but I don't think they did anything with him because, and to this day the reason was, because Richards felt the same way.

When I was with the Orioles, at the end of one year, I think we were flying to Kansas City. Back in those days you would walk out on the tarmac and board the plane. And we were standing out there and the plane flew over where I was standing at and it started sputtering. And we had a pitcher by the name of Connie Johnson and he looked up and said, "And I'll guarantee that airplane is bad," and by heavens it was. So, that plane, they fixed it, and we boarded on it and went to Kansas City. And Richards, we had an off day, and Richards had left by plane, I mean train, the day before. Of course, he doesn't like to fly. So any place that he went, if he could, he would take the train.

I guess he was sympathetic to Jim. I don't think they reprimanded him in any way. Of course, he missed his turn pitching.[21]

The lone bright spot in the four-game set came against Columbus when Fisher upped his record to 6–0, winning the third game of the series 5–4. With an impressive 2.21 ERA in sixty-one innings of work the twenty-year-old lefty had only given up eighteen runs (fifteen earned), struck out forty-eight, and completed all six of his wins. Bill Durney, in his assessment of Fisher to the *Sporting News*, stated, "Fisher has all of the tools." It was evident that he was catching the attention of the Orioles and their manager Paul Richards, who was already hinting at promoting the youngster to the big leagues.[22]

It was evident that Oertel wasn't the answer at third base and skipper Martin was in a quandary trying different pieces, alternating Bobby Adams and Eddie Kazak in Smith's stead. But with Castleman and Burke on the disabled list and Snyder playing hurt, the Marlins' struggles continued over the course of the entire road trip. After leaving Columbus the Marlins dropped two out of three to Buffalo and finally were swept during their three-game series with Rochester, losing two games by scores of 10–0 and 14–2. Miraculously, by the end of the road trip, the Marlins (24–21) were still clinging to first place, a half-game ahead of Buffalo, Montreal, and Rochester. In what seemed to be shaping up as the closest pennant race in years, the standings were so tight that only five games separated the last-place Maple Leafs from the top position.

In order to shore up the infield, General Manager Ryan acquired shortstop Bobby Willis from the Class-AA Chattanooga Lookouts. The move allowed Smith to return to his usual position at third base. Although Smith was suffering from the effects of a nagging spike wound that he acquired on May 20 against Columbus, he was happy to return to his familiar spot at the hot corner.[23] Willis arrived with a less-than-impressive batting average just under .200 that was of some concern, but he was at least a whiz with the glove and the answer to shoring up a leaky defense that had been a culprit in many of the team's recent losses.

Closing out the month of May the Marlins were relieved to return home. Their first opponent would be their rival the Sugar Kings. Lacking a big bat, battling injuries, and lacking depth in the starting staff, the Marlins were hoping for the best, but as Bette Davis famously once said, "Fasten your seatbelts, it's going to be a bumpy night."[24] The Marlins found that the road ahead was filled with potholes, and not even a good set of shock absorbers would smooth the ride they were about to take.

NOTES

1. Cy Kritzer, "38,878 Turn Out for Four Int Openers," *Sporting News*, April 22, 1959, 30; Bob Owens, "Hurrah for Rolf Scheel! He Wronged but We Won," *Miami News*, April 15, 1959.

2. Baseball-reference.com.

3. Bob Owens, "Marlins Split on Baseball Theory," *Miami News*, April 17, 1959.

4. Bob Owens, "Marlins Split on Baseball Theory," *Miami News*, April 17, 1959; *Sporting News*, April 29, 1959, 34.

5. Tommy Fitzgerald, "Blame Marlin Drummer Boy," *Miami News*, April 18, 1959.

6. Baseball-reference.com.

7. Tommy Fitzgerald, "Parsons Saves Miami," *Miami News*, April 19, 1959.

8. *Sporting News*, May 6, 1959, 28.

9. Jimmy Burns, "Pepper Clicks as Grid Hero, Marlins Pilot in Royals' Park," *Sporting News*, May 13, 1959, 32.

10. Lloyd McGowan, "Fisher Pitches to 11–2 Victory as Marlins Pound Out 16 Hits," *Miami News*, April 30, 1959.

11. Ibid.

12. Ibid.

13. Jimmy Burns, "Red-Hot Marlins Complete First Tour with 8–3 Mark," *Sporting News*, May 20, 1959, 29.

14. Baseball-reference.com.

15. Ibid.

16. Tommy Fitzgerald, "Jets in Dream World," *Miami News*, May 12, 1959.

17. Bob Owens, "Oertel May Have Trapped It," *Miami News*, May 15, 1959.

18. Bob Owens, "Marlins Farewell Falls over Thinking Man's Catcher," *Miami News*, May 18, 1959.

19. Ed O'Neil, "Everything Was So Nice . . . Then the Roof Caved In," *Miami News*, May 19, 1959.

20. Ibid.

21. Leo Burke, phone interview with the author, August 22, 2011.

22. Jimmy Burns, "Fisher of Marlins Wins First Six on Five-Day System," *Sporting News*, June 3, 1959.

23. *Sporting News*, June 10, 1959, 48.

24. J. Mankiewicz, *All About Eve* (Twentieth Century Fox, 1950).

TWENTY-FOUR

Chasing Buffalo

With his Marlins off to an unexpected strong start, the always congenial Pepper Martin had grown into somewhat of a celebrity in Miami. Martin's legend was forever cemented in the public's mind when he exploded on the national scene in 1931 by leading the "Gashouse Gang" to the championship. In what would become one of the most famous Fall Classics of all time, the rough-and-tumble and gregarious Martin would bat an incredible .500 and steal five bases, sparking the St. Louis Cardinals on to an upset over Connie Mack's dynastic Philadelphia Athletics. With his laid-back, backwoods charm and sunny attitude peppered with an always-positive appraisal of his club's talent, the local fanship had begun to believe that the Marlins were legitimate contenders for their first-ever title. The press in Miami was especially enamored with Martin, who supplied more-than-ample quotes to fill their bylines. Scanning the various news accounts of the day, one can find little criticism of him as a manager except for the occasional questions related to some of his on-field strategic decision.

In John Heidenry's account of the 1930s Cardinals titled *The Gashouse Gang*, he shares a story that captures the personality of Martin, along with Branch Rickey's assessment of the most colorful of the "Gang."

> Although many of Rickey's plants were true, or at least inspired by fact, others were patently apocryphal, such as the one about the time Martin's wife delivered their third child while Pepper was playing a game. As soon as it was over, Pepper allegedly rushed to the maternity ward, burst into Mrs. Martin's room and shouted, "Darling, great news, we won a doubleheader."
>
> Rickey once told a reporter, "Pepper Martin is the most genuine person I've ever met in my life. There was never an ounce of pretense in the man. He was 100 percent in everything he did. When he fell in love, he fell head over heels. If he wanted a new shotgun, he went out

and bought it, whether he could afford it or not. He went all out in everything he did, and that was why he was such a great ballplayer." [1]

Slick-fielding Bobby Willis harkened back to one of his favorite memories of Martin and how he tried to keep the game as simple as possible. While laughing heartily he shared this story:

> *Bobby Willis*: Well you know Pepper was a clown you know . . . back in those days we enjoyed playing baseball. We loved to play baseball and Pepper was a clown and he could still play at that age, Pepper, I think he was somewhere in his mid-60s [fifty-five] then. I'm not sure. But he could still, you know, reach his foot up and touch his toes over his head. You know he was just a clown and enjoyed baseball.
>
> His steal signal was a wink. He looked at you and winked and that was his steal signal. He was a, you know, none of the fancy 1, 2, 3, 4, 5 whatever signs, you know, he just cupped his eyes and winked at you. That was his steal signal. So, you know he was just an enjoyable person to play around to play ball with. [2]

Vito Valentinetti was a tough kid who grew up playing baseball in the Bronx and was a fierce competitor on the mound, yet he still holds a soft spot for his colorful manager. His memories evoke laughter to this day.

> *Vito Valentinetti*: He was a jolly guy, you know. He rarely got mad and didn't see him get angry at anybody. He would go along, kind of a funny guy, and always playing those tricks with the ball. He used to flip 'em around his back and under his legs and over his head. [3]

Martin played and managed with an enthusiasm for the game that few approached. Although he was rarely seen without an ear-to-ear grin, there were times when the other side of his personality—which housed his fiery nature—would emerge. Although fifty-five years old at the time, Martin's competitive embers were still burning. Fresh in the minds of the older Miami fans was the time that Martin, while managing the Miami Sun Sox, was fined and suspended for two weeks for choking an umpire when he thought his team had been wronged. [4]

Leo Burke vividly recalled the time that his usually fun-loving manager showed his displeasure when one of his treasured props was left damaged on the dugout floor.

> *Leo Burke*: He had this, he always smoked this pipe, and I remember we had a big burly pitcher who pitched. I think he was with the White Sox for a while but he was also with the Washington—what were they called then, the Senators? The Washington Senators and his name was Harry Byrd. Well, anyhow, he came to us to pitch. And he was pitching a game and he wasn't doing too well. . . . Pepper came out and Harry didn't want to come out. And he really raised Cain. . . . He came in and while Pepper was greeting the relief pitcher Harry went over and hit that pipe and broke it. After the game Pepper went to get his pipe and saw that it was broken and he became furious. . . . He challenged the

whole team if any of you guys are man enough to stand up and admit who did it he said, "I'll fight you right here." And nobody did, not even Harry.[5]

Still clinging to first place on May 29, the Marlins held a slim one-half game lead over Buffalo, and a full game over Columbus as they came home to face Havana for four games. The standings showed only four games separated the league-leading Marlins from the bottom-dwelling Toronto Maple Leafs; Havana, barely in second division, was two and a half games to the rear of Miami. Rejoining the club were Leo Burke and Foster Castleman, the latter just starting to take infield practice while Burke prepared to join his teammates on the field.[6]

For the home opener, swingman Bunky Stewart was chosen to square off against Sugar Kings' right-hander, Franklin Delano Roosevelt "Ted" Wieand.[7] Every year the Marlins staff seemed to have one hard-luck pitcher and Stewart was the 1959 recipient. Stewart was among the league leaders, with an ERA south of 2.00, but had a puny 1–3 record, through no fault of his own, based on the poor support he was receiving from his teammates. Stewart was a part of the Senators' contingent with Miami and up to this point had experienced a pretty much nondescript major league career. Somehow, after pitching poorly for the 1952 Chattanooga Lookouts (6–9, 4.58), he received a call from the major leagues and enjoyed a cup of coffee with the Nats, appearing in one game for one inning and allowing a couple of runs. Over five seasons in Washington the slight-of-build southpaw accumulated a 5–11 record and stratospheric 6.01 ERA.[8] Unbeknownst to Stewart, he was winding down his career. Only twenty-eight years old, Stewart was hoping for another crack at the big time, and although he would perform well, he never returned to the big leagues.

After allowing an unearned run in the first inning Stewart settled down. In the seventh inning first baseman Frank Kellert knotted the score by blasting a solo shot, evening the ledger at one apiece. Stewart stayed strong until the eighth inning. He had allowed only two hits but finally was showing signs of fatigue, culminating in a tasty-offering belt-high pitch to Sugar Kings' backstop Enrique "Hank" Izquierdo. Izquierdo jumped all over it and the pitch landed barely fair inside of the foul pole for a double. Wieand then helped his own cause by laying down a successful bunt for a single, followed by Leo Cardenas's RBI single to center-field for what proved to be the difference maker in the Sugar Kings' 2–1 triumph.[9]

Although Artie Kay finished out the eighth inning, retiring all three batters and stranding his two inherited runners, the Marlins failed to mount a comeback. Stewart's record dropped to 1–4, despite a microscopic 1.13 ERA. The Marlins dropped to third place based on Buffalo's 16–9 win against Montreal. Due to rain in Richmond, the Jets were idle but nonetheless picked up half a game, leaving them tied with Miami for third place.[10]

It was a foreboding vision of what was to come as Miami prepared for their Memorial Day doubleheader against Havana. A decent crowd of 6,126 greeted the Marlins as they dashed out to their respective positions on the field. In the stands were a few loyal Sugar Kings rooters waving Cuban flags and cheering on their team in their native Spanish tongue. The Marlins were quickly greeted in the top of the first inning by two Sugar Kings scores, the result of a Carlos Paula double with runners on base. Miami answered the bell in the bottom of the first inning by scoring three of their own runs thanks to an RBI single by Johnny Bucha and another single by Burke that plated two more of his teammates.[11]

Starting pitcher Don Rudolph's struggles were evident early on. After retiring only two batters in the first inning, his manager Preston Gomez strolled to the mound and with little hesitation Gomez tapped his left arm, a signal for Luis Arroyo to enter the game. Arroyo, nearly unhittable all season, went the rest of the short seven-inning affair without much incident, striking out twelve and holding the Marlins scoreless. The Marlins' usually reliable defense proved to be their own worst enemy during the fourth inning, when the Sugar Kings received a gift that couldn't have been more generous than if it were offered tied with a bow. An apparent Rogelio Alvarez fly ball that should have been easily caught dropped between Bobby Willis and Chuck Oertel for a double. The gaffe came back to haunt Miami when Alvarez later scored on a wild pitch and allowed the Sugar Kings to tie the score at 3–3.[12]

The deciding run came off Anderson in the fifth inning when Elio Chacon ran out a base hit that squirted down the third base line. Chacon promptly stole second base and dashed home on Lou Skizas's single, providing the Sugar Kings with the difference maker in the 4–3 victory.[13]

The nightcap proved even more futile as the Sugar Kings upped their win streak to eight games and defeated the Marlins, 5–4. Carlos Paula terrorized Jack Fisher with two doubles and four RBIs. Despite home runs by Burke and Bert Hamric, the usually resilient Fisher dropped his second game in a row, sending the Marlins (24–24) tumbling into fifth place.[14]

The final game against Havana, and to close out May, was salvaged thanks to Artie Kay's continued brilliance out of the pen. After Jim Archer was removed following six and two-thirds innings and holding a 6–3 lead, Wes Stock entered the game but faltered. Stock's struggles to find his command continued when he allowed three runs and retired only one batter before exiting the game with the clubs knotted at six runs apiece. Increasingly, Martin was turning to Kay in tough spots. Kay, in the midst of his finest season in baseball, was up to the task. The twenty-four-year-old Belton, South Carolina, native labored through four innings, carrying the game into the eleventh inning. The Sugar Kings finally flinched when relief pitcher Rudolph walked Bobby Adams with the bases loaded to end the extra inning affair, giving Kay the 7–6 win.[15] Thankfully, the Marlins had ended their seven-game losing skein.

Looking forward to playing Rochester and Buffalo at home, the Marlins were hoping to turn things around. Vito Valentinetti faltered against the Red Wings in the lid-lifter, spotting the visitors a 4–0 lead and prompting Martin to pull him with no outs in the second inning for Harry Byrd. Byrd responded and set down the Red Wings in the second inning without giving up a hit. In the bottom of the second inning the Marlins exploded for five runs. After allowing two runners to reach, starter Bill Greason left one up in the strike zone that catcher Steve Korcheck couldn't ignore and he plastered the offering over the left field fence to cut the lead down to 4–3. Before the inning was over the Marlins had plated two more runs, including Woody Smith's home run, putting Miami ahead 5–4. Smith would later play the role of hero, driving in the deciding run.[16]

Anderson, who had been struggling with issues due to his mechanics, feverishly warmed up in the bullpen and entered the game in the third inning. Anderson had struggled as of late and prior to the game he met up with pitching coach Lloyd Brown to work on his leg motion, the source of his recent troubles. The session paid instant dividends as the "Quiet Man" slowed down the Red Wings' bats, allowing only two runs over the final seven innings and opening up the opportunity for his teammates to outlast the Red Wings, 7–6. Assessing his past troubles, Anderson said after the game, "I had lost my coordination."[17] Everyone was happy to see him return to form.

The remainder of the series proved more troublesome, as Miami dropped the next night's game 5–1, the casualties of excellent pitching by Red Wings' twenty-year-old right-hander Bob L. Miller. It was Stewart's fifth loss of the season despite a glossy 2.19 ERA.[18] After a June 3 rainout the series finale was becoming an all-too-disturbing trend as the Marlins dropped another heartbreaker, losing by the score of 4–3. Stock once again labored to find his command and was rocked for four runs in four innings of work, losing his first starting assignment of the season.[19] Kay tossed four innings of scoreless relief to no avail. As usual, Martin's assessment of Stock, despite his second consecutive poor performance, was upbeat, predicting he would be a winner by the end of the season: "We've got a few things to work out with him on his delivery but he has good stuff and he will be tough before this thing [league race] is decided."[20]

With first place Buffalo in town next, it seemed like homecoming for the Miami fans as many former Marlins, including Dick Bunker, Jimmie Coker, Turk Farrell, Dallas Green, Warren Hacker, Pancho Herrera, Don Landrum, and Hank Mason, filled out their roster, not to mention their manager Kerby Farrell. Although Miamians were known to be low key and appreciative of a good effort, they were more concerned about winning games and gaining some ground in the standings.

In the opener Fisher regained his past form and broke a personal two-game losing streak, pitching seven innings. He allowed four earned runs before turning the reins over to Archer. It was a rare relief role for Archer, who would make only eight such appearances all season. Martin's pitching strategy harkened back to old-time baseball when starting pitchers would occasionally work in critical late-inning situations. Wanting to earn a win in the worst way, Martin was not shy to turn to a starter to secure a victory, reminiscent of the days when Dizzy Dean would be called in on short rest to pitch an inning or two. And in this case Archer did, earning the save as the Marlins cruised to a 6–4 win.

A June 7 doubleheader against Buffalo found the Marlins winning the first game 3–0 behind a rejuvenated Anderson. Anderson's time spent with his pitching coach showed huge dividends, as his knuckler was working to perfection. The "Quiet Man" allowed only five hits over seven and a third innings before turning the ball over to Kay, who finished up the game to earn the save.[21]

In the nightcap, Archer started the short game but received little support from his comrades. Miami outhit their opponents 7–5 but came out on the short end of the stick as ex-Marlin Turk Farrell earned the 2–1 win despite needing some relief help from Ken Lehman to seal the deal. At one point it looked as if the Marlins were going to pull off the sweep. After Bucha's single scored pinch-hitter Adams, with bases loaded in the sixth, Fred Valentine hit a hot smash toward a diving Ruben Amaro at shortstop that looked as if it had eyes. However, Amaro made a beautiful diving stop on the ball that was hit so hard he was able to start the double play with just enough time to nab the speeding Valentine at first base. The play proved to be a back-breaker, snuffing a potential game-breaking inning.[22] The loss left the Marlins (29–29) in sixth place, but on the positive side only three games behind the division leading Bisons and only one-half game behind Rochester and Havana for fourth place.

The remainder of June the Marlins essentially treaded water. The Marlins seemed to have righted their course by starting out their road trip taking three out of five games from Toronto. Vito Valentinetti got the ball rolling in the second game of the series-opening doubleheader in Maple Leaf Stadium after newly acquired Marlin Ron Moeller stubbed his toe in the early contest, falling 4–0. Despite some wildness—including walking six batters—the ex-Senator squirmed his way out of several threats and downed the Leafs in the night game, 5–1.[23] Once again, Kay was called on to pitch the final two innings to preserve the victory. It was Kay's sixth consecutive appearance without being charged with a run. In an eleven-day span he had pitched fourteen and two-thirds innings had had only given up five base knocks, one walk, and all the while striking out six enemy batters.[24] Key offensive contributors were Kellert, Oertel, Valentine, and Willis, who all contributed two base hits. The biggest blow of the night came off the bat of Kellert, a 345-foot shot off of starter Don Johnson.[25]

Inspired by his teammate's previous night's performance, Bunky Stewart was victorious. Despite the chilly conditions in Toronto and the taunting fan base, Stewart was resilient. Among a myriad of boos and a little bench jockeying from the Leafs' bench, Stewart shook off his hard-luck shackles. The wispy lefty received nine runs of support from his *compadres*, a much-appreciated gift. The Marlins played a combination of long ball and small ball as Burke blasted a grand slam in the eighth inning and Hamric, Valentine, and Willis all contributed stolen bases; final score, Marlins 9, Maple Leafs 2.[26]

Playing their second doubleheader in three days, the Marlins split the series finale when Jack Fisher returned to his old form, twirling a complete game four hitter and earning his eighth win of the year. Woody Smith's single, double, and two RBIs were all "Fat Jack" needed for the 3–1 win.[27]

The Marlins wrapped up their northern road trip in less-than-impressive fashion, dropping two out of three games to Montreal. The June 13 match-up proved to be their best offensive performance since April 29, the last time they scored double-digits against this same Royals team. Archer was the beneficiary of the latest offensive outburst, as he cruised to the 10–3 win despite surrendering thirteen enemy hits. Burke continued his timely hitting when he belted his eleventh home run of the year, and Oertel had a perfect 4–4 day that included driving in a pair of runs. Burke was acquiring several positive accolades from around the IL, not only for hitting but also for his newfound defensive prowess at his new position. His teammate Woody Smith exclaimed, "This kid deserves tremendous credit." He added, "I've never seen anybody adapt himself to a strange position so quickly."[28] Even Toronto's Dixie Walker chimed in after being the victim of several highlight reel plays: "He plays second as if he'd been there all his life."[29]

Not only was Burke playing well, but the Marlins' reserve backstop was also making the most of his chance while in the lineup. Dealing with a chipped bone on his finger, backstop Korcheck had been among the hottest hitters on the Marlins. The former football star was taking advantage of regular catcher Bucha's absence. Bucha, receiving some much-needed rest, was reduced to playing only one game on the recent road swing and "Hoss" appreciated the extra work.

Still another recent surprise was the play of Bobby Willis. Batting over .300 on the road trip, he improved his season mark by raising his average from .182 to .267. This didn't escape the notice of his skipper, who after acquiring Willis was singing the praises of his young shortstop when he predicted that if Willis could hit .250, he could make it at the major league level.

Looking ahead to their return home, the Marlins returned to Miami with Toronto, soon to be followed by their countrymen from Montreal. The Canadian contingency always looked forward to a trip down south to escape their country's cool climate, but instead they were harshly greeted with torrential rains with nary a sunbeam in sight. The two teams were able to salvage two of the four games in the homestand. News of a more pleasant nature was Castleman's return to shortstop for the June 16 opening game. Encouragingly, Castleman showed no ill effects from his time on the injured list, going 4–4, all of them singles, in the Marlins' 5–2 loss. [30]

The dismal weather failed to relent with Montreal in town. In total, there was a rain-shortened game against the Leafs on June 17, rainouts against the Leafs on June 18 and 19, a rain-shortened six-inning affair against Montreal in the opener, and a rain delay in the second game of a double dip against the Royals' on June 21; the rain had resulted in cancellation of five of the last six games. The Marlins settled for a split in two decisions with the Royals, earning one impressive win behind Anderson's shutout performance. Apparently the humidity had his knuckleball fluttering like a butterfly, as the visiting Royals only managed six hits in the 2–0 Marlins triumph. It was Anderson's third whitewashing of the year. [31]

The weather may have dampened the spirits of the Marlins faithful, but it was nothing compared to the announcement on June 22 that their recently wed staff ace Jack Fisher received the call from Baltimore to join the Orioles. When informed of his promotion, Fisher simply replied, "I'll be doggoned." For the twenty-year-old Fisher, it was the culmination of a lifelong dream. Not only had Fisher just exchanged vows with the beautiful Judy Mack of Augusta, Georgia, on June 14, but he was also receiving the best wedding present anyone could give him: a promotion to the big leagues. [32] A pitching staff that was already considered lacking in depth, saddled by struggling veterans Mickey McDermott and Valentinetti, led pitching coach Brown and manager Martin to turn to General Manager Joe Ryan to work his magic and fill the void. Fisher finished his one and only season in Miami with an 8–4 record and 3.06 ERA, striking out seventy in ninety-seven innings worked. "Fat Jack" would be hard to replace.

To compensate the Marlins for their loss, the Orioles sent reinforcements by demoting thirty-two-year-old relief pitcher George Zuverink. [33] The six-foot-four, 195-pound ex-Army Corps and World War II vet broke into the big leagues with the Cleveland Indians in 1951, appearing in sixteen games in relief. [34] In 1952 he was sent to Indianapolis (AAA) of the American Association where he stayed for two seasons, putting together a combined record of 25–19. After a look-see with the Cincinnati Reds in 1954 he was traded to the Detroit Tigers and had the opportunity to pitch for the club of his childhood idol, Tommy Bridges. [35] Zuverink (9–13,

3.75) pitched mostly out of the bullpen for the Bengals. In 1955 he joined the Orioles, where he enjoyed his greatest success, leading the American League in saves with sixteen in 1956, and in games pitched in both 1956 and 1957.[36]

Zuverink recalls how he came a long way from being an unsuccessful high-school pitcher to making it in the major leagues.

> *George Zuverink*: When I was around ten years old, I came from Holland, Michigan. Naturally, I was a Tiger fan. I followed them, we only had radio then, and we didn't have no television in those days. I just kept saying that Tommy Bridges was my idol, and I kept saying someday I'm going to pitch for Detroit.
>
> I didn't have much chance of course. I pitched one year in high school and I had no wins and seven losses. But I still wanted to play baseball, but I was in the service during the Second World War in Australia. My job was filling oil, and driving oil, to the planes, you know. So I had some time off in between, and I played on the squadron team, and pitched a no-hit, no-run game. The manager said, "George, did you ever think of playing pro ball?"
>
> I said, "Think about it?" He said, "I'll write to the owner of the St. Louis Cardinals." Sam Breadon, I guess his name was. It was the letter from him that said, "When you get out of baseball I would like to sign you up." So that's how I got started. Just that one game and the right man who was in the right position.
>
> I pitched one year in their organization. I was relief the next year because they had so many guys coming out of the service. And then I pitched semi-pro ball back in Holland.
>
> I thought I did well with Detroit that one year. Freddie Hutchison was the manager. He believed in me and I had a good year there. I had a couple of shutouts. We won an eleven-inning ballgame one to nothing. Then they wouldn't give me a two-year contract. So I went back to the minor leagues and managed there for a little bit. And I forgot who was the guy who took over with us. He was just leaving me at home, and then mentioned my name, and that I did well.
>
> And Paul Richards was in the Coast League when I was in San Diego. I pitched a lot of good ball against him so he got me over to Baltimore. The first thing he did he said, "Let's go out to the bullpen," and he started working with me. He was the only manager that ever did that, that worked with a guy. So he makes you believe in yourself.
>
> I got a lot of articles that were in the paper you know. "Give him the ball. He'll do it."[37]

In an additional personnel move, on the same day General Manager Joe Ryan acquired thirty-year-old curveball artist Herb Moford (2–2, 3.38, 32 IP) from the Boston Red Sox's Triple-A team in Minneapolis. Moford had mostly bounced around the minor leagues since breaking in with the St. Louis Cardinals Class-D Salisbury affiliate in 1947. Moford arrived in the big leagues in 1955 with the Cardinals, posting a 1–1 record with a

7.88 ERA. Coming off his second season in the big leagues with the Detroit Tigers, Moford had failed to impress and finished the season with a disappointing 4–9 log and a 3.61 ERA.[38]

With their new teammates in tow, the Marlins began their road swing by heading north to play Buffalo, Rochester, Richmond, and finally Columbus. Miami (36–34) was holding on to fourth place, still only three games behind Buffalo (39–31), a club quickly beginning to establish themselves as the odds-on favorites to win the IL. It was to be an inauspicious start as the Marlins dropped two games to Buffalo by one run. Nevertheless, payback was sweet as lady justice balanced the scales and the Marlins came out on top of both games of a June 26 doubleheader. Oertel was the hero of the night, thumping three home runs, getting walked four times, and accounting for five RBIs. Miami won the first game, 8–4, when Kay was called on to make a rare start and met the challenge, going seven strong innings and allowing four runs (two earned). Former Marlin Hank Mason absorbed the loss.

In the second game it looked like a sure bet for those wagering on the Bisons to fatten their wallets as the Marlins sent out Valentinetti to face another ex-Marlin, Dick Bunker, in the nightcap. The game went just as if it were scripted, as the Bisons built a 6–2 lead after three innings. Valentinetti was chased after only two innings of work, and when McDermott, with his 10.42 ERA in tow, trudged in from the bullpen in the third inning, the Bisons were licking their lips in anticipation of continuing the onslaught.[39]

Martin had other ideas and, playing a hunch like a riverboat gambler, was soon to be rewarded for his intuition. McDermott's fastball seemed to have gained new life and after eight innings, partially thanks to Oertel's second homer off Bunker on the night, brought the Marlins back from the dead to knot the score at 6–6. "I never saw him so fast," said his beaming skipper.[40]

Both teams traded zeroes until the top of eleventh inning, when Willis, who had earlier entered the game pinch-running for Castleman, found himself leading off third base. Norm Zauchin, who had garnered four hits in the opener but was hitless in the second, launched a high fly ball to left-center field off reliever Don Erickson. Centerfielder Bobby Del Greco had a bead on the ball and after making the routine catch poised for a perfect throw to the plate. Willis broke for home and appeared to be a "dead duck" as the ball was arriving for catcher Joe Lonnett to make the tag ten feet ahead of the scampering Willis. As the ball skipped on the damp grass, the slippery sphere hit Lonnett's glove pocket and bounced away. Willis slid home—the error charged to Lonnett—and the Marlins jumped in front 7–6. McDermott, still in the game, then finished off the stunned Bisons in the bottom of the inning with no incident, earning him a well-deserved win. In total, "Maury" toiled through nine innings of shutout relief, by far his best performance of the year. The stunned crowd in Offerman Stadium could only file out silently in disbelief. Miami (38–36) was back to within three games of first place.[41]

Miami faltered the next night, stymied by future Phillie Art Mahaffey carrying a glossy 12–2 record. Going into Rochester the team bounced back and swept the opening series doubleheader and took three out of four from the Red Wings. The Marlins, at least temporarily staying on the winning track, swept Richmond in three games, before dropping two games in a row to Columbus.[42] Rain seemed to be following the Marlins wherever they traveled. Both their July 1 game in Rochester and the July 5 game in Columbus were cancelled due to rain. This would later pose problems as the Marlins would be forced to play an abnormal number of doubleheaders late in the season.

The Marlins returned to Miami Stadium to start a ten-game homestand beginning July 8 against the southern clubs. First on the bill would be Havana for three games, followed by Columbus for four, then Richmond for three. Although a few scattered showers dusted the area, the 2,740 spectators in attendance weren't to be dissuaded when it came to seeing their hometown boys take on the archrival Sugar Kings.[43]

Miami, now featuring their new "Big Three" of Archer, Anderson, and Stewart, seemed poised to make a move in the standings. In the opening tilt Archer faced the always-tough Mike Cuellar. It was billed as a pitchers' duel, and the contest lived up to its billing. In the top of the first inning, Carlos Paula, who always seemed to be a thorn in the side of the Marlins, singled in Chacon to give the visitors a 1–0 lead. Cuellar remained in control until the sixth inning, when Castleman singled and was followed up by a Smith double, tying the score at one apiece. Cuellar had been wild, walking seven batters and giving up ten hits, but continued to wiggle himself out of several jams. On the other hand, Archer wasn't giving up much and hadn't given up a free pass all night and only six hits. Both teams went into the twelfth inning tied as both pitchers gutted it out. Finally, in the bottom of the twelfth, Cuellar, who had done his best imitation of Houdini all night, couldn't get himself out of this jam. With bases loaded and one out Jerry Snyder stepped up to the plate and knocked a single that scored Frank Kellert. The Marlins had prevailed 2–1. Archer, now 8–4 on the season, was magnificent, going the full twelve innings, striking out eleven, allowing nine hits and no walks. Smith was the hitting star, going 5–5, including bashing three doubles.[44]

The second game was another low-scoring affair. Anderson had already reached the ten-win mark and was slated to face southpaw Walt Craddock. Once again, the crowd of 2,852 was treated to a pitchers' duel. Both teams matched zeroes until the top of the third inning. The pesky Chacon beat out an infield single just ahead of shortstop Castleman's peg. Chacon then moved to second base on an infield out and then to third on a passed ball. Uncharacteristically, Smith then mishandled a roller down the third-base line, allowing Daniel Morejon to advance to third and

Chacon to score. Craddock was cruising along with a no-hitter until the seventh inning, when Castleman broke the ice with a single to center. Smith followed with a double, but the slow-running Castleman was held at third. Kellert then fouled out and Craddock intentionally walked Jerry Snyder to load the bases. With one out, manager Gomez played his infield back to try to turn the double play. With the left-handed Hamric due up, Martin turned to his bench, sending in Bucha to pinch-hit in an effort to get something going. The move proved fortuitous for Gomez as Bucha grounded to slick fielding Leo Cardenas, who promptly started the twin killing. A perplexed Martin, questioning Gomez's strategy, said, "It looked like they were willing to give us a cheap run even though it was the tying one." He added, "But we wouldn't take it." Bucha's tailor-made grounder proved to be the backbreaker and Craddock, mixing his assortment of screwballs and sinkers, pitched nearly perfectly the rest of way, preserving a 1–0 win for Havana. The meetings between the evenly matched combatants had been fiercely competitive, evidenced by the fact that they had each won five games against the other.[45]

The next night's rubber match was your typical Marlins versus Sugar Kings classic. Bunky Stewart and Vicente Amor would go head to head in yet another extra-inning affair. The Sugar Kings built an early 3–1 lead going into the bottom of the sixth inning. Amor had been steady up until then before giving up a double to Smith and a pair of free passes. With no one out, Gomez went to his bullpen and brought in right-sider Raul Sanchez. Both Kellert and Bucha promptly followed each with sacrifice flies tying the score at 3–3. However, Stewart remained sharp through eleven innings, having walked only one batter. Then in the bottom of the eleventh, with one out, Willis, Kellert, and Bucha hit consecutive singles off of Sanchez. Bucha's game-winning base hit set off a celebration at home plate when Willis crossed the plate with the winning tally. The final score showed Miami 4, Havana 3. After the game, the Marlins' exuberant pitching coach Lloyd Brown said, upon hearing that first-place Buffalo and second-place Rochester had lost, "It looks like Bunky's on his way now and we got a [heckava] chance to take it all." Stewart was so jubilant the next day that he was offering to buy ice cream sodas for his battery mate Bucha and hitting and fielding star Smith for playing such a huge role in the win.[46] It was indeed apropos, as this was a sweet win for the Marlins. It was certainly a more innocent time when an ice cream soda was considered a valuable reward.

Just like the Havana series, good pitching and scant offense would dominate the upcoming four-game series versus Columbus and the next three contests against Richmond. A large junior contingent filled the stadium for the July 11 "Youth Day Opener." An encouraging crowd of 4,974 filled the ballpark, lured by an enticing $1 admission fee. Having regained his 1958 form, McDermott took the mound to face off against the Jets' big six-foot-four lefty Joe Gibbon.[47]

Gibbon got off to a shaky start, walking lead-off hitter Oertel, then Snyder. Gibbon became further unhinged when Castleman laid down a sacrifice bunt, which Gibbon fielded but threw late to third, unable to get the fast-moving Oertel. Gibbon then walked the third batter in the inning when Smith drew a free pass, plating Oertel. Zauchin then struck out on a pitch that Danny Baich couldn't handle, allowing Snyder to score from third and Zauchin to take first. After fanning Bucha, Gibbons issued his fifth walk of the inning to Hamric, forcing in the third run of the frame. The Marlins had scored three runs with nary a hit, gaining the upper hand, 3–0.[48]

McDermott pitched brilliantly until the fourth inning, when Baich blasted a solo home run, cutting the Marlins lead to 3–1. With no outs, McDermott lost his composure, giving up a single to Nino Escalara and plunking Tony Bartirome, mostly likely out of frustration. Then, when umpire Lou Dimuro made a questionable call on ball four that loaded the bases, McDermott went into a tirade, yelling profanities that found most of the youngsters in the crowd blushing. Of course, arbiter DiMuro had no intention of changing his call and McDermott was removed from the game and replaced by Kay, who promptly escaped the no-out, bases-loaded jam.[49]

Kay continued his brilliance, striking out six and allowing just a single tally, finishing out the final six innings and preserving what proved to be a Marlins 4–2 victory.[50] The victory set the stage for the next night's performance, as the Marlins won their third game in a row, grabbing the first game of the two-night doubleheader, 3–2. Starter Moford pitched shutout ball until the seventh, allowing back-to-back doubles. Sensing the fatigue in the thirty-year-old veteran, Martin turned to relief specialist Zuverink to cool off the Jets. Zuverink lived up to his billing and, despite allowing a single that tied the score at 2–2, was saving his best work for later in the inning.[51]

In the bottom of the seventh inning, with the bases empty, Zuverink stepped into the batter's box to face Lynn Lovenguth. Zuverink wasn't going to scare anyone with his batting prowess, having acquired a puny .148 batting average in the bigs,[52] but on this day the stars must have aligned. With no ball and two strikes, to everyone's surprise, he launched Lovenguth's next offering deep into the afternoon sky: "I hit it and headed for first. When I saw I was being waved on to second, I said to myself, 'Well, I guess I got a double.' I never dreamed of a home run. As I was coming into second I looked out toward left field and saw the fielder standing by the wall and looking up. I never dreamed of a home run and I was the most surprised person in the ballpark." The blast turned out to be Zuverink's only homer in his career. After finishing the game and earning his first victory of the season, he recalled his last home run came clear back in 1947 playing semi-pro ball in Grand Rapids, Michigan.[53]

Zuverink had the satisfaction of not only driving in the deciding run but also winning his first game as a Marlin.

Miami didn't fare as well in the second game, dropping a nail-biter, 2–1. Byrd, in his return from injury, pitched five good innings before yielding to Kay, who finished out the game pitching two scoreless frames. The Marlins then dropped the series finale the next day, 3–2, despite a valiant effort by Archer, who escaped several jams just to end up the losing pitcher in a complete game effort.[54]

The Marlins proceeded to host Richmond and take two out of three games to close out a successful homestand. Anderson won his eleventh game of the season, combining with Kay to shut out the Vees, 2–0.[55] Miami lost the second game of the series 2–1, but came to win the rubber match as Moford finally lived up to his expectations and twirled a two-hitter blanking the Vees 1–0.[56]

At 50–44 the Marlins were riding a wave of confidence as they prepared for a road trip to Havana. Martin's charges stood only two games behind league-leading Buffalo. As of July 16, the pennant race was still up for grabs in a tight race where even the last-place Sugar Kings (44–52) stood only eight and a half games off the pace. With Moford and Zuverink providing a lift for the departed Fisher and McDermott bouncing back from an early season slump, the fear that the pitching staff depth would be a problem seemed to have stabilized. Of more concern to Martin was his offense, which continued to struggle to scratch out runs. The road ahead seemed sunny, but just like the summer weather in South Florida can change from minute to minute from fair to foul, so it seemed that dark clouds were gathering on the horizon.

NOTES

1. John Heidenry, *The Gashouse Gang* (New York: Public Affairs, 2007).
2. Bobby Willis, phone interview with the author, August 26, 2011.
3. Vito Valentinetti, phone interview with the author, August 23, 2011.
4. Thomas Barthel, *Pepper Martin: A Baseball Biography* (Jefferson, NC: McFarland, 2003).
5. Leo Burke, phone interview with the author, August 22, 2011.
6. *Sporting News*, June 10, 1959, 41; Bob Owens, "Marlins Lease Expires on One Bad Pitch," *Miami News*, May 30, 1959.
7. Owens, "Marlins Lease Expires on One Bad Pitch."
8. Baseball-reference.com.
9. Owens, "Marlins Lease Expires on One Bad Pitch."
10. Ibid.
11. Baseball-reference.com.
12. Tommy Fitzgerald, "Down and Down Go the Marlins," *Miami News*, May 31, 1959.
13. Ibid.
14. Fitzgerald, "Down and Down Go the Marlins"; *Sporting News*, June 10, 1959, 41.
15. Bob Owens, "Marlins' Spy in the Dugout Puts down Cuban Uprising," *Miami News*, June 1, 1959.

16. Bob Owens, "Marlins Winning 'Em Again, Now for That IL Lead," *Miami News*, June 2, 1959.

17. Ibid.

18. Ibid.

19. *Sporting News*, June 10, 1959, 42.

20. Bob Owens, "Chips on the Line for 'Blue' Marlins," *Miami News*, June 5, 1959; *Sporting News*, June 17, 1959, 31.

21. *Sporting News*, June 17, 1959, 31; Bob Owens, "Marlins Take to Road, but Face Quick Defeat," *Miami News*, June 8, 1959.

22. *Sporting News*, June 17, 1959, 31; Owens, "Marlins Take to Road, but Face Quick Defeat."

23. "Vito's Fastball Dazzles Walker," *Miami News*, June 9, 1959.

24. Ibid.

25. "Vito's Fastball Dazzles Walker"; *Sporting News*, June 17, 1959, 32.

26. Don Hunt, "Marlins Sparkle with Bats, Gloves," *Miami News*, June 10, 1959.

27. *Sporting News*, June 17, 1959, 32.

28. *Sporting News*, June 24, 1959, 30.

29. Ibid.

30. *Sporting News*, July 1, 1959, 30.

31. Jimmy Burns, "Fisher Gets Wedding Gift—Joins Orioles from Miami," *Sporting News*, July 1, 1959, 29; *Sporting News*, July 1, 1959, 30.

32. Burns, "Fisher Gets Wedding Gift—Joins Orioles from Miami."

33. "Blue Monday . . . Orioles Recall Fisher," *Miami News*, June 22, 1959.

34. "Blue Monday . . . Orioles Recall Fisher"; baseball-reference.com.

35. Gary Bedingfield, "George Zuverink," February 4, 2007, baseballinwartime. com.

36. Baseball-reference.com.

37. George Zuverink, phone interview with the author, May 3, 2010.

38. Baseball-reference.com.

39. Cy Kritzer, "Marlins Score KO; to Floor Those Bisons Twice," *Miami News*, July 27, 1959.

40. Ibid.

41. Ibid.

42. *Sporting News*, July 15, 1959, 29.

43. *Sporting News*, July 22, 1959, 31, 38.

44. Ibid.

45. Tommy Devine, "'Best in Two Years'—Craddock," *Miami News*, July 10, 1959; *Sporting News*, July 22, 1959, 31.

46. Tommy Fitzgerald, "Marlins Talk Title—Oops! Jets!" *Miami News*, July 11, 1959.

47. Tommy Fitzgerald, "Marlins Win 4–2, Go into Second by .001 Margin," *Miami News*, July 12, 1959.

48. Ibid.

49. Ibid.

50. Devine, "'Best in Two Years'—Craddock."

51. Tommy Fitzgerald, "Be Set for Anything When Marlins Play," *Miami News*, July 13, 1959.

52. Baseball-reference.com.

53. Jimmy Burns, "Zuverink's First Home Run in O.B. Gives Miami Win," *Sporting News*, July 22, 1959, 32.

54. *Sporting News*, July 22, 1959, 32.

55. Fitzgerald, "Marlins Win 4–2, Go into Second by .001 Margin."

56. *Sporting News*, July 29, 1959, 32.

TWENTY-FIVE

Contenders to Pretenders

A trip to Havana usually signaled a good time for all—a welcome respite from dreary stops like Richmond, Columbus, and Buffalo. But increasingly, IL teams approached the Caribbean paradise with apprehension. Although Fidel Castro was firmly in charge—having ousted Fulgencio Batista less than a year ago—bearded soldiers with machine guns were everywhere roaming the streets, an uncomfortable sight for even the stout of heart. The political tension was so thick in the air you could cut it with a knife, but skipper Pepper Martin, always the optimistic soul, did his best to ease his ballplayers' concerns.

Owner George Storer's concern for his players' safety was foremost in his mind. However, he was also consumed with how he could loosen the tightening noose that was choking the local fan base's interest in baseball. Attendance at Miami Stadium, although slightly up from the previous year, was falling way short of projections necessary to keep the team afloat. Storer's promise of not continuing baseball in Miami unless he broke even financially was a reality. Rumors were rampant concerning Miami being part of a possible third major league, the Continental League (CL), coupled with Storer's lifelong ambition of owning a major league team, left local fans believing it might be incentive enough for him to wait and see despite his mounting financial losses. Multimillionaire Bill MacDonald, owner of the Tampa Tarpons of the Class-D Florida State League, reported that he had been approached by members of group representing the CL, but felt that neither he nor Storer would be interested in the proposal. MacDonald expressed his opinion by stating, "In fact, George is not happy with the Marlins—the way they've been drawing with a team in the race—and I wouldn't be a bit surprised if this is his last year running the Marlins. He told me he would give it a good chance this year and it would be his last one if things didn't pick up."[1]

249

For other IL owners, conditions were better. Overall, league attendance was up from the previous year, albeit just barely. During mid-July the league announced an increase of 995 attendees, mostly due to Buffalo's record-setting pace putting them on a track to draw four hundred thousand and breaking their 1957 record of 386,071.[2] Miami's problem continued to be lack of not only fan support but also a complementary stadium lease and concessions contract, making operating profitably extremely difficult.

Storer wasn't the only one contemplating a quick retreat. Sugar Kings owner Bobby Maduro was also ready to shed his responsibilities by making it known he was ready to sell his team. Sounding much like his Miami counterpart Maduro stated, "I've lost money ever since we've been in the International League. I simply no longer can afford to operate under such conditions." Although Castro had offered financial aid to save the club, Maduro didn't feel comfortable accepting funds tied to a proposition that couldn't support itself.[3]

One Marlin who wasn't worried about the situation in Cuba was happy-go-lucky Mickey McDermott. Enjoying one of his frequent all-nighters, the imbibed pitcher once again went south of the law. In the wee hours of the morning on July 17, McDermott led local police on a chase that included speeding sixty miles per hour in a thirty-mile-per-hour zone. After driving almost a mile with lights flashing and sirens blaring behind him, the eccentric McDermott reluctantly pulled over, but not before cruising through a red traffic light. Swaying as he walked, and the smell of alcohol on his breath, he was arrested by Miami police for drunk driving, speeding, and running the red light. It was his third run-in with the law in two and a half years. "Honest, I wasn't drunk. Just had two or three beers," claimed McDermott. After being released on $215 bail and sleeping off his hangover, he rejoined his teammates, anxious to get out of town.[4] Martin was expected to come down hard on the left-hander, but instead was sympathetic toward his plight. "He has a wife and two children and any fine I'd give him would be taking bread out of their mouths. I wouldn't want to deprive them of anything. I've tried to get the guy to straighten out. He's really a wonderful guy," declared Martin.[5]

Although McDermott was a handful to all his managers and owners throughout his career, Martin, who was known to be vehemently opposed to alcoholism, nonetheless held a soft spot for Mickey. No doubt McDermott's drinking evoked memories of many of his teammates from the old "Gashouse Gang," known to bend their elbows more than a few times with spirits in their hands. His problems aside, McDermott had a charming personality that endeared him to almost everyone he met — including the ladies. Armed with a natural down-to-earth sense of humor and an innate gift of lovability, he had a knack for eliciting an almost childlike quality that caused his superiors to protect him despite the headaches he caused.

McDermott recalls in his book, *A Funny Thing Happened on the Way to Cooperstown*, a humorous moment on the field with his manager that captures some of his comicalness:

> Miami was fun. I could be myself. When I wasn't pitching, I often played first base. One day manager Pepper Martin did the mound walk to yank a pitcher who was in trouble. As he was walking him to the dugout, he heard footsteps behind him. He turned. It was me.
>
> "Where are you going? Get back to first base."
>
> "Oh sorry, Skip, I'm so used to being yanked, I thought I was supposed to go, too." I was a very clean pitcher. I took a lot of showers.[6]

> *Jim Archer*: And of course, Mickey McDermott. I'll never forget this guy. Yeah, he pitched for the Red Sox, and his mother-in-law was related to Bart Riley, a criminal attorney. As a matter of fact, Mickey said that he was Al Capone's attorney. And I had been in front of his house in Miami Beach but I never, of course, went in. . . . This guy was amazing to watch for his age; he could throw a baseball like a brick when you caught it. He just had a very strong arm. He was a character. He was drinking later on in his life and he showed up late for a ballgame in Havana one night and Pepper brought him in and talked to him and Mickey come out and he said, "That's the only person in this world that brought tears to my eyes." He said, "He must be something else, [pause] I've been a hard-ass all my life and he actually made me cry." [laughing hysterically][7]

One of McDermott's gifts was his ability to provide comic relief to his colleagues. Stories abound concerning his exploits, and George Zuverink fondly remembers his outgoing, happy-go-lucky teammate.

> *George Zuverink*: Oh, there again, my memory you know. Oh, who's the guy that was with Boston? Mickey [McDermott] was there. Oh, he was still drinking down there. We went to the ballpark one day and Pepper says, "Mickey, I don't think you're ready to play ball. Why don't you go back to the hotel?" After the game we came back and he was just singing away. [laughing] They're not going to stop him anyway, Mickey McDermott, what a guy.[8]

With hopes high and in the midst of a tight pennant race, the Marlins arrived, with McDermott safely in tow, looking forward to gaining ground on front-running Buffalo. Drawing the starting assignment for game one of the critical road trip was Archer to square off against Cuellar. For Havana (45–52) this was a critical series. Still residing in last place tied with Columbus, the grim certainty of dropping completely out of the playoff race was a reality that manager Preston Gomez and his club were not willing to accept.

Most of the Sugar Kings had grown accustomed to the military personnel's presence, but to the visiting Marlins the sight of olive-drab-clad bearded guards carrying machine guns was disconcerting. Trying to relax in the hotel lobby, Archer, battling a case of nerves and admitting he was not feeling well, told his coach Bill Cates, "Better tape my ankle good because I might want to run out of the park fast tonight." It is hard to say whether the atmosphere had an effect on the Marlins' play or not, but what would transpire over the next four games would set the tone for the rest of the season for both squads.

Steve Korcheck recalls that when in Havana you never knew what to expect. Celebrities abounded at the local clubs, but sometimes you crossed paths with luminaries of another variety.

> *Steve Korcheck*: Well, of course, '59, Castro took over and we went to play Havana that year, I'm going to guess, in about April. Maybe even into May. And we stayed at the Havana Hilton, which was Fidel Castro's headquarters. And we were checking into the hotel. They had two .50 caliber machine guns at each side of the entryway. And, you know, didn't give you a hell of a lot of joy.
>
> But anyhow, after we played the night game—of course, you always played the night game—we got back to the hotel. And Pepper Martin and I just happened to be standing together and he looked over and said, "I believe that is Fidel Castro." And you know he had an entourage with him. And he said go talk with him. At the time I had four years of Spanish and was fairly fluent in Spanish. I graduated in college in '54, so a couple of years went by, but I was still fairly fluent.
>
> "So go over there and see if we can talk to him."
>
> I said, "Hell, I don't want to go over there—we'll get shot." And anyhow, I finally did, and found out immediately that Castro was an absolute baseball fanatic. And so Pepper and I went over there and we talked with him until about 5 o'clock in the morning. And . . . just had a great time with him. He just wanted to talk baseball. He didn't say anything about the revolution, or anything.
>
> And Pepper and I said later, Joe Cambria, who was the scout for the Washington Senators in Cuba at the time, because you know Washington was the first team to recruit Cuban ballplayers, and I said, "I wonder if Joe Cambria had signed Castro to a contract if it might have completely changed world history."
>
> [Did he speak to you in English?]
>
> No, he spoke broken English. You know when I went over I talked Spanish. Don't get me wrong, I wasn't real fluent, but enough where I could speak it. And he sort of spoke broken English back then. Most of our conversation was broken English with a little bit of Spanish interspersed, I think.
>
> But it's amazing, Sam, that's my one great recollection of playing with the Miami Marlins.[9]

Adding to the tension was the eeriness of a near-empty Gran Stadium. Castro was scheduled to make one of his famous speeches and the local population stayed home glued to their televisions. Archer's prediction proved prophetic. Unable to find the strike zone, he allowed three runs in the first inning without recording an out. Trailing 3–1, with the bases loaded, Martin turned the ball over to veteran Harry Byrd, who masterfully worked out of the jam without allowing any further damage. After the Marlins had trimmed the lead down to 3–2 in the third inning, Leo Burke tied the score in the fourth, hammering his sixteenth home run of the year. The Sugar Kings tacked on a single run in the sixth inning, and another in the seventh inning when Elio Chacon hit a laser over center-fielder Fred Valentine's head for a triple off of Zuverink, and scored when the next batter, Tony Gonzalez, followed by driving a ball deep to the outfield for a sacrifice fly. Miami's rally in the ninth inning came up short. After cutting the Sugar Kings' lead to 5–4 with two outs, reliever Luis Arroyo came into the game to face pinch-hitter McDermott, who weakly grounded out to end the game.[10]

The rest of the four-game set proved just as troublesome for the Marlins. The following night Miami outhit the Sugar Kings 6–4, but fell short in the run column. Walt Craddock had one of his best performances of the year, earning a complete game win and shutout as the Sugar Kings prevailed, 3–0. Craddock only struck out one enemy hitter, but his control was impeccable, failing to give up a free pass and allowing only one extra base hit to Jerry Snyder.[11]

Closing out the series on July 19, in front of only 1,576 diehard *fanaticos*, the Marlins dropped both ends of the doubleheader by the scores of 4–3 and 4–1. In the first game, after Bunky Stewart had allowed three runs to score in the fourth inning, he was yanked in favor of McDermott. McDermott's fastball was working to perfection and when Miami came back to knot the score in the fifth inning at 3–3, spurred by a McDermott two-run homer, it looked as if Miami would prevail. Nonetheless, skipper Gomez turned to one of their own weapons from the bullpen, Ted Wieand. The big right-hander from Walnutport, Pennsylvania, matched the irrepressible McDermott at every turn. Going into the extra frame Miami failed to score, but in the bottom of the eighth catcher Jesse Gonder found a kink in Mickey D's armor, driving a game winning single to right field with two outs and ending the contest in Havana's favor, 4–3.[12]

The nightcap was anticlimactic, as Miami finished with a whimper by losing 4–1. Raul Sanchez, known around the league as generously using the doctored horsehide, earned the complete game win holding Miami to only six hits while striking out the same number. For the Marlins the frustrations continued, as their offense had failed to score more than four runs in any single game since July 6. Foster Castleman, who was limited to only pinch-hitting duties due to his ongoing knee problems, was anxiously looking forward to returning to Miami and relieving the light-hitting Bobby Willis at shortstop.[13]

Coming back to Miami to kick off a seven-game homestand against Rochester and Buffalo, the Marlins (50–48) found themselves barely clinging to second place, having dropped five and a half games behind the now red-hot Bisons.[14]

With John Anderson suffering from a pulled shoulder muscle and Archer nursing a bad back, Martin was forced to turn to one of his relievers, the steady Zuverink. Making his first start since 1955, Zukerink made a case that maybe he had been miscast in his role as a long man out of the bullpen. The stifling humidity, combined with a drop off the table sinker, put the kibosh on the visitors as Zuverink pitched a four-hit, seven-inning complete game 3–0 win. Zuverink wasn't the only player on the diamond debuting in a new role. McDermott, sporting a glossy .364 batting average, made his first appearance playing first base for the ailing Frank Kellert and Norm Zauchin.[15]

The Rochesterians, who left the batting box mostly frustrated in the first game, returned for the nightcap on a mission. Led by big six-foot-two right-hander Bob Keegan, the Red Wings evened the ledger by taking the second game, 3–1. Although the Marlins outhit their opponents 8–7, they failed to cash in with runners in scoring position, stranding nine.[16]

Again, Martin turned to his bullpen performers for help and called on Artie Kay. Kay, making the most of the opportunity, rose to the occasion in the third game and repeated Zuverink's performance by recording another 3–0 shutout. Kay was flawless, allowing only two hits, walking one, and striking out four. With some much-needed help from Castleman's two-run home run in the third inning off of starter Cal Browning, it proved to be more than enough offense and the Marlins cruised past the Red Wings despite only collecting five of their own hits on the night.[17]

The fourth game set the tone for the rest of the homestand, as Miami took one of its worst defeats of the season, going down quietly, 12–4. With Buffalo coming to town next, the three-game homestand was critical if the Marlins were to stay in the race. Although still in second place, the Marlins (52–50) were barely treading water and trailed the Bisons by a full five games.

The series proved to be a disaster for the Marlins as Bisons starters Ken Lehman, Art Mahaffey, and Warren Hacker all were dominant through the three-game sweep. Marlins swingman Byrd was the most frustrated hurler when he lost his third straight one-run decision in the July 24 opener, 1–0.[18] The Marlins had hoped to capitalize on the absence of one of the Bisons' starters when it was announced that Bisons star Pancho Herrera was being detained in Havana with visa problems. Instead, his replacement, thirty-seven-year-old Jack Phillips, banged out two hits and scored the winning run.

The lid-lifter proved to be an omen. The Marlins crashed in the second game, falling 8–1, and followed up the next night losing 5–3, putting Martin's charges under the .500 mark and in third place, half a game behind the hard-charging Havana club. For all intents and purposes, it appeared the Marlins (52–53) had written off their chances of winning the IL and instead were hoping for a first division finish at best. "They gave it more than the expected effort," said Martin following the sweep, hinting to the press that there was little chance of catching the Buffalo Bisons.[19]

Enjoying a welcome day off, the Marlins were looking at a grueling northern road trip that included stops in Toronto, Montreal, Buffalo, and Rochester. If Miami had any chance of staying in the playoff hunt, they would have to earn at least a split of the sixteen games that lay ahead.

Odd as it seems, the Marlins' hitters were eager to hit the road, where favorable venues provided more conducive environments for batters. Over the course of the season Marlins hitters had struggled at home, hitting thirty points lower than when away. In addition, hitting home runs at a rate of over two to one (forty-eight on the road and twenty-three at home on July 27) when escaping the confines of Miami Stadium, sluggers like Woody Smith and Leo Burke welcomed the occasional long ball. One Marlins ballplayer, not mentioned by name in the *Miami News*, was quoted as saying, "We'd be ten games ahead with the players we have if we were in any other park in the league." He added, "For one thing it's next to impossible to hit the ball out of the park here."[20]

Indeed, around the league, known as a pitcher's dream ballpark, Miami Stadium was a graveyard for hitters. Two factors in particular were obstacles to hitters. For one, the infield grass was cut high, and teamed with the constant wetness that prevailed in the spring and summer months, many hard-hit balls were slowed down considerably, giving infielders added time to field them and put out would-be hitters in their tracks. Second, the prevailing winds that always seemed to be blowing in toward home plate discouraged many a long drive that would have easily escaped in other parks around the league.[21]

Before boarding their flight to Toronto, the Marlin players bid adieu to Steve Korcheck, who was recalled by the Washington Senators. In turn, they greeted their newest backstop, fresh-faced twenty-one-year-old Danny Bishop, en route to Toronto.[22] The year before, Bishop proved he was capable not only with the stick but also as a fine handler of pitchers. Coming off the 1958 season, in which he hit .280 for Class-C Aberdeen of the Northern League, he had also called signals for future major leaguers Steve Barber, Bo Belinsky, and Herm Starrette.[23] General Manager Joe Ryan was hinting there were even more moves in the works.

Travel is always hard on ballplayers and Miami showed the effects of their long flight, dropping the series opener despite banging out eleven base hits. The game started out promisingly enough as Miami jumped to an early 5–0 lead. In the bottom of the fifth, Archer showed the effects of his injured back, giving up five runs in the fifth inning. McDermott came on in the sixth inning and only aided in the melee by throwing more gas on the fire as the Maple Leafs tagged him for six runs in an inning of work. Before the smoke had cleared the Leafs had coasted to an easy 15–8 win.

Martin tried Anderson the next night but the ailing knuckleballer had to be pulled after only two-thirds of an inning after giving up three runs in rapid procession. Fortunately, Artie Kay stepped up again and held down the fort until his teammates could mount a comeback, pitching six and two-thirds innings and only allowing a couple of runs. So strapped was Martin's bullpen that he had to turn to starters Archer and Moford to seal the win. Moford earned the hard-fought 6–5 victory, pitching the final three innings of the eleven-inning affair without giving up a run. Johnny Bucha's single in the final inning proved the difference maker.[24]

The pitching staff was taxed to the limit and the offense was continuing to be inept at putting runs on the board. The club experienced one of its worst road trips of the year. Toronto nearly swept the Marlins by taking three out of the four games. Especially frustrating was the series-ending defeat in which Anderson went nine strong innings only to lose the game in the extra frame, 2–1, when Bert Hamric's attempt at a shoe-string catch of a Hector Rodriguez line drive came up short, allowing pinch runner Tim Thompson to score.[25] Making matters worse, the loss sent the Marlins into second division.

One-run defeats followed Miami like a stray puppy dog looking for a bone. Montreal followed by winning three of five games; two of the contests were decided by one run. Bob Keegan in particular continued his mastery over Miami on August 8, blanking the Marlins 5–0 for his fourth win in five tries on August 8.

First-place Buffalo followed, taking two out of three contests. By this point the Marlins must have felt like they were bitten by a nest of snakes. As an example of how bad things had gotten, in the series-opening game the usually dependable Bobby Willis booted two balls in the fourth inning that led to a couple of unearned runs. The miscues proved to be the difference in Buffalo's 8–6 triumph and negated Hamric's and Oertel's home runs. Hamric, a notorious streak hitter, had endured a horrible 4–52 slump earlier in the year but had been on a tear as of late, blasting five dingers in the last week, but all for naught.[26] Prior to the second game against Buffalo, newly arrived catcher Bishop suffered a finger injury while taking infield practice, and Bucha, who was scheduled for some rest, was forced into action. Bucha's own hand was so banged up he was forced to dip it in an ice bucket between innings to cut the pain.[27] And in the *pièce de résistance,* despite suffering from a horrible toothache, starter Chris Short quieted the Marlins' bats, earning his twelfth win by the score of 5–1.[28]

Closing out the miserable road trip the Marlins were once again robbed—not only on the field but also off the field in Rochester. The Red Wings captured three of the four games, and two contests were decided by single runs again. The August 9 doubleheader turned into a nightmare when Miami dropped the opening game in thirteen innings. It was probably the most unusual loss of the year. Moford, in late relief, pitched more than five innings of no-hit ball going into the thirteenth inning and hit with an errant pitch the lead-off batter Lee Tate. Moford regained his composure, retiring the next two batters before intentionally walking two batters and then plunking Charley James to force in the winning run. The final tally showed Red Wings 5, Marlins 4.[29]

Fortunes didn't improve during the night game. Zuverink was pounded for three runs—including a Luke Easter solo homer in the first two innings—leading a frustrated Martin to turn to his depleted bullpen. The Marlins mounted a comeback, cutting the lead to 3–2 on a Burke sacrifice fly and RBI single by Valentine but came up short as Howie Nunn, who later would have a short career as a nondescript relief pitcher, slammed the door in the seventh inning, preserving the complete game win, 3–2.[30]

On July 15 the Marlins were within one game of Buffalo for the IL lead. In just over three weeks they had tumbled to seventh place, thirteen games behind the league-leading Bisons. Just before the Marlins (57–64) were set to leave town, as if things were bad enough, some local thieves broke into the Marlins' locker room and helped themselves to the team's equipment. The losses amounted to thirteen gloves, forty-eight new baseballs, seven bats, three jackets, four pairs of baseball shoes, and $15 belonging to the clubhouse boy.[31] What wasn't on the police report were the Marlins' playoff hopes, which had been all but snatched in plain sight.

Although the situation looked bleak, General Manager Ryan wasn't throwing in the baseball cap just yet. Always the wheeler and dealer, the optimistic general manager lived up to his promise to find help. In an effort to bolster the lineup, shortstop Jose Valdivielso[32] was acquired from the Washington Senators, catcher Walter Brady was obtained from Class-A Allentown,[33] and former Marlins hurler Bob Conley was purchased from Buffalo[34] to help shore up the mound corps. Conley in particular had been a cog in the Marlins' starting rotation just the year before, going 12–11 with a 2.94 ERA, but had fallen on hard times in Buffalo. It was hoped that a change in venue might spark his return to respectability.

Ryan, always looking to broker a transaction and disappointed by Frank Kellert's lackluster performance, sold the big Oklahoman to Vancouver of the PCL. Kellert, who was expected to provide considerable "punch" in the lineup, more resembled Judy, batting only .245 with a paltry six home runs and twenty-four RBIs in seventy-seven games. In a further move to complete the trade for Brady, the Marlins shipped Vito Valentinetti to Triple-A Minneapolis.[35]

Miami's faint hopes of making a run for the final playoff position rested on a successful sixteen-game homestand against Toronto, Montreal, Columbus, and Richmond. In order to have a shot, Miami would have to leapfrog both Rochester (59–63) and Montreal (60–63) in order to have any chance of catching Richmond (61–61) and Columbus (61–61), currently tied for fourth place.

Bolstered by a day of rest, the Marlins opened up their August 11 homecoming in front of a meager 2,652 paying customers. Although attendance for the year was up by about seven thousand, it was far below the expectations that Storer had projected he would need to keep running the club. The Miami press continued badgering Storer to announce whether he was going to keep the club in Miami and retain ownership, but he remained defiantly silent. Throughout the season, as various articles were alluding to a possible expansion of professional baseball into a third major league—or, as it would come to be known, the Continental League—Miami was often mentioned as a possible candidate. Increasingly, the press was calling on Storer to state his intentions. Would he retain ownership in hopes of securing a new franchise in the upstart league? Would he keep the club in Miami as a member of the IL? Or would he sell the team to a local investor? Tommy Devine, a popular columnist for the *Miami News*, summed it up best when he stated, "Storer is the only radio man I know, who thinks silence is golden."[36] Ultimately, Storer would not divulge his intentions until late that same year.

Although the continued rumors provided fodder for the fans in the seats, the Marlins players gave them little thought and instead were more focused on what was taking place on the playing field. Starting out by taking three out of four from Toronto, and two of three from Montreal, it lit a small flame of hope that another late season turnaround might be in the works. The highlight between the Marlins and the Canadians was when the hometown team took both ends of an August 16 doubleheader, dropping Montreal 11–2 in the opener behind Byrd's complete game performance. Bunky Stewart matched Byrd's feat in the second game, picking up the complete game victory, 4–1.[37] Both Canadian teams were sent packing and aspirations were renewed, but with reservations. Troublesome Columbus and a hard-charging Richmond club were next on the agenda. The Marlins had to be encouraged as they had dominated the Vees during the year, taking fourteen of their previous eighteen meetings.

As usual the Jets proved to be a thorn in the Marlins' side. The three-game series proved to be full of pitching duels and nail-biters. An age-old nemesis, Lynn Lovenguth, was called on to oppose Herb Moford in the opening game. Moford, not up to the task, left the game in the sixth inning, leaving the Marlins trailing, 3–1. Fortunately, Artie Kay registered another fine performance in relief, squelching a possible game-breaking rally and retiring the last two batters in the sixth inning. Miami rallied in the bottom of the ninth inning when Burke singled, chasing Lovenguth and forcing Jets manager Cal Ermer to bring in the right-handed throwing Don Williams to face the next batter, Oertel. Conceding the run, and with the infield playing back, Oertel hit a grounder that resulted in an infield out but scored Burke and moved Valentine to third. With one out and Valentine dancing on third, Ermer again went to his bullpen and this time to left-hander Al Jackson to face Castleman. Jets catcher Danny Baich nervously kept one eye on the pitcher and the other on the jittery Valentine, who kept faking his way home. Valentine's ploy worked and he so upset Baich that the next pitch eluded the catcher. Thinking the ball had got by him and not noticing that the ball had grazed the batter's and umpire's legs, Valentine started to rush home. Baich had, however, kept the ball in front of him and it looked as if Valentine would be caught up between third and home. But Baich's peg to Jackson hit Valentine in the leg and bounced away, allowing Valentine to finish racing home and knotting the score at 3–3.[38]

The momentum seemingly shifted in Miami's favor until the tenth inning when Byrd faltered. After a Ken Hamlin double, Ken Jaciuk singled, bringing Hamlin home and putting the Jets ahead, 4–3. Jackson silenced the Marlins in the bottom of the tenth inning and a dejected Byrd walked off the mound having suffered his twelfth loss of the season. The Marlins had now dropped eleven of fifteen games to Columbus.[39]

The next evening's proceedings weren't much better for the Marlins as they dropped their second consecutive one-run decision by a 5–4 tally. One blast by Jets left fielder Bob Thorpe, a three-run home run off of Anderson, was a crushing blow that left everyone in the Marlins organization, including General Manager Ryan, shaking their heads. Ryan went as far as to ask whether it was possible to beat the Jets, which elicited his response: "It can't be done."[40] Richmond (66–67), having beat second-place Havana (69–63) the last two nights, now stood in fourth place, one and a half games ahead of Miami (64–68).

The *Miami News* sportswriter Tommy Fitzgerald highlighted a note to the Jets at the top of his sports column: "We know you're enjoying your stay in Miami and surely you'd love to play us every day. But, after all fellas . . . ain't you ever heard of charity."[41] Feeling sorry for the Marlins, the Jets did their best imitation of Mother Teresa in the last game of the series, handing Miami a 2–0 win. Archer honed in on his pinpoint control and contributed another one of his many fine performances of the year by holding the Jets to four hits while striking out four and not allowing a single walk.[42]

The Marlins' performance against Columbus was disappointing. If there was any chance to make a run for the final playoff spot, it was now and against their closest competitor, Richmond, for the coveted final playoff spot. A confident Martin was hoping he would get enough hitting to support his chosen starters for the series: Byrd, Stewart, Moford, and Anderson.

Ominous, angry thunderclouds greeted both teams on arrival at Miami Stadium on the morning of August 21. It wasn't long before the skies opened up and torrential rains followed. Puddles gathered on the infield dirt as many of the players happily made plans for a much-anticipated day off. Although only 1,574 paying customers had shown up, Ryan was not in the mood to let a single gate receipt get away if he could help it.

Bill Durney made a suggestion to Ryan that a helicopter hovering over the infield might solve the problem of the hopelessly drenched infield. Ryan swiftly picked up the telephone and placed a call. It wasn't long before a helicopter was hovering over the park. The whirlybird dropped to about six feet over the field and in short time the giant spinning blades dried out the red dirt.[43] Although Satchel Paige was conspicuously absent as a passenger, the pilot earned the MVP for the day and the contest proceeded.

Bill Durney Jr. remembers the difficulty that the wet summers in South Florida presented by the field conditions being up to the task.

> *Bill Durney Jr.*: In August, every day at four-thirty there was a horrendous storm that came through. That was one of the big lessons I learned from my dad. My dad says you play every game you possibly can because you don't want the people getting used to that you may not play. Because Miami was terrible for, especially rush hour if you were going home in rush hour traffic and you have plans to go to the game and it's raining, people shut down right then and say, "Well, they're not playing tonight." What we used to do, we used to when that was located next to I-95 or whatever, we used to when the storm came up at four-thirty, five o'clock at night we turned the lights on then just to let the people know we were playing. And we played every possible game you could possibly get in. And I remember playoff games there they used to bring helicopters in to dry out the infield. I'm sure going over news accounts you will see pictures of that. That always made the news when you do that. Just blow the water off the infield.
>
> That field was amazing. That water it would pool up and drain right through.
>
> We did nothing. It was a natural field but it was on pea rock and once the water got through the top soil it was gone. And I mean you could have a, you could have an inch of rain in a half hour and hour later the place was dry. So, you know, you just made every effort you possibly could to get a ballgame in.
>
> Never gave people any doubt you were going to play. Half your games, you know, you were going to lose the crowd if that was the case. Once that season rolled in, every day looked like a possible rainout.[44]

Following the dramatic exit of the helicopter, the Marlins players — and the few fans left in their rain-soaked seats who braved the weather — wished that the game had been postponed. Facing Vees ace Chris Short, the Marlins' bats seemed as waterlogged as the outfield grass. Mustering only six singles, and despite a gutsy performance by Byrd, the final score showed the Vees upending the Marlins, 3–1. The big blow of the evening came on Deron Johnson's two-run homer in the eighth inning.[45]

The first game proved to be a presage to the rest of the series, as the Marlins dropped all four games. The usually reliable Stewart was hammered the next evening, quickly giving up four walks and five hits in only three innings of work. Despite Burke's twenty-first home run of the year, breaking the team record previously held by Pancho Herrera, the Vees' offense proved too much, pounding out ten hits in the 8–2 win.[46]

The August 23 doubleheader put a dagger in the hearts of the Marlins' playoff hopes. Moford and Vees righty-throwing Jim Bronstad matched zeroes until the fifth inning when the Virginians' second baseman Tony Asaro singled in teammate Fritz Brickell for the only run of the game. Anderson fared no better in the nightcap—no fault of his own, as he received little offensive support. The only Marlins run for the evening was a solo home run by Valentine. Anderson held the Vees to five hits, striking out five and failing to issue any base on balls in six innings, only to see Artie Kay falter in the seventh inning and give up a couple of scores. For all intents and purposes the Marlins were finished. The usually laid-back Ryan, visibly upset after the game, threatened to curtail lucrative offseason incomes of some of his players. "I am going to refuse permission to some of the Marlins to play winter baseball if they're as tired as they look," the livid general manager stated to the press. He added, "I'll find out who's really tired." Martin, however, was unperturbed in his assessment: "They all tried, and I admire them for it."[47]

It was obvious that the Marlins were just playing out the string. Although the club was not mathematically eliminated, currently trailing the fourth-place Virginians by five and a half games, it appeared that they had thrown in the towel. All but three of Miami's remaining seventeen games were left to play on the road, starting with their archrivals the Sugar Kings, and there was a hint that Martin's lackadaisical management style and frustration in the clubhouse were taking their toll.

The Marlins were clearly a different team the second half of the season. Losing Jack Fisher to the Orioles, nagging injuries to their frontline pitchers Archer and Anderson, and the overall lack of depth coming off the bench all played a part in their lackluster performance, while some of the club's struggles could also be directly traced to the deteriorating relationship between a group of the veteran players on the team and Martin.

To further Ryan's frustration, the Marlins closed the season with a whimper, dropping eleven of their final seventeen games. The ultimate humiliation came at the hands of Columbus, who swept a five-game set that included shutting out the Marlins twice.

The final home game of the season saw the Marlins fall to Havana, 4–2. The season-ender was always reserved to honor the players and this night was no exception. Woody Smith was voted by the local sportswriters and broadcasters as the team's Most Valuable Player for the third consecutive season after batting .274, with sixteen homers and seventy-eight ribbies. In the fan voting, Fred Valentine earned honors as the team's most popular player, but he was absent from the festivities after being called up by the Orioles to finish out the season. Valentine closed the season with a .257 average, but led the club in runs (82), hits (158), triples (11), and stolen bases (28). John Anderson (12–9, 2.74 ERA, 204 IP) was given the award for the team's most valuable pitcher despite only winning one game after July. Another notable highlight was Artie Kay's performance. Despite a lackluster 7–6 record, Kay won the IL's ERA title, sporting a 2.08 mark having toiled 160 innings.[48]

Burke failed to add any home runs to the team record after the Richmond massacre in August. Despite his impressive season of twenty-one home runs to go along with seventy RBIs, he set a dubious IL record by striking out 146 times, breaking the previous record held by Luke Easter (140).[49] Notwithstanding this, Burke, along with Jack Fisher, Wes Stock, Fred Valentine, and George Zuverink, were Marlins who saw action in the big leagues, albeit mostly expanded roster recalls in September. Sadly, Woody Smith, despite another productive season, was overlooked once again by the parent club. Smith, now thirty-two years old, was considered old in baseball years, and the focus of the Orioles and Paul Richards was continuing to develop younger players, building what would one day become the Baltimore Orioles dynasty. One youngster in particular was already at the big-league level playing the hot corner and would make quite a name for himself down the road as the "Human Vacuum Cleaner," gobbling up balls hit his way with skillful prowess few had ever seen before. His name was Brooks Robinson.

A postscript to the season in what shaped up to be a dogfight of a pennant race turned out to be a near runaway for Buffalo. Although Columbus made a late-season run, mostly thanks to feasting on the Marlins all season, they fell short by five and a half games to the Bisons. Much like Miami's playoff run in 1957, entering the postseason with a losing record, Richmond repeated the act and surprised the Bisons in the initial round of playoffs by taking four of five games. In the other series, Havana, a last-place finisher the year before, pulled off another upset, sweeping the favored Columbus Jets. Havana, led by future major league stars Mike Cuellar, Leo Cardenas, and Tony Gonzalez, then took home their first IL title by knocking of Richmond in six games. Ultimately, the Cinderella Sugar Kings would shock the world and defeat the much-favored Minneapolis Millers in the Junior World Series, four games to three. To Marlins fans, it must have been painful seeing the success of their biggest rivals come to fruition. The people of Havana were dancing in the street and in Miami all they could say was "Maybe next year."

Final Standings:

	W	L	GB
Buffalo	89	64	–
Columbus	84	70	5½
Havana	80	73	9
Richmond	76	78	13 ½
Rochester	74	80	15½
Montreal	72	82	17½
Miami	71	83	18½
Toronto	69	85	20½

NOTES

1. Tommy Fitzgerald, "Says Storer Feels Same," *Miami News*, July 28, 1959.

2. Cy Kritzer, "Shag Hails Bisons as Tops on Defense," *Sporting News*, July 29, 1959.

3. Jimmy Burns, "Maduro Ready to Sell, Castro Offers New Aid," *Sporting News*, July 29, 1959.

4. *Sporting News*, July 29, 1959, 32; Tommy Fitzgerald, "'Innocent'" Mickey Nabbed Again," *Miami News*, July 17, 1959.

5. Fitzgerald, "'Innocent'" Mickey Nabbed Again."

6. Howard Eisenberg and Mickey McDermott, *A Funny Thing Happened on the Way to Cooperstown* (Chicago: Triumph Books, 2003), 154.

7. Jim Archer, phone interview with the author, February 21, 2010.

8. George Zuverink, phone interview with the author, May 3, 2010.

9. Steve Korcheck, phone interview with the author, April 11, 2010.

10. *Sporting News*, July 29, 1959, 32; Bob Owens, "Tommygun, Ghost Park Too Much for Marlins," *Miami News*, July 18, 1959.

11. *Sporting News*, July 29, 1959, 32.

12. *Sporting News*, July 29, 1959, 32; Bob Owens, "Wanted: Hitters Who Hit; Apply Miami Stadium NOW," *Miami News*, July 20, 1959.

13. *Sporting News*, July 29, 1959, 32; Owens, "Wanted: Hitters Who Hit; Apply Miami Stadium NOW."

14. Owens, "Wanted: Hitters Who Hit; Apply Miami Stadium NOW."

15. Tommy Fitzgerald, Bob Keegan Polished Off Marlins," *Miami News*, July 22, 1959.

16. *Sporting News*, August 5, 1959, 32; Fitzgerald, "Bob Keegan Polished Off Marlins."

17. *Sporting News*, August 5, 1959, 31–32.

18. "Bisons Hold Hex over Byrd," *Sporting News*, August 5, 1959, 32.

19. Bob Owens, "Marlins Battling for Top 4 Finish," *Miami News*, July 27, 1959.

20. Bob Owens, "Marlins Hitting Better on Road," *Miami News*, July 28, 1959.

21. Ibid.

22. Ibid.

23. Baseball-reference.com.

24. Don Hunt, "Bucha Confuses 'Em after Hit Wins Game," *Miami News*, July 30, 1959.

25. *Sporting News*, August 12, 1959, 27, 34; Don Hunt, "Leafs Bounce Marlins into Second Division," *Miami News*, August 1, 1959.

26. Cy Kritzer, "Byrd, Luck Still Down, Loses to Bisons," *Miami News*, August 5, 1959.

27. Cy Kritzer, "Bucha Courage Praised in Defeat of Buffalo," *Miami News*, August 6, 1959.

28. Cy Kritzer, "Burke Another Colavito?," *Miami News*, August 7, 1959.

29. "Marlins Lost All but Their Tickets Home," *Miami News*, August 10, 1959.

30. Ibid.

31. *Sporting News*, August 19, 1959, 32.

32. "Sports Scene about Miami," *Miami News*, August 8, 1959.

33. Bob Owens, "Zauchin behind Plate?" *Miami News*, August 11, 1959.

34. "Transactions," *Sporting News*, August 19, 1959, 25.

35. "Transactions," *Sporting News*, August 19, 1959, 25.

36. Tommy Devine, "Radio Man Believes in Silence," *Miami News*, August 21, 1959.

37. Bob Owens, "Marlins Face Only First Division," *Miami News*, August 17, 1959.

38. Tommy Fitzgerald, "Fred's Bat, Glove Fell Bit Short," *Miami News*, August 19, 1959.

39. Ibid.

40. Tommy Fitzgerald, "What Do You Have to Do to Beat That Columbus," *Miami News*, August 20, 1959.

41. Ibid.

42. *Sporting News*, September 2, 1959, 27, 36.

43. Jimmy Burns, "Helicopter Used to Dry Off Miami Park after Rainstorm," *Sporting News*, September 2, 1959, 32.

44. Bill Durney Jr., phone interview with author, December 21, 2010.

45. *Sporting News*, September 2, 1959, 28.

46. Tommy Fitzgerald, "Marlins Deflated as Vees Reduce Playoff Chances," *Miami News*, August 23, 1959.

47. Bob Owens, "Marlins Just Going through the Motions . . . Ryan," *Miami News*, August 24, 1959.

48. *Sporting News*, September 16, 1959, 30; baseball-reference.com.

49. *Sporting News*, September 2, 1959, 36.

Part V

1960

TWENTY-SIX

Old MacDonald Had a Farm Team

George Storer—or, as the press sometimes dubbed him, "Silent George"—finally broke his silence and announced the news of the fate of the Marlins. The taciturn owner had lived up to the promise that he had made almost a year ago: if the Marlins did not at least break even, he would sell the team with the stipulation of keeping the club in Miami. Although the financial bleeding had slowed, bean counters' numbers don't lie, and the Marlins' books reflected that the club was in the red for 1959 in the amount of $52,500. The divorce was final.

Storer, who no doubt had been shopping around his team for a while in the anticipation of luring a buyer, didn't look far to find the team's new owner: his close friend Bill MacDonald. On the evening of January 2, 1960 it was formally announced that MacDonald agreed to the purchase of the club at an undisclosed amount somewhat less than what Storer had originally paid for the Marlins. General Manager Joe Ryan assessed the situation when he said, "Mr. Storer has had a lot of problems with the ball club." He added, "Not only has he lost money on the team itself but he has had keen disappointments with the concession company. He felt the return from his investments were ridiculously low."[1] Ryan's statement was an understatement, to say the least.

Like Storer, MacDonald was a self-made millionaire. Although both men were exceptionally wealthy, they were polar opposites in personality. Storer was business-like and aloof whereas the unassuming MacDonald—a self-proclaimed extrovert—was warm and generous to a fault. MacDonald was the modern version of Dickens's character Fezziwig from *A Christmas Carol*, minus the Welsh wig. A large rotund man with a perpetual smile on his face and a warm, firm handshake for everyone he met, he enjoyed life to the fullest hilt. A doting father who spoiled his two children, he was also generous toward friends and associates and was known for handing out gold cufflinks like Santa hands out candy canes during the Yule season. Scrooge's account of old Fezziwig can easily be attributed to MacDonald when he says, "He has the power to render us happy or unhappy; to make our service light or burdensome; a pleasure or a toil . . . the happiness he gives, is quite as great as if it cost a fortune." [2]

MacDonald was born in Butte, Montana, in 1908 and by his own admission was a descendant of sheep thieves. As a young man he felt the need to escape the mining town he grew up in and go somewhere he could exploit his gift of gab and business sense. At the time, Chicago was a growing, bustling metropolis that was brimming with opportunities and MacDonald seized his chance. He began working as a bus conductor for the Chicago Motor Coach Company, which gave him the opportunity to do what he liked best: to talk and meet people. When his supervisor, a man named Paddy, informed him he was going to be a driver, MacDonald told this story in a 1964 interview with *Sports Illustrated*: "It was the Fourth of July. A jillion people got on and got off. It was ding, stop, and dong, go. I never got out of second gear. I must have lost five pounds. When I got back I told Paddy he could keep his glamorous driver's boots and fancy uniform. I wanted to be a conductor and stand in the back and ring the bell and holler, 'low bridge!' and meet the people. 'Me bucko,' said Paddy, 'a driver you are and a driver you'll be.'" MacDonald summed up his decision by adding, "If I hadn't been so impulsive, today I'd have 36 years' seniority and the choice of routes, a Polish wife, two kids and only a couple more payments on a refrigerator." [3]

Free to pursue his dreams, MacDonald opened his first business during the height of the Depression, a ticket agency offering travelers transportation from Chicago to New York in twenty-eight hours or your money back. Needless to say, and according to MacDonald, he never issued a refund. When train fares dropped, MacDonald wisely got out of the business and sold out to the Santa Fe. Within a couple of years the money was nearly gone and, not a man to stay in one place too long, he made his way to Miami. Always looking for an opportunity, he sold his Buick coupe and for $750 bought the parking concession rights at the Dempsey-Vanderbilt Hotel on Collins and 21st. [4] In quick succession MacDonald parlayed his profits, investing in the dry-cleaning business, restaurant management, trucking, and finally selling mobile homes and building the largest mortgage company then in San Juan, Puerto Rico. [5]

Residing in a ritzy home in Bal Harbour with his wife Victoria, his two adopted children, two Rolls Royce autos, and a fifty-foot yacht named "Snoozie," MacDonald was familiar to Floridians not only for his various business ventures but also for his ownership of the Class-D Tampa Tarpons. One of the things he was most proud of was turning around the struggling Tarpons and developing them into the pride of the Florida State League. MacDonald loved the sporting life and besides being an avid golfer, he owned a stable of racing horses and enjoyed fishing the Atlantic waters for trophy marlin. One source of great pride was displaying his trophy catches on the wall of his house. It was not unusual to see the corpulent MacDonald smoking a cigar while holding a Coke in one hand and talking about his latest catch or eye-catching chip shot on the course all at the same time.[6] With the newest addition to his collection of endeavors, MacDonald had now landed the biggest marlin he had ever bagged, and just like hooking the large sporting fish, it was not going to be an easy proposition hauling it in and making it a trophy to admire.

Before liquidating the Marlins, Storer left two final fingerprints on the organization. First, he signed a full working agreement with the Baltimore Orioles securing Miami as their only Triple-A affiliate. Second, he addressed the club's much-needed leadership change. Pepper Martin had expressed an interest in returning to the team for another season, but it was no secret that the Orioles and Ryan and Storer were not happy with how the club had performed in 1959. Although the "Wild Horse of Osage" was popular with the team's fan base, his lackadaisical form of managing and failure to control a few of his troublesome veterans, like Mickey McDermott and Windy McCall, ultimately proved to be his downfall. It was time for a change and Storer had made up his mind to hire a manager who stressed teaching, discipline, and a hard-nosed approach to the game. He found his man in Al Vincent.

Vincent had a reputation as a firebrand leader with a no-nonsense approach to the game. After accepting the position Vincent told the press, "Some might have considered me a little too tough and demanding. I've never been one to get along with a player who doesn't show that he wants to play. If he doesn't comply with my wishes then I guess I get pretty stubborn." Given the chance to manage again, Vincent gave up the Orioles coaching position (hitting instructor and first-base coach) that he had held since 1955 to return to the minor leagues and guide the Marlins and many of the young prospects ticketed for arrival in Baltimore. Vincent had last managed in 1954 in the Brooklyn Dodgers organization at Class-AA Fort Worth, and in total had spent thirty-two years in professional baseball. Vincent began his playing career in 1928, breaking in with Class-D Talladega Indians as a second baseman and proceeded to rise as high as Triple-A ball, playing for Buffalo and Toledo. In 1937 he called it quits as a full-time player, although he did play part-time for a few seasons, before accepting his first manager's position in 1937 with Class-A-1 Beaumont of the Texas League. He quickly gained a reputation as an excellent tutor to young ballplayers and climbed his way up the minor league ladder.[7] After two consecutive losing seasons, the Miami supporters were hoping to see that this new style of management would turn the team around.

Leo Burke, who played under both Martin and Vincent, recounts the differences between Martin's style of managing and a sterner Vincent:

Leo Burke: Oh yeah, they were very different. Pepper was much more laid back, but he was very much from the old school. I know we had a couple of boys on that team, when he was there, that were former major leaguers and they were sort of hard to control. And Pepper was intent on changing their habits. And in most cases it didn't work.

Al was very disciplined and he was very astute in what he was doing, you know. But he didn't put up with anything either. He was more serious in his ways. He was, I would say it was much more pleasurable playing for Pepper than it was Al, although the results wouldn't have been any different.[8]

MacDonald was intent on letting the professionals run matters on the field while he prepared for spring training with a Marlins roster that was a combination of youth and experience. Although seasoned veterans like Jim Archer (twenty-seven), Harry Byrd (thirty-five), Billy Hoeft (twenty-seven), Dick Hyde (thirty), Woody Smith (thirty-three), Herb Moford (thirty), and Norm Zauchin (twenty-nine) were in the mix, more often than not Vincent would be depending on fresh new faces like Jerry Adair (twenty-two), Angelo Dagres (twenty-four), Dick Luebke (twenty-five), Barry Shetrone (twenty), and $110,000–bonus baby Dave Nicholson (nineteen) to carry the load.

Nonetheless, before the pitchers and catchers were scheduled to report, MacDonald was faced with the business end of dealing with the city of Miami and the Jacob Brothers and Florida Sports Service Inc. to find an equitable arrangement in running his new club. If MacDonald had any hope of making a go of it in Miami, he needed the income from concessions to survive. In February, MacDonald reached an agreement with city of Miami to lease Miami Stadium for $50,000 with a renewal option for four additional years. As part of the agreement, MacDonald requested that he be given full concessionary rights, thus ridding himself from the yoke bestowed by the Jacob Brothers. MacDonald went as far as threatening to move the team if he was not given the concession rights. The city agreed and MacDonald had cleared a major hurdle.[9]

With the last hint of winter hanging in the air the prospective Marlins slowly filtered into spring training camp at Miami's Flamingo Park, anxious for another season to commence. Expectations were high in Miami with the influx of a talented young group of Orioles farmhands. Hopes were that this group would spur the team to greater heights. Experts like Cy Kritzer, in his *Sporting News* preseason picks, were a little less optimistic and predicted the Marlins to be a dark horse in the IL pennant race: "Al Vincent, another new pilot, may have a real sleeper in the Miami Marlins. Fred Valentine, who should be an improved hitter, will team in the outfield with Barry Shetrone and Al Nagel, the Texas League batting champion." Kritzer added one ominous note that Marlins fans were not used to hearing: "The Marlins need more pitching."[10]

Returning to anchor the staff for another season were veterans Jim Archer, Harry Byrd, Artie Kay, Herb Moford, and Bunky Stewart. Archer's 13–10 record and 2.81 ERA were an aberration and didn't reflect just how dominating he was during the 1959 season. A victim of lack of run support due to an anemic offense, the sleek Virginian from Max Meadow nonetheless completed sixteen of his twenty-eight starts, all while recording three shutouts. Vincent further expected bigger and better things from veteran Byrd, who had flashes of greatness the year before but was inconsistent. Byrd's struggles could be traced to a slow start, which led to a disappointing 8–16, 3.52 record. However, hard-luck Bunky Stewart (6–11, 2.91) and Herb Moford (7–7, 2.10) felt Archer's pain and came into camp with aspirations of better results in the win-loss column in 1960.[11]

While most of Vincent's concerns surrounded his staff, the real excitement in spring training camp revolved around the herd of young bucks seeking to make their marks. Capturing a majority of the headlines was the twenty-year-old bonus baby, Dave Nicholson. Part of a bidding war involving several clubs, it was reported that Nicholson originally signed on the dotted line with the Orioles for $135,000.[12] Nicholson, at six-foot-two and 215 pounds, was a chiseled specimen right out of the Athenian Greek Gods League who quickly gained a reputation for his moonshots and propensity to whiff with his all-or-nothing swing. The kid from St. Louis was cut from the same mold as future sluggers like Rob Deer and Gorman Thomas. One of the most highly touted prospects ever in the Orioles system, he was coming off a monster second season in the minors, having hit thirty-five home runs while batting .292.[13]

Nicholson was projected to start and be part of what many considered the top outfield in the IL, albeit an overcrowded one. Joining him roaming the pastures of Miami Stadium would be Angelo "Junior" Dagres, Al Nagel, Barry Shetrone, and the not-to-be-forgotten Fred Valentine, back for his second tour of duty in Miami.

Dagres's claim to fame is that he was the only known Orioles rookie to be signed and put on a major league uniform on the same day. After a brief tryout supervised by Paul Richards, Dagres caught the eye of his evaluator after displaying his hitting prowess and running a 6.2 in the sixty-yard dash. Dagres's memories of that day are as clear as if it was yesterday.

> *Angelo Dagres*: In Massachusetts, that's where they take all of the prospects [referring to the Cape Cod League]. I was up there and I burned the league up. I hit .422. I led the league in home runs and everything else. And I took those credentials, and the scouts were there, and we were going around. At the time there wasn't a draft and I just went out, and you know going club to club, I ended up signing with Paul Richards.
>
> But the thing that impressed him, at the time, was when I went to Baltimore. They had me run the sixty-yard dash. And I did that in 6.2.

Then they timed me going down to first base and I had to do it after I did the 6.2. Harry Brecheen, who at one time was a pitching coach for the Orioles was there. Yeah, the "Cat." A great guy, he took the watch and showed it to Paul Richards. And Paul Richards says, [laughing] "You better do that again." So I had to do it again. I did a 6.2 something else. It was 6.2. And finally I had to go down to first base and they had me do it. And then I went down on a bunt and they timed me in 3.25. . . . He said I was the greatest prospect he had seen. [14]

At the tender age of twenty-one years and fresh out of Rhode Island University, where he set several records in baseball and basketball, Dagres made his major league debut on September 11, 1955, by beating out a potential double-play ground ball and collecting his first major league run batted in. Used sparingly the rest of the season, he nonetheless represented himself well, batting .267 while driving in three runs in fifteen at-bats. [15]

Hoping to join Dagres as a starter was his teammate from the previous season, Alfred Nagel. Both pasture workers were graduates out of Class-AA Amarillo Gold Sox, of the Texas League (TL), where they had been involved in a heated 1959 batting race. Ultimately, Nagel came out the winner, edging his teammate by batting .344 to Dagres's .336. Nagel in particular was an intriguing prospect, having blasted twenty-seven four-baggers and driving in 123 runs while earning Rookie of the Year honors in the TL [16]

Although not as proficient hitting the long ball, Barry Shetrone filled out the trio of outfielders, coming over from Triple-A Vancouver, where he hit a very respectable .293 and scored seventy-four runs in 110 games. [17] The twenty-one-year-old Shetrone, mostly a singles hitter, was expected by his skipper Vincent to be a top-of-the-order hitter, along with Valentine, and set the table for sluggers like Burke, Woody Smith, and hopefully Nicholson or Nagel.

Rounding out the crop of youngsters was an impressive shortstop who would acquire what would probably be the most colorful nickname by any of the Marlins: "Casper the Friendly Ghost." Given the moniker by one of his teammates due to his pasty complexion and his almost snowy-like blond hair, [18] the talented ex-Oklahoma Aggie was known for his slick fielding but seeming lack of earnestness toward his craft. In *Baseball Digest*'s annual Spring Scouting Report, a stinging assessment was handed out on Jerry Adair. The article stated, "This boy needs to change his thinking. Could become an outstanding infielder if he is willing to pay the price. Has fine all-around ability, but lacks seriousness." Another graduate from Amarillo, Adair batted .309 the previous season while driving in seventy-three for the Gold Sox. [19] The Orioles' brain trust were hoping that disciplinarian Vincent could knock off of few of the rough corners and focus Adair on the prospect of becoming the Orioles' regular shortstop or even second baseman.

With the team almost set coming out of spring training, the parent club sent a couple of reinforcements to Miami to fortify the roster. A veteran of eight major league seasons, Billy Hoeft and slugging catcher Gene Green were added to the roster.[20] Hoeft, a tall, six-foot-three, lanky southpaw, enjoyed his greatest big league success with the Detroit Tigers in 1955 (17–7, 2.99 ERA) and 1956 (20–14, 4.06 ERA). The Oshkosh native also led the American League in shutouts with seven in 1955.[21] His steady decline, due to arm troubles, was of some concern, but the Orioles brass was hoping he would find his sea legs again. He would ultimately reinvent himself as a quality reliever after the 1960 season.

Hoeft's new batterymate, Gene "The Animal" Green, was all too familiar to Marlins fans, having tormented them over three previous seasons (1956, 1957, and 1959) as a member of the Rochester Red Wings. Green's reputation as a hitter was never in question, since he hit twenty-three, twenty, and nineteen homers over the aforementioned seasons, not to mention batting over .300 in two of those seasons and just missing a third, batting .299 in 1957.[22] Although proficient in the batters' box, Green had been slowed by knee injuries and was suspect as an outfielder and below average as a catcher. It was hoped that his bat would make up for his deficiencies in the field.[23]

With Opening Day just one day away, and based on an impressive spring training in which the Marlins had tucked away fourteen wins, Vincent's charges appeared ready to make a statement. "I don't know of any club in the league I'd swap them for," said the self-assured Marlins skipper when assessing the upcoming season's outlook.[24] With a lineup that featured speed, youth, depth, and power, the Marlins looked good on paper, but the results on the field are what counts. It wouldn't take long before the quality of this team would manifest itself, and the stakes, as well as the future of Marlins in the IL, were hanging in the balance, with the consequences to be determined.

NOTES

1. Paul Cox, "Marlins Are Sold," *Miami News*, January 3, 1960.
2. Charles Dickens, *A Christmas Carol* (London: Chapman & Hall, 1843).
3. Gilbert Rogin, February 17, 1964, www.sportsillustrated.cnn.com/vault/article/magazine/MAG1075648/index.htm.
4. Ibid.
5. David Remnick, *King of the World: Muhammad Ali and the Rise of an American Hero* (New York: Random House, 1999).
6. Ibid.
7. Jimmy Burns, "Vincent to Crack Whip as Marlins' New Field Boss," *Sporting News*, December 16, 1959; baseball-reference.com.
8. Leo Burke, phone interview with the author, August 22, 2011.
9. "Miami Park Lease Approved—With Concession Rights," *Sporting News*, February 10, 1960, 19.

10. Cy Kritzer, "Wide-Open Race in Int Nod Goes to Bisons, Vees," *Sporting News,* April 20, 1960, 35.

11. Baseball-reference.com.

12. Bill Bryson, "Only One of Ten Pays Off," *Baseball Digest,* April 1958, 5, 7.

13. Baseball-reference.com.

14. Angelo Dagres, phone interview with the author, October 24, 2010.

15. Dan Guttenplan, "Reflections on What Could Have Been," *Newburyport Daily News,* August 20, 2010, www.newburyportsnews.com/sports/x332266741/Reflections-on-what-could-have-been.

16. Baseball-reference.com; "The Scouting Report," *Baseball Digest,* March 1960, 8.

17. Baseball-reference.com.

18. United Press International, "Birds' Friendly Ghost Cause of Nightmares," *Star News* (Wilmington, NC), August 30, 1962, 19.

19. "The Scouting Report," *Baseball Digest,* March 1960, 7.

20. Tommy Fitzgerald, "Marlins Get Hoeft, Green from Orioles," *Miami News,* April 18, 1960.

21. Baseball-reference.com.

22. Fitzgerald, "Marlins Get Hoeft, Green from Orioles."

23. Baseball-reference.com.

24. Tommy Fitzgerald, "Vincent Endorses Opening Marlins," *Miami News,* April 20, 1960.

TWENTY-SEVEN

A Soggy Start

Seventy-seven-year-old Frank "Shag" Shaughnessy had held his post as the IL's president since 1936 and, needless to say, had seen numerous changes to the league, most of them overseen by himself.[1] His most challenging season was on the horizon and ultimately it would prove to be his last year at the helm of his beloved IL. Still dealing with the instability in Havana due to the volatile revolution in Cuba that would ultimately force the transfer of the Havana franchise to Jersey City, financially challenged markets in Columbus and Miami leading to league-wide speculation of the viability of baseball in those cities, and continued intrusion foreseen by the advent of television cutting into attendance league-wide, 1960 would prove more than enough to ultimately lead the future Canadian Hall-of-Famer into retirement.

Like many of the players who passed through the IL, Shaughnessy had also enjoyed a major league career, albeit a very brief stay, with the Washington Senators (1905) and Philadelphia Athletics (1908). Following his playing career he accepted a position at McGill University to coach football and in the offseason managed semipro teams in Hamilton and Ottawa. After coaching briefly for the Detroit Tigers, he was employed as the manager of the Montreal Royals of the IL. "Shag," as he was more popularly known, was an innovator and top-rate administrator, and while in Montreal he introduced night baseball and devised the "Shaughnessy Plan" that organized a four-team playoff system that kept fan interest high and kept the turnstiles turning when otherwise they would have been stagnant. So effective was his playoff scheme that it was quickly implemented through most of the other minor leagues. It wasn't long before "Shag" garnered the post of league president and guided the IL through the difficult Depression and war years when interest in baseball waned.[2]

As was the custom, Shaughnessy chimed in with his preseason picks for the upcoming season. No doubt not wanting to quash the hopes of any of the multitude of supporters of the eight members of the IL, the longtime head of the league forecasted a tight race between seven teams, with Montreal pulling up the rear based on the Dodgers spreading their talent between three of their Triple-A affiliates. Miami was seen as a strong candidate to grab one of the playoffs spots based on the quality of young talent the Orioles were pouring into the Marlins under the scrutinizing gaze of their new field general Al Vincent and his coaches Bill Cates and Bobby Hogue.[3]

The new ownership, under the watchful eye of Bill MacDonald, was anxious to make a splash bigger than Flipper to celebrate the new-look Marlins. The city fathers of Miami, Miami Beach, and Hialeah announced the day as "Miami Marlins Day." The festivities that kicked off Opening Day included a parade beginning at 11:30 am that launched at 17th and Flagler, making stops at all the aforementioned cities. To make sure everything went off without a hitch, Ernie Seiler, a City of Miami recreation director and curator of the Orange Bowl Parade, was hired to organize the curtain raiser.[4]

As the weather so many times does in South Florida, the rains came down on MacDonald's parade in more ways than one. Starting at midday, and perhaps an omen of things to come during the upcoming season, the foreboding gray skies overheard opened up, letting loose heavy rains. The downpour refused to yield as game time approached, dampening the spirits of many as they opened up their umbrellas and folded newspapers over their heads for protection. But the loyal fans who braved the showers were treated to the biggest Opening Day celebration since Bill Veeck's extravaganza in 1956. Loud music, fireworks, and even a jumping donkey that had more spring in his heels than Fred Valentine performed a jumping act over the left field fence that entertained the 4,765 hardy spectators. By rough estimate, ownership and sportswriters surmised that half of the customers expected for the game were turned away by the foul weather.[5]

With MacDonald and his wife in attendance, sitting in their field-level box seat, they both looked on as Miami Mayor Robert King High was introduced to the crowd. And with a mix of applause and a few boos from dissenters the first ball was launched, followed by the customary playing of the national anthem—and then the comforting sound of "Let's Play Ball" rang out. Fans with transistors radios tuned in to a new voice on the radio: WGBS's program director Bob Martin. Martin was substituting for Bill Durney, who was laid up in a bed in Mercy Hospital due to his continuing battle with high blood pressure. Martin had last worked the mike ten years prior as a Number 2 man on radio for the Boston Red Sox. Although Martin did his best, there was no doubt the fans missed the venerable Durney's call of the game.[6]

Opening Day Starting Lineups:

Buffalo Bisons	*Miami Marlins*
CF Solly Drake	2B Jerry Adair
LF Don Landrum	LF Fred Valentine
3B Wayne Graham	CF Barry Shetrone
RF Bob Bowman	3B Woody Smith
C Joe Lonnett	1B Norm Zauchin
1B Fred Hopke	RF Dave Nicholson
2B Bobby Morgan	SS Ron Samford
SS Bobby Wine	C Roger McCardell
P Ken Lehman	P Jim Archer
Manager: Kerby Farrell	Manager: Al Vincent

Eager to start the season off on the right foot, Vincent named his ace Jim Archer to face Bisons southpaw Ken Lehman. Archer's chief weapon was his control, as he did not have a big strikeout pitch and lived and died on the corners. Mixing his highly effective curveball with a change of pace and occasional fastball to keep the batters off balance, Archer was a finesse pitcher in every sense of the word.[7]

Fred Valentine wasted no time delighting the eager Miami supporters. After lead-off hitter Adair was retired in the bottom of the first inning, the speedy left fielder promptly poked a single for the first Marlins hit. Barry Shetrone followed by smacking a gapper, ending up at third base with a triple, plating Valentine and spotting the Marlins a 1–0 lead.[8]

The lead was short-lived when Buffalo tied the score in the top of the second inning. After Archer surrendered a walk to Bob Bowman and a double to Joe Lonnett, the control specialist uncharacteristically unleashed a rare errant toss past Roger McCardell, allowing Bowman to cross the plate unmolested. Buffalo broke the game open in the third inning, exploding for five runs, two of which were the result of a hit batsman and a walk. Archer, who only had three wild pitches and four hit batsman the previous year, was pulled after only two and a third innings, giving way to Vito Valentinetti, now in his second stint with the club.[9]

Miami cut the lead to 5–2 in the fifth inning when Norm Zauchin cracked a colossal blast to the deepest part of centerfield, just short of clearing the fence, scoring Shetrone. The gods must have been impressed by the Greek's impressive blow, because the rain that had slowed to a drizzle throughout the game started to come down in sheets, causing a twenty-minute delay before relenting. The respite had little effect on the Marlins' fortunes, as Buffalo had added one more run before the showers came and proceeded to close the deal after seven innings when the game was called, producing a 6–2 victory.[10]

Whether it was a soggy ball or opening night jitters, Archer wasn't himself from the beginning, giving up four walks to go along with a wild pitch and hit batsman. Buffalo's edgy manager said after the game, "You aren't gonna see many nights when that [Jim] Archer is so wild." Indeed, it was one of few performances that Archer would serve up during the 1960 campaign. Vito Valentinetti came on and performed admirably in relief, but the hometown team failed to generate a comeback and let the fans go home disappointed, leaving them with the consolation of having suffered through such nasty weather only with the memory of a jumping donkey and their soaking wet clothes.[11]

Even though the Opening Day loss was frustrating, the Marlins were still looking forward to a fifteen-game homestand that they hoped would get them out of the gate faster than MacDonald's prize racing horse Royal Native. Sadly, the script didn't quite work out as well as the director planned.

Buffalo continued to stifle Miami bats, sweeping the three-game set. In the second game of the homestand, Vincent opted for Gene Green to make his first start of the season as his catcher. Although McCardell was a fine backstop and called a strong game, Vincent was hoping that despite Green's defensive deficiencies behind the plate he would provide offsetting offensive numbers to justify the shift. Green, who had served previously as a backup catching option for Rochester in three seasons with the Red Wings, was not seen as a viable option to play in the outfield with a stable full of young upcoming speedster types more adept at chasing down fly balls. Facing future Phillies mound star Art Mahaffey, Green and his teammates fared no better than the night before, collecting five measly hits as Gene Green got the collar in the 5–3 defeat.[12] Closing out the series, four ex-Marlins came back to haunt Miami Stadium faithful when Dallas Green and Don Erickson teamed up to throttle the Marlins again on six hits, earning a 5–4 win. And Fred Hopke, having found his stroke, hit a key two-run home run in the fifth inning that knotted the score before another, Don Landrum, stroked the game difference maker, a sacrifice fly in the sixth inning.[13]

Rains returned to Miami the next two nights, forcing cancellation of both games with Rochester. Play resumed against the visiting Red Wings with an April 25 doubleheader, finally seeing the Marlins snap out of their funk and sweep the twin bill. Billy Hoeft proved his mettle, shutting down the Wings in the seven-inning opening game, holding the visitors to three hits in the 4–1 win. Bunky Stewart was tested, but earned a hard-fought victory in the nightcap 5–3. Gene Green's bat paid huge dividends as he blasted a home run in the first game and topped his earlier performance by crushing a grand slam in the second game, giving him five RBIs on the night.[14]

Heavier-than-usual spring rains continued to dampen the fields of Miami Stadium. The Marlins' spirits were equally waterlogged, as the team's fortunes mirrored the daily forecast. A 3–10 start wasn't what Marlins management—or their fans—envisioned, and fan apathy had already taken hold. The majority of game attendance numbers began to drop below the one thousand mark, and 2,500 was considered a big crowd for weekend match-ups. The formidable Maple Leafs wasted little of their energy dispensing the forlorn Marlins in four straight games. Outscored 18–7 in the set, Vincent had yet to find a lineup that clicked and continued to platoon not only his six outfielders but also Green and McCardell behind the plate. Only the infield of Smith (3B), Ron Samford (SS), Jerry Adair (2B) and Norm Zauchin (1B) had so far escaped Vincent's tinkering hand. Eventually that would change.

Montreal followed up the Leafs' performance by taking three out of four as Vincent continued to tinker with his lineup, trying to find some kind of magic combination to turn around the club's fortunes. Two Marlins who were especially frustrated with the platooning system were outfielder Dagres and backstop McCardell. Dagres in particular remembers that it was tough for him to find his groove, splitting time with the other guys. McCardell's displeasure would come to a head later in the season.

> *Angelo Dagres*: Al would platoon me. He would platoon me and the other guys. He was one of those platoon people. And that hurt me because it took a lot of at-bats from me. Yeah, he used to platoon everybody all the time.[15]

Before leaving town for their first road trip—the always troublesome northern swing against Toronto and Montreal—General Manager Ryan responded to the club's poor showing by making some moves, beginning with trading Johnny Bucha to San Diego of the PCL for Jim "Hot Rod" McDonald. Bucha had seen little action, and in fact he had only one at-bat to show so far for the season. The hard-nosed catcher was growing increasingly frustrated after being dropped to third-string catcher on the depth chart.[16] There was no doubt that Bucha was looking forward to a change of scenery, with hopes of plying his trade in sun-drenched San Diego (Bucha would appear in only four games for San Diego, going 3–3 before calling it quits in baseball). A fan favorite in Miami for his hard-nosed, never-back-down persona, Bucha would leave a lasting memory with the locals and be remembered as one of the most popular players to grace Miami Stadium.

In receiving McDonald, the Marlins were hoping the ex-major leaguer, who had spent time previously with the Red Sox, Browns, Yankees, and White Sox, would shore up a bullpen that had been anything but impressive early in the season. In 136 appearances in the big leagues, "Hot Rod" had been used more as a reliever eighty-one times and carried with him a 24–27 record on his resume.[17] The usually reliable Artie Kay

and Dick Luebke, the primary relief options for Vincent, were both struggling. An impatient Joe Ryan was anxious to shore up a few of the holes
in the leaky Marlins boat.

In addition to McDonald, the parent Orioles demoted Anderson. Anderson, who had been used sparingly by Baltimore, was sure to be used
more regularly by Vincent and would ultimately play the role of swingman. Offensively, the Marlins were staying put in hopes that their youngsters would snap out of their early season funk. With the exception of
Barry Shetrone and Al Nagel, who were toying with the .300 mark early,
the rest of the players in the club were still trying to find their groove.

The adding together of a couple of new faces, and a day off before
hitting the road for the first time, caused everyone on the team to be
apprehensive. The Marlins had dug themselves into an early hole and the
prospect of picking up wins on the road was an uncertain prospect at
best. But as the club was about to discover, home cooking isn't always
what it's cracked up to be and sometimes the vittles are more satisfying
away from home.

NOTES

1. Canadian Baseball Hall of Fame and Museum, www.baseballhalloffame.ca.
museum/inductees/frank-shaughnessy/.

2. Ibid.

3. Tommy Fitzgerald, "Tight 7–Team Race Predicted For I.L.," *Miami News*, April
16, 1960.

4. Tommy Fitzgerald, "Parade, Big Show Kicks Us Off," *Miami News*, April 16,
1960.

5. Ed O'Neil, "Marlins Don't Like the Water," *Miami News*, April 21, 1960; Tommy
Fitzgerald, "Ball Club's Opener Great . . . For Flotilla," *Miami News*, April 21, 1960.

6. Morris McLemore, "Yesterday's Favorites, Today's Long Hair," *Miami News*,
April 21, 1960; "Durney Out of Hospital," *Sporting News*, May 4, 1960.

7. Bill James and Rob Neyer, *The Neyer/James Guide to Pitchers* (New York: Fireside,
2004), 121.

8. Fitzgerald, "Ball Club's Opener Great . . . For Flotilla."

9. Ibid.

10. Ibid.

11. Fitzgerald, "Ball Club's Opener Great . . . For Flotilla"; *Sporting News*, May 4,
1960, 31.

12. Bob Owens, "Six Outfielders, Only 3 Can Play," *Miami News*, April 22, 1960.

13. Tommy Fitzgerald, "Marlins Have Hit .190 in 3 Losses," *Miami News*, April 23,
1960.

14. "Green's Socks, Hoeft's Arm Lead Marlins to First Win," *Sporting News*, May 4,
1960.

15. Angelo Dagres, phone interview with the author, October 24, 2010.

16. Tommy Fitzgerald, "Relief Pitching Fails Again," *Miami News*, May 3, 1960.

17. Baseball-reference.com.

TWENTY-EIGHT

Road Sweet Road

The always troublesome northern road trip loomed ahead for the Marlins, with stops in Toronto and Montreal and a brief sojourn in Richmond before returning to Miami. Year after year hopes were always that the Marlins would get off to a fast start and carry the momentum through to the season's end with a championship in hand. However, this proved to be the case less often than not. Invariably, the Marlins found themselves perennially clawing and fighting late in the season to try to make up for lost ground and coming up short.

Landing at the Toronto airport, the usual icy cold northerly winds welcomed the team as they trudged across the open tarmac to the terminal, an ominous greeting from the last remnants of "Old Man Winter." Toronto, which traditionally had been an independent club stocked with ex-major leaguers and longtime minor league stars, was coming off its first losing season since 1950. Traditionally, the Maple Leafs were front-runners and under the fiery leadership of Dixie Walker had been a dominant team in the IL. Nevertheless, 1959 was a different story and the aged club slumped to an unsatisfactory 69–85 record.[1] Hoping to breathe new life into his club, Leafs owner Jack Kent Cooke made a surprising move during the offseason by signing a working agreement with the Cleveland Indians, breaking from their independent status. With the change came a new skipper, Mel McGaha, and lots of new faces. The fresh-faced Leafs featured a talented roster of young pitchers like Frank Funk (twenty-four) and Wynn Hawkins (twenty-four) to go along with a complement of veterans like Al Cicotte (thirty), Ron Negray (thirty), Steve Ridzik (thirty-one), and Pat Scantlebury (forty-two).[2] Under McGaha's tutelage the team would ultimately prove to be the best in the league and arguably one of the best minor league teams of the 1960s.

Twenty-six-year-old right-hander Wes Stock drew the first assignment to face Leafs ace Al Cicotte in the first game. Up to this point in the season, Stock, who was counted on as one of the bulwarks of the staff, had been anything but. In the four appearances he had worked—over nine and a third innings—he had given up seven runs (five earned) and had yet to earn a victory. Stock relied heavily on his slider, but had so far found his bread-and-butter pitch more often in the enemy batters' roundhouse than eluding their bats.

With 15,178 raucous loyal aficionados filling the seats for the Toronto home opener, the Marlins were greeted with a shower of boos that were so loud the steel girders reverberated like a tuning fork on a high C note. Al Vincent had scheduled an afternoon workout prior to the game that was supposed to put some charge in the Marlins' bats, but, as so often occurred, it did little to kick-start them out of their malaise.

It was a pitcher's night. The kind of evening that batters dislike because of the coldness that hangs in the air and the sting that contact with the ball leaves in their hands. Both pitchers breezed through the first seven innings with little complaint of the weather. Stock had one scare in the first inning when Clyde Parris hit a wind-aided line drive that had extra base hit written all over it. Dagres, utilizing his speed, had other plans for the ball and at the last second, heading back at high speed, reached up to snag the sphere just in time. It was the first of two defensive gems he would record on the night.[3]

In the eighth inning the Marlins' fortunes changed. Norm Zauchin ripped a laser shot down to third base that eluded Parris. With no outs Stock then laid down a perfect sacrifice bunt, moving Zauchin to second and bringing Fred Valentine to the plate. Cicotte then fanned Valentine and, looking to escape the inning unscathed, faced Dagres. Dagres, looking to make contact, punched a ball in the hole between first baseman Steve Jankowski and second baseman Sparky Anderson. Jankowski reached the ball, but was unable to get a handle on it. Instead of holding the ball and freezing Zauchin on third base, Jankowski threw to first over the head of Cicotte and into the stands, allowing Zauchin to score. It would prove to be all the offense the Marlins needed. Even though Gene Green added his third home run of the season with a ninth-inning solo shot, the Leafs went down quietly on just five hits as Stock earned his first shutout and complete game victory of the season in the 2–0 win.[4]

Enjoying an off day, Vincent continued to schedule afternoon workouts with his hitters, trying to break his recruits out of their early season offensive doldrums. Vincent, trying to encourage Zauchin, who was mired in yet another funk, suggested to the veteran, "Level out that swing." He later chided, "Well, at least you got a chance hitting that way. Before, it was an almost automatic out."[5]

For all the effort and extra work that Vincent put his batters through, they had little to show for it. Running up against Leafs flame-thrower

Steve Ridzik, they were simply overmatched. On a cool May 6 evening, Billy Hoeft, designated as the starter, matched Ridzik toe to toe for seven innings. Hoeft was masterful and carried a no-hitter going into the seventh before Jackie Waters connected on a hanging slider for a two-run home run, giving the Leafs a 2–0 edge. Ridzik dominated Miami, stingily holding the Marlins to a paltry four base hits and not allowing any enemy runners to advance past second base.[6] All in all, Vincent couldn't be too down in the dumps, knowing that he had at least managed a split against the league's top team.

With Montreal due up next, the seemingly dormant bats that seemed to be in hibernation suddenly showed life against the Royals. The first game of the three-game set saw Miami bust loose for thirteen hits, including every regular scratching out at least on base hit in the 6–3 win. Vincent was especially pleased to see John Anderson, making his first start since being demoted by Baltimore, looking like the Anderson of old. His fluttering knuckleball danced around the Royals' bats all night, earning the "Quiet Man" his first win in the 6–3 decision.[7]

Vincent's charges followed up Anderson's performance the next day by taking both ends of a doubleheader to celebrate Mother's Day. Billed as "Miami Day" in Delorimier Stadium, the appropriately named promotion was indeed Miami's day. As part of the festivities Commissioner B. E. Hearn presented the Royals with a palm tree that was planted just beyond the centerfield wall. To the delight of the 8,443 Montreal devotees, Miss Miami Sandy Guthrie circulated through the crowd, handing out oranges and glad-handing with all the moms and no doubt a few of the dads in attendance.[8]

Getting back to baseball, in the early contest, aided by two RBIs by Green, Jim Archer pitched a gem, frustrating the hometown boys, 3–1. Doing his best imitation of Houdini, Archer worked out of several jams and, despite giving up ten hits, was able to leave nine of the enemy base runners stranded to earn the hard-fought win. More important to Vincent was the fact that Archer had conquered his earlier control woes by allowing only one free pass in nine innings of work.

The nightcap proved to be a thriller, but at the pitchers' expense. Before the night was over eleven hurlers would appear (four by Miami and seven by Montreal). Unlike the first couple of games, this match proved to be a real slugfest. Montreal struck first, tagging starter Valentinetti for four runs in the first three innings and spotting the Royals a 4–0 advantage. Montreal starter Dave Hoskins cruised through the first three innings unscathed before faltering in the fourth and fifth innings, allowing the Marlins to trim the lead to 4–3. Miami evened the score in the sixth inning, and both teams traded scores until the thirteenth inning, when Woody Smith stepped up to the plate to face longtime IL star Babe Birrer. Birrer had stifled the Marlins for the past two innings but this time he met his match, as Smith promptly drilled a solo shot over the left field wall, giving the Marlins a 9–8 edge. Artie Kay working his fifth inning of relief and, anxious to get some much-needed rest, shut down the Royals in the bottom of the thirteenth to end the marathon and collect a much-deserved win. It was the third straight game that the Marlins had double figures in hits, much to the pleasure of the players and coaches.[9]

Before returning to Miami the Marlins had one last stop in Richmond and in the process they returned to their old form. Kay, making a rare start, was hung with the lid-lifting 5–1 loss thanks to a Jim Pisoni three-run homer.[10] The Marlins failed again during the next night's contest, partially due to a McCardell base running blunder where he failed to touch first base on a sure double. The deflated Marlins were only able to put together three hits. Stock, who had struggled early in the season, struck out eight, including five in a row that all went to no avail in the 2–0 loss.[11] In the finale, Al Nagel stroked out four hits in five at-bats and drove in five runs, playing a major role in the Marlins' 9–2 victory. Nagel, on a tear, increased his league-leading batting average to .364.[12]

Vincent continued to tinker with his lineup, now focusing more on his infield. Continued frustration with Zauchin's lack of hitting, Leo Burke was inserted at first base to spark the offense. In an effort to apparently strengthen the defense, Vincent shifted his regular second sacker Adair to shortstop and in the process moved Ron Samford from short to second, a move he would stick to for most of the rest of the season. It seemed like an odd strategy, and when Vincent was asked about the reason for the change, he stubbornly refused to offer any explanation.[13]

Adair would later arrive in the majors as a shortstop, but eventually shifted back to second base and established himself as one of the best defensive players at his position in the 1960s. Adair, born in Lake Station, Oklahoma, had Cherokee and Irish blood coursing through his veins but was more famous for wielding his leather than his war club. He may not have instilled fear into the hearts of major league pitchers, but defensively he was a whiz and ultimately set a major league record in the span of eighty-nine games, from July 22, 1964, to May 6, 1965, by handling 458 chances with nary a miscue.[14] All-time Adair has the tenth best fielding percentage by a second baseman (.9939) and in 1964 only committed five errors during the entire season, stacking up with such luminaries as Hall-of-Famers Roberto Alomar, Ryne Sandberg, and Joe Morgan.[15]

With some measure of their self-confidence restored the last-place Marlins (8–13) returned to Miami Stadium to first face their rivals from Havana, to be followed by Richmond and Columbus. In what would prove to be a repeating pattern over the course of the entire season, Miami's propensity to lose in their home yard would become both perplexing and frustrating.

Keeping the ball in Miami Stadium, arguably the toughest home run park in the IL, had never been a problem for most Marlins hurlers, with the exception of Billy Hoeft, who was increasingly the victim of an abnormal amount of the long ball. The May 13 home opener against the Sugar Kings was an evening affair dubbed as "Black Cat Night," featuring a group of young ladies dressed as witches. Bill MacDonald, taking a page from Bill Veeck's own book, brought in bewitching damsels to stroll through the crowd carrying signs depicting a step ladder, black cats, and the number thirteen in hopes of jinxing the visitors. Unfortunately, the hexes seemed to work in reverse and the results weren't any different for Hoeft, as Felix Torres and Jim Pendleton both went yard, sending Hoeft down in flames, 7–1. Baltimore's field director, Eddie Robinson, was a former first baseman and no stranger to the long ball during his thirteen-year major league career. He was especially puzzled by Hoeft's performance based on his history of giving up few homers in the past—an average of about one blast per ten innings.[16] Robinson commented, "He was certainly no gopher ball pitcher up there," referring to his big-league experience. In twenty-eight and two-thirds innings, Hoeft had already allowed six blasts, accounting for twelve runs.[17]

Vincent had planned on pitching Anderson the next night to face the always tough Orlando Pena, but did an about-face and surprised one of his veterans. Vito Valentinetti, in anticipation of a night off, showed up early to get in some running in preparation of a start later in the week. What Valentinetti hadn't planned on was Vincent naming him the night's starter at the last minute. Having already struggled early in the season, Valentinetti was caught off guard by the decision. In the process of carrying out his off-day pregame workout, Valentinetti had burned up precious energy running wind sprints and he wasn't prepared to make his best effort.[18] Nevertheless, Valentinetti, a fierce competitor and anxious to prove himself big leagues, took to the mound, but before throwing his first pitch he received an unusual request from his manager.

> *Vito Valentinetti*: I went to the ballgame one day and he says, "Come on down; I want to talk to you in the runway." He said, "I want you to throw all fastballs. Don't throw anything but a fastball."
>
> I said, "It's senseless. I'm trying to win a ballgame and he wants me to throw fastballs."

Later in the season he was asked again to throw only fastballs.[19]

> *Vito Valentinetti*: Well, later on I figured the front office wanted to know what kind of fastball I got, you know. So, whatever happened? What in the hell happened, later on and a little later in the season not too long after that incident that he asked me to throw all fastballs, I was traded to Portland, Oregon. The furthest point in the United States from Miami to Portland, Oregon. They did it, I think, just to stick it to me. . . . Well, I don't know if he got word from the front office, but he told me to throw more fastballs in a game. His idea was taking orders from Paul Richards or somebody else in the organization. I don't know.[20]

Valentinetti, running on fumes early, flamed out and spotted Havana a 4–0 lead before hitting the showers after only two innings of work. The Marlins countered with two runs of their own in their half of the second after Burke and Adair drew walks and Valentine and Shetrone followed with singles, plating both runners and trimming the score to 4–2. The Marlins continued to chip away at the lead with solo home runs by Ron Samford in the sixth inning and a dramatic blow by Burke that traveled 380 feet over the National Bohemian sign in the ninth inning, sending the game into extra frames.[21]

Coming on in relief in the third inning, Dick Luebke held the Sugar Kings at bay, tossing five scoreless innings before yielding to Kay in the eighth inning. Both squads traded zeroes into the fourteenth inning. Miami looked on the verge of winning the game and appeared to have the victory in their back pocket after loading the bases with no outs, but couldn't score against Havana's flaky left-hander Luis Arroyo and his elusive screwball in the bottom of the fourteenth frame. Arroyo coaxed Kay into hitting into a force out before inducing Valentine to hit into a double play. Seemingly inspired by Arroyo's bases-loaded jam escape, the Sugar Kings finally got to a bone-weary Kay and plated two runs in the top of the fifteenth inning on Rogelio Alvarez's RBI double and a rare Woody Smith throwing error. Havana held on to a hard-earned 6–4 win.[22]

With four games left at home the Marlins surprised even themselves by taking the last game against Havana 5–1 behind another stellar pitching performance by Archer. Trying to motivate his team, a determined Vincent, under the watchful eye of the Orioles field director Eddie Robinson, donned shin guards and a catcher's mask to work with Shetrone and Valentine prior to the game on their bunting skills. "With their speed, they each could add 10 or 12 hits a season on bunts if they just laid down the ball right," said the wiry skipper. His efforts proved fruitless as the season wore on.[23]

Having won only four of sixteen home games, a frustrated Vincent continued to focus on his woeful offense, hoping to give his pitching staff some relief. At least for one of the Marlins, Dave Nicholson, Vincent's batting drills worked. Nicholson had failed to find his footing early in the season and was struggling with a miserable .217 batting average just a week ago. Against fourth-place Richmond, in the opening game of the series, big six-foot-three starboard-throwing Jim Bronstad took the mound against Wes Stock. Stock had lost the week before to the same Bronstad, but this time the results were reversed. In the bottom of the sixth, with Adair inching off first base, Nicholson got ahold of a Bronstad offering that he couldn't pass up and planted it over the left field wall, giving the Marlins a 2–0 lead. It was big Nick's first homer of the season. Miami tacked a couple more runs on in the seventh inning thanks to a Woody Smith double and errant throw by Jesse Gonder that brought

Smith home. The happiest player in the park—other than Stock, who earned the shutout—was Nicholson, who, thanks to his recent mini-streak of five hits in his last ten at-bats, had raised his average up to .277.[24]

It would prove to be Miami's first extended win streak at home: four in a row. The Marlins continued to experience good fortune when they edged the Vees 2–1. They then came back the next game and, thanks to a Zauchin home run and some newfound muscle, crushed the visitors 12–5 on University of Miami Night.[25] Bettering their record to 12–15 and escaping the basement, the Marlins vaulted past both Montreal and Richmond into sixth place.

Changes affecting the club were both on the field and off the field. Not surprisingly, Baltimore recalled Dave Nicholson to sit on their bench rather than languish on the pine in Miami. In exchange, the Orioles sent down pitcher Walter "Rip" Coleman. Working on a thirty-day option with the Marlins, the Orioles' brass decided to recall their $100,000 prospect despite their disappointment with his hitting and failure to adjust to Triple-A pitching.[26] Although Nicholson would eventually establish himself in the big leagues and enjoy a seven-year career with the Baltimore Orioles, Chicago White Sox, Houston Astros, and Atlanta Braves, like many bonus babies of the era he would fall short of the high expectations that were placed on him by the fans.[27]

Eager to help the Marlins turn their season around, the Orioles sent Jim Busby as reinforcement. Expected to be a stabilizing force on the team, Busby had already spent ten seasons in the big leagues with the Chicago White Sox, Washington Senators, Cleveland Indians, and Orioles. Known more for his defensive skills than his prowess with the Louisville Slugger, Busby brought veteran leadership to a club that was sorely missing that type of presence since the loss of Johnny Bucha and Foster Castleman (both were released early in the season).[28]

Off the field, Bill MacDonald was becoming increasingly frustrated with his latest sports distraction, and became more and more involved with his prize three-year-old filly racehorse Royal Native and vested financial interest in Miami Tropical Park. Attendance was lagging behind expectations and despite an aggressive campaign to draw community support and numerous promotions to entice fans into the park, on most nights fewer than two thousand fans were in the stands. To make matters worse, the long-standing battle between the Marlins and Florida Sports Services (the Jacob Brothers) reared its ugly head again when Circuit Court Judge George Holt ruled that a concession contract signed with the Miami Baseball Company five years ago that had been inherited from George Storer's time as owner was still valid. This was a major blow to MacDonald, since concession sales amounted to a large part of income generated by the team. This essentially guaranteed that the club would run in the red for yet another season.[29] The loss of sales from hot dogs, peanuts, and popcorn along with other sundry items ranked second as the biggest contributing factor—trailing lack of attendance—leading to the demise of Triple-A baseball in Miami.

With one game left against Richmond and four games ahead with fifth-place Columbus, the Marlins looked like a club poised to climb into first division. What happened next was a portent of what was to come for the remainder of the season.

The Marlins had few opportunities to impress sizable crowds, but the finale against Richmond was a perfect opportunity to impress the locals and possibly drum up some excitement. An ingenious marketing gimmick that was hatched under the Storer regime and adopted by MacDonald's staff was the strategy based on the theory that the quickest way to a man's heart is through his stomach. The Marlins and grocery chain Food Fair collaborated to form one of the premier promotional affairs of the season, dubbed as "Food Fair Night." Ducats for the evening contest were distributed to customers for free with purchase of groceries at Food Fair, and fans attending the game were eligible for food giveaways. It was a guarantee of a full stadium, as evidenced by the better-than-expected crowd of 11,214 filling Miami Stadium. It turned out to be the largest numbered attendance in Miami Stadium since July 15, 1956.[30]

Taking the hill for the Marlins was Vito Valentinetti, assigned to take on the Vees' hottest hand, big Eli Grba. Grba was part of the New York Yankees' staff the previous year and so far was pitching like he was ready to return to the big club, having won three games while losing only one. On the other hand, Valentinetti was still trying to find a groove. With roster cuts looming that required teams to bring down their rosters to twenty players, Valentinetti certainly felt the pressure to impress General Manager Joe Ryan and extend his stay.[31]

For all the support the Marlins received, the team turned in one of their worst performances of the year. Valentinetti was pulled after facing only seven batters and allowing four runs. The usually reliable pitching staff struggled and the Vees pounded out ten hits against Valentinetti, Kay, Stewart, and Luebke. Combined with six walks and miscues by Samford (who had shifted to shortstop), second baseman Burke, and pitcher Kay, the result was ten unearned runs—an unexpected gift for the Vees. Even Richmond pitcher Grba got into the act, blasting a grand slam off of Kay, only adding insult to injury. By the time the crowd had thinned out, with only a few loyal rooters remaining, the scoreboard told the sad tale: Richmond 14, Miami 4.[32]

The Marlins finished up their homestand as deflated as a week-old balloon. The always troublesome Columbus Jets made short work of the downtrodden Miamians, sweeping the four game series. It seemed as if a dark cloud was hovering over the Marlins. First, Zauchin, suffering from bronchitis, aggravated his situation during infield practice and was coughing up blood, forcing him onto the injured list.[33] This was soon to be followed up by recently acquired pitcher Rip Coleman's refusal to report and he was ultimately sold to Toronto for $15,000. To the Marlins' dismay, he would finish the season in Toronto, posting a 9–8 record and 2.71 ERA.[34]

Although the first two games were decided by scores of 3–2 and 1–0, the inability of Marlins hitters to come through in the clutch was becoming an all-too-familiar theme, not to mention various base-running blunders and the failure to lay down bunts. Among the many struggling batters were Woody Smith, in the midst of his worst season, hitting only .215 (1 HR, 15 RBIs), Zauchin (.198, 1 HR), Adair (.221, 0 HR), Green (.230, 3 HR), Burke (.239, 2 HR), and Valentine (.232, 3 SBs). Although the rookie corps was expected to experience some growing pains, General Manager Ryan made no bones about what the team's real struggles were all about and wasn't holding back any punches when he said, "The trouble has been that the veterans have not been carrying the youngsters in the early stages."[35]

It all hit rock bottom in the series finale doubleheader, when the Marlins were pounded into submission, 14–1, in the second game of the twin bill. It was the most lopsided loss in Marlins history.[36] Mired in a five-game losing streak, it was almost a relief that the upcoming road trip to Havana, Columbus, Buffalo, and Rochester lay ahead. Now residing in seventh place, Miami (12–20) was one game ahead of Montreal, who currently languished in the basement. If they could take any solace at all, it was in the fact that things couldn't get any worse. Or could they?

NOTES

1. Bill O'Neal, *International League: A Baseball History 1884–1991* (Austin, TX: Eakin Press, 1992), 381–83.

2. Baseball-reference.com.

3. Don Hunt, "Marlins Stock Rises," *Miami News*, May 5, 1960.

4. Ibid.

5. Don Hunt, "Lengthy Marlins Drill Keyed to Weak Hitting," *Miami News*, May 6, 1960.

6. Don Hunt, "Marlins' Weak Hitting Gives Toronto Victory," *Miami News*, May 7, 1960.

7. Lloyd McGowan, "Royal Day for Marlins—2 Victories," *Miami News*, May 9, 1960.

8. McGowan, "Royal Day for Marlins—2 Victories"; *Sporting News*, May 18, 1960, 34.

9. McGowan, "Royal Day for Marlins—2 Victories."

10. Shelly Rolfe, "Hit Batsman Beat Marlins—Vincent," *Miami News*, May 11, 1960.

11. Special to the *Miami News*, "'Patsy' Virginians Scuttling Form," May 12, 1960; *Sporting News*, May 25, 1960, 32.

12. Special to the *Miami News*, "Al Nagel's .364 Leads IL," May 13, 1960.

13. Ibid.

14. Royse Parr, "Jerry Adair," Society for American Baseball Research, 2009, http://bioproj.sabr.org/bioproj.cfm?a=v&v=l&bid=40&pid=45.

15. Lyle Spatz and the Society for American Baseball Research, *The SABR Baseball List & Record Book* (New York: Scribner, 2007).

16. Baseball-reference.com.

17. Tommy Fitzgerald, "'Gopher' Pitches Again KO Hoeft," *Miami News*, May 14, 1960.

18. Ibid.

19. Vito Valentinetti, phone interview with the author, August 23, 2011.

20. Ibid.

21. Tommy Fitzgerald, "Marlins Succumb, 6–4 to Sugar Kings in 15th," *Miami News*, May 15, 1960.

22. Ibid.

23. Tommy Fitzgerald, "Vincent Wears Guards," *Miami News*, May 16, 1960.

24. Tommy Fitzgerald, "Vees Wish Dave Rested More Often," *Miami News*, May 17, 1960.

25. Bob Owens, "Nicholson Called Up by Orioles; Marlins Get Coleman, Victory," *Miami News*, May 18, 1960.

26. Ibid.

27. Baseball-reference.com.

28. Jimmy Burns, "Miami Inks Busby to Stabilize Kids," *Sporting News*, May 25, 1960, 31.

29. "Marlins Lose Hot Dog Battle," *Sporting News*, May 25, 1960, 32.

30. "Grocery Night Lures 11,214, Miami's Top Crowd Since '56," *Sporting News*, June 1, 1960, 30.

31. Bob Owens, "'Summit' Meeting on Player Cut," *Miami News*, May 20, 1960.

32. Ibid.

33. Special to the *Miami News*, "Zauchin Out Three Days," May 22, 1960.

34. Tommy Fitzgerald, "Homer Succeeds after Bunt Fails," *Miami News*, May 21, 1960.

35. Special to the *Miami News*, "Ryan Doesn't Blame Vincent," May 26, 1960.

36. Tommy Fitzgerald, "Fast Jets Find Marlins Taking Their Sunday Nap," *Miami News*, May 23, 1960.

TWENTY-NINE

Vincent Feels the Heat

When your team isn't winning, the hometown fans are quick to look for someone to lay the blame on. The Marlins roster was full of candidates and based upon the level of play exhibited so far on the field, some of it was justified. Although the players were frustrated, probably the most vexed man on the field was Al Vincent. Unlike his predecessors in the dugout, Vincent hadn't exhibited the ability to connect with Miami fans on a personal level, and was in turn viewed as standoffish by many. In short, Vincent, whether through the fault of ownership or his own lack of motivation to reach out, had so far failed to build a rapport with the local supporters. It soon would set him up for abuse from the cranks in the stands that didn't set well with the newest skipper.

Managers are always second-guessed and put under the microscope by the fans. No manager escapes some type of ill treatment, but at the same time he does earn some level of respect from the public—unless, of course, he proves to be utterly incompetent. In general, most of the Marlins' past field generals—Don Osborn, Kerby Farrell, and Pepper Martin—had enjoyed a good relationship with the fans and experienced very little backlash from the seats or the press. Osborn was like a parent's firstborn child. Since he was the first face of the new Marlins, he was accepted with open arms and, in the eyes of most fans, could do little wrong. He was diplomatic and, although firm with his players (with the exception of Satchel Paige), he was open with the fans and spent many hours off the field promoting his club and glad-handing with fans at speaking engagements and various off-field promotions. Farrell, although less savvy with the public, was open with the press and portrayed the image of a brilliant tactician who coaxed his team to play at a competitive level. Farrell also made a strong effort to please the press, almost to the point of letting them influence his on-field decisions. And

Pepper Martin was the mischievous and lovable baseball hero who endeared himself to everyone with his wonderful sense of humor and his laid-back charm. He was adored by the blue-collar fans for his gritty, dirt-under-the-fingernails style and appreciated by the white-collar types for his old-school work ethic. He expected his players to give 100 percent while at the same time enjoying the game with the enthusiasm of a youngster. But Vincent, although an astute baseball man and wonderful teacher, was seen by fans as distant. So when words began to be exchanged between Vincent and rooters behind the dugout, the target of the Marlins' shortcomings began to fall squarely on the back of the man who they thought was at fault for the team's failures.

Miami was given the opportune chance by the league schedule makers of starting out the season by playing twenty-four of their first thirty-two games at home. A perfect opportunity that should have gotten the season off to a fast start was instead squandered when the team dropped seventeen of their twenty-four home dates. It didn't take long before more than a few frustrated ticket holders aimed their poison arrows at the dugout, only to be met by the angry curse-laden retorts of Vincent. Although Vincent had taken away some of the abuse from the players, it was now being heaped on him exponentially.

The first hint of a problem came out on May 26, when the *Miami News* reported that there were rumors that the fans were circulating a petition asking for the removal of Vincent as manager. General Manager Joe Ryan was quick to respond that the rumors were not true and that he was satisfied with the job Vincent was doing managing the club and that no reprimand would be handed down. It was an uncomfortable situation and Vincent himself announced that going forward he would manage from the dugout instead of the third-base coaching box, which was the custom at the time.[1]

It was almost a relief to hit the road for Havana. However, the Marlins found the atmosphere in Cuba as inhospitable as Batista sitting across the table from Castro. With armed troops roaming the streets and the constant echo of gunfire sounding in the distance, many of the Marlins players would have gladly traded their ball caps for combat helmets and a quick trip back to Miami.

The Marlins appeared a little shaky on the field and dropped the opener 3–2 despite a valiant effort by starter John Anderson. Struggling with ongoing back pain, Anderson was betrayed by a wild pitch that allowed the winning tally to cross the plate in the tenth inning. It was especially discouraging since it was the team's fourth consecutive loss in one-run decisions and sixth straight loss overall.[2]

The next night the old adage, "When something can go wrong it usually does," and the Marlins were the recipients of Mr. Murphy and his law. With Woody Smith breaking out of his funk and blasting his second home run of the year and starting pitcher Vito Valentinetti adding one of his own taters, you would think the Marlins would have caught a break. Unfortunately, starter Jim Archer's pitching wasn't as sharp as Smith's and Valentinetti's batting eye. The Sugar Kings thumped four of their own long balls to down the Marlins, 11–7. The Marlins, working on their worst losing streak of the season, had now dropped seven straight.[3]

Mercifully, the Marlins ended their losing skein the final night in Havana with almost no help from their offense. Miami's only hit of the night came in the ninth inning when Fred Valentine's single broke up Bob Miller's bid for a perfecto. Oddly, the single didn't result in the winning run. The Marlins' only score came in the first inning when Jim Busby walked, took second on a wild pitch, and later scored when Sugar Kings' first baseman Rogelio Alvarez couldn't handle a Leo Cardenas peg from the hole. Wes Stock, who was finding out that the only way he could usually win was by hurling a shutout, scattered six hits and helped his own cause by striking out nine enemy batters in the 1–0 win.[4]

The Marlins enjoyed the next day off before resuming play against the Columbus Jets on May 27. Two players appreciative for the extra day off were Norm Zauchin, still recovering from his bronchial ailment, and Al Nagel, who was struggling with a viral infection. Never one to sit on his hands, General Manager Ryan also made another roster move, selling Valentinetti to the Portland Beavers of the PCL. It would prove to be the spunky and proud Italian's last stop in his professional career.[5]

To show you how much baseball has changed since Valentinetti's days, whereas players now are treated to first-class accommodations, he wasn't even issued a plane ticket out of town to get to his next destination, but instead reported to the team in the old-fashioned way: trekking across the United States in his own station wagon.

> *Vito Valentinetti*: I was shipped off to Portland and I got in my car in Florida, but my family is in New York. And it must have taken me about a week. I had two guys who hung around the hotel, and one guy wanted to get off in Vegas and the other guy, I don't know where we dropped him off. But one of them didn't drive, and there were two of us driving, and we took that station wagon all the way to Vegas. I don't remember stopping. And when I got to Vegas, [pause] when I got to Portland they called it the longest car ride I took to get there. It took me about seven days, I guess. I don't know when I dropped that guy in Vegas.[6]

Waiting on arrival at the Columbus airport were heavy rains and a cancellation at Jet Stadium for the opener of the series. Ballplayers traditionally enjoy any bonus days in the year that they are given and in this case it was a welcome relief. The Marlins, dating back to last season, had dropped nine straight to the Jets and the additional respite might just be what the doctor ordered to break the hex.

Sending out Billy Hoeft, with a less-than-exemplary 1–4 record, against right-hander Tom Cheney, who had only lost one game all season, didn't bode well for a turnaround, but the ex-Tiger would be up to his A-game on this evening. With a little support from Gene Green, who smacked his fourth home run of the year, a two-run shot in the fifth inning, it proved the difference maker as the Marlins came out on top, 4–2. Al Vincent was encouraged mostly by Hoeft's ability to avoid the "gopher ball" that had so plagued him all season.[7] However, Vincent's elation over Hoeft's performance was somewhat diminished when he learned after the game that one of his most productive hitters, Barry Shetrone, would be lost for an extended period due to a dislocated shoulder, the result of an awkward slide, and Fred Valentine was also out with a torn leg muscle.[8]

The Marlins took three out of four from Columbus, and proceeded to drop all three games in Buffalo, then closed out the road trip by taking three of four from Rochester before heading back to Miami with a 7–7 record on the aforementioned road swing and a 19–27 record overall, leaving them in seventh place. So far, Wes Stock had been the club's most consistent starting pitcher, but had only three wins to show for all his efforts. All of his victories had come via a shutout, leaving the beleaguered youngster scratching his head, wondering if his teammates had something against him.

In an effort to bolster his sagging offense, and offset the injuries to outfielders Shetrone and Valentine, General Manager Ryan signed twenty-nine-year-old veteran free agent Joe "Rabbit" Caffie. In 1951 Caffie was signed by the Cleveland Indians from the famous Negro League club Cleveland Buckeyes at only twenty years old. He began his career with the Duluth Dukes of the Class-C Northern League and in 1952, while starring for the Dukes, Caffie utilized his blinding speed and finely tuned batting eye to earn the Northern League MVP award, batting .342 and knocking eighteen triples. The "Rabbit's" breakout season earned him a spot on Triple-A Indianapolis and aspirations of realizing his big-league dreams. Caffie later became a journeyman, but a legitimate star at the Triple-A level, stopping along the way in Syracuse, San Diego, Buffalo, St. Paul, and Montreal before landing in Miami. Caffie enjoyed a brief fling at the major league level with the Cleveland Indians in 1956 and 1957, appearing in forty-four games over the two seasons and presenting himself well by batting .291. However, by 1960 Caffie was nearing the end of his playing days and, following a brief trial with Montreal, he was snapped up by Ryan, who held out hope that the "Rabbit" might revive his career in Miami.[9]

In spite of Ryan's moves to jolt the club out of its doldrums, Vincent was increasingly feeling the pressure due to his inability to turn the club around and mount an extended win streak. It was becoming evident that the losing and negative fan pressure was weighing heavily on the ex-

Oriole coach. Vincent, unlike some managers, was quick to put the blame on his charges' shoulders if warranted. His latest scapegoats were catchers Roger McCardell and Gene Green. "I'm fifty-three years old, but I could go behind the plate and do a better job than those fellows have been giving me," said an opinionated Vincent. He added, "I don't ask what they are hitting . . . just what are they catching . . . and it's not enough." McCardell's technical difficulties were especially perplexing behind the plate. After enjoying a cup of coffee with the San Francisco Giants the previous season, he seemed ready to acquire some further seasoning and was on the verge of a breakout year in the minor leagues that left him ready for a quick turnaround to the majors. McCardell's troubles were not only with his defense but also at the plate. The ex-Giant was limping along with a .231 average and had exhibited little at the plate, having produced a scant two ribbies in sixty-five at-bats. His fellow batterymate Green could be excused for some defensive lapses, as he was a converted outfielder to catcher who was never a defensive wiz behind the plate anyway. "The Animal" could usually be counted on to provide ample offense to negate his shortcomings in the field, but so far had done little to accomplish this by chipping in a modest five home runs and a .280 batting average, figures below the Marlins' brass's expectations.[10]

Ripping his two catchers publicly did little to inspire Vincent's troops against their next opponents, the last-place Montreal Royals and red hot Toronto Maple Leafs. Although Stock pitched his usual shutout, only allowing three hits to earn a 2–0 win in the opener,[11] both Hoeft and Herb Moford dropped tough decisions, Hoeft by the score of 5–4, victimized by Mike Goliat and Gordon Windhorn home runs,[12] and Moford on the wrong end of a 2–0 shutout thanks to a couple of errors by the usually dependable Zauchin.[13] And for all his struggles with the long ball, Hoeft received the call he had been waiting for from Baltimore to return to the Orioles, leaving the minors behind. Hoeft would go on to reestablish himself in the big leagues as a relief pitcher with the Orioles, Giants, Expos, and Cubs, adding twenty-two more wins to his log and twenty-two saves before retiring in 1966.[14]

Miami fared no better against the Maple Leafs, dropping three of the four-game set. The Marlins' only victory came in the series lid-lifter on "Green Stamps Night" when they licked the visitors, 3–1. Bunky Stewart pitched a masterful two-hitter and received some much-needed support from his teammates to the tune of ten base knocks. Ironically, Stewart was nearly cut loose and released by the Marlins just a few days before but received a reprieve when a couple of his fellow hurlers came down with sore arms.[15]

Like geese flying north for the summer, the Marlins gathered their belongings, flapped their wings, and headed north to face Montreal and Toronto again. Joining his new teammates on the trip was little five-foot-five sparkplug Albie Pearson. His demotion came as a result of Jim Busby being recalled by the parent Orioles. His teammates must have thought one of the jockeys from Flamingo Park had boarded the wrong flight, but they were mistaken. Pearson, probably the smallest player in the majors, made a big splash in 1958 with the hapless Washington Senators, winning the Rookie of the Year Award while batting .275 and reaching base at a .354 clip. However, in 1959 the sophomore jinx got the best of the mighty-mite, and after slumping to .210 he found himself traded to the Baltimore Orioles. A bad back and case of tattered confidence had slowed Pearson, but Paul Richard and Al Vincent felt they could help Pearson return to the level he enjoyed in 1958 and a trip to Miami was just the cure.[16]

Given a second chance, a focused Pearson was thankful for the opportunity to play in Miami and resurrect his career. Under the tutelage of Vincent and through lots of hard work, his industrious manager would lay the groundwork for Pearson's successful return to the major leagues.

> *Albie Pearson*: Al Vincent probably was the key guy. He and Paul Richards were very close. I recall Al working with me all the time. In fact we'd go out to the ballpark, in the old Miami ballpark, and worked during the hot day before I was injured down there. Just work and he was more than willing to help me. I appreciated Al for that time.
>
> At that time they wanted me too. [pause] I know that Paul Richards and Al, they were very close. In fact, I played golf with them both. They both loved golf but anyway I remember that they wanted me to begin to work with a Willie Mays basket catch. And I worked in the outfield there in Miami. Rather a strong memory of Miami is of being hit fungoes by Al until my eyes were coming out of my head until I could see out of my back.[17]

The opening series in Montreal was billed by Montreal sportswriters as the "Cellar Classic." Following an always welcome day off, the Marlins, with their newest teammates Caffie and Pearson in tow, jumped back into the fray and promptly dropped both ends of a doubleheader, 7–1 and 6–3. The twin losses were disappointing, but the play of Pearson in centerfield impressed everyone. Not only did he collect his first two hits as a Marlin but he also made a defensive gem in the second game, snaring a Dick Sanders drive against the wall to deny a sure extra base hit, and then throwing a perfect relay to Ron Samford, who doubled up ex-Marlin Jerry Snyder at first base. Unfortunately, Moford and Stewart were unequal to the task, as the Royals drew to within one game of the Marlins and an escape from the cellar.[18]

Rains pelted the field all of the next day and only 862 stout-hearted fans showed up on a dank night to witness what would prove to be a lopsided affair. Artie Kay, making one of his eight starting appearances on the year, was called on to face lanky right-hander Rene Valdes. Lacking command, Valdes wasn't up to snuff and the Marlins chased the Royals' starter after only five innings, building a 6–0 lead. Royals relievers could do little better as every Marlin in the starting lineup collected at least one base hit, with the exception of Zauchin. Pearson continued to impress his new manager, collecting four base hits. Caffie, exacting revenge on his ex-team, one-upped his colleague by connecting for two home runs and also garnering four hits on the night. A gloating Vincent took credit for one of his new acquisitions when he said, "I took him because I remember how he beat us in May." He added, "They told me the boy was through although he won the league batting championship three years ago. I didn't believe it. How could that guy be through at twenty-nine years of age?" And although Kay was only adequate on the mound, giving up six runs, he helped his own cause by chipping in with a single and a double in what turned out to be Miami's best offensive performance of the year in the 17–6 thrashing.[19]

In an uncharacteristic reversal, the Marlins came back the next night as listless as a wind-beaten flag. Archer continued to struggle and saw his record drop to 2–6. Recently acquired Jim "Hot Rod" McDonald fared about as well as Montreal's relief corps did the night before by allowing six runs in only one inning of work. Needless to say, the "Hot Rod" days were numbered in Miami, as he would only appear in six games total before exiting. The final results showed Montreal 12, Miami 0.[20]

Leaving Montreal to finish a four-game stand in Toronto, the Marlins were perched precariously only percentage points ahead of Montreal from sharing the IL basement. While Montreal was rained out against Havana, the Marlins must have wished for the same reprieve against the front-running Toronto Maple Leafs. Pearson, who had been exemplary in the field since arriving, did a rare about-face and lost a sure fly ball out in the lights during the fourth inning, allowing Toronto to score three runs and secure the lead. Stock, although not as sharp as usual, pitched the complete game but failed once again to win due to lack of support as the Leafs dropped Miami 6–2 and sent the visiting Marlins spiraling into last place.[21]

Just when it looked like the road trip was about to go into disaster mode, a new acquisition by General Manager Ryan would step up and stem the tide. Rodolfo "Rudy" Arias made his mark in IL history, tossing a seven-inning no-hitter against Rochester on August 17, 1958, pitching for his home town Havana Sugar Kings. Arias pitched so impressively in Havana that it earned him a promotion to the Chicago White Sox the next year and ultimately a trip to the 1959 World Series against the Los Angeles Dodgers. Although Arias failed to make an appearance in the Fall Classic, he finished up the season with perfect 2–0 mark and 4.09 ERA in thirty-four relief appearances. In 1960 the Cuban star returned to Triple-A for the San Diego Padres before being acquired by Ryan for the rest of the season to pitch in Miami. Although Arias only appeared a solitary season in the majors, he would end up hanging around professional baseball until 1966, finishing up with the Poza Rica club in the Mexican League.[22]

Toronto, last in the league in batting average, found few pitches in Arias's selection to their liking. Held to a meager four hits, it took Arias two hours and ten minutes to record a 2–0 shutout and earn his first victory for his new club. Facing Rip Coleman, the ex-major leaguer who had earlier in the season refused to report to Miami, Woody Smith (who had recently been demoted to batting eighth in the batting order and mired in a season long slump) took out his frustrations by banging out a solo home run and RBI double to provide the Marlins with all the offense they would need.[23]

Closing out the northern road swing the next day, the Marlins split the double-dip finale by winning the first game, 4–1, and then taking a beating in the second game, 7–2.[24] In front of 11,215 hostile rooters, Moford pitched a complete game in the opener, scattering nine hits and getting support from veterans Caffie and Smith, who both drove in a couple of runs. Bunky Stewart fared less well in the late match, giving up two walks, two singles, and a three-run home run to Don Dillard that in total accounted for five runs. Stewart was pulled by Vincent after retiring only one batter and the beleaguered manager turned to McDonald and Luebke to finish out the remainder of the seven-inning affair.[25]

The headline on the *Miami News* sports page said it all the next day, "Marlins Return to Hated Home." A 15–15 road record, although not overly impressive, is usually an indicator that if the team plays well on the road, they should do even better on their home turf—a recipe for a playoff contending club. However, the Marlins' 9–22 ledger at home was a disturbing reminder that this Marlins' club was far from being a contender and no one had any answers why they had struggled so mightily at home. Now residing in last place (24–37), eighteen and a half games behind Toronto (40–16), the season was melting away faster than a snow cone on Miami Beach in June. Still not satisfied with the makeup of his club, Ryan wasn't done making changes to the roster and was trying his best to salvage what was quickly becoming a lost season. But for Bill MacDonald, the changes that he was contemplating had much bigger consequences, and as he became more impatient with his team's results and apparent lack of interest by the community in the Marlins, his eyes began to focus elsewhere. The future of Triple-A baseball in Miami was hanging in the balance and changes were in store, although few were taking notice.

NOTES

1. Special to the *Miami News*, "Ryan Doesn't Blame Vincent," May 26, 1960.
2. "Int Items," *Sporting News*, June 1, 1960, 30.
3. Special to the *Miami News*, "Marlins Serving 'Em Up," May 25, 1960.

4. Special to the *Miami News*, "Ryan Doesn't Blame Vincent."

5. Special to the *Miami News*, "Marlins Glad Jet Going Up," May 28, 1960.

6. Vito Valentinetti, phone interview with the author, August 23, 2011.

7. Special to the *Miami News*, "Ends Jets String Over Marlins, 4–2," May 28, 1960.

8. "Ends Jets String Over Marlins, 4–2"; "Injuries Jolt Marlins Outfield," *Sporting News*, June 15, 1960.

9. Nick Diunte, "Joe Caffie, 80, Former Cleveland Indians Outfielder Started in the Negro Leagues," examiner.com, August 27, 2011, www.examiner.com/baseball-history-in-national/caffie-80–former-cleveland-indiand-outfielder-started-the-negro-leagues; baseball-reference.com.

10. Tommy Devine, "Catching Flop Give Vincent Big Headache," *Miami News*, June 3, 1960.

11. "Marlins' Stock Consistent All Four Wins via Shutouts," *Sporting News*, June 15, 1960, 30.

12. Tommy Fitzgerald, "Gopher Ball Ruins Hoeft," *Miami News*, June 9, 1960.

13. Tommy Fitzgerald, "And Another Marlin Fails His Way Up," *Miami News*, June 10, 1960.

14. Fitzgerald, "And Another Marlin Fails His Way Up"; baseball-reference.com.

15. Cy Kritzer, "Miami Ends Bisons' Woes," *Miami News*, June 3, 1960.

16. Baseball-reference.com.

17. Albie Pearson, phone interview with the author, May 17, 2010.

18. Special to the *Miami News*, "Pearson Gave All in Defeat," June 15, 1960.

19. Special to the *Miami News*, "Marlins Avoid Basement," June 16, 1960.

20. Special to the *Miami News*, "Vincent Asks for Shutout," June 17, 1960.

21. Special to the *Miami News*, "Bumbling Marlins Now Last," June 18, 1960.

22. Society for American Baseball Research, "Ramirez, Jose," 2009, bioproj.sabr.org; baseball-reference.com.

23. Special to the *Miami News*, "Angry Smith Leads Marlin Uprising, 2–0, June 19, 1960.

24. Special to the *Miami News*, "Marlins Return to Hated Home," June 20, 1960.

25. Ibid.

THIRTY

Vincent Takes Refuge and MacDonald in Over His Head

On June 27 the eight team owners, accompanied by their general managers, trekked north for their yearly IL meeting. Greeting the business-like group, as had been the case for many years, was Frank Shaughnessy. The topics of conversation swirled not only around the Havana situation and possible relocation of the team to Jersey City but also around potential moves of clubs that were struggling to make ends meet. At the forefront of speculation of a possible transfer were the Miami Marlins. Although widely hailed in 1956 as a coup for the IL and seen as having the potential to boom league attendance, Miami had failed to draw the numbers that were projected and had seen a steady decline in attendance every year despite playing in a state-of-the-art minor league facility.

Accompanying General Manager Joe Ryan to this year's league meetings was a representative from San Juan, Puerto Rico, fueling rumors that an imminent move was in the works. With the expected move of the Havana Sugar Kings to Jersey City in July just over the horizon, it appeared as if the league was planning on keeping its ties to the Caribbean intact. When asked whether it meant Miami was considering moving from the confines of Miami Stadium to more southern climes, Joe Ryan commented, "Not necessarily, other clubs might move."[1]

Bill MacDonald was quiet on the matter, but made it known early that he might absorb small losses if the team showed it could be viable financially in the long run. Seemingly distracted by his own stable of racehorses and his financial interests in Miami's Tropical Park, it was becoming increasingly apparent that Triple-A baseball in the "Magic City" was in dire straits.

The players, and especially Albie Pearson, were supposed to feel welcome on what was tabbed as "Welcome Albie Night" to honor their newest acquisition. The only problem was that Pearson had left the team temporarily in Toronto to fly to Baltimore and move his family to Miami. The promotion, now without its star, was called off at the last minute and instead the Marlins were greeted by a scant crowd of 2,064 for their June 21 doubleheader against Rochester.

The Marlins' play was lukewarm at best for the June 21 matches as they split the twin bill by edging the Red Wings in the first game, 5–3, and dropping the late affair, 6–0. Artie Kay, starting the short first game, lasted only one and a third innings. He left the game with the Marlins trailing 3–0. Bunky Stewart, taking over for Kay, was exemplary in a strong effort, going five and a third scoreless innings and holding on until his teammates were able to mount a comeback in the victory thanks to a home run by Gene Green and two RBIs apiece by Ron Samford, who also homered, and Norm Zauchin. Herb Moford retired the last batter to earn the save and preserve Stewart's hard-fought win.[2]

Jim Archer's struggles continued in the late affair as his record fell to 2–7. Given little support by his teammates to the tune of only two base hits, his opponent Willard Schmidt hardly broke a sweat in the 6–0 shellacking.[3]

Ryan, not one to give up on a season, was still making moves prior to and after the game. Staying in touch with White Sox brass, he acquired catcher Dick Brown on option. Brown came with excellent credentials, having served as the backup catcher with the Cleveland Indians during the 1957–1959 seasons while batting a respectable .263, .237, and .220 as well as flashing some power, blasting sixteen home runs in 471 at-bats over the course of those same three seasons.[4] Brown had also served as Herb Scores's catcher in Florida at Lake Worth High School in 1951 and 1952, bringing along with him some local interest.[5]

Vincent, unimpressed by the play of Roger McCardell and recognizing Gene Green's defensive deficiencies behind the plate were not compensation enough for his bat, was happy with the type of move that allowed him to strengthen the Marlins up the middle. Moving Brown behind the plate would allow Green to move to first base, where his defensive lapses would be less noticeable. However, it left Zauchin without a job. Zauchin, who found himself unable to hit himself out of a paper bag, was hitting a meager .221. He was flapping in the wind and most certainly trade-bait for any takers.[6] Ryan was more than willing to part with Zauchin, now relegated to a backup position, and his $15,000-a-year salary, which at the time was among the highest in the IL.

The Marlins' struggles at home seemed to have subsided, at least temporarily, as they split four game sets with both Rochester and Buffalo. As predicted, Dick Brown was inserted as the regular backstop and Green shifted to first. Offensively the team continued to struggle, but Brown began to act as a stabilizing force behind the plate and the pitching staff was reaping the benefits. Although the Marlins treaded water at home and were playing better as of late, the fan abuse toward Vincent continued as angry rooters vented their frustrations and heaped the blame on the manager, who continued to take refuge in the dugout instead of his usual place inside the third base coaching box.

Unfortunately for Vincent, his troubles were not confined to the fans—they extended off the field as well. In the locker room there continued to be friction with a couple of players who didn't see eye-to-eye with their skipper and his authoritarian style. On June 28, little-used catcher McCardell refused to accompany his teammates on their road trip to Rochester. "Since you have two other catchers my services will not be missed," said the frustrated catcher to General Manager Ryan.[7]

Vincent's troubles continued on July 5 when platooned outfielder Angelo Dagres was suspended for a day for what Vincent saw as showing indifference on the field. A fielding error and lack of perceived hustle on a single that turned into a double against Richmond proved the difference in the 10–9 loss. "I just know he's through with this club," stated the angry manager following the game. Although Dagres was batting a lustrous .317 at the time, Vincent decided that he no longer wanted the former Oriole in his club. Despite his tirade, cooler heads prevailed in Baltimore and Vincent was ordered to keep Dagres, who returned to the lineup just a couple of days later.[8]

July proved to be a troublesome month all around. Besides the discontented players, a rash of injuries began to take their toll. Joe Caffie (jammed hand), Green (sore right hand), and Pearson (pulled leg muscle and back pain) all missed playing time due to their assorted ailments.[9] On top of that John Anderson (back), Barry Shetrone (shoulder), and Fred Valentine (leg muscle) were still recovering from their own strains and pains, forcing Vincent to further juggle the lineup on a daily basis. The Marlins' lot became so bad that even players Ryan was acquiring to fill the void were arriving with their own physical problems in tow.

At one point in early July Vincent had only seven active pitchers on his roster at his disposal. Nearly half of his pitching staff spent time on the disabled list with a variety of ailments, from sore arms to strained backs.[10] On July 3, in hopes of getting reinforcements, Ryan acquired relief specialist Dick Hyde from the Washington Senators and in return sent peeved catcher McCardell and ineffective "Hot Rod" McDonald to the Nats,[11] thus shedding the club of some unhappy warriors. In the landmark and amusing book *The Great American Baseball Card Flipping, Trading and Bubble Gum Book*, with tongue-in-cheek descriptions, Brendan Boyd and Fred Harris colorfully depict Hyde's style by saying, "Dick Hyde was the last of the legitimate submarine pitchers. . . . Sometimes, in fact, it looked as though he was throwing the ball from between his legs."[12]

The bespectacled down-under right-hander was only two years removed from his breakout season in the big leagues, a year in which he was arguably the best relief pitcher in the American League, appearing in fifty-three games, posting a 10–3 record, 1.75 ERA, with eighteen saves. He also led the league in games finished with forty-four. Hyde was so dominant that he finished twelfth in MVP voting in a time when relief pitching wasn't recognized for its importance as it is today.[13] Nonetheless, since 1958 he had struggled with arm problems and, upon arrival in Miami, was battling a sore wing. It was hoped that Hyde would take up the mantle of relief ace from the beleaguered Artie Kay, who had yet to find the same form he flashed in 1959.

Ryan stayed busy throughout July looking for lightning in a bottle while continuing to acquire reclamations projects. Soon after acquiring Hyde, Arnie Portocarrero, formerly with the Philadelphia/Kansas City Athletics and now Baltimore, was shipped to Miami. Portocarrero, like his teammate Hyde, was hoping to resurrect his career. The husky right-hander experienced his best season in the majors in 1958, when he put together a glossy 15–11 with a 3.25 ERA for the Orioles.[14] He had since fallen on hard times and found himself in Miami looking for a ticket back to the show.

Another Ryan acquisition was consummated on July 16 when thirty-two-year-old Ruben Gomez was optioned to the Marlins from the Philadelphia Phillies.[15] The former New York/San Francisco Giants star pitcher burst onto the scene in 1953, winning thirteen games and losing eleven as a rookie in 1953. Gomez proved even more invaluable the next season as the Giants took the NL pennant and then upset the heavily favored Cleveland Indians in the World Series by sweeping them in four games. It was to be Gomez's (17–9, 2.88 ERA) best season in the bigs, which included a win in the World Series. Gomez started the 1960 season, his second with the Phillies, trying to recapture his past glory, but instead proved ineffective: in his twenty-two appearances and one start he went 0–3 with a 5.23 ERA.[16] Sent down by the parent club to Buffalo, the Puerto Rican with a reputation for his nasty screwball was getting little work and had only a 2–2 record for all his efforts. It was hoped that a change of scenery would prove to be a godsend for Gomez in Miami. The Marlins were a club that was going nowhere, but he would at the very least get regular work on the mound. It wasn't long before Vincent inserted him in the starting rotation.

Several more completed transactions came to their conclusions before the month of July. Wes Stock received the call that he was hoping for from the Orioles, closing out his ledger in Miami with an impressive 8–6, 2.25 ERA record in 128 innings. Half of Stock's wins came by shutouts, and if he had pitched on a contending club, he undoubtedly would have enjoyed a double-digit winning season.[17] In addition, Al Nagel (61 G, 205 AB, .228, 2 HR, 12 RBI), who looked so promising in spring training, had failed to deliver the goods and was demoted to the Nashville Volunteers of the Class-AA Southern Association.[18]

Before the month of July came to its merciful conclusion, General Manager Ryan was able to shed the team of underachieving Zauchin. Although several players had come and gone over the years, few players came with more expectations than Norm Zauchin, only to fall short. Standing six-foot-four and 220 pounds, many thought he would be Miami's version of Luke Easter or Rocky Nelson, but instead, over parts of the two years he spent with the Marlins, the burly slugger produced a less-than-spectacular eleven home runs, forty-five RBIs, and a microscopic .233 batting average.[19]

With two months left to play in the season, the hapless Marlins (44–60) were mired in last place, twenty-five and a half games behind the first-place Leafs and eight and a half games behind Buffalo for the final playoff position. The *Miami News* had begun to show the IL standings in reverse order every time the team would slip into the basement and fan apathy was reaching new lows. Of the fifteen home games played in Miami during the month of July, only two contests drew better than two thousand fans, and two games on July 26 and July 29 drew a measly 802 and 871 paying customers, respectively.[20] You might say that the Marlins had gone to the dogs, but even the Miami Beach Kennel Club, hosting summer dog races, was outdrawing the Marlins' home games by a 4–1 ratio.[21]

The Marlins weren't the only team having their share of problems. The recent shift of the Sugar Kings from Havana to Jersey City found baseball fans in the area showing little interest, and when Miami came into town to play their biggest rivals for the July 22–24 series, only 6,034 locals bent the gates for the four games. As distressing as this appeared, Miami and Jersey City were part of the ever-increasing lack of interest in minor league baseball across the nation. Cities like Charleston, Indianapolis, Louisville, San Diego, Salt Lake City, Seattle, and Vancouver, all longtime minor league bastions, were drawing similar numbers and their operators shared the same concerns as MacDonald. It was a reflection of what many minor league teams were experiencing, due mostly to the onset of television, which allowed the general public access to major league baseball and in many ways eroded the local loyalties to minor league teams that were strong in the past. In just ten years the number of minor league leagues had dropped from a high of fifty-eight down to twenty in 1960.[22] To many it seemed that the minor leagues were dying on the vine.

Owner Bill MacDonald, in a discussion with *Miami News* columnist Tommy Devine, was frank and open about the Marlins' situation when he stated, "When I bought the club last December, I went into it with my eyes wide open. If I could have foreseen how bad things were going to be, I never would have touched it." The upfront owner added, "I didn't expect to make money, but I hoped the operation for the first two years could break even. But in a crapshooter's parlance, I've thrown a pair of sixes and the roll is going to cost me $125,000 this season."[23]

MacDonald further admitted that he had gotten in over his head, thinking that the same recipe for success that had worked in Tampa with his Class-D Florida State League Tarpons would translate in Miami. One of the usually upbeat owner's complaints was "When I need player help from Tampa, I can go out and buy the talent I need." He added, "That doesn't work in the International League. The players who could help us aren't for sale, so we find our hands tied." In addition, MacDonald stated that he wasn't happy with his working agreement with the Baltimore Orioles and wished he had instead chosen to operate as an independent. He also went on to cite factors such as the high $50,000 stadium rental amount, a total absence of television and radio revenues, a bad spring training deal with the Orioles that cost the Marlins money before the season started, and the inability to control their own concessions as severely limiting profits and constraining the viability of the team.

MacDonald had also made the same mistake that his predecessor Storer had when putting out a face of the Marlins to the public. Joe Ryan had always played two roles: one of the shrewd and knowledgeable baseball man behind the scenes and the other as the face of the Marlins to the public. Although Ryan was a valuable administrator, and one of the best in the business, he lacked the imagination, magnetism, and salesmanship to ingratiate him to the public. Ryan couldn't be faulted for trying; he simply was more effective working behind the scenes, where he was the most comfortable and effective.[24] What made the 1956 version of the Marlins so successful was the charisma of Bill Veeck, and Bill MacDonald's seemingly endless enthusiasm and ability to sell baseball to almost anyone was unfortunately lost to his many other distractions.

MacDonald was publicly stating that he was considering other options for the 1961 season, although he hedged his remarks by saying a late season turnaround could persuade him to reconsider. Once again MacDonald specified Puerto Rico as his first option: "They dangle a $50,000 or $60,000 television fee before you and that money is yours before you move in. They guarantee a minimum of 1,000 box seats . . . that's 70,000 admissions itself. If they got a club, a new ball park would be built." Already MacDonald was laying the groundwork for a change of venue and strong Puerto Rican business interests were beginning to sway him in the direction of establishing a team in the Caribbean to replace the now-displaced Havana Sugar Kings.[25]

On the playing field the season-long feud between Al Vincent and the fans had so degenerated that the prickly skipper rarely came out of the dugout during a game. Whatever connection he might have earned with the fan base was almost nonexistent and the results were negative publicity that the Marlins could ill afford.[26] Although both MacDonald and Ryan publicly defended Vincent, the lack of diplomacy he exhibited and his failure to apologize for any offensive actions, including the recurring bouts of cursing he continued to direct toward the fans, were not to be excused by the few faithful still populating the stands. Coupled with a last-place standing and dreadful record at home, just like a newly set-off air-raid horn, the warning sounds were progressively getting louder, announcing that the future of professional baseball in Miami was waning. But was anyone listening?

NOTES

1. *Sporting News,* July 6, 1960, 30.
2. Tommy Fitzgerald, "Help Comes, Zauchin Now Trade-Bait," *Miami News,* June 22, 1960.
3. Ibid.
4. Baseball-reference.com.
5. Fitzgerald, "Help Comes, Zauchin Now Trade-Bait."
6. Ibid.
7. Jimmy Burns, "Miami Catcher Refuses Trip, Miffed over Lack of Action," *Sporting News,* July 6, 1960.
8. "Pilot Fires Miami Slugger—Orioles Order Him Retained," *Sporting News,* July 20, 1960, 31.
9. Special to the *Miami News,* "Sinking Marlins 'Tired and Whipped,'" July 9, 1960.
10. Ibid.
11. Special to the *Miami News,* "Dick Hyde Purchased by Miami," July 3, 1960.
12. Brendan C. Boyd and Fred C. Harris, *The Great American Baseball Card Flipping, Trading and Bubble Gum Book* (New York: Little, Brown, 1973).
13. Baseball-reference.com.
14. Ibid.
15. "Marlins Get Ruben Gomez," *Miami News,* July 17, 1960.
16. Baseball-reference.com.
17. Tommy Fitzgerald, "Veale Just Too Tough," *Miami News,* July 21, 1960; baseball-reference.com.
18. Fitzgerald, "Veale Just Too Tough."
19. "Zauchin Sold to Buffalo," *Miami News,* July 31, 1960; baseball-reference.com.
20. Tommy Devine, "Marlins Share Gate Misery with Rivals," *Miami News,* July 25, 1960.
21. Tommy Devine, "What Baseball Needs . . . Is a Good $2 Bet," *Miami News,* July 15, 1960.
22. Devine, "Marlins Share Gate Misery with Rivals."
23. Tommy Devine, "Bill's Dice Rolling Wrong, Club Loss to Be $125,000," *Miami News,* July 12, 1960.
24. Tommy Devine, "'Nothing That Will Appeal to Fans,'" *Miami News,* July 14, 1960.
25. Devine, "What Baseball Needs . . . Is a Good $2 Bet."
26. Devine, "'Nothing That Will Appeal to Fans.'"

THIRTY-ONE

Playing Out the String

At the beginning of the season, Vincent named Jim Archer to be his number-one starter. Although he faltered in the season preview, it was thought to be only a blip on the radar and the twenty-eight-year-old Virginian would soon regain the form he flashed in 1959 when he led the staff in wins (thirteen), innings pitched (208), and complete games (sixteen), and also tied with several others in shutouts (three). By the time June had rolled around, Archer (2–5) was still in a funk and it seemed as if IL hitters had his number. Commiserating around the batting cage one day, Norm Zauchin approached Archer to tell him that he was telegraphing his pitches. Apparently Archer was exhibiting certain mannerisms that tipped off enemy batters to what was coming next, and Archer took the feedback to heart.[1]

As August rolled around, Archer had completely turned around his season and corrected the idiosyncrasies that had plagued him early. Although the Marlins were providing little support offensively, he had been on a tear and improved his record to eight wins and seven losses. On a staff that had lost their best starting pitcher, Wes Stock, to the Orioles, it was welcome news to Al Vincent to see his ace back to form and ready for what would be the most brutal run of the season.

Archer was not the type of hurler who relied on overpowering batters and instead lived and died on the corners of the strike zone. Archer harkened back to his youth and how he was able to develop the abilities to place the ball pretty much where he wanted.

> *Jim Archer*: Well, I started out, I guess, when I started walking. It seemed like I always had a baseball in my hand. As I get a little bit older, I was born and raised in a little country town in a four-room house, and we had a stove in the center of the house that kept the whole house warm.

And we had a well and we drew our water from the well. That well was on a concrete slab, and the concrete slab it was about eight by ten square, but it was about eight to ten inches high on one end and I used to throw the baseball up in there and pretend that I was pitching. I could throw where I could get a groundball back and I could throw it where I could get a fly ball. That's the way I played back and forth until I wore the cover off the baseball, then I would tape it with black tape.

It seemed like I was always throwing something. I got in trouble for throwing rocks. [laughing][2]

Early season rainouts had become an ongoing problem all year and although the players appreciated a day off here and there they were about to pay the price for all of those cancellations. Over the course of the next two weeks the Marlins would play twenty games; six of those dates would be doubleheaders, not to mention the majority of the games to be played on the northern road swing, and with a staff that was already short-handed due to various injuries, the Marlins' hopes of escaping the cellar looked bleak. To make room on the roster, the Marlins had already dealt Artie Kay to their upcoming opponent Rochester, and Dick Hyde, brought in to take his place, was working hard but struggling to recover from his arm woes.

Opening up in Rochester, the Marlins were facing a team that they were experiencing rare success against and had previously beaten eight out of thirteen times. Vincent sent Herb Moford to the hill to face southpaw Cal Browning on a hot humid night in front of 3,292 fans inside Silver Stadium. Hoping to bolster their sagging offense, the Marlins recalled a familiar face in Bert Hamric from Double-A Chattanooga of the Southern Association to join them for the rest of the season.[3] Hamric had seemingly regained his stroke, batting .266 with twelve home runs and a team-leading seventy-six RBIs, and was counted on to do better than the previous season in Miami, when he hit only .224 with fourteen homers and sixty RBIs.[4]

In the opener Miami's defense proved to be as porous as a Tarpon Springs sponge. They committed four errors in the field, including miscues by Ron Samford, Jerry Adair, and Dick Brown. The four errors amounted to one less than the number of hits they garnered for the entire night, but Gene Green did club out his tenth round-tripper of the season. Coming in for relief the last three and a third innings, Artie Kay gained some satisfaction by stifling his ex-mates and slamming the door in their faces to preserve the 3–2 win.[5]

Archer followed up the next night with another strong performance, giving up only five hits in seven innings of work. Barry Shetrone and Gene Green both homered, but when Archer worked himself into a jam in the eighth, Vincent pulled him in favor of Hyde. After the first two Red Wings batters singled, Ben Mateosky strolled to the plate to face Hyde and promptly singled to right field, knotting the score at 2–2. An intentional walk, a single, and an infield out surrendered by Hyde led to a Rochester 4–2 lead. The Marlins could only muster one more run and for the second night in a row dropped a one-run decision; this time the tally showed 4–3.[6]

Ruben Gomez continued to impress his new teammates, mixing his legendary screwball with sliders and fastballs to shut down the Red Wings in the third game of the series, 7–0. Allowing only three hits, the wiry Puerto Rican upped his season record to 4–3. Shetrone homered for the second night in row and added three RBIs, providing more than enough support for Gomez, who helped his own cause by also stroking a couple of base hits.[7]

The Marlins failed to earn a series split, dropping the final game to Rochester, 8–5. Although the Marlins outhit the Red Wings 12–9, and Shetrone homered for the third game in a row, the team's failure to hit with runners in scoring position proved to be the straw that broke that camel's back and led to the Marlins' downfall.[8]

Battered and bruised, the Marlins began the most rugged part of the schedule by playing the first of six doubleheaders to be played over the next eleven days. Buffalo, always an inviting park for hitters, proved to be just that. Vincent, as was his habit all during the season, brought his hitters to the park early for extra batting practice and this time with positive results.[9] In the double-dip opener Miami built a quick 6–0 lead behind home runs by Gene Green and Dick Brown. Going into the bottom of the second inning the herd came thundering back. Portocarrero began to unravel and allowed Buffalo to score single runs in the second and third and a pair in the fourth. In the bottom of the sixth inning, with a 7–4 lead, it looked as if the Marlins had the game in the bag, but Portocarrero continued to struggle and allowed the Bisons to tie the score. In hopes of saving the game Vincent called on Archer to preserve the win, but the Virginia native faltered, giving up three quick hits and allowing the Bisons to take an 8–7 lead. The slim margin would ultimately hold up as the Marlins failed to touch reliever Max Surkont, who earned the save. The Bisons' pitching staff was so stretched on the evening that ex-Marlin Bob Bowman was pressed into service as a reliever doing middle duty. Bowman would, before the season's end, appear in four games that season for former Marlins manager Kerby Farrell.[10]

Miami earned some satisfaction that same evening, coming back to win the nightcap behind Herb Moford's gutsy nine-hitter. Aided by Jerry Adair and Ron Samford homers, the Marlins coasted to an easy 8–3 win in the second game. Vincent praised his catcher Dick Brown for taking the reins as team leader by saying, "Our club has lacked a field leader. Brown seems to be the man now. The players look up to him, especially after last night."[11]

The Marlins' failure to win one-run games continued when Buffalo won the third game of the series, 8–7. It was the Marlins' sixth straight loss in games decided by a single tally and this one came in familiar fashion. With a 6–1 lead going into the bottom of the sixth inning, starter John Anderson appeared on the way to an easy victory. But a big blow by pinch-hitter Billy Taylor doubling in two runs chased Anderson from the game. Vincent called on Hyde to put out the fire, but found that the once-dominant closer only threw more gasoline on the fire, allowing the Bisons to storm back and gain the 8–7 win. Hyde was so ineffective that he even walked a pitcher, pinch-hitter Ken Lehman, and, to add insult to injury, made a throwing error on a Bobby Wine bunt that proved to be the difference-making run. [12]

Before leaving for their next stop in Buffalo, the Marlins split the doubleheader finale. Lying ahead was the Marlins' most brutal stretch of the season. They would be pushed to the limit in a seven-game series against league-leading Toronto. For the next three days the Marlins and Leafs would play doubleheaders before concluding the series with a single game. Following the Toronto series the Marlins would move on to Montreal for a five-game set. Mercifully, there would only be one doubleheader to play in Delorimier Stadium.

With seven games in four days ahead of them the Marlins' pitching staff would prove their mettle against an elite Toronto Maple Leafs club. Having lost confidence in his relief corps, Vincent was calling on all his starters to go as long as they could.

In the first of three consecutive doubleheaders, Bunky Stewart worked quickly and efficiently, shutting down Toronto in a seven-inning affair that took only one hour and twenty minutes to complete. The Leafs managed only two hits off the little lefty, falling 3–0. In the nightcap Gomez continued to shine, not only with his hurling but also with his bat, working overtime into the tenth inning to earn a hard-fought win. The slight Puerto Rican helped his own cause by driving in a couple of runs. Local fans got their money's worth of entertainment as Toronto starter Bob "Riverboat" Smith and Gomez got into a bean ball war. After Gomez hit Smith in the back, Smith retaliated the next inning by plunking Gomez. Unfortunately for "Riverboat," his equalizer backfired on him and after Adair walked, Fred Valentine singled to bring home Gomez and cut the Leafs' lead to 4–3. Woody Smith would later triple in the eighth inning, scoring Green in what would ultimately be the tying run and sending the game into extra frames. Miami tallied a couple of runs in the top of the tenth to come out on top, 6–4. [13]

Toronto got their revenge the next night when Anderson, despite pitching a complete game, was bested by Bob Chakales, 4–2. Portocarrero followed with a poor performance, lasting only five and two-thirds innings in a disappointing 10–9 slugfest loss. In an all-too-familiar scenario, Miami's bullpen faltered again when Dick Hyde surrendered four runs in the ninth inning and blew what had been a 9–6 Miami lead. [14] Final tally showed Leafs 10, Marlins 9.

Both bone-tired teams sloshed their way through their third straight double dip. Pitching on sheer determination, Rudy Arias in the short game and Moford in the late affair both pitched complete games. Vincent, now hesitant to use any of his relievers, left Arias in the game despite giving up five runs, resulting in a 5–3 loss. Moford fared better in the late game. Moford's own two-run single in the sixth inning proved to be the back-breaker as the Leafs fell by a 6–3 score.[15]

Although the Marlins (50–69) were still residing in last place, one of their charges was quietly turning heads around the league. Gene Green, upping his batting average to .298 after an uncharacteristically slow start, had as of late been on a tear. Trailing league-leading hitter Jim Pendleton of Jersey City by only four points, there was talk that the Marlins' most productive hitter might soon be receiving a call from Baltimore. Besides his glossy batting average, Green was among the league RBI leaders with sixty-four and had collected sixteen round-trippers to boot.[16]

Putting the proverbial cherry on top, the Marlins finished on a high note, taking the rubber match. Using their seventh different starter in the series, Vincent once again asked for the supreme challenge of his pitchers to finish the game to the end and Archer was more than happy to oblige. Relying on his pinpoint control, Archer went the full nine innings and allowed only three hits and a walk while striking out eight, easily handing the Leafs a 6–0 blanking.[17] It was one of Archer's three shutouts of the season and probably his best performance as he evened his record at 9–9.[18] The win allowed Miami to close within one game of Columbus and they had escaped the basement before moving on to Montreal.

Like the Marlins, the Royals were experiencing their own problems with attendance and viability as a baseball market. Unlike the Marlins, the Royals' roots in the IL were deep and stretched back to 1890, when the Buffalo Bisons pulled up stakes and made their home in 1890. Montreal took a brief hiatus from the IL after 1917, but returned again in 1928 when the Jersey City franchise was purchased and Delorimier Stadium was built to house the prodigal sons. Beginning in 1939 the Royals began their marriage with the then Brooklyn Dodgers, the team that they would become most associated with until the arrival in 1969 of their own team, the Montreal Expos. Unbeknownst to most fans in the geographically opposed cities, both clubs were in their final death throes as members of the IL. Montreal's tradition as the jewel of the Dodgers' minor league system had now shifted to Spokane and the once rich vein of talent the Dodgers had supplied was slowing to a trickle, handicapping the franchise's ability to compete.[19]

Coming into the four-game series beginning on August 13, the Marlins were still languishing in last place, but were only one and a half games behind Montreal. Not intimidated by the road, the Marlins set their eyes on escaping the nether regions; for all intents and purposes, their playoff hopes were dashed and they were a longshot at best to see postseason play.

Stewart was thus far a disappointing 0–3 against Montreal for the season, and once again met with a rude awakening. First baseman Joe Altobelli, who would by season's end lead the IL in both homers and RBIs, led the Royals' hitting parade by crushing his twenty-ninth homer of the year. Just for good measure he added a double and a triple, plating four runners, which proved Stewart's undoing in the 8–3 loss. It was especially frustrating since seventh-place Columbus dropped both ends of a doubleheader to Buffalo and a win would have allowed the Marlins to escape last place.[20]

Miami bounced back the next night behind Gomez, who upped his season record to 6–3, but, more important, was now 4–1 with the Marlins. Both Adair and Joe Caffie doubled to set the table for a two-run first inning. It was all the offense Gomez would need as he held the Royals to a scant four hits, cruising to the end in the 8–1 yawner win. Gomez continued to show his proficiency at the plate by clubbing a double and setting an example for more than a few of his teammates—like Woody Smith and Fred Valentine, who were still mired in slumps.[21]

Away from home since July 31, the Marlins concluded their road trip by splitting a doubleheader finale with Montreal, winning the first game 5–3 and losing the night game 6–0. With a long flight ahead and Buffalo coming into town the next day, the Marlins were running on fumes.[22]

One of the Marlins not worse for the wear, Herb Moford, strolled confidently into Miami Stadium, refreshed after having last started a game five days ago on August 10. Working his breaking balls to perfection, Moford held the visiting Buffalo Bisons to two hits while garnering his fourth blanking of the season, 4–0. Bisons skipper Kerby Farrell lamented after the game, "He's one of the best in the league on throwing breaking stuff." The forlorn skipper further exclaimed, "And we don't have a breaking ball hitter on our team."[23]

Moford's gem set the tone for the rest of the series as the Marlins nearly swept the Bisons in the four-game set. The only loss came in the first game of the next night's doubleheader. Uncharacteristically, Portocarrero brought his best stuff to the park, only to match zeroes with the Bisons' Hank Mason and Max Surkont for ten innings before leaving the game with the score tied 0–0. Dick Hyde remained strong in relief until the fourteenth inning before coming unglued, allowing Jackie Davis to homer and three additional runs to cross the plate. The final score: Bisons 4, Marlins 0.[24]

Miami bounced back in the late game, edging the Bisons 1–0 on Stewart's five-hit shutout. The Marlins' hero of the night was catcher Dick Brown, who caught both ends of the doubleheader, amounting to his sixty-second and sixth-third straight appearances since being acquired from the White Sox. Gene Green gushed praise on his teammate following the game: "You ought to spread it all over the paper how much guts that guy's got." Brown, who had proven to be an iron man in every sense of the word, announced to the press, "I guess Al would take me out if he wanted to but I'd rather catch them all." Vincent wouldn't change his mind and Brown would prove to be so durable that he appeared behind the plate catching every game for the Marlins until the close of the season.[25]

The Marlins' good fortune continued at home in mid-August as they bested their longtime nemesis Red Wings, taking three of five games. Although the Marlins were in the midst of their most successful home-stand of the season, Vincent continued to feel the abuse from the local fans, and during a Saturday night affair it resulted in some vicious mud-slinging. No pun intended, as you will see.

A disgruntled fan named Walter Mudd, sitting in a box seat, began to loudly voice his opinions concerning Vincent's ability as a capable man-ager and offered his thoughts that Vincent should return to Baltimore to coach. "I told him he wasn't capable of managing a ball club but I didn't curse him," claimed Mudd. This reportedly set off Vincent and he went into a rage, verbally abusing his target and stating he would be there long after Mudd was gone. For once, Marlins' broadcaster and public relations director Bill Durney defended the beleaguered manager by saying, "The guy was sitting in the general admission section and came down for the sole purpose of telling Vincent he was stupid. What can you expect a manager to do, just grin and say thank you?"[26]

Vincent's failure to make the Marlins a contender and his frustrations with the club's underachievement were a reflection of what the season had become. Unfortunately for Vincent, most of the fan abuse was being heaped on his shoulders, and the constant mistreatment was grating on his psyche, further isolating him from the few fans who were still show-ing up at the games. Although the Marlins' recent success had, at least temporarily, pulled them out of the league basement and into sixth place, any hope of postseason success had long since faded and it seemed as if the team was merely playing out the string and trying to avoid falling into last place again.[27]

Back on the road again the Marlins would meet their once-hated ri-vals, the now relocated and renamed Jersey City Jerseys. Although the rivalry no longer held its geographical importance, the two teams had bad blood between them.

An August 23 doubleheader started with a heated battle between the bitter enemies. The resilient veteran Jim Archer, who once sported an uninspiring 2–7 record, had since done a complete 180–degree turn and was now flashing a 10–9 mark. On the other side of the diamond, ex-Marlin and infamous "Dalton Gang" member Seth Morehead prepared to face one of the hottest hurlers in the IL. Both teams battled tooth and nail through a scoreless six innings in the short game before Shetrone,

Green, and Caffie touched Morehead for three consecutive singles, handing him the 1–0 defeat. It was a typical hand-wringer dominated by pitching as the former Sugar Kings managed six hits to the Marlins' four, but
were unable to string any of their base knocks together.[28]

The second game found the Jerseys gaining some semblance of revenge, outdistancing their opponents, 8–4. Gomez, who had been money
in the bank all season, had his poorest performance of the year when he
allowed eight runs in six and one-third innings. The Marlins' defense
took most of the blame for Gomez's failures, allowing five unearned
runs. Errors by Adair, Burke, and Gomez and two misplayed balls by
Valentine were the chief culprits.[29]

Not all news was bad news. Moford, keeping in step with Archer,
won his sixth consecutive game the next night, hurling his fifth shut-out
of the year, a 2–0 win. Both Brown and Green drove in runs during the
Marlins' puny six-hit performance, but it was more than enough to send
the Jerseys to the cleaners. The Marlins, on a rare winning skein, had now
won eight of their last twelve games. At 61–75, with eighteen games
remaining to play, the sixth-place Marlins now stood seven and a half
games behind fourth-place Buffalo.[30]

It was the shortest road trip of the season (three days), but the Marlins
were not up to the task against Jersey City. It would prove to be the last
meeting between the two teams on the road and the former Sugar Kings
took great pleasure in earning the hard-fought 4–3 victory. True to form,
Dick Hyde took another defeat in relief, dropping his season ledger to
0–5.[31] Interestingly, the five-year rivalry would end up in a draw, with
both teams winning fifty-five times.

The returning Marlins were little concerned with the rumors, now
reaching a fever pitch around the club, concerning their possible relocation. Still playing in front of crowds sometimes numbering less than a
thousand, a discouraged MacDonald announced that the chances of the
team relocating the next season were 50–50. With losses amounting to an
estimated $132,000, not even a multimillionaire like "Big Bill" wanted to
continue to operate in the red.[32] In Tommy Fitzgerald's column of the
August 25 *Miami News*, MacDonald announced in no uncertain terms
that he had had it: "Let somebody else take a shot at it. I'd be delighted to
sell the franchise if somebody else wanted to give it a try." He did offer a
morsel of hope that the team might stay by adding, "Before moving the
franchise, I feel the civic thing to do is to give somebody in Miami a
chance to keep it here." MacDonald was still talking about moving to
Puerto Rico, but was widening his scope to include Norfolk, Virginia,
and Jersey City, New Jersey.[33]

Whatever hopes the Marlins' dim playoff chances held were quickly
squandered. Miami dropped two of three to Columbus, three of four to
Richmond, and finally three of four to Jersey City. Although the Marlins
enjoyed some consolation in that they hadn't slipped into last place, some

of the more productive players were hoping for a call from Baltimore to showcase their talents for next year.

Last Home Game Starting Lineups:

New Jersey Jerseys	*Miami Marlins*
SS Elio Chacon	CF Albie Pearson
2B Yo-Yo Davalillo	SS Jerry Adair
LF Jim Pendleton	LF Barry Shetrone
C Chuck Dotterer	CF Fred Valentine
3B Daniel Morejon	1B Gene Green
RF Ray Shearer	2B Ron Samford
3B Felix Torres	C Dick Brown
SS Lou Jackson	3B Leo Burke
P Seth Morehead	P Dick Luebke
Manager: Nap Reyes	Manager: Al Vincent

On September 5 the Marlins dropped their last-ever home game as a member of the IL and last meeting ever against Havana/New Jersey. It was a pitiful sight to see, with only 738 paying customers peppered throughout the stands of Miami Stadium in what should have been a night that they honored their soon-to-be-departed heroes. It was fitting that the Marlins played their rivals in their home finale, but something was missing. Absent from the starting lineup was thirty-three-year-old Woody Smith. Finishing out his most disappointing season in his career, he sat observing from the sidelines as Leo Burke minded his property on the hot corner. Smith, although still able to flash impressive leather, had seen his numbers drop to alarming lows (.213, 11 HR, 49 RBI).[34] Yet despite the lack of productivity, Smith remained beloved and one would be hard pressed to find anyone sharing a discouraging word about the man who was the face of Marlins baseball.

In typical season fashion the Marlins blew a sixth-inning 4–3 lead. Despite banging out nine hits—only two were for extra bases, doubles by Pearson and Brown—the Marlins were unable to string together a strong rally and fell short, to the dismay of the locals. For losing pitcher John Anderson, who came on in relief of Dick Luebke, it was a welcome end to his most exasperating season as a pro. He, like his teammate Woody Smith, had spent all or part of the last five seasons in a Marlins uniform, and had also suffered through his worst season as a pro. Battling back problems, he never found the form he had experienced in 1959, and his 2–10 record and astronomical 5.96 ERA did nothing but add agony to an already hard-to-swallow lost campaign.[35]

Even harder to digest was the failure by owner Bill MacDonald. The jolly man who had so optimistically predicted after purchasing the Marlins from George Storer that the team would be a force to be reckoned with, and anticipated how he would turn the floundering franchise around in a couple of years, had failed. The same Marlins that saw over 288,000 fans turn out during their 1956 inaugural season had sadly seen their attendance drop to 120,922 by the end of 1960.[36]

MacDonald thrust the final death blow by announcing that he wouldn't be returning for the 1961 season and would be pulling up stakes for greener grass somewhere else. "I won't be back . . . I can't think of anything that could cause me to change my mind," said MacDonald. It was the age-old story of a successful businessman who loved baseball and thought he could make it work just like his other business ventures. Throwing out the window all the lessons he learned in the business world, MacDonald had let his heart sway him. Despite all his good intentions, he was defeated before he even began. Unlike his predecessor, it only took MacDonald a year to figure out that it was time to throw in the towel. The once optimistic owner stated, "Misery loves company and I have it. The International League as a whole is having a bad year. There won't be a single club which will make money."

On September 11 the Marlins played their last game in Richmond. It was a five-inning, rain-shortened affair—an inning for each year the Marlins inhabited Miami Stadium and the IL. Thanks to a Burke grand slam off of Vees left-hander Ed Dick, the Marlins prevailed. Fittingly, Woody Smith homered in his last at-bat as a Marlin. It was an appropriate ending for Forrest "Woody" Smith. It was his heroic way of saying goodbye and thank you to Miami. The solo blast proved to be the difference maker as the Marlins came out on top 5–4 before the downpour mercifully ended their season.[37] To the surprise of no one, the Orioles failed to call up Smith in September. By now the old pro was resigned to the fact that he wasn't going to realize his major league dream.

For a few of Smith's teammates, the 1960 season would serve as a launching pad to their future careers. Adair, who had a cup of coffee with the Orioles in 1959, returned again to Baltimore for a late season call-up and by 1961 would become the O's regular second baseman, going on to a successful thirteen-year career in the big leagues with the Chicago White Sox, Boston Red Sox, and Kansas City Royals.[38]

Albie Pearson regained his confidence and in 1961 was drafted by the expansion Los Angeles Angels, where he would reestablish himself as one of the premier lead-off hitters in the American League.[39] Although his back problems would eventually return to haunt him and ultimately cut his career short, he remembered his time in Miami as a launching point that prepared him for his successful return to the majors. Pearson remembered his back problems and how he overcame adversity to continue his career.

Albie Pearson: It did end my career, but actually it was kind of a blessing in disguise because when the Angels were formed and the Orioles had [pausing]—because my back was pretty bad, and they [Baltimore Orioles] were not going to put up with it then. So at the end of 1960 when I was playing with Miami, the Marlins, my last year, the Angels were formed. And I was put on Triple-A Rochester's roster. And so when the Angels were formed I decided to write a letter to Gene Autry and Fred Haney. Fred Haney was the general manager. Gene Autry was the owner. And I just told them, you know what my back, which has clearly been bad, it feels great and I would like an opportunity to be part of the playing pool for the Angels because I was born and raised in Southern California and I would like to go home.

And so Fred Haney, working with Gene Autry, along with Billy Rigney, who was my first manager there with the Angels, in fact my only one through six years there, he decided to put me in the draft pool and I was the twenty-eighth and last player drafted by the Angels from the Orioles system and had the opportunity to be there.

My back was solid for six years and then it broke down again and that ended my career. But I just wrote a letter saying, "Hey, give me a chance to play." And I got a chance to come home and be part of the Angels. In fact, I had a chance to be part of the first Angel team ever. Even, if I recall, I scored the first run, and it was part of the historical time with the Angels in 1961.

Again back to Miami. I really, when I say, I enjoyed my time there. It was a time for me to make a comeback and do some things . . . that second year when I hit two or three something [hit .301 in 1960]. Yeah, that was a time in Miami when, if I recall, that during that time the confidence. [pause] And I don't know but I'm sure you've heard the term many times through baseball players, really the key to play well is being confident. And my confidence after having been Rookie of the Year and quote "sophomore jinx" I had about ten ounces of it. When I went down to Miami my confidence returned and I was able to hit the ball and perform well enough where my confidence—where I felt that I could play any place.[40]

Dave Nicholson, although a disappointment in the little time he spent in Miami, continued to be plagued by his big swing and a large hole in his strike zone. However, his ability to hit home runs bought him time and that skill ultimately translated into a seven-year major league career in which he totaled sixty-one round-trippers.[41]

Wes Stock ended up making seventeen appearances in relief for the Orioles, winning two and losing two with a 2.88 ERA. Stock hung around the big leagues as a relief pitcher. He later became more famous as a pitching coach with Kansas City/Oakland Athletics (1967, 1973–1976), Milwaukee Brewers (1970–1972), and Seattle Mariners (1977–1981).[42]

Other Marlins who appeared in the big leagues in Baltimore that season were John Anderson, Jim Busby, Gene Green, Billy Hoeft, Arnie Portocarrero, and Barry Shetrone.[43]

And, much to the delight of Walter Mudd (the disenchanted Marlins fan), his wish to have Vincent dismissed as manager came to fruition, but with a caveat—Vincent didn't disappear altogether. Following the 1960 season he left the Orioles organization and hooked up with the Philadelphia Phillies' coaching staff for the 1961–1963 seasons. He also landed a similar job with the Kansas City Athletics from 1966–1967 before leaving major league baseball. Vincent's career didn't end there. In 1974 he accepted a position at Lamar University and served as the team's special assistant coach for the next sixteen seasons. He was inducted into the Cardinals Hall of Fame in 1980 and received the ultimate honor when Lamar University's baseball field was named in his honor, along with Bryan Beck: Vincent-Beck Stadium.[44]

Final Standings:

	W	L	GB
Toronto	100	54	–
Richmond	82	70	17
Rochester	81	73	19
Buffalo	78	75	21½
Havana/Jersey City	76	77	23½
Columbus	69	84	30½
Miami	65	88	34½
Montreal	62	92	38

NOTES

1. Tommy Fitzgerald, "Bryant Says Pitch-Calling Overvalued," *Miami News*, June 9, 1960.
2. Jim Archer, phone interview with the author, February 21, 2010.
3. Special to the *Miami News*, "Chance to Gain Playoff Makes Marlins Nervous," August 2, 1960.
4. Baseball-reference.com.
5. Special to the *Miami News*, "Chance to Gain Playoff Makes Marlins Nervous."
6. Special to the *Miami News*, "Same Script: Marlins Lose," August 3, 1960.
7. Special to the *Miami News*, "Gomez Is Like Money in Bank," August 4, 1960.
8. "Battered Marlins' Shuffle to Buffalo," *Miami News*, August 5, 1960.
9. "International Items," *Sporting News*, August 17, 1960.
10. Special to the *Miami News*, "Spirit of Brown Catching, Al Says," August 6, 1960.
11. Ibid.
12. Special to the *Miami News*, "Marlins Lead 6–1, Bisons Win, 8–7," August 7, 1960.
13. Special to the *Miami News*, "Marlins Find a Soft Spot," August 9, 1960; *Sporting News*, August 17, 1960, 30.

14. Special to the *Miami News*, "Toronto Fans Learn Why Marlins Are 8th," August 10, 1960; *Sporting News*, August 17, 1960, 30.

15. Special to the *Miami News*, "Orioles to Call on Gene Green?" August 11, 1960.

16. "Orioles to Call on Gene Green?"; *Sporting News*, August 17, 1960, 30.

17. Special to the *Miami News*, "Stewart Gets Call Tonight," August 12, 1960.

18. "Stewart Gets Call Tonight"; baseball-reference.com.

19. Bill O'Neal, *International League: A Baseball History 1884–1991* (Austin, TX: Eakin Press, 1992), 305–11.

20. Special to the *Miami News*, "Marlins Regain Old Form," August 13, 1960.

21. Special to the *Miami News*, "Marlins Slug Montreal, 8–1," August 14, 1960.

22. *Sporting News*, August 24, 1960.

23. Ibid.

24. Tommy Fitzgerald, "Marlins Hate Marathons," *Miami News*, August 18, 1960.

25. Ibid.

26. Paul Cox, "Vincent Abused Him, Fan Claims," *Miami News*, August 23, 1960.

27. Ibid.

28. Special to the *Miami News*, "Moford Goes Tonight," August 24, 1960.

29. Ibid.

30. Ibid.

31. *Sporting News*, September 7, 1960, 29.

32. Jimmy Burns, "MacDonald Says Miami's '61 Chances Now Are Only 50–50," *Sporting News*, August 31, 1960, 32.

33. Tommy Fitzgerald, "Marlin Owner Declares He's Had It," *Miami News*, August 25, 1960.

34. Baseball-reference.com.

35. Tommy Fitzgerald, "Baltimore to Give Vincent a Chance to Watch a Winner," *Miami News*, September 6, 1960.

36. Tommy Devine, "Clues Clear in Baseball 'Murder' Case," *Miami News*, September 6, 1960.

37. Special to the *Miami News*, "It's All Over Now for Marlins," September 12, 1960.

38. Baseball-reference.com.

39. Ibid.

40. Albie Pearson, phone interview with the author, May 17, 2010.

41. Baseball-reference.com.

42. Ibid.

43. Gary Gillette and Pete Palmer, *The ESPN Baseball Encyclopedia*, 5th ed. (New York: Sterling, 2008).

44. "Vincent-Beck Stadium," LamarCardinals.com, http://www.lamarcardinals.com/facilities/vincent-beck-stadium.html.

THIRTY-TWO

The Final Chapter

On November 28, 1960, the IL announced their formal approval allowing the Marlins to relocate and pull up stakes for their move to San Juan, Puerto Rico.[1] Fan reaction to the loss of the Marlins was mostly apathetic silence, a sad commentary on a proud team that would ultimately lay the groundwork for professional baseball's birth in the Magic City when the Florida Marlins arrived in 1993.

The city of Miami fathers made a last-ditch effort to keep the team by offering a $10,000 reduction in the stadium rental fees, but it was to no avail. The token offer was quickly tossed aside by team owner Bill Mac-Donald, whose previous season losses amounted to over $150,000. The team packed up their bags for their new southern climes.[2]

Flush with excitement and holding a fresh working agreement with the St. Louis Cardinals in hand, MacDonald headed to San Juan confident that his new Marlins would be the success he had hoped for when he bought the team from Storer. However, his optimism would be short lived. Despite acquiring stadium rental for a mere $1 and broadcasting rights amounting to approximately $75,000, few Puerto Ricans made their way to the ballpark and, coupled with outrageous travel expenses, it only took until mid-May for the IL fathers and MacDonald to figure out that the move was ill advised and that the franchise would have to be transferred out of San Juan to avert financial disaster.[3]

Although not an ideal site, the IL ultimately approved the Marlins' relocation to Charleston, West Virginia. In a strange PR move, the team retained the name "Marlins," to the confusion of more than a few fans. It can be safely said the mountain streams and lakes of West Virginia were without any of the fighting game fish, but a clever front-office person with the team attributed the new Marlins' logo to a popular hunting rifle used by locals in the area, saving the club the expense of outfitting the team in new uniforms.[4]

Meanwhile in Miami, Miami Stadium was as quiet as a church mouse with no tenant. Although the Orioles played their home spring training games at the stadium, the otherwise buzzing park stood silent for the summer of 1961.

It wouldn't take long for baseball to return, and by 1962 the Class-D Florida State League (FSL) reinstituted minor league baseball in Miami with their newest affiliate, taking on the familiar Miami Marlins name under the watchful eye of their parent club, the Philadelphia Phillies. Although a much lower classification of play than what fans were used to, and missing many of the recognizable names the locals had become accustomed to seeing grace the diamond, many hardcore fans were happy to see their summer entertainment card once again filled.

The following season the FSL moved up to Class-A. The Marlins kept their popular moniker while still taking up residence in the friendly confines of Miami Stadium. In 1966 the Baltimore Orioles signed a working agreement with Miami, but kept the name the same until 1970, when they changed the name to reflect the parent club, switching the team to the Orioles, a name they would keep for the next eleven seasons. In 1982 the Marlins name returned, as the team no longer had a working agreement with Baltimore. No team name changes occurred with the club again until 1989. The new tag of "Miracles" was adopted and stayed attached to the club through the 1991 season. The last season that minor league ball would grace the fields of Miami Stadium was 1991, as the city anxiously awaited the christening of major league baseball's grand entrance in 1993. Although the "Marlins" nickname would once again be resurrected, the new team name would reflect a more statewide appeal under the name "Florida Marlins."[5]

As for the vast majority of the original ballplayers, they went their various ways, never to return to Miami, except for two who made their triumphant returns just a few years later. In 1969, seven years after hanging up his cleats and closing out a brilliant seventeen-year minor league career, Woody Smith returned to the dugout, making his managerial debut as the skipper of the Marlins' Class-A FSL affiliate. Smith proved as adept at managing as he had been at handling the hot corner, guiding the Marlins/Orioles to four straight league championships from 1969–1972 and compiling a 335–201 record along the way. Still suffering that itch to play, the forty-two-year-old Smith made appearances in twelve games, batting .290 in forty at-bats during his first season as a manager before finally retiring his Louisville Slugger for good.[6]

Despite the success that Smith enjoyed as a manager and his ability to garner titles, the Baltimore Orioles fired Smith without explanation at the conclusion of the 1972 season. It was a hard pill to swallow for Smith and he remained bitter over his dismissal. "Bitter? Hell yes I'm bitter," said

Smith later. "I worked hard at Miami and suddenly they fire me, without a word of explanation. A guy would have to be a complete fool not to be bitter when he knows he's done a good job and still gets fired for no reason."[7] The cold manner in which the Orioles handled the situation hurt most, and it was another disappointing episode in the career of a man who gave his heart and soul to the game he loved.

Smith's former infield partner Pancho Herrera also returned to Miami for two seasons in 1968 and 1969, joining his ex-teammate across the diamond in 1969 for one last season together. The thirty-four-year-old Herrera spent the early part of the year plying his trade in the Mexican Southeast League, which concluded its season in July, before returning to his home, which was now based in Miami.[8]

Bill Durney Jr., another one who returned to Miami, had moved from pitching, batting practice, and acting as ballboy to running the club. He remembers the contribution that Herrera made to the Marlins during his two-year stint.

> *Bill Durney Jr.*: And another guy probably off one of those clubs was Pancho Herrera. I brought Pancho back to A-ball back in '68. He'd played in Mexico every year and their season would end in July. And I would bring him back for the last part of July and August to play for us. He'd hit ten home runs for me, being that short period of time, and was great with the young kids on the club and do a real good job for me. That was one connection besides Woody . . . Pancho was just a great big kid and heart.[9] [Actually hit four home runs in 1968 and four home runs in 1969][10]

The one constant that remained the same through five decades was Miami Stadium. Although baseball continued to be played for more than thirty years, a cloud of dismay seemed to engulf the stadium, and with it began the slow decline and eventual demise of the once proud jewel of minor league baseball. Although there were many reasons why baseball died a slow death in Miami, some of the future troubles of Miami Stadium could be attributed to the slow deterioration of the surrounding neighborhood encircling the ballpark that brought with it a perception of being a crime-ridden area. The development of Interstate 95, which diverted traffic and hurt accessibility to the park, didn't help.[11]

In 1987, a last-ditch effort to save Miami Stadium was launched, including renaming the park "Bobby Maduro Stadium." The man who brought organized baseball to Cuba and championed professional baseball in Miami for so many years had died that same year and the Miami City Commission voted unanimously to rename the stadium in his honor. Almost as an omen of impending doom, the newly christened Bobby Maduro Stadium was painted in large letters across cheap plywood and bolted unceremoniously to the façade. By 1990 the Orioles skipped town for better digs farther north in Florida.[12]

With little public resistance, the former Miami Stadium was demolished in 2001. It took a mere two months to bring down what was once the jewel of the minor leagues. The dream that Jose Aleman Jr. had optimistically envisioned to be a stepping-stone toward luring major league baseball south was now gone. Aleman Jr., ahead of his time in projecting Miami as a major league city, did not live to see the coming of major league baseball in 1993. On July 31, 1983, a mentally distressed and severely depressed Aleman Jr. found a 9mm semiautomatic weapon and opened fire on four family members, killing his sixty-nine-year-old aunt. A now reclusive, broken man who had squandered his family fortune, Aleman Jr. fired at police and threatened to kill his mother before shooting himself in the head a split second before a police bullet struck him in the stomach. "The poor kid could have gone out a millionaire," said Al Rubio, a former Sun Sox general manager.[13]

Today, on the corner of Northwest 23rd Street and 10th Avenue, all that remains of Miami Stadium is the name attached to an apartment complex where there once stood a proud baseball park. The neighborhood that surrounds the complex is shabby and few, if any, who live in the apartments have any memories of the ballpark or its significance to the community.

Today in the city of Miami, new excitement has replaced the distant memories of baseball past. Where the Orange Bowl once stood there is now a gleaming modern stadium equipped with a retractable roof and luxury box seats, a reflection of modern baseball ready to be launched for the 2013 season. It is the same location where Satchel Paige, on a magic evening on August 7, 1956, held court pitching one of the most famous games in minor league history, only a scant few miles from where Miami Stadium was located.

The few men and women who are old enough to remember the original Marlins carry with them loving memories of the team that once proudly represented Miami and in many ways laid the groundwork for the newly christened Miami Marlins of today. In the old-timers' minds' eyes they can still see Woody Smith flawlessly one-handing a tapper just inside the third-base chalk line and whipping a bullet across the field to the extended glove of Pancho Herrera just in time to nip the runner at first base. Or Don Cardwell sending a whistling fastball toward home plate, freezing the enemy hitter, poised at the ready on a called strike three. It is Pepper Martin smoking his pipe in the dugout and Satchel Paige going into his double wind-up before heaving one of his cleverly named pitches to Gus Niarhos or Clyde McCullough squatting behind the plate, the pitch always arriving just where he wanted it. It's Bob Micelotta and Benny Tompkins combining flawlessly for another double play and Don Landrum reaching up at the last second, robbing another would-be hitter of a sure extra base hit. And it is Tim Anagnost waiting at home plate as Bob Bowman, or Cal Abrams, or Ed Bouchee round third base, the young batboy's hand outstretched, waiting to greet them at home plate for a celebration of another Marlins' home run. So if you happen to be in the area of Northwest 23rd Street and 10th Avenue on a quiescent South Florida night and you close your eyes, quiet your mind, and listen ever so carefully, you might still hear the crack of the bat, the rising roar of the crowd, and the soothing voices of Bill Durney and Sonny Hirsch echoing softly on the breeze as you drift back in time.

NOTES

1. Miami News Wire Service, "Adios, Marlins, Adios," *Miami News*, November 29, 1960.
2. Jimmy Burns, "Cards Set with MacDonald, but Team May Leave Miami," *Sporting News*, October 12, 1960, 6.
3. Jimmy Burns, "Puerto Rico Club Tabbed as Boost for Int Loop Gate," *Sporting News*, December 7, 1960.
4. Bill O'Neal, *International League: A Baseball History 1884–1991* (Austin, TX: Eakin Press, 1992), 259.
5. Baseball-reference.com; Kevin M. McCarthy, *Baseball in Florida* (Sarasota, FL: Pineapple Press, 1996).
6. McCarthy, *Baseball in Florida*.
7. Gene Williams, "Woody Smith Remains Bitter," *Miami News*, April 18, 1973.
8. Society for American Baseball Research, "Ramirez, Jose," http://bioproj.sabr.org/bioproj.cfm.
9. Bill Durney Jr., phone interview with the author, December 21, 2010.
10. Baseball-reference.com.
11. Luis Yanez, "Miami Stadium: Field of Broken Dreams," *Miami Herald*, May 11, 2007, www.miamiherald.com/460/v-print/story; Robert Andrew Powell, "Rough Diamond," *Miami New Times*, August 15, 1996, www.miaminewtimes.com/content/printVersion/236865.
12. Powell, "Rough Diamond."
13. Ibid.

Appendix 1

Roll Call

Ted Abernathy (1959)
Cal "Abie" Abrams (1956–1957)
Jerry "Casper the Friendly Ghost" Adair (1960)
Charles "Red" Adams (1957)
Robert "Bobby" Adams (1959)
John "The Quiet Man" Anderson (1956–1960)
Jim Archer (1959–1960)
Rudolfo "Rudy" Arias (1960)
Toby Atwell (1956)
Roger Bean (1959)
Danny Bishop (1959)
Marv Blaylock (1957)
Henry Bolinda (1957)
Ed Bouchee (1956)
Bob Bowman (1956)
Walter Brady (1959)
Richard "Dick" Brown (1960)
Johnny "Fake Catch" Bucha (1957–1960)
Richard "Bunks/Dick/Youngblood" Bunker (1957–1958)
Leo Burke (1959–1960)
Jim Busby (1960)
Harry Byrd (1959–1960)
Joe "Rabbit" Caffie (1960)
Bob "Sugar" Cain (1956)
Don Cardwell (1956, 1958)
Thomas Casagrande (1956)
Foster Castleman (1959)
Bubba Church (1957–1958)
Mel Clark (1956)
Jimmie Coker (1958)
Jim Command (1956)
Bob Conley (1956–1959)
Angelo "Junior" Dagres (1960)
Pompeyo "Yo-Yo" Davalillo (1956–1957)
Bill Davidson (1959)

Karl Drews (1959)
Don Erickson (1956)
Chuck Essegian (1957–1958)
Richard "Turk/Dick" Farrell (1956)
Jack "Fat Jack" Fisher (1959)
Robert Frederick (1958)
Ruben Gomez (1960)
Glen Gorbous (1956)
Sid Gordon (1956)
Mackey Grasso (1958)
John "Johnny" Gray (1958)
Dallas Green (1957–1958)
Gene "The Animal" Green (1960)
Jim Greengrass (1957)
Bob Greenwood (1956)
Warren Hacker (1958)
Bert Hamric (1958–1960)
Chuck Harmon (1958)
Mickey Harrington (1957)
Dick Harris (1958)
Roy Hawes (1956)
Mel Held (1959)
Francisco "Pancho/Panchon/Frank" Herrera (1957–1958)
Dorrel "Whitey/Wild Child" Herzog (1957)
Phil Hewitt (1956)
Arthur Hirst (1958)
William "Billy" Hoeft (1960)
Ray Holton (1956–1957)
Fred "Fatboy" Hopke (1958)
Earl Hunsinger (1956–1957)
Richard "Dick" Hyde (1960)
Wilbur "Moose/Shorty/Wib" Johnson (1956–1958)
Howard "Howie" Judson (1957)
Arthur "Artie" Kay (1959–1960)
Edward "Eddie" Kazak
Frank Kellert (1959)
Thornton Kipper (1956)
Dick Kokos (1956)
Steve "Hoss" Korcheck (1959)
Bill Lajoie (1959)
Don Landrum (1957–1958)
Gene Lary (1959)
Leigh Lawrence (1959)
George Lerchen (1956)
Angelo LiPetri (1956–1958)

Stu Locklin (1957)
Richard "Dick" Luebke (1960)
Robert "Bob" Mabe (1960)
Clarence Maddern (1957)
David Mann (1956)
Henry "Hank" Mason (1957–1958)
John "Windy" McCall (1957–1959)
Roger McCardell (1960)
Clyde McCullough (1957)
Mickey "Maury" McDermott (1958–1959)
Jim "Hot Rod" McDonald (1960)
Jack Meyer (1957)
Bob "Mickey" Micelotta (1956–1958)
Ed Mierkowicz (1956)
Bob Miller (1958)
Ron "The Kid" Moeller (1959–1960)
Herb Moford (1959–1960)
Seth "Moe" Morehead (1956)
Earl Mossor (1958)
Alfred "Al" Nagel (1960)
Gus "Gussie" Niarhos (1956)
Dave Nicholson (1960)
Larry Novak (1956–1957)
Charles "Chuck/Ducky" Oertel (1959)
Jim "Bear" Owens (1956)
Satchel "Satch" Paige (1956–1958)
Charles Parsons (1959)
Carlos Paula (1956)
Albie Pearson (1960)
Duane Pillette (1956)
Tony Ponce (1956)
Arnold "Arnie" Portocarrero (1960)
Tom "Money Bags" Qualters (1956–1957)
Don Richmond (1956)
Saul Rogovin (1957)
Dario Rubinstein (1957)
Ron Samford (1960)
Rolf Scheel (1959)
Roman "Ray" Semproch (1957)
Barry Shetrone (1960)
Forrest "Woody" Smith (1956–1960)
Gene Snyder (1956–1958)
Jerry Snyder (1958–1959)
Jack Spring (1956)
Veston "Bunky" Stewart (1958–1960)

Wes Stock (1959)
Haywood Sullivan (1957)
Ben "The Professor" Tompkins (1956–1958)
Virgil "Fire" Trucks (1959)
Leonard Tucker (1959)
Robert "Bob" Usher (1958)
Jose Valdivielso (1959)
Fred "Squeaky" Valentine (1959–1960)
Vito Valentinetti (1959)
Fred "Freddie" Van Dusen (1958)
Jim Westlake (1956)
Robert "Bobby" Willis (1959)
Robert "Bobby" Young (1957–1958)
Norm Zauchin (1959–1960)
Edward Zinker (1956)
George Zuverink (1959)

Appendix 2

Season-by-Season Statistics

Team Batting	Age	G	PA	AB	R	H	2B	3B	HR	RBI	SB	BA	OBP	SLG
Abrams, Cal*	32	129	585	454	100	126	17	3	10	50	6	.278	.422	.394
Anderson, John	26	8		5		1	0	0	0			.200		
Atwell, Toby*	32	4		8		0	0	0	0			.000		.000
Bouchee, Ed*	23	144	613	496	78	146	22	7	17	94	1	.294	.415	.470
Bowman, Bob	25	126	484	412	63	114	23	4	19	79	2	.277	.368	.490
Cain, Bob*	31	2		1		0	0	0	0	0		.000		.000
Cardwell, Don	20	33	89	82	11	15	5	2	2	17	0	.183	.227	.366
Casagrande, Thomas	26	1		1		0	0	0	0			.000		.000
Clark, Mel	29	63	197	182	16	41	5	3	1	9	2	.225	.272	.302
Command, Jim*	27	42	141	121	13	25	3	0	3	7	0	.207	.319	.306
Davalillo, Yo-Yo	25	50	183	166	18	42	8	0	0	8	3	.253	.275	.301
Farrell, Turk	22	23	57	52	3	6	2	0	0	3	0	.115	.145	.154
Gorbous, Glen*	25	79	235	210	20	55	5	1	3	29	2	.262	.309	.338
Gordon, Sid	38	55	176	140	23	33	8	0	4	23	0	.236	.392	.379
Greenwood, Bob	28	19	24	21	0	0	0	0	0	0	0	.000	.125	.000
Hawes, Roy*	29	5		19		3						.158		
Hewitt, Phillip	19	1		4		1						.250		
Holton, Ray	30	55	194	174	10	43	2	1	1	20	0	.247	.300	.287
Johnson, Wilbur	26	65	168	142	23	35	1	0	0	11	2	.246	.333	.254
Kipper, Thornton	27	23	18	16	2	2	0	0	0	0	0	.125	.125	.125
Kokos, Dick*	28	4		7		0	0	0	0			.000		.000
Lerchen, George#	33	8		14		4						.286		
LiPetri, Angelo	26	35	20	19	1	2	0	0	0	2	0	.105	.150	.105
Mann, David#	23	28	81	70	12	18	3	3	1	8	1	.257	.358	.429
Micelotta, Mickey	27	146	560	488	62	115	20	2	12	51	4	.236	.320	.359
Mierkowicz, Ed =	32	120	410	357	39	84	16	1	8	47	3	.235	.327	.353
Morehead, Seth*	21	30	69	61	3	7	0	0	0	3	0	.115	.182	.115
Niarhos, Gus	35	78	260	207	29	45	9	0	0	14	0	.217	.368	.261
Novak, Larry*	24	102	342	306	38	80	6	0	14	46	1	.261	.318	.418
Owens, Jim	22	15	39	36	1	4	0	0	0	0	0	.111	.111	.111
Paige, Satchel	49	37	42	38	1	6	2	0	0	6	0	.158	.200	.211
Paula, Carlos	28	11	42	38	3	6	0	1	0	3	2	.158	.214	.211
Ponce, Tony#	34	15	12	11	1	1	0	0	0	0	0	.091	.167	.091
Qualters, Tom	21	35	16	10	3	2	0	0	0	0	0	.200	.429	.200
Richmond, Don*	36	21	61	57	4	13	3	0	1	7	1	.228	.262	.333
Smith, Woody+	29	149	573	501	68	134	23	6	19	83	1	.267	.342	.451
Snyder, Gene	25	28	36	30	1	4	0	0	0	1	0	.133	.161	.133
Spring, Jack	23	31	31	29	3	5	1	0	0	3	0	.172	.200	.207
Tompkins, Ben	27	139	552	495	56	123	23	2	9	53	2	.248	.304	.358
Westlake, Jim*	25	7		20		5						.250		

* denotes left-handed batter or left-handed pitcher, # denotes switch-hitter, + denotes stats for two teams, = denotes stats for three teams

Source: baseball-reference.com

1956 Miami Marlins Statistics

Team Pitching	Age	W	L	ERA	G	GS	CG	SHO	IP	H	R	ER	HR	SO	BB
Anderson, John	26	1	2		4										
Bolinda, Henry	24	0	1		6										
Cain, Bob*	31	0	0		2										
Cardwell, Don	20	15	7	2.85	30	28	10	4	205	174	74	65	14	139	90
Conley, Bob	22	0	0		7										
Erickson, Don	24	0	0		2										
Farrell, Turk	22	12	6	2.50	23	17	7	1	144	128	47	40	4	64	56
Gorbous, Glen	25	0	0		1										
Greenwood, Bob	28	4	5	4.96	18	6	1	0	69	69	44	38	3	34	40
Hunsinger, Earl	22	0	0												
Kipper, Thornton	27	2	5	6.35	23	1	0	0	51	66	39	36	3	27	27
LiPetri, Angelo	26	4	4	2.95	31	1	0	0	61	49	20	20	2	52	30
Morehead, Seth*	21	8	13	2.87	30	28	8	1	188	178	73	60	11	168	68
Owens, Jim	22	5	7	2.86	15	14	6	1	104	94	42	33	4	62	57
Paige, Satchel	49	11	4	1.86	37	10	2	2	111	101	29	23	4	79	28
Pillette, Duane	33	0	0		3										
Ponce, Tony	34	1	1	2.92	15	3	0	0	40	45	18	13	2	10	5
Qualters, Tom	21	5	5	3.38	34	5	0	0	80	76	42	30	2	50	39
Snyder, Gene*	25	6	4	3.82	27	20	1	0	106	84	57	45	4	91	88
Spring, Jack*	23	6	6	4.06	30	13	3	1	93	105	51	42	9	47	38
Zinker, Edward	27	0	1		3										
Total		80	71												

1956 Miami Marlins Statistics (continued)

Team Batting	Age	G	PA	AB	R	H	2B	3B	HR	RBI	SB	BA	OBP	SLG
Abrams, Cal*+	33	137	553	467	71	130	33	5	1	41	7	.278	.386	.377
Adams, Red	35	16	10	5	0	0	0	0	0	0	0	.000	.167	.000
Anderson, John	27	19	16	14	0	2	0	0	0	0	0	.143	.200	.143
Blaylock, Marv*	27	41	171	139	18	35	4	4	2	15	2	.252	.379	.381
Bolinda, Henry	25	3		4		0						.000		
Bucha, Johnny	32	79	267	243	26	67	6	1	6	26	0	.276	.332	.383
Bunker, Richard*	22	28	52	38	4	5	0	0	0	1	0	.132	.277	.132
Church, Bubba	32	18	37	36	3	9	0	0	0	1	0	.250	.250	.250
Conley, Bob	23	11	19	18	1	1	0	0	0	0	0	.056	.105	.056
Essegian, Chuck	25	32	104	92	13	18	2	0	3	8	0	.196	.279	.315
Green, Dallas*	22	3		3		1						.333		
Greengrass, Jim	29	5		14		2						.143		
Harrington, Mickey	22	4		9		2						.222		
Herrera, Pancho	23	154	646	566	77	173	25	6	17	93	14	.306	.377	.461
Herzog, Whitey*	25	77	300	257	48	70	14	5	2	25	6	.272	.358	.389
Holton, Ray	31	2		3		0						.000		
Hunsinger, Earl	23	24	18	18	0	0	0	0	0	1	0	.000	.000	.000
Johnson, Wilbur	27	10	16	10	2	3	0	0	0	0	1	.300	.533	.300
Judson, Howie	31	20	35	32	3	6	3	0	0	5	0	.188	.182	.281
Landrum, Don*	21	140	582	541	70	159	19	17	3	41	14	.294	.331	.409
LiPetri, Angelo	27	15	6	5	0	1	0	0	0	0	0	.200	.333	.200
Locklin, Stu*	28	75	281	250	26	75	10	4	4	29	0	.200	.365	.420
Maddern, Clarence+	35	76	213	186	22	54	12	1	4	25	0	.290	.366	.430
Mason, Hank	26	35	19	12	0	1	0	0	0	1	0	.083	.214	.083
McCall, Windy*	31	14	13	12	0	3	0	0	0	0	0	.250	.308	.250
McCullough, Clyde	40	88	275	233	16	50	9	1	4	23	3	.215	.320	.313
Meyer, Jack	25	7		15		2						.133		
Micelotta, Mickey	28	143	526	449	51	97	14	5	9	60	1	.216	.319	.330
Novak, Larry*+	25	125	432	377	48	91	14	2	11	46	1	.241	.324	.377
Paige, Satchel	50	40	37	33	0	1	0	0	0	1	0	.030	.059	.030
Qualters, Tom	22	46	71	63	2	4	0	0	0	2	0	.063	.119	.063
Rogovin, Saul	33	14	20	19	0	5	0	0	3	1	0	.263	.250	.263
Rubinstein, Dario	25	1		5		2						.400		
Semproch, Ray	26	37	64	62	1	7	0	0	0	4	0	.113	.111	.113
Smith, Woody	30	155	636	570	63	158	17	2	14	73	3	.277	.343	.388
Snyder, Gene	26	20	25	24	0	2	0	0	0	1	0	.083	.083	.083
Sullivan, Haywood	26	17	68	60	7	12	4	0	2	8	0	.200	.294	.367
Tompkins, Ben	28	108	360	320	37	80	9	3	2	30	0	.250	.317	.316
Young, Bobby*	32	105	408	371	44	91	19	3	7	31	5	.245	.291	.369

* denotes left-handed batter or left-handed pitcher, # denotes switch-hitter, + denotes stats for two teams

Source: baseball-reference.com

1957 Miami Marlins Statistics

Team Pitching	Age	W	L	ERA	G	GS	CG	SHO	IP	H	R	ER	HR	SO	BB
Adams, Red	35	1	2	3.77	16	3	0	0	43	46	24	18	6	19	15
Anderson, John	27	3	4	2.82	19	4	2	0	51	51	19	16	3	23	24
Bolinda, Henry	25	0	1												
Bunker, Richard*	22	6	10	3.55	28	24	5	1	147	147	71	58	9	81	70
Church, Bubba	32	5	6	3.69	18	14	4	0	100	103	48	41	7	50	22
Conley, Bob	23	4	3	3.91	11	9	2	1	53	54	25	23	5	24	17
Green, Dallas	22	0	1		2										
Hunsinger, Earl	23	2	2	3.04	24	9	0	0	71	55	25	24	3	66	58
Judson, Howie	31	6	6	3.42	19	13	4	1	92	102	42	35	9	33	38
LiPetri, Angelo	27	1	0		14										
Mason, Hank	26	4	5	4.04	35	2	0	0	69	60	35	31	2	45	39
McCall, Windy*	31	0	1		12										
Meyer, Jack	25	3	2	3.51	6	6	3	0	41	34	16	16	5	26	24
Paige, Satchel	50	10	8	2.42	40	8	5	1	119	98	35	32	15	76	11
Qualters, Tom	22	11	12	3.29	46	16	4	3	186	179	77	68	9	73	51
Rogovin, Saul	33	3	5	4.11	13	9	1	0	57	72	28	26	4	22	21
Semproch, Ray	26	12	4	2.76	37	17	9	3	176	158	63	54	7	95	70
Snyder, Gene*	26	4	6	4.44	18	14	2	1	73	62	42	36	3	45	70
Total		75	78												

1957 Miami Marlins Statistics (continued)

Team Batting	Age	G	PA	AB	R	H	2B	3B	HR	RBI	SB	BA	OBP	SLG
Anderson, John	28	31	30	25	2	4	1	0	0	1	0	.160	.250	.200
Bucha, Johnny	33	95	283	251	18	70	13	1	7	34	0	.279	.345	.422
Bunker, Richard*	23	29	51	44	1	7	0	0	0	5	0	.159	.245	.159
Cardwell, Don	22	21	56	53	5	11	2	0	2	7	0	.208	.236	.358
Coker, Jimmie	22	104	348	309	32	76	13	1	8	33	7	.246	.327	.372
Conley, Bob	24	30	76	67	2	4	0	0	0	0	0	.060	.087	.060
Essegian, Chuck	26	81	328	298	36	74	13	1	15	44	2	.248	.305	.450
Frederick, Robert	22	8		11	0							.000		
Grasso, Mickey	38	2		3	0							.000		
Gray, Johnny	30	8		9		1						.111		
Green, Dallas*	23	36	66	57	6	9	2	1	1	1	0	.158	.250	.281
Hacker, Warren	33	13	30	28	2	6	0	0	0	0	0	.214	.214	.214
Hamric, Bert*	30	71	243	206	26	45	4	0	5	26	3	.218	.329	.311
Harmon, Chuck	34	36	135	126	12	26	2	2	0	11	4	.206	.246	.254
Harris, Dick*	22	7		8		2						.250		
Herrera, Pancho	24	121	497	436	72	123	17	3	20	66	11	.282	.356	.472
Hopke, Fred*	21	28	94	83	7	17	2	0	1	5	2	.205	.298	.265
Johnson, Wilbur	28	15	49	41	6	11	1	1	0	1	1	.268	.375	.341
Landrum, Don*	22	151	633	560	65	140	24	6	4	45	9	.250	.318	.341
Mason, Hank	27	43	19	15	1	3	0	0	0	1	0	.200	.250	.200
McCall, Windy*	32	40	18	15	0	1	0	0	0	0	0	.067	.176	.067
McDermott,Mickey*	29	56	144	131	13	25	6	2	1	12	0	.191	.252	.290
Micelotta, Mickey	29	127	444	379	35	76	10	3	4	28	1	.201	.308	.274
Miller, Bob	32	4		1	0							.000		
Mossor, Earl*	32	12	5	5	1	1	1	0	0	0	0	.200	.200	.400
Paige, Satchel	51	28	32	29	1	2	0	0	0	2	0	.069	.069	.069
Smith, Woody	31	151	617	539	77	157	33	4	13	29	4	.291	.360	.440
Snyder, Jerry	28	99	373	340	35	106	13	5	0	25	6	.312	.343	.379
Stewart, Bunky*	27	16	14	10	1	1	0	0	0	1	0	.100	.231	.100
Tompkins, Ben	29	72	223	202	33	55	8	3	2	16	2	.272	.333	.371
Usher, Bob	33	115	434	397	40	109	17	2	6	43	3	.275	.328	.373
Van Dusen, Fred*	20	22	68	48	9	8	0	0	1	5	0	.167	.382	.229
Young, Bobby*	33	59	200	178	7	45	5	0	1	10	2	.253	.310	.298

* denotes left-handed batter or left-handed pitcher, # denotes switch-hitter

Source: baseball-reference.com

1958 Miami Marlins Statistics

Team Pitching	Age	W	L	ERA	G	GS	CG	SHO	IP	H	R	ER	HR	SO	BB
Anderson, John	28	4	5	3.23	31	9	4	1	103	100	40	37	6	48	38
Bunker, Richard*	23	9	8	2.85	26	19	6	2	136	113	52	43	12	69	75
Cardwell, Don	22	12	5	2.34	20	19	12	3	150	106	42	39	6	131	48
Church, Bubba	33	0	0		3										
Conley, Bob	24	12	11	2.94	30	27	12	4	190	174	69	62	12	82	55
Frederick, Robert	22	1	4	4.50	8	6	2	0	32	30	16	16	2	16	10
Gray, Johnny	30	2	2		8										
Green, Dallas	23	7	10	3.74	31	22	5	0	159	135	73	66	12	103	70
Hacker, Warren	33	5	6	3.11	13	11	2	2	81	70	31	28	5	52	11
Hirst, Arthur*	25	0	1		1										
LiPetri, Angelo	28	0	0		4										
Mason, Hank	27	4	2	3.06	42	5	0	0	100	92	36	34	7	60	37
McCall, Windy*	32	4	4	3.49	38	0	0	0	67	56	31	26	7	42	36
McDermott,Mickey*	29	5	6	1.86	17	10	4	1	92	62	23	19	6	57	34
Miller, Bob	32	0	0		3										
Mossor, Earl	32	0	1		12										
Paige, Satchel	51	10	10	2.95	28	15	7	1	110	94	44	36	8	40	15
Snyder, Gene*	27	0	1		2										
Stewart, Bunky*	27	0	2	5.21	16	3	0	0	38	41	25	22	5	9	15
Total		75	78												

1958 Miami Marlins Statistics (continued)

Team Batting	Age	G	PA	AB	R	H	2B	3B	HR	RBI	SB	BA	OBP	SLG
Abernathy, Ted	26	2		2		1						.500		
Adams, Bobby	37	15	41	39	3	12	3	1	0	7	0	.308	.317	.436
Anderson, John	29	31	77	72	0	10	1	0	0	4	0	.139	.162	.153
Archer, Jim	27	37	77	67	3	11	1	0	0	3	0	.164	.197	.179
Bean, Roger	22	4		10		2						.200		
Bishop, Danny#	21	7		13		3						.231		
Brady, Walter	24	25	89	77	3	21	1	0	0	6	0	.273	.356	.286
Bucha, Johnny	34	101	361	331	25	85	15	1	1	32	0	.257	.308	.317
Burke, Leo	25	136	497	456	43	100	14	3	21	70	2	.219	.276	.401
Byrd, Harry	34	42	70	61	3	10	1	0	0	2	0	.164	.215	.180
Castleman, Foster	28	121	460	409	53	128	25	0	6	34	2	.313	.371	.418
Conley, Bob+	25	14	12	11	0	1	0	0	0	0	0	.091	.091	.091
Davidson, Bill	21	9		6		0	0	0	0			.000		.000
Drews, Karl	39	2		1								.000		.000
Fisher, Jack	20	15	40	37	4	10	0	0	0	2	0	.270	.300	.270
Hamric, Bert*	31	146	581	510	58	114	14	7	14	60	8	.224	.305	.361
Held, Mel+	30	24	9	8	0	1	0	0	0	0	0	.125	.125	.125
Kay, Arthur	24	55	43	37	3	3	0	0	0	1	0	.081	.081	.272
Kazak, Eddie	38	7		26		9						.346		
Kellert, Frank	34	77	283	237	23	58	12	0	6	24	0	.245	.356	.371
Korcheck, Steve	26	52	154	131	11	25	3	0	3	20	0	.191	.283	.565
Lajoie, Bill*	24	26	93	81	8	17	0	0	1	7	0	.210	.290	.247
McCall, Windy*	33	6		1		0	0	0	0			.000		.000
McDermott,Mickey*	30	68	128	120	10	30	1	0	5	8	0	.250	.297	.383
Moeller, Ron*	20	4		1		0	0	0	0			.000		.000
Moford, Herb	30	16	40	39	3	5	0	0	0	1	0	.128	.128	.154
Oertel, Chuck*	28	148	600	539	72	148	20	4	11	56	4	.275	.337	.388
Parsons, Charles	27	4		3		0	0	0	0			.000		.000
Scheel, Rolf	26	3		4		1						.250		
Smith, Woody	32	156	638	563	67	154	49	2	16	78	3	.274	.341	.453
Snyder, Jerry	29	58	151	140	11	28	2	1	0	7	0	.200	.243	.229
Stewart, Bunky*	28	31	39	36	3	6	0	0	0	0	0	.167	.167	.167
Stock, Wes	25	6		4		1						.250		
Trucks, Virgil	42	4		1		0	0	0	0					.000
Tucker, Leonard	29	18	45	39	6	5	0	0	0	1	1	.128	.227	.128
Valdivielso, Jose	25	17	30	29	1	2	0	0	0	2	0	.069	.067	.069
Valentine, Fred#	24	155	678	614	82	158	25	11	11	39	28	.257	.319	.388
Valentinetti,Vito	30	15	10	9	1	0	0	0	0	1	0	.000	.000	.000
Willis, Bobby	27	88	182	174	20	45	3	0	0	8	3	.259	.274	.276
Zauchin, Norm	29	68	198	165	19	40	7	1	6	26	2	.242	.364	.406
Zuverink, George	34	30	9	8	1	3	0	0	1	2	0	.375	.444	.750

* denotes left-handed batter or left-handed pitcher, # denotes switch-hitter, + denotes stats for two teams

Source: baseball-reference.com

1959 Miami Marlins Statistics

Team Pitching	Age	W	L	ERA	G	GS	CG	SHO	IP	H	R	ER	HR	SO	BB
Abernathy, Ted	26	0	0	9.00	1				2	3	2	2		1	1
Anderson, John	29	12	9	2.74	30	29	10	3	204	187	72	622	9	95	41
Archer, Jim*	27	13	10	2.81	36	28	16	3	208	216	78	65	11	129	43
Byrd, Harry	34	8	16	3.52	42	24	9	1	202	188	85	79	21	114	65
Conley, Bob+	25	1	4	6.59	11	9	1	0	41	49	32	30	11	17	10
Drews, Karl	39	0	0		2										
Fisher, Jack	20	8	4	3.06	12	12	7	0	97	81	36	33	4	70	39
Held, Mel+	30	1	5	3.83	24	2	0	0	54	56	26	23	8	31	15
Kay, Arthur	24	7	6	2.08	55	6	2	1	160	124	53	37	11	94	44
Lary, Gene	25	0	0		6										
Lawrence, Leigh	25	0	0		3										
McCall, Windy*	33	0	0		5										
McDermott, Mickey*	30	3	7	5.66	23	7	0	0	70	91	52	44	5	43	32
Moeller, Ron*	20	0	1	3.86	3				7	6	3	3		5	4
Moford, Herb	30	7	7	2.10	16	14	6	3	107	77	30	25	6	61	28
Parsons, Charles	27	2	0		4										
Scheel, Rolf	26	0	1		1										
Stewart, Bunky*	28	6	11	2.91	31	18	7	1	127	120	56	41	7	59	51
Stock, Wes	25	0	1	9.00	6				15	21	19	15		9	13
Trucks, Virgil	42	0	1	3.86	4				7	7	4	3		0	9
Valentinetti, Vito	30	1	3	7.97	15	7	1	0	35	43	35	31	6	22	27
Zuverink, George	34	3	4	2.95	30	4	2	2	55	49	21	18	3	33	15
Total		71	90												

1959 Miami Marlins Statistics (continued)

Team Batting	Age	G	PA	AB	R	H	2B	3B	HR	RBI	SB	BA	OBP	SLG
Adair, Jerry	23	152	638	602	78	160	29	2	6	35	12	.266	.297	.350
Anderson, John	30	30	25	21	2	5	1	0	0	2	0	.238	.333	.286
Archer, Jim*	28	35	67	61	2	6	0	1	0	2	0	.098	.125	.131
Arias, Rudy*	29	19	47	43	4	9	1	0	0	2	0	.209	.244	.233
Brown, Dick	25	89	363	338	37	82	14	2	13	50	2	.243	.287	.411
Bucha, Johnny	35	1		1		0						.000		
Burke, Leo	26	125	436	377	50	96	14	0	15	54	2	.255	.349	.411
Busby, Jim	33	27	106	94	13	26	6	1	1	7	0	.277	.324	.394
Byrd, Harry	35	7		5		0						.000		
Caffie, Joe*+	29	80	229	206	21	45	11	0	4	24	4	.218	.288	.330
Dagres, Angelo*	25	93	215	192	27	51	5	2	1	17	2	.266	.344	.328
Gomez, Ruben+	32	26	50	44	4	10	1	0	0	4	0	.227	.292	.250
Green, Gene	27	136	532	460	51	126	19	2	18	77	0	.274	.360	.441
Hamric, Bert*	32	15	35	34	5	7	0	0	0	1	2	.206	.229	.206
Hoeft, Billy*	28	9		19		1						.053		
Hyde, Dick	31	20	4	4	0	2	0	0	0	0	0	.500	.500	.500
Kay, Arthur+	25	62	27	22	3	3	1	0	0	0	0	.136	.269	.182
Luebke, Dick	25	41	21	20	0	1	0	0	0	0	0	.050	.050	.050
Mabe, Bob	30	2		1		0						.000		
McCardell, Roger	27	36	92	82	7	18	8	0	1	3	0	.220	.297	.354
Moeller, Ron*	21	3		2		0						.000		
Moford, Herb	31	35	74	66	2	9	1	0	0	5	0	.136	.149	.152
Nagel, Alfred	27	61	205	180	18	41	4	0	2	12	0	.228	.303	.283
Nicholson, Dave	20	18	56	50	4	13	3	1	1	4	1	.260	.339	.420
Pearson, Albie*	25	53	213	176	26	53	5	2	1	13	4	.301	.412	.369
Portocarrero, Arnie	28	14	28	25	0	4	2	0	0	1	0	.160	.222	.240
Samford, Ron	30	151	589	544	49	138	19	7	10	62	5	.254	.303	.369
Shetrone, Barry*	21	91	333	273	38	70	5	5	9	28	7	.256	.379	.410
Smith, Woody	33	142	552	478	36	102	17	2	11	49	0	.213	.305	.326
Stewart, Bunky*	29	30	36	28	3	4	0	0	0	3	0	.143	.250	.143
Stock, Wes	26	21	48	40	0	3	0	0	0	1	0	.075	.119	.075
Valentine, Fred#	25	114	453	395	39	100	21	6	2	28	6	.253	.330	.352
Valentinetti, Vito	31	9		7		2						.286		
Zauchin, Norm+	30	123	407	363	39	78	7	2	8	31	2	.215	.289	.311

* denotes left-handed batter or left-handed pitcher, # denotes switch-hitter, + denotes stats for two teams

Source: baseball-reference.com

1960 Miami Marlins Statistics

Team Pitching	Age	W	L	ERA	G	GS	CG	SHO	IP	H	R	ER	HR	SO	BB
Anderson, John	30	2	10	5.96	30	11	4	0	83	101	60	55	9	36	36
Archer, Jim*	28	11	12	3.33	35	26	12	3	189	185	77	70	17	111	40
Arias, Rudy*	29	7	9	3.57	19	16	7	1	121	121	58	48	12	52	37
Byrd, Harry	35	3	1		7										
Gomez, Ruben+	32	7	6	2.27	14	12	9	1	103	78	32	25	5	70	28
Hoeft, Billy*	28	4	5	3.09	9	8	3	0	64	54	24	22	11	43	17
Hyde, Dick	31	0	5	5.29	20	0	0	0	34	37	23	20	1	24	15
Kay, Arthur+	25	8	6	3.26	61	8	4	0	174	159	81	63	13	92	65
Luebke, Dick*	25	2	4	3.44	41	4	1	0	102	87	44	39	13	71	41
Mabe, Bob	30	0	0		2										
McDonald, Jim	33	0	0		6										
Moeller, Ron	21	0	2	3.86	3				7	6	3	3		5	4
Moford, Herb	31	11	12	2.94	35	26	14	5	208	174	80	68	17	101	61
Portocarrero, Arnie	28	2	2	3.67	12	10	1	0	76	73	33	31	8	20	19
Stewart, Bunky*	29	7	10	3.98	30	15	4	3	113	116	57	50	12	55	40
Stock, Wes	26	8	6	2.25	21	15	8	4	128	102	41	32	9	102	34
Valentinetti, Vito	31	1	2		9										
Total		65	88												

1960 Miami Marlins Statistics (continued)

Bibliography

BOOKS

Barthel, Thomas. *Pepper Martin: A Baseball Biography*. Jefferson, NC: McFarland, 2003.

Boyd, Brendan C., and Fred C. Harris. *The Great American Baseball Card Flipping, Trading and Bubble Gum Book*. New York: Little, Brown, 1973.

Broeg, Bob. *One Hundred Greatest Moments in St. Louis Sports*. St. Louis: Missouri History Museum, 2000.

Clavin, Tom, and Danny Peary. *Roger Maris*. New York: Touchstone, 2010.

Dickens, Charles. *A Christmas Carol*. London: Chapman & Hall, 1843.

Eisenberg, Howard, and Mickey McDermott. *A Funny Thing Happened on the Way to Cooperstown*. Chicago: Triumph Books, 2003.

Ercalono, Patrick. *Fungoes, Floaters and Fork Balls: A Colorful Baseball Dictionary*. Englewood Cliffs, NJ: Prentice-Hall, 1987.

Figueredo, Jorge. *Cuban Baseball: A Statistical History, 1878-1961*. Jefferson, NC: McFarland, 2003.

Gillette, Gary, and Pete Palmer. *The ESPN Baseball Encyclopedia*, 5th ed. New York: Sterling Publishing, 2008.

Heidenry, John. *The Gashouse Gang*. New York: Public Affairs, 2007.

James, Bill. *The New Bill James Historical Baseball Abstract*. New York: Free Press, 2001.

James, Bill, and Rob Neyer. *The Neyer/James Guide to Pitchers*. New York: Fireside, 2004.

Linn, Ed, and Bill Veeck. *Veeck—As in Wreck*. New York: University of Chicago Press, 1961.

Lipman, David, and Satchel Paige. *Maybe I'll Pitch Forever*. Garden City, NY: Doubleday, 1962.

McCarthy, Kevin M. *Baseball in Florida*. Pineapple Press, 1996.

Nemec, David, and Dave Zemen. *The Baseball Rookies Encyclopedia*. Washington, DC: Brassey's, 2004.

O'Neal, Bill. *International League: A Baseball History 1884–1991*. Austin, TX: Eakin Press, 1992.

Peary, Danny. *We Played the Game*. New York: Black Dog & Leventhal, 1994.

Remnick, David. *King of the World: Muhammad Ali and the Rise of an American Hero*. New York: Vintage, 1998.

Ribowsky, Mark. *Don't Look Back: Satchel Paige in the Shadows of Baseball*. New York: Simon & Schuster, 1994.

Shlain, Bruce. *Baseball Inside Out*. New York: Penguin, 1992.

Snyder, John. *Cubs Journal: Year by Year and Day by Day with the Chicago Cubs Since 1876*. Cincinnati, OH: Emmis Books, 2005.

Spatz, Lyle, Society for American Baseball Research. *The SABR Baseball List & Record Book*. New York: Scribner, 2007.

Tye, Larry. *Satchel: The Life and Times of an American Legend*. New York: Random House, 2007.

Watkins, Clarence. *Baseball in Birmingham: Images of Baseball*. Charleston, SC: Arcadia, 2010.

NEWSPAPERS AND PUBLICATIONS

Baseball Digest
The Citizen
Miami Herald
Miami News
Montreal Gazette
Palm Beach Post
Sporting News
Syracuse Post-Standard

PERSONAL INTERVIEWS

Tim Anagnost
Jim Archer
Bob Bowman
Richard Bunker
Leo Burke
Mel Clark
Angelo Dagres
Bill Durney Jr.
Dick Getter
Johnny Gray
Dallas Green
Fred Hopke
Earl Hunsinger
Wilbur Johnson
Steve Korcheck
Bob Kuzava
Stu Locklin
Butch McCord
Bob Micelotta
Albie Pearson
Tom Qualters
Ray Semproch
Jack Spring
Benjamin Tompkins
Bob Usher
Vito Valentinetti
Bobby Willis
George Zuverink

WEBSITES

Baseballhalloffame.ca.museum
Baseballlibrary.com
Baseballinwartime.com
Baseball-reference.com
Basketball-reference.com
Bioproj.sabr.org
Brainyquote.com
Examiner.com/baseball-history
Hardballtimes.com
Iowa.dnr.gov
Lamarcardinals.com
Miamiherald.com
Miaminewtimes.com
Minorleaguebaseball.com
Sports.espn.go.com
Sportsillustrated.cnn.com

Index

About the Author

Sam Zygner is chairman of the Society for American Baseball Research, South Florida Chapter. He received his MBA from Saint Leo University and his writings have appeared in *La Prensa de Miami* (newspaper) and the *SABR Baseball Research Journal*. Sam is a lifetime Pittsburgh Pirates fan. He is married, with three children and four grandchildren.

9 780810 891388